THE
PRACTICAL
GARDENING
HANDBOOK

THE PRACTICAL GARDENING HANDBOOK

Arthur Billitt
David Papworth
Philippa Back
Peter Blackburne-Maze
Ken March

Originally published as four separate volumes
The Flower Garden
The Herb Garden
The Patio and Windowbox Garden
The Greenhouse Garden
by Octopus Books Ltd

First published in Great Britain
in this format in 1991 by
Ivy Leaf
Michelin House
81 Fulham Road
London SW3 6RB

Reprinted 1994

This edition produced exclusively for Bookmart Ltd

ISBN 0 86363 035 9

Printed in Hong Kong

CONTENTS

NOTES

For convenience, ease of growing symbols have been incorporated in the A-Z sections.
They can be interpreted as follows:

  *Easy to grow plants
 **Plants which require more than average care
***Temperamental or difficult to grow plants

These symbols are appropriate as long as the correct conditions are
provided.

GUIDELINES FOR SUCCESS

STARTING FROM SCRATCH

The perpetual hurry of life tempts most of us to start seed sowing or planting out bedding plants into the flower garden before the ground has been thoroughly and properly prepared. This is a sure way to disappointing results.

If you are starting with a brand new garden plot, the first thing to do is to remove all rubble and builders' waste, which, if left on the soil, soon turns it sour. Then you must plan the garden lay-out. Remember that few flower gardens are complete without a lawn, but just where you site it will inevitably affect the position of the flower beds, and therefore, ultimately how much or how little sunshine the flowers themselves will receive. North- and east-facing beds will always be less successful than those that face south and west because they are that much colder.

THE RIGHT TOOLS FOR THE JOB

I am a great believer in lightweight, but strong garden tools. The heavier the tools, the more energy is required to use them. The principal tools that a flower gardener needs are a spade and fork for digging the ground, incorporating compost and manure, lifting plants etc., a cultivator for knocking down the clods of earth in the spring and a rake for raking over the ground to make it even and level, ready for sowing or planting; a little fork and trowel for planting out, a hoe and a border fork for controlling weeds and a good pair of secateurs.

My spade must have a thin blade and a wooden shaft. I would not buy a stainless steel one; the stainless steel is a visual luxury that increases the weight. Spades are of course, made in several sizes; never buy one that is too big for your particular manpower on the assumption that you will cover the ground more quickly with it. Many have tried, only to suffer disappointment and backache.

The cultivator I favour is three-pronged with broadened ends to the tines. Again it is lightweight so it really requires very little energy on my part to use. In addition to this long-handled one, short-handled versions are available, generally intended for use by the physically handicapped or by children. I find them most useful in closely planted areas.

The secret of success in preparing seed-beds is to get a really fine tilth, and this is where the rake comes into its own. I like one with a 30-cm-(12-inch-) head. For dealing with those weed seedlings, again with as little effort as possible, I use a dutch hoe. This implement can be bought with various widths of blade; a very wide one is not really suitable for use in flower borders. Instead select one with a 13 cm (5 inch) wide blade. For use in the herbaceous border and amongst roses, I find a border fork most valuable, particularly for loosening obstinate weeds. Mine has a wooden handle and good sturdy tines.

For pruning roses or cutting down herbaceous plants at the end of the season, you will need a pair of secateurs. Make sure they fit comfortably into your hand, are not too heavy to handle and are sufficiently strong and sharp to make a good, clean cut.

SOIL TYPES

Soils vary greatly both from the kind of earth of which they are comprised and their mineral content. Whilst it is not necessary to analyse your soil minutely, it is important to understand its properties otherwise you will not know which plants will grow happily.

Basically the differences in soil types are related to the ratio of sand and clay in their make-up. Increases in the sand content makes the soil lighter and more porous. It warms up quickly, but also dries out more quickly, and it tends to be quite short of nutrients. Addition of organic material such as compost or peat helps to retain moisture in the soil and gives it more substance. Clay soils, with low sand content, tend to be wet and cold early in the season. Winter digging, with the clods left rough to weather, makes the preparation of the soil in spring easier and also improves the drainage. Work in some well-rotted compost or manure while doing the winter digging. Once a clay soil has been well cultivated and plants have become established in it, they will grow well, for it is very fertile.

Digging with the right weight spade (top) and preparing the seed bed with a rake

Using a long-handled cultivator (top) and weeding with a dutch hoe

Garden soils may be acid or alkaline and you can discover which yours is by checking on the plants that are growing (if the garden is already established) and then looking up what conditions they favour. By and large a chalky soil has a high alkaline content, clay soils tend towards alkalinity and sandy soils have a higher acid content. Soil with a high acid content can be corrected with applications of garden lime, while digging peat into alkaline soils will help to redress the balance. However, bear in mind

that you cannot change this aspect of your soil for ever; you have to repeat the applications regularly or the soil will merely revert back to type. If it is not too overtly one way or the other, it is generally better to live with the overall soil, and then if you want to grow plants that are really not happy with the prevailing conditions, you can treat the soil individually for them.

PREPARING THE FLOWER BEDS
All digging is best done in the late autumn or

winter when the heaviest clay soils particularly benefit and can be made easy to work if the turned over clods are exposed to the winter elements. The water within them freezes, splitting them open. When you are digging, it is a good idea to incorporate some well-rotted garden compost or manure into the bed to enrich it. In the spring, it is then a comparatively easy job to attack the turned over clods with the cultivator and knock them down into smaller lumps. A work over with the rake will give an acceptable tilth for seed sowing or planting. Lighter soils can be dug in the spring without too many problems, but again, it is really better to dig them over in the autumn. If you were to dig a sandy soil in a dry spell in the spring, the loss of moisture incurred as the soil is turned over may well cause it to become excessively dry, thereby increasing the need for artificial watering later.

It is during this deep digging operation that you want to make sure you remove the roots of all perennial weeds such as couch grass, thistles, docks, nettles and the like. Annual weeds can be dealt with later on when they start emerging as little seedlings (see page opposite).

FERTILISERS – FEEDING AND MULCHING

There are few flowers and plants that do not benefit at some time or another from a little additional feeding. In many instances, this can be applied to the ground before planting – for example when planting herbaceous plants sprinkle some bonemeal or general fertiliser into the planting holes. Alternatively feed plants during their growing season.

A balanced garden fertiliser will contain ingredients to supply the three major plant growth nutrients, which are nitrogen, phosphates and potash, plus, possibly trace elements such as iron, magnesium, manganese etc. Organic fertilisers based on natural ingredients are usually more expensive and somewhat slower in action than inorganic ones, but are still preferred by some people. Both inorganic and organic fertilisers are available as powders, granules or liquids. To avoid waste, never exceed the recommended dosage or dilution rates and wait until the winter rains have ended. Apply to the soil around the plants.

Fertiliser formulations for applying to the foliage – known as foliar feeds – are available. They should be sprayed on the plant when the weather is cool – either in the morning or the evening. This approach to plant feeding can be valuable in an emergency when plants are under stress for some unusual reason such as long periods of dry or very hot weather.

Herbaceous plants and shrubs such as roses will also benefit from a spring 'mulch' which helps to preserve moisture in the ground, as well as helping to keep down weeds as they have to force their way up through the thick covering. Simply put a layer of peat, or compost round the base of the plants. It will soon be hidden as the new growth emerges.

COMPOST MAKING

Well-made, well-rotted compost is an invaluable component of the flower garden for when returned to the beds it helps to maintain fertility. It is important to make as much of it as you can even though, apart from lawn mowings and leaves there is not going to be a great deal of waste plant material to use for compost making in the flower garden.

We make our compost by a slow but sure method which takes about twelve months in all and costs virtually nothing. It is a simple procedure; put a 13-15-cm (5-6 inch) layer of green material directly onto the soil in the wired-in compost bin. On top of this put a sprinkling of garden soil (this supplies the necessary micro-

For a good compost, build up layers of waste sprinkled alternately with soil and garden lime

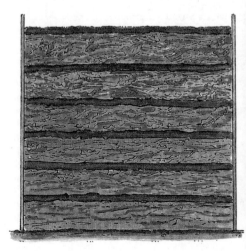

Alyssum saxatile and Aubrieta

organisms which will work on the waste material) and then another 13-15-cm (5-6 inch) layer of vegetation waste. Top with a sprinkling of garden lime. From then on, repeat these layers until the compost bin is full. If you have no general waste material, but only grass, it would be wise to use a recycler which prevents the compost from becoming slimey. Your compost would then be ready after about six months.

FLOWER BED MAINTENANCE

Apart from feeding and mulching plants, two things are necessary to keep the flower beds in good condition – watering and weeding.

There will inevitably be times during the summer when some, if not all, your plants need your help if they are to get all the water they need. Start by making sure the ground in which you plant them is moist, and water the young plants as they are getting established in a new position. Thereafter, water as necessary, but do not wait until the plants start to wilt before giving them water as it could then be too late to achieve recovery. The best time to water is in the evening; this is when the plants derive the maximum benefit. If this is really not convenient, do it early in the morning, but never in the middle of the day when the sun is at its hottest. Do not just dribble water on the surface round the plant; that will only bring the roots to the surface and ultimately will cause more stress to the plants than giving them none at all. Make sure that the water goes right down to the roots by giving the ground a prolonged soaking. Bear in mind that once you have started watering established plants during a dry spell, you must keep on watering them regularly. By and large it is better to prepare the soil so that it is really moist and water-retentive.

It is obviously necessary to control the weeds in any flower garden, both so the plants are shown off to their best advantage and to ensure they do not suffer or become smothered. The secret of continuous weed control in any bed is to go round with a hoe regularly, starting as early as the beginning of March – to disturb the weeds before they have time to make any foliage or start seeding. An old saying among experienced gardeners is 'one year's weed seeding will save seven years weeding'.

It is important that the roots of some plants should be disturbed as little as possible (see in the A-Z listings), in which case you should weed round them by hand.

CULTIVATION AND ROUTINE CARE

CHOOSING THE RIGHT PLANTS

Success in gardening becomes so much easier when the plants you want to grow like both your soil and the climate that prevails in your area. Problems and disappointments occur when the desire to grow specific flowers is so strong that it causes one to disregard these two vital growing factors. Rhododendrons, azaleas and camellias are a case in point; they all like an acid medium, so to attempt to grow them on a chalky soil for example, would be asking for trouble – or a great deal of expense to try to overcome the problem by changing the basic nature of your soil.

There are few climates in the world where so many plants can be grown as here in the U.K., but as the winter frosts vary so greatly in intensity, the permanent planting of half-hardy subjects is generally unsuccessful, certainly in the colder areas. If you want to grow them and preserve them through the winter, be prepared to take care of them in one way or another during the winter (see page 14).

If you are new either to gardening or to your district and are therefore unsure just what will and will not flourish in your soil and climate, a peep over the fences down the road or a few visits to local gardens should answer your queries about what to plant initially. Experiments can come later. In selecting your plants, do make sure you site them carefully in relation to their need for full sunshine or partial shade. By doing so, you should be able to fill all the odd corners in the garden, thereby providing the maximum amount of interest and colour. Aim, too, to spread colour throughout the garden and choose plants that have varying flowering times so that you have a cheerful display from May to September. Try to get a good balance of shapes, mixing tall plants with those that are bushy, rather than putting all those with upright growth habits together. Obviously you should put the tallest plants at the back of a bed, but avoid too many upright subjects, unless you are deliberately trying to give the effect of height. You will achieve a much softer overall effect by not planting your flowers in regimented straight lines.

GROWING YOUR OWN PLANTS

All sorts of plants are on sale at nurseries and garden centres in the spring under the heading of 'bedding plants'. Generally speaking, this is an expensive way to buy most plants, as clearly the nursery has done all the initial work and will be charging for their time. In any event, you will

have far more fun and achieve greater satisfaction in your gardening if you raise your own plants. This you can do either by growing them from seed, or by taking cuttings or small pieces of rooted material from established plants. Before we look at these various forms of propagation, though, a word about bedding plants, for they do have a place in many flower gardens. They are a way of getting colour quickly and safely into your flower beds and you can buy exactly what you want, in the numbers you want. As a general rule, do not buy these plants until well into May, so that with the danger of frost past, you can plant them out quickly. Many garden centres offer plants for sale far too early, with the result that if you plant them immediately, they will suddenly be killed off by a late frost.

A well organized greenhouse can be a tremendous help to the flower gardener

GROWING FROM SEED

Great numbers of plants can be raised from seed; depending on how hardy (i.e. ability to withstand cold and frost) the subject is, you can either sow seed outside or start it off indoors.

Outdoor cultivation

Seed of hardy annuals, hardy biennials and hardy perennials can all be sown straight into the ground outside. Hardy annual seeds can be sown where the plants are required to flower. The ground should have been dug in the autumn as recommended on pages 5-6, then broken up with a cultivator in the spring. The aim is to get the soil into a really fine, workable stage, so that it crumbles easily in your hand. Rake it over just prior to sowing to make sure you have a really fine tilth with no large stones or clods of soil on the surface. Then either broadcast the seeds over the ground or draw out shallow drills with the edge of the hoe or rake and scatter the seeds along these. The seeds of many annuals are quite small and it is important not to cover them with too much soil.

Always read all the directions on seed packets. You will find that mid-April is the best time to sow most hardy annuals, but do wait for good weather to get the right sowing conditions – that is a fine, dry top tilth with moist soil underneath.

When the seedlings appear and are large enough to handle, thin them out by pulling out the weaker ones.

The seeds of hardy biennials and perennials are more usually sown in a seed bed rather than straight into the place where they are intended to flower. This is because they will generally take some time to become established and it is more sensible therefore to fill the flower beds with flowering annuals in the meantime. Use a small patch of the garden as a seed bed; it should be in a light and sunny, but well-protected position. The soil should be in good condition – warm and full of nutrients. Rake it over to prepare it for seeds as you did the garden, to produce a fine tilth free from stones. It should be free from weeds as the seedlings may have to stay put for some long time before being transplanted. The procedure for growing these is the same as for hardy annuals; sow the seeds at the times recommended on the seed packets and thin out seedlings so that those you

ABOVE: *Sow seed in shallow drills (top) and thin out to leave the stronger plants*
RIGHT: *For indoor cultivation, sow seed in an electric propagator (top left) or in a seed tray (top right). Thin out to leave about 28 seedlings (bottom left). The plants can be hardened off in a cold frame (bottom right)*

want have sufficient room to grow unhampered. If the weather is dry, make sure that the seed bed is kept moist. Transplant the seedlings at the recommended times.

Indoor cultivation

All plants that are categorised as being half-hardy will need to be started indoors. The kitchen window sill can be a suitable site for seed trays, providing the house temperature does not drop dramatically during the night when central heating goes off. For raising seedlings on a small scale, it is probably worth investing in a small electric propagator. It should be fitted with a built-in thermostat which holds the temperature at 16°C (62°F). Even if you have a heated greenhouse, a propagator of this type will keep the heating costs down as there will be no need to heat the whole greenhouse. Again, read the directions on the seed packets to find out the right time for sowing, as this will vary considerably. Begin by filling the seed trays with a seeding compost (see page 13), which should feel moist. Sprinkle the seed over this and cover with another very fine layer of sifted compost. Keep the compost moist as the seedlings start coming up; you can speed up germination by covering the trays with polythene. Thin out the seedlings either by pulling out the weaker ones or by transplanting the tiny plants. This is known as *'pricking-out'* and the important thing to remember is not to put too many seedlings into each seed tray. I find that 28 is about the right number for a standard tray and will give you good strong plants to transplant. Once in these trays, the seedlings must be placed in a good light (i.e. no longer in the propagator) otherwise they will soon become weak and drawn, but they must still be kept in a warm place. When the plants get too big for the trays, you should pot them into small individual pots filled with potting compost (see page 13).

Before planting out into their flowering positions, they must be *hardened off*. This means getting them used to the climate gradually before they have to withstand it all the time. You can either put them in a cold frame (which should be in a sheltered position protected from cold winds) or you can put them out into the garden by day and bring them back indoors at night. Remember that if they are exposed to frost at this time, they will die.

Planting out
This should be done when all danger of frost has gone and the plants are healthy and well established. Make sure the compost around their roots is very moist, then dig a hole in the garden where you want them to be. Remove the plant from the pot and put it in the hole with as much of the growing medium around the roots as possible. If the soil is inclined to be dry, water the plants immediately in order to help them get established quickly.

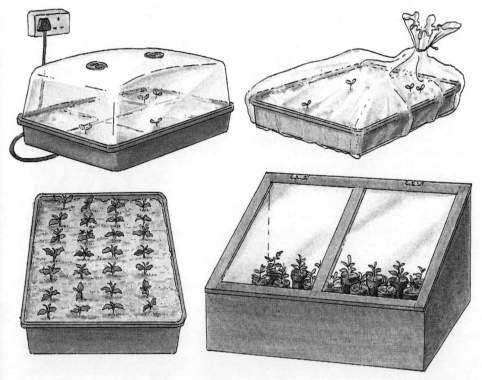

OTHER METHODS OF PROPAGATION

Although many perennials can be grown from seed, once you have the plant in your garden, you will want to propagate it by taking cuttings, by layering, or by dividing the roots to give 'rooted offsets'.

Taking cuttings

Some hardy perennials, such as lavender, can be propagated from non-flowering shoots taken during the late summer. You can either take a soft cutting or a heel cutting. The former is a cutting taken immediately below a leaf joint. For a heel cutting, remove the shoot with a heel of the harder stem from the parent plant. For both types, remove a few bottom leaves before dipping the cut end in a rooting powder or solution. The cuttings are then inserted into a pot filled with moist seed compost or into a special rooting bag. Place the pot or rooting bag into a plastic bag to prevent drying out. Make sure that the plastic does not rest on the cutting and remove it when rooting has taken place.

Chrysanthemums and dahlias can be propagated from cuttings taken during early spring. For this purpose the chrysanthemum stools (roots) or dahlia tubers are housed in warm conditions, ideally in a greenhouse, to produce young growth early. These young shoots are then cut off and potted into a pot filled with moist seed compost.

Without heat outdoor chrysanthemums and many other perennials can be propagated from root cuttings, that is, individual shoots removed from the stool with a few pieces of root still attached.

ABOVE: A soft cutting is taken immediately below a leaf joint

CENTRE: A heel, or semi-hardwood cutting is taken by removing the shoot with a heel attached to it from the parent stem

RIGHT: Dip the cut end of any cutting in a rooting powder or solution, then put the cuttings round the edge of a pot filled with moist potting compost. Cover with a plastic 'tent' to prevent the compost from drying out. Support the plastic with hoops of wire so that it cannot touch the cuttings, and remove it as soon as the cuttings have rooted

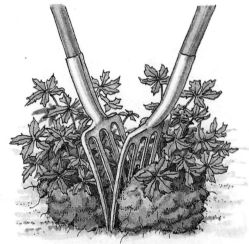

Pin down a shoot to be layered and cover with soil and a stone

Divide a plant by using two forks placed back to back in the plant

Layering

Another propagation method, especially suitable for carnations and pinks, is layering. This involves pinning down a non-flowering shoot and covering it with soil. I often use a stone or piece of tile to hold the shoot down. The layered shoot is left attached to the parent plant until well rooted. It is then cut off and planted.

Division of plants

This is suitable for most perennials, and is best carried out in late March/early April when the plant should just be moving into new growth, so that the risk of failure with the rooted offsets is minimal. Dig the plant right out of the ground, then place two forks back-to-back in the plant and carefully prise it into pieces. Select the best young outside rooted pieces for planting straight back where you want them. Discard the older central root material.

SEED AND POTTING COMPOSTS

A special type of compost is needed for germinating seeds as tiny seedlings need relatively small amounts of plant nutrients until they have developed the root systems to cope with them and sufficient above ground growth to need them. Later on the plants will need the higher nutrient levels of a potting compost.

Peat-based seed and potting composts are now more popular than those formulated with loam, the main difference between them being weight. Peat composts are much lighter and cleaner to handle but they do need more careful watering. Once a peat compost dries out it can be difficult to wet again to the right moisture level for either seedlings or plants.

All seed and potting composts tend to generate free nitrogen if stored for long periods. Free nitrogen in a compost can cause root damage so it is wise to buy from a supplier who has a rapid turnover.

CARE OF GROWING PLANTS

Besides the watering and feeding mentioned in the previous chapter, most flowers, perennials in particular, need some routine care if they are to achieve their full potential. Tall plants, for example, should be supported to protect them from being blown over in strong winds or battered down by heavy rain. Support them before any damage occurs, for once they have fallen over the stems will either break or bend so badly that permanent damage will be unavoidable. Support can be given by pushing canes, or a few pea sticks, into the ground around the plants and tying round the stems loosely with garden twine. In the case of single-stemmed

19

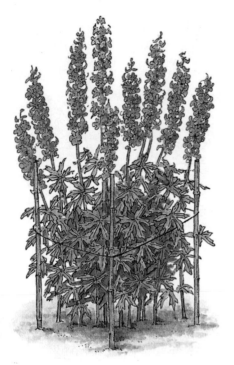

Support a clump of tall plants by pushing canes into the ground and tying twine loosely round canes and plants

very tall flowers such as sunflowers, secure to the support cane using a plant tie. Some bushy type plants can be supported merely by pushing twiggy sticks into the ground around them as they are growing. These will provide sufficient support without tying round them.

Many flowers, particularly those of biennials and perennials will flower more than once in a season if you pick or cut off the flower heads as soon as they have died. This is known as *deadheading*. By removing the dead flower heads, you stop the plant putting its energy into making seeds and it can use it instead to produce more flowers. If you want to collect seeds to sow, then you must leave the flower heads to ripen into seed heads.

Apart from roses (see page 68), pruning is not a big activity in the flower garden. The pruning generally takes the form of cutting the stems of perennials right back down to the ground in the autumn so that they are clean and tidy.

OVERWINTERING

Hardy perennials that are to stay in their positions in the flower beds or herbaceous border through the winter need very little care. At the end of their flowering time, when the foliage has also begun to die back, cut them right down to the ground so that no more than 5 cm (2 inches) of stem is showing above the soil. Clear away all dead foliage from the ground around them leaving it really clean. This makes sure that there is no waste material to rot around the plants, nor is there a potential breeding ground for insects.

Tender plants are adversely affected by excessive wet and very low temperatures during the winter. A sheet of raised glass over a small plant, or a blanket of loosely tied bracken or straw around a larger plant goes a long way to ensure their survival. Plants which die down completely such as fuchsias can also be covered with a layer of bracken or straw to protect their roots from frost.

Some plants which grow from tubers, corms, rhizomes or bulbs may need lifting and storing in a dry, airy, frost-free building through the winter. Lift them in the autumn, shake off the soil and store.

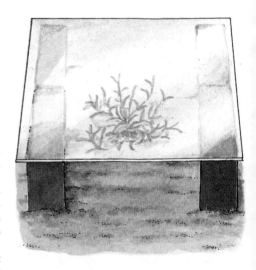

A small, tender plant can be protected from excessively wet or cold weather by placing a raised sheet of glass over it

Make a 'blanket' of loosely tied straw or bracken to enclose a large, tender plant completely for protection from winter weather

In this very colourful garden, exceptionally effective use is made of different sizes and types of containers filled with a profusion of flowering plants

CONTAINER FLOWER GARDENING

A patio or small paved area can be an attractive and colourful part of the flower garden, provided the plants are tended properly. Most plants can be grown successfully in pots and containers, but you must give them all the care and attention they will inevitably need.

Plants grown in containers can provide bright splashes of colour and interest and it is also an excellent way of being able to have those plants in your garden that do not like your type of soil. The smaller varieties of rhododendron, azalea and camellia are ideal subjects for growing in pots or containers provided these are filled with lime-free compost. Remember you must feed and water container-grown plants even in rainy weather, as most of the compost will be covered by foliage.

21

COMMON PESTS AND DISEASES

Whilst it is true that there are many garden pests and diseases and that some of them are fairly common, this need not be of great concern or worry to the amateur gardener. The secret of success in the fight against all of them is a watchful eye and a little basic know-how about the envioronment and the weather that encourages them. I would suggest a careful and observant daily walk round the garden, during which, with a sharp eye, you will soon spot any insect damage. You will quickly recognise, too, insects that feed on the sap they suck from the leaves, making a mess of the plants generally.

Sucking insects such as aphids (greenfly etc.) first appear almost singly on a plant, but if left undisturbed they multiply at a terrific rate and the plant becomes virtually 'lousey' in a few days. Hence on sight of the first one or two, take immediate action with an appropriate insecticide to eliminate them before too much damage is done. Generally speaking, sucking insects

Greenfly on rose shoot (1), leafminer on chrysanthemum (2), capsid bug on dahlia (3), narcissus fly (4)

are killed by skin absorbtion of the insecticide (a contact insecticide) whilst caterpillars are eliminated by digesting the sprayed insecticide.

In the case of diseases on plants it is somewhat different as once fungus diseases are established it is too late to affect a complete cure. Most plant diseases invade with little or no warning; by the time you have noticed them, they are established and the damage will have been done. Preventative spraying is therefore essential and must be done at the right time according to the manufacturer's directions for the fungicide you are using. Take notice of any disease problems in your garden as they occur and then take action against them next year.

COMMON PROBLEMS ON FLOWERS

Anemone: Both the DeCaen and the St. Brigid anemones are, on occasion, subject to attack by aphids (greenfly). They effect their damage by sucking the sap out of the young leaves. In addition, caterpillars and cutworms occasionally chew the buds, leaves and stems. Simple and safe control for all the pests is an insecticide based on two vegetable ingredients, potenone

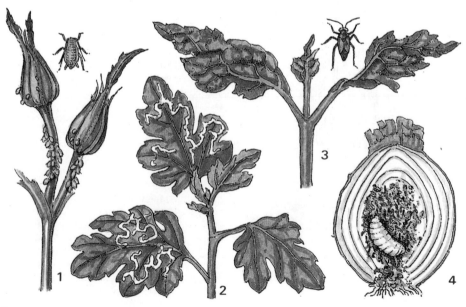

(the active ingredient of derris) and quassia (made from tree bark). Grey mould (botrytis) may cause rotting of flowers and buds early in the season particularly if the weather is wet. Prevention is the best idea; spray on a dry day with a product based either on carbendazim or thiram.

Anthirrhinum: Sucking insects of various types can cause leaf distortion and stunting of the growth here. Immediate action is advisable; spray with dimethoate and permethrin. Never use a fungicide based on malathion as anthirrhinums are very sensitive to it. Downy mildew disease which curls the leaves can be prevented by spraying with a fungicide based on thiram. Anthirrhinum rust is sometimes a problem in the south of England and is more difficult to control. Growing rust-resistant varieties is the best solution to the problem.

Asters: Attacks by aphids (greenfly) are very common and occur almost immediately after the asters have been planted out in the spring. The attack causes the leaves to curl up and the plants receive a considerable check in growth. Another pest is the capsid bug which punctures the leaves, thereby distorting them. As a preventive to both, spray with malathion a few days after planting out. Losses from foot rot disease also often occur soon after planting. To guard against it, water the ground with cheshunt compound solution. Never plant asters on the same spot two years in succession.

Begonias: Powdery mildew, which causes white powdery spots or patches on the leaves and stems, can be a problem but will only occur when the weather is continually cold and damp. At the first sign of such trouble, spray with a fungicide based on thiram and repeat at weekly intervals.

Chrysanthemums: Several sucking insects, such as aphids, capsid bugs and leaf miners, attack outdoor chrysanthemums. Leaf miners inject their eggs into the leaves and on hatching, the larvae burrow disfiguring trails through the leaves. Earwigs can also be troublesome. All these insects can be controlled with an insecticide based on HCH. Grey mould (botrytis) is a moist, warm weather problem causing damage to the blooms. Remove any affected blooms, then spray the plants with a thiram based fungicide which will also prevent powdery mildew.

Daffodils (all narcissi bulbs): The most serious

Blackspot and powdery mildew on rose (top) and antirrhinum rust

problem stems from the narcissus fly laying its eggs in May or June in or near the holes left by the dead foliage. The hatched larvae then tunnel into the bulbs, resulting in serious flower reduction (blind bulbs) and actual loss of bulbs. To reduce the risk of this egg-laying, remove the foliage just before it is completely dead, hoe or rake the surface to fill the holes, then water the area with an HCH insecticide. If the bulbs are later lifted for replanting discard any with soft necks. After replanting repeat the HCH insecticide treatment over the planted area.

Dahlias: These popular flowers are subject to attacks by aphids (blackfly particularly), capsid bugs, caterpillars and earwigs. We use a combined formulation of HCH, derris and thiram as a spray, which not only controls the pests but also prevents disease problems such as grey mould (botrytis). A simple earwig trap can be made by placing a 8 cm (3 inch) flower pot filled with dried grass upside down on top of the support stakes. Deal with the earwigs hiding in the pot each morning by holding the inverted pot above a bucket of hot water and tapping it.

Delphiniums: Greenfly can be a problem, but it is powdery mildew which coats the leaves and stems that is far more serious and it is liable to break out at any time during the season. Prevention is better than an attempted cure. Start early in the season whilst the plants are still small, by spraying with a combined spray of carbendazim and dimethoate plus permethrin. Both of these are systemic, and if sprayed at three weekly intervals will keep delphiniums clean. If powdery mildew is a recurrent problem, an application of garden lime and super phosphates early in the year should help to reduce the scale of the trouble.

Dianthus (carnations, garden pinks, sweet williams): Two forms of aphids can attack these outdoor plants. One sucks the sap from the leaves and causes stunted growth and distortion; spray with malathion immediately the pest is sighted. (The same spray will control thrips and carnation fly, the latter tunnels into the leaves and stems.) The other aphid infests the roots and is more difficult to control. The first sign is generally wilting during a dry spell, in which event drench established plants with an insecticide based on dimethoate. In the warmer and dryer parts of the country, carnation rust may occur starting first on the lower leaves as brown spore clusters. A fungicide based on thiram repeated at ten days intervals will keep the young foliage reasonably clean.

Gladioli: The most dreaded pests here are thrips – very tiny insects which suck the sap from the stems and leaves, turning them streaky and, finally brown. The pests will also feed on the flowers, making white flecks appear in the petals. Spray as soon as possible with an insecticide based on HCH. If the corms are lifted for replanting in the spring, dry them off very quickly but store at a temperature slightly below 10°C (50°F), otherwise the thrips will multiply on the corms. To control any aphids and caterpillars spray as for dahlias.

Hellebores: Early in the season white fly may appear in quantity on the flowers and foliage. Spray regularly from then on with dimethoate and permethrin until about the middle of June.

Leaf spot disease can disfigure the flowers and cause large black patches on the leaves. Remove and burn infected leaves and flowers, then spray with a liquid copper fungicide.

Hollyhocks: Rust has become a serious problem in many areas on established plants and no fungicide has yet been found to control it effectively. The raising of new plants each year and preventive spraying with a thiram based fungicide from seedling stage onwards is currently the only answer.

Irises (Flag Irises): At Clack's Farm, we have found leaf spot disease to be a constant problem. It starts in the spring with brown, oval-shaped spots which quickly enlarge, badly damaging or completely killing the infected leaves. Repeated applications of a fungicide based on carbendazim or buprimate and triforine may control it. The incidence of the disease is related to the local climate; in the southeast where it is drier it may not be a problem.

Michaelmas Daisies: Few plants are more prone to powdery mildew than Michaelmas daisies but with the new systemic fungicides it is possible to control it, providing preventive spraying starts well ahead of the first signs of the disease. Spray with a fungicide based on carbendaxim at fortnightly intervals. Should there be any sign of insect damage, change to a fungicide containing HCH and thiram. This will then control sucking and leaf-eating insects as well as controlling disease.

Pansies: A race of very small aphids attack pansies with deadly consequences. However, a routine spraying programme with malathion will prevent disaster. Stem rot disease can cause losses after planting out, but can be deterred by sprinkling 4% calomel dust in the planting hole. I have found that planting on fresh ground each year is the best insurance.

Petunias: There are no real pest problems but on some soils foot rot disease may occur. This, too, can be reduced by planting on a different site each season. Where this is not possible, a pre-planting watering of the soil with cheshunt compound solution does help to reduce losses.

Polyanthus and Primroses: A minute pest, the bryobia mite can cripple the plants, as can the red spider mite, too. Both pests deplete the foliage of sap and when this happens the plants are soon in serious trouble. Spray early with an insecticide based on dimethoate and permethrin or malathion.

Roses: The pests on roses are numerous – aphids (greenfly) caterpillars, leaf hoppers, thrips, sawfly larvae, etc. One or another is bound to turn up sometime during the growing season. To make sure that none escape, when they do arrive I use dimethoate and permethrin as an insecticide because it is effective against both the sucking and the leaf-eating insects. It maintains its effectiveness for about three weeks. In listing the diseases, black spot must be number one and it is widespread, especially in the cleaner air areas. The first symptoms appear as black spots in the older leaves; as the season progresses so does the extent of the disease, bringing about early leaf fall. It is this that depletes the health of the roses and unless some steps are taken to control the disease matters go on from bad to worse. The action I take is as follows; regular collection of infected fallen leaves because, although partially decayed, in the spring they release spores of the disease and so spread it still farther afield. I skim the soil with a spade so that the remaining debris gets buried, and prune the bush roses before Christmas instead of the third week in March, spraying them after pruning with a liquid copper fungicide. Thereafter, I repeat the spray treatment in early March when the buds are swelling and during the season I add carbendazim systemic fungicide to the insecticide spray. This is not only an additional aid in the battle against black spot but also excellent for the prevention of mildew.

In the south where the summers are warmer and drier, rose rust with its orange coloured postules occurs – the postules turn brown later in the season. Repeated spraying with thiram beginning in early spring as a preventive measure can be recommended.

Wallflowers: These are members of the cabbage family, so when the seed is sown during the summer it is wise to sprinkle bromophos in the seed drills to prevent cabbage root fly maggots feeding on the roots of the seedlings.

SLUGS AND SNAILS

At certain times of the year, especially in wet spells, both slugs and snails can do a lot of damage. Careful use of slug baits will reduce the populations but these are generally poisonous to domestic pets. An alternative way of

A simple earwig trap (top), see under Dahlia; and a slug trap

killing this pest is to sink a plastic container level with the soil, fill it with beer and put a large leaf over it. Empty it in the morning and repeat daily until you catch no more slugs in it. Far more important, however, is to remove the slugs' living quarters which may be areas of accumulated rubbish, uncontrolled vegetation, slabs of stone – in fact any hiding place where the conditions are cool and damp.

SOIL PESTS

All soil houses many insects, some of which are friendly and some harmful. Generally speaking the ones that move quickly are the gardeners' friends as they feed on other soil insects. The slow movers are the ones that stay put to feed on plant roots and stems. Usually you can leave well alone, but if you notice a real infestation in the soil, water it with a dilute HCH insecticide.

THE FLOWER GARDENER'S YEAR

The growing season from March to September will always be the busiest time for the flower gardener, but October to February should not be an inactive or uninteresting period of the year. It is during these five months, when the weather is occasionally kind, that the autumn clearing up, the winter digging, any alterations to the lay-out of the garden, rose planting, etc. are best carried out. These shorter day activities maintain the flower garden in good condition and incidentally, also keep the gardener fit.

January: Time to finish winter digging. The workability in the spring of the heaviest soils will be improved if the frost is allowed to get into the turned-up clods. Such digging also reduces slugs by exposing their eggs.

February: Usually the coldest month of the year but if it turns mild you could plant roses. Finish tidying up the herbaceous border by cutting down all dead stems; apply a light dressing of general fertiliser before lightly forking the soil, without disturbing any roots, between the plants. Sow begonia and geranium seed in a heated propagating frame.

March: With the ground well prepared and reasonably dry, this month could be the best time to plant herbaceous subjects and roses without the risk of losses. Remove the dead leaves from bearded irises and apply a general fertiliser to the ground about them, very lightly forking it in without disturbing their roots. Prepare a plot in full sun for dahlias; they will love it if it has been deeply dug with some well-rotted compost well beneath the surface to hold the moisture. Increase snowdrops now by lifting them complete with green foliage, then dividing and replanting them. Lily bulbs can be planted now, the fresher they are the better (see also September). Towards the end of the month is a good time to plant gladioli corms; if you put them 15-20 cm (6-8 inches) down they will probably survive next winter's frosts without lifting. They will also stand up to the winds better without extra support. It is time to give roses their first application of a balanced rose fertiliser. Sow half hardy annuals such as petunias, etc. indoors and remember they will need steady warmth for successful germination, so it is advisable to put them in a propagating frame.

April: Time to be out and about with the sprayer. If you have euonymus in the garden, begin by spraying this shrub as it is the host plant of overwintering blackfly. A regular inspection for the emergence of any aphids now will prevent major trouble later on. This is the month when annual weeds start to emerge and build up amongst the bulb foliage; hand weeding now will prevent seeding. Where there is less density of plants, start a weekly routine with the hoe. Even if the weeds have not yet emerged they will be in the white thread stage below the surface of the soil. Sow hardy annual seeds in the open but not before seed areas have been well prepared – made weed free and raked level to a reasonably dry fine tilth. Take care to sow evenly and thinly. Time to sow sweet-peas or plant out those raised under cover. Start hardening off petunias, marigolds, etc.

May: Keep on watching out for greenfly etc. particularly on roses and take action immediately when necessary. Add a systemic fungicide to the insecticide when spraying roses to prevent mildew.. If the weather turns dry, any roses planted in March will appreciate a can of water in the evening. In the south, wait until the third week in the month before planting out begonias, petunias and other half-hardy subjects. Farther north it is wise to delay still further until all risk of frosts have passed. If your soil is poor, a little garden fertiliser worked in before planting out will be a great help.

June: When you are spraying against greenfly, do not forget that they may be breeding in the hedges around the garden, so spray them as well. Be particularly diligent with the hoe during dry and warm days; the sun then makes sure that the weeds die immediately they are up-rooted. Dead-head roses daily to ensure continuous flowering. Cut sweet-peas before the blooms start to fade; if allowed to set seed before cutting, the plants will soon cease to produce more flowers. Lift any daffodils you wish to move for re-planting later in the season; do not dry the bulbs in direct sunshine. Towards the end of the month, sow wallflowers and sweet williams in shallow drills in a seed

bed for transplanting later. Remember the importance of watering young, recently bedded-out plants during hot dry spells.

July: By the middle of the month the first flush of roses will be nearly finished and it is time for another application of rose fertiliser after cutting each stem back to a strong outward facing bud. This is a good time to lift bearded irises if they have been down for three years or more. Select the strongest, single-rooted rhizomes for re-planting (if possible on a fresh site), but give the ground an application of a general fertiliser first. Remove the dead flowers from lilies unless you wish to save the seed. A good time to sow polyanthus and primroses outside in very shallow drills, preferably in a shady spot.

August: Herbaceous plants will need attention – dead-heading and general tidying. Take cuttings of border carnation, pinks, rock roses, etc., for rooting in pots, using a seed compost or a small rooting bag. Make sure that the cuttings are shaded and that the compost does not dry out. Take cuttings of your favourite roses.

September: Early this month, transplant wallflower and sweet william seedlings into a nursery bed or directly into the flower bed, depending on the space available. The move and extra spacing will encourage them to make bushy plants. Time to plant lilies – freshly lifted lily bulbs do best but beware of any showing signs of having dried out. Most lilies appreciate

Plan to have colour throughout the year

moist conditions but with good drainage and some dappled shade. During the month, clear away hardy annuals running to seed.

October: Take advantage of fine weather days to get rid finally of the residue of the hardy and half hardy annual bedding plants. Add all the debris to the compost heap. Early flowering and spray chrysanthemum stools will overwinter better if they are lifted towards the end of the month and put in a cold frame. After the first autumn frost, lift dahlia tubers and store them for the winter. Plant spring flowering bulbs.

November: Whilst the weather outside may not be too inviting this is the month for improving your garden soil. Whenever possible, dig it with a spade and leave it rough for the winter. Now is the best time to plant roses but do have the ground prepared ready for them.

December: Follow my example and prune your bush roses before Christmas. It is not yet time to put the spade away if there is still some open ground to be dug. When all is finished, the garden may look somewhat bare. An hour or two spent with a seed catalogue indoors and the posting of an order will make sure that you are indeed ready for next year, providing of course, that you have remembered to clean and oil your garden tools before putting them away.

Happy Gardening next year.

BULBS, CORMS AND TUBERS

For most of us bulbs are associated with the spring flowers, such as tulips and daffodils. If you choose carefully, however, it is possible to have a great variety of flowers from spring through summer to autumn, all grown from bulbs, corms or rhizomes.

There are a few golden rules when growing plants of this type. Always plant at the depth recommended by the suppliers, and find out, too, what kind of conditions – sun or shade – and the type of soil each individual likes. All bulbs need good drainage and the dead foliage should be quickly cleared away when the plant has finished flowering. If obeyed, these two rules prevent rotting of the bulbs and any build up of disease.

ALLIUM*

There are many different types of allium, or ornamental onion, some with flowering stems so tall that they need support to keep their flowerheads off the ground whilst others are sufficiently small to make them suitable for the rock garden. Planted amongst low-growing shrubs, the taller alliums make effective unusual displays. In common with all members of the onion family they appreciate well drained soil and as much sunshine as possible. Allium seed-heads are just as attractive as the flower-heads.

Allium aflatunense grows to 75 cm (2½ ft) tall, and with its large purple-lilac heads is exceptionally ornamental. It flowers in late May. *A. caeruleum* grows to 60 cm (2 ft) high and is widely available. It is a graceful plant with cornflower blue flower-heads carried on strong wiry stems. It flowers in June. *A. cowanii* grows to 60 cm (2 ft) high and has fine heads of pure white flowers which appear at the end of May. *A. moly* grows only to 30 cm (1 ft) high and is an old garden favourite. It has umbels of golden yellow flowers which appear in June.

Early autumn is the best time to plant all varieties. Once planted, leave them to multiply until the clumps become overcrowded. At this point, lift the bulbs and replant them separately. Sow seed outside in a seed bed immediately after it has ripened or, if you buy it, try to make sure it is as fresh as possible. Leave it for a season before pricking the seedlings out into a bed.

ANEMONE*

We grow *Anemone coronaria* from corms – the 'De Caen' and 'St Brigid' strains are selections that have evolved over the years to provide us with some of the most colourful of all early blooming flowers. Being natives of the warmer Mediterranean climate, they still need some special care and protection for quality and quantity flower production. In the south-western areas of Cornwall and Devon, they flower happily outside during the early months of the year, but elsewhere they will need protecting with cloches if they are to flower early. In all situations, plant in well-drained soil where there is plenty of sunshine. For spring flowering, plant the corms in September/October. The foliage will die down after flowering. Allow the corms to multiply without disturbance to give increased flowering in the following seasons.

'De Caen', the single flowered anemone, is usually offered as a mixture of brilliant colours but named varieties are available in separate colours. 'St Brigid' has semi-double flowers and is not quite so free flowering. Seed of both can be purchased for sowing any time, January to June, in a greenhouse or cold frame.

Among the small flowered varieties for rockery and wild gardens is the easy-to-grow *A. blanda* which reaches a height of 10-15 cm (4-6 inches) and has blue flowers that bloom in March/April. It is delightful and is even successful when planted in semi-shade. *A. blanda atrocaerulea* is another small one with lovely blue flowers. It increases rapidly after planting. Separate colours are available such as 'Charmer' – pale pink, 'Radar' – bright carmine and 'Splendour' – white. You can also buy these as a mixture.

BEGONIA**

Tuberous-rooted begonias need special care to get them into flower by planting-out time (June). For success, it is necessary to have a greenhouse, a propagating frame or some other facility with good light where the temperature does not drop below 18° C (65° F). Start the tubers in March by putting them hollow side uppermost in a moist peat compost. At this time, they can be spaced quite close to one another, but soon afterwards when growth starts, each plant will need a 2.5-cm (5-inch) half pot at least. Prepare the ground outside where you want them to flower by digging in some well-rotted compost or peat to hold the moisture. The plants will grow well in partial shade provided they are never short of water. For the best blooms feed with a liquid tomato fertiliser every fortnight. At the end of the season, after the first frost damage to the foliage, lift the tubers and dry them indoors. Store in a frost-free, airy place until March.

At Clack's Farm, we started with Begonia 'Non-Stop' mixed seed and raised plants from the seedlings in the greenhouse heated to 18° C (65° F). These we planted out in June. At the end of that season, we lifted the tubers and have since started them up into new growth, as explained above, each spring. The seed may be expensive but it is an investment in tremendous beauty. Most other varieties are only really suitable for greenhouses.

CHIONODOXA*
Commonly known as Glory of the snow, these early spring flowering bulbs, with their dainty small star-shaped flowers artistically arranged on

A beautifully coloured Colchicum speciosum

slender stems, are natives of the high mountains in Asia Minor. Plant them in the autumn in ordinary well-drained soil where they will be able to have a full view of the sun, and leave them undisturbed. They will multiply rapidly to be a sheer delight every year. Our *C. luciliae* with its vivid blue, white-centred flowers has just done this. *C. luciliae* 'Rosea' has pure pink flowers and can be recommended, as can *C. gigantea* with large pale blue blooms.

COLCHICUM**
Autumn flowering colchicums can be used to advantage in a shrub border or even in rough grass. The flowers are held on naked stems, and they do make an attractive splash of colour. Whilst the flowers themselves take up only a small space, the large leaves can smother nearby plants in the spring. They also look untidy before they die back. These are two good reasons why it is important to choose the planting site carefully. The best effect is obtained when the corms are planted in clumps in August/September

Lily of the Valley, Convallaria majalis

and are then left for years.

C. *autumnale* (sometimes called the Autumn crocus) is a European native, much appreciated by autumn visitors to France, particularly to the foothills of the Alps. Its crocus-like flowers are a soft rosy lilac. The dark rosy purple flowers of C. *cilicium* appear slightly later. C. *speciosum*, in its several forms, such as 'Album' – a white, 'Disraeli' – a deep mauve and 'Lilac Wonder' – a pinkish lilac with a white throat – is probably best for garden planting.

CONVALLARIA*
Lily of the Valley
This well-known plant is famed for its graceful sprays of perfumed, bell-shaped flow-

ers. It grows rampantly with us in the shade of a stone wall where the sun is never able to dry out the soil. It can generally be established in partial shade or even out in the open provided the soil never completely dries out. To ensure the right growing conditions, prepare the ground by digging in a liberal quantity of well-rotted compost. The best time to plant is September/October; make sure that each crown is planted with the point upwards. When the bed becomes overcrowded – which it will do after some years – lift and replant the bulbs after replenishing the ground with compost. C. *majalis* is the standard white form. It grows some 15-20 cm (6-8 inches) high. C. *majalis* 'Rosea' has pink flowers but it can be less vigorous.

CROCOSMIA*
This is closely related to montbretia and indeed is often mistaken for a giant and improved form of it. Perhaps this is not altogether surprising as montbretia was one of its parents. It is a plant that needs sunshine to flower well – in shade it does no more than just survive – and it does best in a light well-drained soil. If grown in the north it would appreciate the shelter of a south facing wall.

We started with a few corms of C. *masonorum* which grows to 75 cm (2½ ft) and we now have several well established clumps. The richly coloured flame-orange flowers on arching stems make a superb display from July to September, and it is excellent for cutting, too. A newer variety, C. *Lucifer*, has even finer and more colourful flowers of an intense brilliant flame red. These appear in June/July, and the plant grows to 90 cm (3 ft).

The best time to plant is March. When the clumps become overcrowded lift and divide them, then re-plant if possible on fresh ground which has had some well-rotted compost incorporated.

CROCUS*
The 'heralds of the spring' – crocus will grow in any type of soil. While the large-flowered crocus may be the most spectacular, we should not forget the small-flowered species which flower in February/March. Try C. *chrysanthus* mixed; they will quickly multiply and give an increasing display as the numbers build up. The same can be said for the large-flowered varieties; we grow 'Queen of the Blues',

'Pickwick' – pearly grey with dark centres and striped dark lilac, 'Jeanne d'Arc' – snow white, 'Remembrance' – a large violet purple and 'Large Yellow'. The last one was raided by sparrows until we discouraged them by no longer feeding them! October/November is the best time to plant.

CYCLAMEN**

The hardy cyclamen, *C. neapolitanum* is an exquisite plant which flowers in the autumn long after its foliage has died down. The tiny pink or white flowers are perfect miniature cyclamen on slender stems. They are fascinating to watch as they seem almost to dance in a slight wind. There can be few more beautiful sights in any garden than masses of these delightful flowers in a low golden autumn sunlight

The exquisite, miniature Cyclamen neapolitanum

especially if they cover a large area under a beech tree.

The secret with these treasures is to plant the corms (slight depression upwards) in the late summer, barely covering them with soil. They prefer a well drained situation where they are not likely to suffer scorching from hot sunshine. From then on, hand weed around them carefully so as not to disturb either the corms or the seedlings (see below). In a few years, the cyclamen will have extended their territory considerably. Seed is available; sow it in a cool greenhouse any time from October to March. Plants grown in this way will probably start to flower in their second or third year.

DAHLIA**

These are half-hardy, tuberous rooted perennials which require a sunny position in rich fertile soil, that is moisture retentive and well prepared.

As all parts of the plant are frost sensitive, planting must be delayed until the risk of spring frost has ended; this means late May/early June. Dahlia tubers can be planted out but it is more advisable to use tubers that have been started off in the greenhouse. However, best results of all are obtained with rooted cuttings from forced tubers, started in a warm greenhouse and hardened off before planting out. These methods are for the various decorative and exhibition types, which vary in height from 45 cm – 1.8 metres (18 inches – 6 ft). All but the shortest varieties need staking and tying during the growing season. For mass bedding-out dahlias can be raised from seed in a temperature of 15° C (60° F). 'Chi-Chi' mixed has a considerable range of colours in flowers and foliage.

At the end of the flowering season, bury the tubers at least 30 cm (1 ft) deep under a thorn

hedge or beside a fence, where they should be safe from rotting and frost.

ENDYMION NON-SCRIPTA* Bluebell

Our native bluebell is wonderful when seen in the spring as carpets of blue in a country setting or in a wild garden. However, it is wise to think twice before planting bluebells in a border; they spread so rapidly, both by multiplication of the bulbs and by seeds, particularly if the soil suits them.

ERANTHIS**

Winter Aconite

The winter aconites, E. hyemalis, are one of our earliest and brightest spring flowers. A wonderful bright golden yellow colour, they are rather like large buttercups on short stems set in rings of leafy bracts. Grown in masses they are stunningly cheerful. Plant the nobbly tubers, in spring, not more than 5 cm (2 inches) deep, in small groups. If the soil is good and inclined to be moist, they will soon spread. Always hand weed the area; never use a hoe. Any disturbance will prevent tubers multiplying and spreading over a much larger area. Ideal for naturalising under trees.

FRITILLARIA**

There are two species within this group of hardy bulbs that are of particular interest to the gardener: F. imperialis (Crown imperial) and F. meleagris (Snake's head). Both do best in well-drained moist soils. They should be planted either in full sun or in slight shade, after which they should be left undisturbed for years. We mark

their growing area with canes so that we know just where they are as there is no visible growth above ground between July and January and the slightest damage to an emerging stem in February will mean loss of flowers. The bulbs are fleshy, easily damaged and must be planted as fresh as possible from August to October. Plant Crown imperials 15-20 cm (6-8 inches) deep and Snake's heads 10-15 cm (4-6 inches) deep. We have two varieties of Crown imperials, both of which grow to 90 cm (3 ft). They are 'Lutea Maxima' which has deep yellow blooms and 'Rubra Maxima' which has brick red flowers. The Snake's heads which are much lower growing at 25 cm (10 inches) high are C. meleagris mixed. They have charming drooping bell flowers in many variations of chequering. All flower in April.

GALANTHUS*

Snowdrop

The 'Fair Maids of Feburary', this is the first outdoor bulb to flower and no garden is complete without them. Whilst they will grow and succeed in moist soils, they do best in heavy loams with plenty of moisture. Left undisturbed they multiply freely until, if grown in a border, they may need lifting and dividing to maintain maximum flower production. The time to lift and replant snowdrops is a couple of weeks after flowering whilst the foliage is still green. If dry bulbs are bought they should be very fresh; plant them straight away.

There are numerous varieties; G. nivalis is the com-

mon snowdrop and is usually chosen for naturalising in the grass and in shade under shrubs. For open ground it is better to plant the large-flowered varieties, such as G. elwesii or G. nivalis 'Viridapicis' with its green-tipped petals. My favourites are 'Mr. S. Arnot' which has large single flowers and G. nivalis plenus with large double flowers.

GLADIOLUS*

All gladioli do best when planted in a sunny position where the soil has been well prepared. Some old compost or manure dug in also helps as does good drainage. The corms are frost sensitive so the time to plant is late March/April. The depth is important and always plant at least 15 cm (6 inches) or even deeper; then unstaked flower stems do not topple over and if you are prepared to take something of a risk, the corms can be left in the ground through the winter. If not planted as deep as this, the corms need lifting in the autumn. Dry them off quickly indoors and store in a frost free airy place.

In addition to the large-flowered varieties, the more dainty primulinus and butterfly types appeal to me.

HYACINTHUS*

Hyacinths

Once hyacinths have been planted and left undisturbed, they will flower without fail each spring although after several years the quality of the flowers does deteriorate. They prefer a medium soil with good drainage. We regularly plant out our forced 'Christmas' hyacinths, they recover quickly and will flower for several seasons afterwards without lifting.

IPHEION**

This bulb plant, with its grass-like foliage, flowers from March to May. Its single flowers have six petals and they measure 3-5 cm (1½-2 inches) across. They are carried on 15-20 cm (6-8 inch) stems. Ipheion are natives of Mexico, and as a result they need a sheltered position in sun or slight shade plus good drainage and plenty of humus. September/October is the time to plant. Do not allow the bulbs to dry out before planting. Ipheion 'Wisley Blue', which has large violet blooms is probably the best.

IRIS*

Amongst the many bulbous iris the best known is probably *I. reticulata* which grows 15-20 cm (6-8 inches) tall. It is often planted with good effect in rock gardens, and it produces its purple-blue flowers in February/March. The variety 'Cantab' is a lighter blue than 'J.S. Dijt' which is a near purple. *Iris danfordiae*, with its vivid yellow flowers, needs planting at least 12.5 cm (5 inches) deep to prevent the bulbs splitting up into non-flowering bulblets. The tall Dutch iris which grows 75 cm (2½ ft) high is excellent for cutting in June. If left undisturbed it will flower for years provided it too, has been planted about 12.5 cm (5 inches) deep. In fact, the same is true of the Spanish and English iris. All iris do best in a rich moist soil.

LEUCOJUM* Snowflake
These hardy bulbous plants,

The beautiful Lilium regale

with snowdrop-like flowers, do well in any garden soil, whether they are planted in sun or partial shade.
L. aestivum – grows 50 cm (20 inches) tall and in spite of its common name – Summer Snowflake – actually flowers in March/April. It has pure white bells on each stem. *L. vernum*, smaller at 15 cm (6 inches) tall, is the spring snowflake, and it flowers soon after the snowdrop. It requires a moist cool peaty soil. Plant bulbs in late summer.

LILIUM**

This is a very extensive family of hardy lilies and we are more than grateful that our Clack's Farm lime-free soil suits most of them. The lilies' soil requirements are good drainage but with moisture retention (achieved by digging in plenty of compost). The ideal situation is for the bulbs to be in light shade, but with the flower heads out into the sunshine. Flowering from June until August, we have several varieties, such as 'Pirate', 'Enchantment', 'African Queen', 'Green Dragon' and many others. In July, we enjoy *L. regale*, which, with its yellow throated white flowers, is the easiest to grow. All these lily bulbs should be planted 15 cm (6 inches) deep as they are stem-rooted. The one we have to nurse most carefully is *L. candidum* (Madonna Lily). Plant this one with its 'nose' close to the surface and mulch with compost in spring.

All lily bulbs should be planted while they are as fresh as possible and you should allow them a few years to settle down. Sow seed immediately after harvesting in seed trays and keep outside in autumn.

MUSCARI*
Grape Hyacinth
These small, well-known bulbous plants thrive in a sunny position, in fact they multiply so rapidly that it is advisable to lift and replant the largest of the bulbs each year. Plant in the autumn. *M. botryoides* 'Heavenly Blue' with sky-blue flowers is the best form. *M. botryoides* 'Album' is white.

NARCISSUS*
These are the hardy spring flowering bulbs which include the daffodils, jonquils and various species and hybrids. To many people the terms, 'daffodils' and 'narcissus' mean two different plants, but strictly speaking they are one and the same. All narcissi do well in most garden soils and a late summer planting allows the bulbs time to develop good root systems before the soil cools down. Our outstanding large golden-yellow trumpet daffodils include 'Golden Harvest' and 'Rembrandt' but there are long lists to choose

Nerine bowdenii is very colourful

from in the bulb catalogues. The superb 'Ice Follies' has attractive off-white flowers, and amongst the pure white, 'Mount Hood' is one of the best. We are also very fond of 'Fortune', which is a large-cupped variety with a reddish corona. Just some of the Narcissi varieties are 'Geranium', 'Cheerfulness', and 'Actaea'.

When you purchase bulbs make sure that the 'nose' of each bulb is firm. Plant early in the autumn and after flowering, let the foliage die naturally before cutting down.

NERINE**
Unfortunately only one species – *N. bowdenii* which grows 60 cm (2 ft) high – is hardy enough to be planted outside in this country. It requires a warm sunny position; ours does well in front of a south facing wall. It likes a light soil, particularly if given a summer mulch of well-rotted compost to supply nutrients. The foliage dies down during the summer and the large umbels of delightful pink flowers appear on naked stems in early autumn. Plant bulbs 10 cm (4 inches) deep in April.

RANUNCULUS*
Buttercup
R. acris 'Flore-pleno', the double yellow buttercup, which grows 75 cm (2½ ft) tall, is suitable for a herbaceous border provided it can have a position in full sun or half shade in moist soil. Other colours are available as a mixture. Plant the corms with their claws downwards in February/March. To propagate, divide and then replant the corms in the spring.

SCILLA* Wild Hyacinth

This is another small bulbous plant that is well worth a place in any rock garden. It likes a well drained soil with a little added peat to hold the moisture. Its bell-like flowers appear in March.

There is a choice of several varieties; *S. siberica* 'Spring Beauty' which grows 15 cm (6 inches) tall and is a bright blue; *S. campanulata* mixed, taller at 35 cm (14 inches) and *S. tubergeniana* which has blueish-white flowers and grows only 10 cm (4 inches) high. Plant the bulbs as fresh as possible in late summer or early autumn. All are suitable for naturalising.

TRILLIUM* Wood Lily

The common name of this plant gives some indication of the growing conditions required – namely a moist soil, rich in humus and a position in light shade. *T. grandiflorum* (Wake Robin) grows 30 cm (1 ft) high and has short arching stems to carry its large three-petalled flowers that measure 5-7 cm (2-3 inches) across and appear in late spring. *T. undulatum* (Painted Wood Lily) grows 30 cm (1 ft) tall; its flowers have white petals that are reddish purple at the base and its coppery red foliage is an extra feature.

Plant the rhizomes as fresh as possible in late summer. Lift and divide them after the foliage has died down.

TRITONIA*

Closely related to freesia and Crocosmia, *Tritonia crocata* is somewhat less hardy, which is not surprising as it is a native of South Africa. In the U.K. it

can only be regarded as a possible flower garden plant in the warmer areas. In those parts, it needs a light, well-drained soil and a sunny sheltered position. Its 60 cm (2 ft) spikes of bright orange flowers appear in May/June. Plant the corms in March for flowering a year later.

TULIPA* Tulips

Under this title there is the extensive genus of popular spring flowering bulbs with heights ranging from about 15 cm (6 inches) to 75 cm (2½ ft). Because of this variation, it is important to find out about the growth habit of the various types. Any good garden soil will suit tulips, but they like an open sunny position. While most hybrid tulips, such as the tall Darwins and May-flowering varieties,

The unusual flowers of Trillium grandiflorum

deteriorate if left in the ground from season to season, some of the species persist well, and in fact, will multiply freely. For long-term planting, try *T. fosteriana* 'Madame Lefeber', which grows 45 cm (18 inches) tall and is a striking vivid scarlet, *T. greigii* 'Red Riding Hood', which grows 15 cm (6 inches) tall or *T. kaufmanniana* (Waterlily tulip) 30 cm (12 inches) tall. 'The First' is an exceptionally early variety and has pure white blooms tinted carmine-red on the reverse of the petals. It grows to 20 cm (8 inches).

To make your choice, I suggest you look through a bulb specialist's catalogue and order early so that you can plant in October.

ANNUALS

Annuals are plants that can be grown from seed to flower and die and in the same season. (HHA) in the text indicates that the subject is not completely hardy in our climate, consequently it is one that needs special treatment. Begonias, petunias and marigolds are good examples: their seed requires warm conditions early in the season for germination, and similar conditions to produce good plants, which are on the verge of flowering, towards the end of May, ready for planting outside when the risk of spring frosts is over. (HA) in the text indicates that the seed can be sown outdoors where the plants are intended to flower. There is a great variety within this group which means that with a few packets of seed it is possible to produce plenty of summer colour in the garden at little cost.

AGERATUM* (HHA)
Soft cushion-like flowerheads are the feature of this beautiful edging or bedding annual. Given a moisture-retentive soil and a sunny position it will flower from early summer until the first frosts. Water it if there is any danger of the ground getting dry and deadhead when the flowers die.

The height of the different varieties varies from 15-45 cm (6-18 inches). The taller varieties provide a useful cut flower. The colours also vary from a clear blue of 'Blue Mink' to bluish-mauve of 'Blue Blazer' and lavender blue of 'Blue Bouquet'. Sow in February/March under glass and keep at a temperature of 10-15°C (50-60°F) to germinate.

ALYSSUM* (HA)
This small ever-popular edging plant, Alyssum maritimum, is suitable for growing in the rock garden and in the crevices of paving or stone walls. It flowers continuously throughout the summer in any ordinary soil in a full sun position. It grows to a height of 10-15 cm (4-6 inches) and popular varieties are 'Little Dorrit' – white, 'Snowdrift' – white, 'Rosie O'Day' – pink and 'Royal Carpet' – purple.

Sow under glass in February/March and keep at 10-15°C (50-60°F). Sow in open ground in April/May.

AMARANTHUS* (HHA)
The red version of Amaranthus caudatus is commonly known as 'Love Lies Bleeding'. It is tall enough to grow in the centre of an annual bed or border. The flowers occur in long graceful tassels from July to October, and are ideal for cutting as they last well in water. The green variety 'Viridis' in particular is prized by flower arrangers. Other varieties include 'Crimson' and 'Tricolor Splendens'.

Amaranthus grow to 75-90 cm (2½-3 ft) and favour a sunny position. An ordinary soil is adequate but more impressive growth will result from planting in a deep rich soil. Sow under glass in March and keep at 15°C (60°F) or in March/May outside.

ANCHUSA* (HA)
Anchusa capensis is a biennial from which a strain has been developed for use as an annual. A good blue in the flower garden can be scarce at midsummer, but from July to August, anchusa can fill the gap with its large forget-me-not-like flowerheads of an intense blue. Sow seeds in March/May in open ground and transplant groups to the border. Growing to a height of 23 cm (9 inches), it is also ideal to grow in a container. A good variety is 'Blue Angel'.

ARCTOTIS*
African Daisy (HHA)
This grey-green leaved plant has large daisy-like flowers which come in a wide range of both pale and bright colours from late June until the first frosts. Some flowers have zones of contrasting colour towards the centre making them particularly striking. A good choice for a dry sunny position, after planting out, pinch out the growing tips at about 15 cm (6 inches) to encourage branching and cut or dead head after the blooms have died to encourage further flowering. They grow to a height of 30-75 cm (1-2½ ft), and the taller varieties may need some twigs for support.

Arctotis makes an attractive if short-lived cut flower. Sow in February/March under glass and keep at a temperature of 10-15°C (50-60°F).

BEGONIA SEMPERFLORENS** (HHA)

This is a fibrous-rooted begonia. Grow it as an annual, then at the end of the season lift the plants and pot them for further flowering indoors. The germination and early stages of growing are not the easiest but by planting-out time this begonia is generally a real survivor. The fleshy leaves help it through dry spells and it is equally at home in sun or light shade. Even deeper shade does not suppress it altogether. Plant it in the front of a border, or in any sort of container. It varies in height from 15-38 cm (6-15 inches). Masses of small flowers in shades of red and pink through to white are produced from June until the first frosts. The foliage may be green or bronze.

There are many seed mixtures which achieve a complete carpet of colour. Recommended varieties are 'Happy Choice', which has large flowers, 'Organdy' – mixed, 'Danica' – mixed, or available in individual colours of red, rose and scarlet, 'Ambra' – in various single colours, and 'Picotee' – white edged pink. Sow under glass from January to March and keep at a temperature of 20-25°C (68-78°F). The seed is very small, but try to sow as thinly as possible and do not cover with compost. Prick out when the seedlings have two sets of true leaves. As a precaution against damping off disease, water the trays of seedlings from below by standing in water just until

Ageratum 'Blue Mink' is a good colour

the surface of the growing medium becomes damp.

BRACHYCOME* (HA)

Brachycome iberidifolia, the Swan River Daisy, produces fragrant cineraria-like flowers of blue, pink, purple and white shades from June to September. Growing to a height of 23 cm (9 inches) it is useful for group planting in the border. Sow in March/May in open ground.

CALENDULA*
Marigold (HA)

This old English flower will thrive in any open position. It rewards the sower with a glorious summer show of orange and yellow shades for almost no effort. The large double-daisy-type flowers look colourful and last well in water. Growing to 30-60cm (1-2ft) high, recommended varieties are 'Radio' – deep orange, 'Lemon Queen' – yellow and 'Fiesta Gitana' – a colourful mixture. Sow in open ground from March to May. If you want to change the plants in a bed, the prolific self-seeding of marigolds could create something of a 'weed problem'. Once allocated an area, self-sown seedlings will go on flowering satisfactorily.

CALLISTEPHUS*
Aster (HHA)

Callistephus chinensis is an annual belonging to the same family as the perennial Michaelmas daisy. Although it had been a great favourite over the years, the high incidence of aster wilt disease had become a deterrent to many gardeners. Relatively recent successes in the breeding of strains with an acceptable degree of wilt resistance has changed this situation. Asters flower according to the variety from July until the first frosts. Recommended varieties are 'Milady' – dwarf varieties in colours of rose, blue, white and mixed, 'Lilliput' – miniature pompon and 'Super sinensis' single. All are excellent for bedding out. There are several forms ranging from the tall, feathery-headed ostrich plume type to the chrysanthemum flowered ones, including those with incurving petals. There are also those with miniature pompom flowers and – probably the best of all for weather resistance and flower arranging – the single

sinensis strain. Height ranges from 20-60cm (8-24 inches); tall ones are ideal for cutting.

Sow under glass in March/April and keep at 15-20°C (60-68°F) to germinate. Plant out in well drained soil in a sunny position. Watch out for curling leaves – a sign of aphid attack to which the young plants are particularly prone. It has a stunting effect and adversely affects flowering prospects.

CENTAUREA*
Cornflower (HA)

Centaurea cyanus is an easy annual for any well-drained, sunny site. The cornflower is a sturdy border and cut-flower plant, and may be either true cornflower blue or red, pink, purple or white. The taller varieties, growing up to 90 cm (3 ft) high, may need support. Sow seeds from March to May or in September where they are to flower the following year. Do not try to transplant.

Another species is *C. moschata* or Sweet sultan. Its powder-puff flowers of yellow, pink, purple and white are sweetly scented and good for cutting. It grows to a height of 60 cm (2 ft). Sow seed in April/May where it is intended to flower.

CHRYSANTHEMUM*
(HA)

Large groups of the single flowered chrysanthemum, *Chrysanthemum carinatum*, growing 75 cm (2 ft) tall make impressive mid-border plantings and also supply long-lasting cut flowers. Colours include bronze, yellow, red, purple and white. Some varieties have zones of contrasting colour around the flower centre.

All do well in sunny positions, but make sure the soil never dries out around the plants' roots as this sometimes results in collapse. Seed should be sown in the open from March to May. Pinching out the leading shoot encourages branching and increases flower production. Seed mixtures are available.

CLARKIA* (HA)

This annual will do well in most soils, situated either in sun or partial shade. With its naturally branching habit it quickly covers the planting area and then flowers continuously from July to September. *Clarkia elegans* grows up to 60cm (2 ft) high and produces long double flower spikes in shades of purple, red, pink and orange to white. *Clarkia pulchella* grows to 45cm (18 inches) high and has double and semi-double flowers of white, violet and rose. Sow seed from March to May directly into the position where it is intended to flower.

COREOPSIS* (HA)

This will succeed in any well-drained soil–a light type being preferable – in a sunny position. It is a good choice in an industrial area because it will tolerate a polluted atmosphere. Depending on variety, plants reach 30-60cm (1-2ft) and produce daisy-like flowers continuously from July to September. Colours range from the more common yellow to crimson and scarlet. Those with petals contrastingly blotched towards the centre are particularly attractive. I sow seed mixtures in situ from March to May.

COSMOS* (HHA)

This is a tall-growing plant and very useful to bring colour to the back of the flower border. It has attractive finely cut foliage and bright dahlia-like flowers which are ideal for cutting. Cosmos will stand a dry season and is an ideal subject for a light, poor soil. Some support could be needed by flowering time which is in August and September.

Seed can be sown in a cool greenhouse, but I sow in situ in April/May. Although described as a half-hardy plant, shedded seed often survives the winter. It is certainly worth leaving self-sown seedlings; just thin them out and leave them to flower where they appear. Our choice is 'Sensation Mixed' which grows to 90 cm (3 ft).

DAHLIA** (HHA)

The bedding type of dahlia is usually grown as an annual. As such it has become one of the most valuable of the late summer flowerers. Blooms, in forms and colours similar to those of the larger border dahlias, appear in profusion from July going on until they are cut down by the first frosts. Dead-heading and cutting for decoration encourages the formation of more flowers. 'Chi Chi' and 'Redskin' are good colour mixtures.

For best results, a well-cultivated soil is necessary and the plants need watering well during dry spells. They grow only to a maximum height of 39 cm (15 inches) so no staking is needed.

Sow seed in the greenhouse at a temperature 15-20°C (60-68°F) in March and prick out,

The delicate mixed colours of Centaurea cyanus, the cornflower

putting eighteen seedlings in each standard sized tray. Plant out the small plants at the end of May/beginning of June after all danger of frost.

DELPHINIUM* (HA)

Larkspur, *Delphinium consolida*, is the annual delphinium, often grown especially for summer flower arrangements. Its tall slender stems are covered with pink, blue or white flowers from June to August. The double sorts are particularly beautiful. 'Stock flowered' mixture is one of the best especially for cut flowers. It grows to 90 cm (3 ft).

Godetia has very beautiful flowers produced in great profusion

Seed may be sown in the open from March to May but if you want early flowers, sow in the previous September. The plants do best in a good moisture-retaining soil in full sun. Water them during dry spells.

DIANTHUS* (HHA)

Some of the newer varieties of the annual *Dianthus chinensis* are a must for a brilliant summer show. 'Heddewigii' has single flowers in scarlets, reds, pinks, mixtures and white, produced in succession from June until the first frosts. Other outstanding varieties are 'Queen of Hearts', which grows to 30 cm (12 inches) and has scarlet-red flowers and 'Snow Fire' which has white flowers with bright scarlet centres, and is a little smaller at 20 cm (8 inches). The bushy plants appreciate a neutral to alkaline soil in a position that gets plenty of sunshine. Sow under glass at a temperature of 15-20°C (60-68°F) in February/March for planting out at the end of May.

DIMORPHOTHECA* (HA)

Dimorphotheca aurantiaca is a bright daisy-like flower from South Africa commonly known as 'Star of the Veldt'. It loves a dryish border, but do not plant it in shade as its flowers only open in bright light. I sow in the open from March to May where I intend it to flower. For a glorious display sow *D. aurantiaca* hybrids.

ECHIUM* (HA)

Echium plantagineum has a long flowering season. If sown early it will start to flower in late May and go on continuously until the autumn. The bees love its lovely bell-like flowers that come in shades of blue and pink. Most sites and soils are suitable but flowering is freer in full sun. Sow in the open where intended to flower from March to May. We sow 'Dwarf Hybrid' mixture, which grows to 30 cm (12 inches) high.

ESCHSCHOLZIA*

Californian Poppy (HA)
Grown as a hardy annual, *E. californica* produces masses of orange-yellow poppy flowers from June to October. 'Balerina' mixed is an interesting variety which has semi-double flowers with fluted petals.

The poppy does best in the poorer sandy soils and is just right for a dry sunny border. Self-sown seedlings will flower well in succeeding seasons. Sow in situ outdoors from March to May.

GAILLARDIA* (HHA)

Give G. pulchella a mid-border position where it will flower freely from July to October, providing, also, incidentally, a good flower for cutting. Try 'Suttons Large-flowered Mixed' which grows to 75 cm (2½ ft) or 'Goblin' (dwarf bedder), which is half the height at 38 cm (15 inches). Varieties with large flower heads will need support.

I sow seed in the greenhouse in March and keep at a temperature of 15°C (60°F) planting out at the end of May/ beginning of June. The plants do well in sun or light shade in almost any soil although a well-drained soil is best.

GAZANIA** (HHA)

This is a half-hardy annual from South Africa that loves sunshine, in fact its brilliant daisy flowers close at night. Seed mixtures are available which give flowers of yellow, pink and red shades as well as the more usual orange.

I sow in the greenhouse heated to 15-20°C (60-68°F) in March for planting out at the end of May/beginning of June. It likes a well-drained sunny position.

GODETIA* (HA)

G. grandiflora is easy to grow and flowers prolifically in any soil. The plants are bushy and grow quickly, so they will soon cover the ground in the flower border. Clusters of poppy-type flowers are produced in profusion from June to August. Try 'Tall Double Mixed' which grows to 60 cm (2 ft) or 'Double Azalea-flowered Mixed' which grows to 35 cm (14 inches). I sow seed in an open sunny position in April where intended to flower, barely covering the seed.

HELIANTHUS* (HA)

There are many daisy-like flowers among the annuals but this plant – H. annuus, the sunflower – must be the most spectacular. From the tallest varieties, 3.2-4 metres (8-10 ft) stems topped by flowers measuring 30 cm (12 inches) across, are by no means unusual. These giants need lots of sun and a good, well-drained soil with plenty of water during dry spells. Support the stems with strong stakes. Shorter varieties are available, needing lighter support, and they will flower impressively in the centre of a bed or towards the back of the flower border but remember

The sunflower, Helianthus, is a most spectacular garden flower

The sweet pea, Lathyrus odoratus

the heads will always turn to face the south. The flowering period is from late July to September, and recommended varieties are 'Giant Yellow' which grows 2 metres (6 ft) high and 'Sunburst', which has mixed colours and grows to 1.2 metres (4 ft) tall. Sow in the flowering positions in April/May.

HELICHRYSUM* (HA)

The Strawflower, *H. brac-teatum*, is certainly attractive in the garden as a bedding plant but its great value is to the flower arranger for drying. Again, the flowers are daisy-like in shape but the petals are shiny and somewhat like straw. Flowers are produced from July to September and blooms for drying should be cut just as they are opening. If they are cut when fully open, seed development continues and the flower centres are spoilt. Try growing 'Hot Bikini' – a bright red and 'Bright Bikini' – a colourful mixture, both of which grow to 30 cm (12 inches) high. To dry remove all foliage from the stems and then hang them, flower heads downwards in small bunches in a shady cool airy place. Sow seed in March/May in open ground. A sandy soil in full sun is best.

HELIOTROPIUM* (HHA)

Many people know this as Cherry pie. Its sturdy naturally branching plants bear forget-me-not-like flowers from May to October. The dark green to almost purple foliage of some varieties makes a useful contrast both to its own flowers and to other foliage in the bed. 'Marine', which grows 38 cm (15 inches) high is an outstanding variety. Sow in the greenhouse at a temperature of 15-20°C (60-68°F) in February/March and plant out into any well-drained soil in a sunny position.

HELIPTERUM* (HHA)

This is often listed by seedsmen as *Acroclinium*. It has a delicate daisy flower well suited for planting in the summer flower border and for drying for winter decoration. Its flowers, which appear in July and August and again have strawy petals, are ideally suited for drying; this is done in the same way as Helichrysum. 'Sandfordii' is an attractive yellow variety, growing 30 cm (12 inches) high.

I sow seeds direct into their flowering position in April/May. Poorish soil and a sunny site produce the best flowers.

IBERIS* Candytuft (HA)

This pretty border plant, *I. umbellata*, bears many clusters of pink, white or purple flowers. Being so easy to grow makes it one of the best for a child's first packet of seed. The plant will thrive in most ordinary garden soils. If successional sowings are made from March to May where it is intended to flower, the flowering season can extend from June to September. 'Giant Hyacinth' – a white and 'Red Flash'– a vivid carmine red are both successful varieties.

IMPATIENS**
Busy Lizzie (HHA)

The Busy Lizzie, *I. sultanii*, is perhaps more often thought of as a pot plant than a bedding subject. However when used for bedding brilliant splashes of colour and a complete ground cover can result, with continuous flowering from June to October. The tender horizontally growing stems which are so vulnerable when pot grown spread out quite safely over the surface of the garden soil. Impatiens will grow in any ordinary soil in sun or light shade provided it is never short of moisture. Try 'Futura' mixed.

Sow seeds in March/April under glass and keep at a temperature of 15-20°C (60-78°F). We use equal parts of peat and sand seed compost mixture and do not cover the seed. Never let the compost dry out after germination.

LATHYRUS*
Sweet Pea (HA)

The sweet pea, *L. odoratus*, is a great favourite. From June to September the lovely flowers in shades of red, pink, salmon, blue, lavender and white are a delight in the garden and for indoor flower arrangements. The tall 'Spencer' varieties all need sticks or some form of support as does 'Jet Set' mixed which grows 90 cm (3 ft) tall. 'Snoopea' mixed 30-38 cm (12-15 inches) tall and needs no support, making it excellent for a border. As for all mem-

bers of the pea family, an alkaline soil is required. Sow seed in January to March under glass at a temperature of 15-20°C (60-68°F) or in April/May in open ground.

LAVATERA* (HA)

The Annual Mallow, *L. trimestris*, is an erect plant, which grows to around 75 cm (2½ ft) tall, branches naturally and is a good space filler. The wide petals of its pink or white flowers form a beautiful open trumpet up to 10 cm (4 inches) across and appear from July to September. Recommended varieties are 'Silver Cup' which grows 60 cm (2 ft) tall

The annual mallow, Lavatera trimestris

and 'Mont Blanc' which is white and a little shorter at 50 cm (20 inches) tall. Sunny sites on ordinary soils are suitable. Sow the seed in situ in April.

LIMONIUM*
Statice, Sea Lavender (HHA)

The sprays of small yellow, pink, lavender, blue and white flowers decorate this plant from July to September. They are excellent for drying if you cut them just as they begin to open. 'Rainbow' mixture is a recommended variety: it grows 45 cm (18 inches) tall. Any ordinary soil is suitable for this plant. I sow seed from January to March under glass at a temperature of 15-20°C (60-68°F) for planting out at the end of May.

LOBELIA* (HHA)

The compact form of this plant which grows about 10 cm (4 inches) high makes it ideal as an edging plant. The trailing varieties are excellent for containers and hanging baskets. Recommended varieties are 'Cambridge Blue' – a sky blue, and 'Crystal Palace' – a deep blue, while 'Blue Cascade Pendula' is the one for hanging baskets. To enjoy a long period of flowering the plants should not dry out.

I sow seed in the greenhouse at a temperature of 18-20°C (65-68°F) from January to March and prick out in tiny clumps of four or five to plant out at the end of May.

MALCOMIA*
Virginian Stock (HA)

The low growing drifts of small rose, lilac and white sweet-scented flowers of M. maritima appear very quickly after sowing the seeds of this plant. For a continuous show, make successional sowings of mixed seed from March to May in a sunny position where you want it to flower.

MATTHIOLA*
Night-scented Stock (HA)

This well-known plant, M. bicornis, is not much to look at during the day but at night it opens its pale lilac flowers and gives out a sweet heavy scent. It is especially fragrant on a still warm evening. Sow seed from March to May where you want it to flower in any garden soil in sun or partial shade.

MESEMBRYAN-THEMUM** (HHA)

The Livingstone Daisy is a sun-loving, succulent-leaved native of South Africa which spreads brilliance over the driest of sunny sites. Masses of bright red, pink, orange, yellow and white daisy flowers appear continuously from June to August. A position in full sun is essential as the flowers only open when it shines. Try growing 'Sparkler', which grows to 10 cm (4 inches).

I sow seed in the greenhouse at 18-20°C (65-68°F) in February/March for planting out at the end of May.

MIMULUS** (HHA)

The native growing area of mimulus, the Monkey Flower, is boggy so it is well suited to planting in damp places and light shade. Flowers mainly in shades of gold or blotched mahogany are produced freely from June to September. After the initial flowering, pinch back the leading shoots to encourage branching and ensure continuous flowering.

I sow in the greenhouse at temperature of 15-20°C (60-68°F) in February/March for planting out at the end of May into as moisture-retentive a soil as possible.

MOLUCCELLA**
Bells of Ireland (HHA)

The tall flower spikes of M. laevis reach up to 90 cm (3 ft) and consist of tiny white flowers, each surrounded by a light green shell-like calyx. They are highly valued by flower arrangers for drying and cut flower use. The plant will survive in any garden soil in an open sunny position, but dryish conditions seem to give the best results. Sow seeds under glass in March at 15°C (60°F) to plant out at the end of May.

NEMESIA* (HHA)

This is an early flowering annual which puts on a show from the end of May to August. Growing to a height of 20-30 cm (8-12 inches) it is a good subject for beds and borders. 'Carnival Mixed' produces compact plants of glorious colours. Keep the soil moist if the plants are to flower well for a long time.

I sow under glass in March at a temperature of 15-20°C (60-68°F) for planting out at the end of May. Do not allow to stand in the tray any longer than need be. Tray-bound plants do not become bushy in the way they should.

NEMOPHILA*
Baby Blue Eyes (HHA)

This annual, N. insignis, has a useful spreading habit and from June to August it forms a carpet of bright blue, white-centred saucer-shaped flowers. It may be grown in sun or partial shade, but it likes a good moisture-retentive soil. Sow in March in the open where you want it to flower.

NICOTIANA*
Tobacco Plant (HHA)

Beautiful trumpet-shaped flowers borne from late June to September and generally very fragrant are the feature of this plant. Older varieties open in the evening only, and while newer varieties do open during the daytime as well, the breeding in of day-long opening seems to have resulted in the loss of scent. Blooms stand up to rain well, although the taller varieties growing up to 90 cm (3 ft) need some support. The newer, free-flowering dwarf varieties do

Nemesia with its rich colours

not need support. Choose from 'Evening Fragrance' – mixed colours growing 90 cm (3 ft) tall, 'Crimson Rock', growing 45 cm (18 inches) tall and 'Lime Green' growing to 75 cm (2½ ft) tall.

Sow seeds under glass in March at 15-18°C (60-65°F) for planting out in late May.

PAPAVER* Poppies (HA)

Tall stems support the cupped yellow, red, orange and white heads of these flowers as they sway in the breeze from June to August. Recommended varieties are 'Shirley Poppy' which produces single or double flowers and grows 60 cm (2 ft) high and 'Paeony-flowered' Mixed which grows to 90 cm (3 ft) high. I sow seed in April in good ordinary soil in full sun.

PETUNIA* (HHA)

Petunias, with their trumpet-shaped flowers, are available in many colours, some with white edgings or star markings and bicolours. Some of the newer varieties are earlier, freer flowering and more weather resistant than their predecessors. Try 'Resisto Rose' and 'Red Joy' plus other colours in the same series.

Sow under glass in early March at a temperature of 15-20°C (60-68°F) for planting out at the end of May. To ensure good plants, the seedlings should never receive a check at any time. Prick out before they become drawn. Plant in any good garden soil preferably after it has been well cultivated to allow an easy root run, thus enabling the plants to take up all the moisture they need. Water well between the plants during dry spells.

PHACELIA* (HA)

P. campanularia is a small bushy plant, growing only 23 cm (9 inches) high; flowers from June to September. The flowers are deep blue and bell-shaped and the foliage gives off a fragrance when pinched. This plant does best in a light well-drained soil and is well suited for small informal sowings towards the front of the flower border. I make successive sowings from March to June where I want it to flower.

PHLOX* (HHA)

Phlox drummondii is an easily maintained bedding plant which is equally suitable for container planting. Dense heads of yellow, red, pink, purple, lavender and white flowers from July to September. Sow under glass in March at 15°C (60°F) for planting out at the end of May.

45

PORTULACA** (HHA)

This is a somewhat neglected annual which deserves wider use. It is a neat plant with succulent foliage that enables it to withstand a degree of drought. It can really only be said to grow 15 cm (6 inches) tall as the stems tend to lie along the ground. Semi-double flowers with prettily ruffled petals in shades of most colours (except blue) appear successively from June to September. The flowers wait for sunlight before opening fully and then form a complete carpet of colour and decorative foliage. Recommended varieties are $P.$ grandiflora 'Double Mixed' or F_2 and 'Calypso'.

Sow under glass in March at a temperature of 18°C (65°F), and never overhead water the seedlings – instead water from below by placing the trays of seedlings in water. Plant out at the end of May in a sunny position in any ordinary soil.

SALPIGLOSSIS** (HHA)

This plant is so beautiful and exotic to look at that it gives the impression it is harder to grow than it really is! Trumpet-shaped flowers, some attractively veined, are carried on slender stems and open in succession from July to September. At a height of 45-60 cm (18-24 inches) it is a striking mid-border plant; try growing F_1 'Splash'. Water in dry weather to maintain flowering. Sow seed under glass in February at 18°C (65°C) to plant out at the end of May.

SALVIA* (HA and HHA)

Salvia horminum (HA) is an unusual bushy plant which produces brightly coloured terminal bracts of blue, pink, purple or white. These are the plant's real attraction as they outshine the much smaller flowers. The plant makes a striking addition to the flower border. Sow under glass in March at a temperature of 15-18°C (60-65°F) for planting out at the end of May.

Salvia Splendens (HHA), although not one of the easiest of subjects to grow, still remains a firm favourite. The flower spikes – usually red or scarlet – are always brilliant and appear from July until the first frosts. Recommended varieties are 'Carabiniere' – scarlet-red, growing 38 cm (15 inches) tall and 'Volcano' – an intense bright red, which grows to the same height. Keep a watch out for slugs. Sow seed under glass in February at 15-18°C (60-68°F) for planting out in late May.

TAGETES* Marigold (HHA)

In its various forms all of which are easy to grow, this is a most accommodating annual. Tagetes erecta, the African marigold is the tallest and largest flowered. It begins its flowering a little later than the smaller types as big plants take longer to mature. However the show provided by the large lemon-yellow to bright orange blooms from June until the first frosts is always splendid. Try 'Gay Ladies' mixed which grows 45 cm (18 inches) tall. T. patula, French marigolds, are compact, bushy and very free flowering. They flower from late May until the first frosts and can completely clothe the planting area with masses of individual, long-lasting blooms. There are singles, doubles and variants in plenty; try 'Queen Sophia', which is an outstanding double. Amongst the new Afro-French marigolds 'Suzie Wong', 'Moll Flanders' and 'Nell Gwyn' are all excellent, and grow to a height of 30 cm (12 inches). Tagetes tenuifolia pumila is the plant commonly known as tagetes. Small bushy plants with finely cut foliage are covered with small single gold, lemon or mahogany daisy-like flowers from July to September. It is a particularly good edging plant; try 'Golden Gem'.

Tagetes as a group require very little heat for germination. I sow all types in the greenhouse in March at a temperature of 15°C (60°F) for planting out at the end of May.

TROPAEOLUM*
Nasturtium (HA)

Do not dismiss the nasturtium, T. majus, as being too ordinary; trailing varieties cover banks, fences or any 'eyesore' with cheerful, colourful efficiency from June to September with minimum demands on soil or gardening skill. The dwarf varieties will grow happily in any sunny spot in need of colour. Try 'Gleam' hybrids, which have double flowers and grow 38 cm (15 inches) tall and 'Mixed tall single' a climbing variety which grows up to 1.8 metres (6 ft). Sow in situ, April to Mav.

VERBENA* (HHA)

The heads of primrose-like flowers in shades of red, pink, blue and white, often faintly scented, are borne in profusion by these sturdy little plants from June until the first frosts. Outstanding varieties are 'Derby Salmon Rose' and 'Derby Scarlet'. Sow seed under glass in February at temperatures of 15-20°C (60-68°F) for planting out at the end of May.

XERANTHEMUM* (HA)

X. annuum is one of the best plants to grow for the production of everlasting flowers. Growing to a height of 60 cm (2 ft), the strawy-petalled white, pink, lilac or purple daisy-like flowers keep their true colours for years if cutting and drying are carried out properly (see under *Helichrysum bracteatum*,

page 36). Sow March to April where you want them to flower, in a good light soil.

ZEA*
Ornamental Maize (HHA)

This plant, *Zea mays japonica*, produces an ornamental corn cob which can be cut when fully ripe for drying and winter decoration. Try 'Strawberry Corn' which grows to 60 cm (3 ft).

Sow under glass in March at a temperature of 15-20°C (60-68°F). Plant out at the end of May in a sunny spot and fertile soil, putting plants in a square block to assist pollination and the formation of seed.

ZINNIA** (HHA)

Z. elegans is a bright, sun-loving annual which flowers from July to September. Some varieties are quite tall, growing up to 90 cm (3 ft), but the strong stems and firm flower heads are excellent for cutting. Try 'Ruffles Mixture' or select separate colours; they grow 60 cm (2 ft) high.

Sow in the greenhouse in March at a temperature of 15-18°C (60-68°F) for planting out at the end of May. If possible, plant into a rich well cultivated soil in a sunny but sheltered position.

The marigold, Tagetes

BIENNIALS

All the plants in this list will flower properly in the season following that when the seed was sown. However it is important to sow the seeds during the period recommended on the seed packet as the length of daylight determines when and how the flowering will occur. Seed of biennials sown too early may produce flowers of very poor quality towards the end of that season instead of their best blooms as nature intends the year after the seed germinates.

ALTHAEA* Hollyhocks
Whilst hollyhocks can be grown as annuals or perennials it is more usual nowadays to treat them as biennials. By doing so it is possible to minimise the risk of hollyhock rust, a disease which becomes a scourge on old plants especially in the warmer and dryer parts of the country.

Sow the seed outdoors in May or June in a well prepared seed bed. Space out the strongest seedlings so as to get strong plants for planting out in late summer. Hollyhocks do best in dry, sunny positions especially when they have the protection of a wall or fence; that is why I always associate them with cottage gardens.

Both the double and the single varieties come true to colour from seed. If you enjoy watching bees at work, grow Sutton's 'Single Brilliant-Mixture'; the bees simply love the wide open flowers. For double flowers, Chater's 'Double Mixed' is an excellent selection. 'Summer Carnival' also produces a good mixture of fully double flowers which grow low down the stems.

BELLIS* Daisy
The common species, Bellis perennis, is the well-known, un-loved lawn weed, but there are various large-flowered and double minia-ture varieties well worth considering giving space in the flower garden. For example Bellis perennis 'Monstrosa' with its double flowers that reach 5 cm (2 inches) or more across and have a colour range from white through pink to scarlet red, makes an excellent bedding plant. It is at its best in May/June, and is sometimes catalogued as 'Goliath Mixed'. Among the miniature varieties are 'Pomponette' which has tightly quilled double daisies in shades of red, rose and white; 'Lilliput' which has crimson flowers; 'Dresden China' which has pink; 'Red Buttons' – carmine-red, and 'Rob Roy' – red. The advantage of growing 'Dresden China' and 'Rob Roy' is that neither produces seeds to cause an unwanted plant-weed problem. Instead they have to be propagated by division of parent plants, so are available from nurseries as bedding plants.

Sow the seeds of other varieties outside in June in shallow drills in a seed bed. Transplant them to their permanent quarters in September.

CAMPANULA MEDIUM*
Canterbury Bell
These are the traditional Canterbury Bells, which with their 'cups and saucers' are still great favourites in cottage gardens. I feel that they merit a place, if only a small one, in any flower garden. Special seed mixtures are available of 'Calycanthema', which grows up to 75-90 cm (2½-3 ft) high and has softly coloured flowers in white, rose and various shades of blue. Dwarf Bedding Mixture seed is available for plants that only grow 45 cm (18 inches) high, but the flowers, although produced in a similar colour range, have single blooms without 'saucers'. However we have grown one of these mixtures, namely 'Bells of Holland', and found the dome-shaped plants looked attractive when bedded out in a border.

Sow the seed in May/June outdoors, thinly in shallow drills in a seedbed. Transplant in September.

CHEIRANTHUS*
Wallflower
Wallflowers, Cheiranthus cheiri, are particularly popular as late spring and early summer flowering bedding plants. They need to be well grown and established as bushy plants to stand the winter if they are to make a really good colourful and fragrant show in the spring. Being members of the brassica family they appreciate a soil with some calcium in it; it is necessary to add

garden lime to acid soils. This not only helps to grow good plants, but it also helps to prevent the disease club root attacking them.

For best results sow the seed in May/June, thinly in shallow drills in a seed bed. When the seedlings are large enough to handle, transplant them into rows 15-20 cm (6-8 inches) apart. At the same time, in order to ensure bushy plants pinch out the tips of the growing points. In October lift the plants and plant them where you want them to flower, bearing in mind they prefer a sunny position. The ground should have been well dug over and prepared, and limed if necessary.

There are numerous varieties to choose from; most of them make plants that grow 35-45 cm (15-18 inches) tall and which should be spaced about 30 cm (12 inches) apart. Our favourite single colour varieties are 'Fire King' – a brilliant scarlet; 'Blood Red' – with a colour that is true to its name; 'Vulcan' – a deep crimson and 'Cloth of Gold' – a yellow variety. For really startling displays in many colours plus plenty of fragrance, try either 'Persian Carpet' or 'Colour Cascade'. These mixtures always look superb in small gardens.

Seed of dwarf varieties that grow about 22 cm (9 inches) high in the usual range of colours is available and these, of course, can be planted a little closer together.

The Siberian Wallflowers, C. × allionii, which grow about 30 cm (12 inches) high and have brilliant orange spikes of flowers, can also be planted slightly closer together than the tall wallflowers. The pro-

The popular Sweet William, Dianthus barbatus

cedure for growing them from seed is the same as for ordinary wallflowers.

DIANTHUS BARBATUS*
Sweet William

In recent years Sweet Williams have been greatly improved – some of the new varieties have really brilliant combinations of colour in massive clusters of flowers and there are some excellent varieties in single colours, too. Whichever type you grow, sow the seed outdoors in May/June in shallow drills in a seed bed, and transplant them into their flowering positions in October. Plant them 20-25 cm (8-10 inches) apart in bold blocks for the best effect. To do well they need a well-drained soil, a sunny position and if the soil is inclined to be acid, a little garden lime added when preparing the bed.

The tall varieties grow up to 45 cm (18 inches) high and good ones to chose are 'Giant Auricula Eyed Mixed', 'Pink Beauty Improved', 'Scarlet Beauty' and 'Messenger Mixed'. A hybrid known as 'Sweet Wivelsfield' has large clusters of flowers in many colours. Among the dwarf varieties, which grow up to 25 cm (10 inches), 'Indian Carpet' in a glorious mixture of colours is outstanding.

DIGITALIS* Foxglove

Once introduced into your garden and allowed to seed you will soon have legions of seedlings every spring. If these are thinned out, they will make grand plants for flowering the following season. Whilst our native *Digitalis purpurea* is beautiful and interesting when seen growing wild in a woodland setting, it is wise to start in a garden with a packet of 'Excelsior' strain seed. From this you will get plants that are some 1.5 metres (5 ft) tall, with large spikes of flowers. Their joy is that they come in a far greater range of colours – white, cream or pink to purple – all with delightfully spotted throats. The more recently introduced 'Foxy' strain is similar but not so tall; it does well in partial shade where the soil does not dry out even in high summer.

May or June is the time to sow the very fine foxglove seed. Broadcast it over a well-prepared seed bed and lightly rake over the soil to cover the seed. When the seedlings are large enough to handle, space them out so they are 15 cm (6 inches) apart. Plant them out in September.

LUNARIA* Honesty

Lunaria annua is a must for the flower arranger's garden, and the real interest will be in the stems of silvery seed pods produced at the end of the summer. These are always in great demand for dried winter floral arrangements. Whilst the variety with purple flowers is generally the most popular, there are others which have white or pink flowers. The colour of the flowers, incidentally, make no significant difference to the quality of the seed pods. You will only need to sow honesty once if you allow the seed to shed; in fact seedling production is so prolific that it can become a weed.

To make a start sow the seed outside in May/June where you want it to flower. Thin out to 30 cm (12 inches) apart.

MYOSOTIS*
Forget-Me-Not
The ever popular Forget-me-not, *M. alpestris*, is a native

The bright, purple flowers of honesty, Lunaria annua

flower of Great Britain which, in the hands of the plant breeders, has been greatly improved for decorating our gardens. Even when grown without the company of other plants, the dainty flowers carried on thin stems are a delight in April and May. When seen flowering amongst a bed of tulips in full flower they make a sight never to be forgotten. There are varieties in colours other than blue, such as 'Carmine Red' and 'Victoria White', but for me a Forget-me-not must be blue. 'Royal Blue' which has rich dark blue flowers and grows 30 cm (12 inches) tall, is an excellent choice and there is a dwarf form of the same variety. It grows only 18 cm (7 inches) tall and has a more bushy growth habit. Plants will seed freely after flowering to produce plenty of seedlings.

To make a start, sow the seed in April or May outside in a seed bed for transplanting in September. The alternative is simply to sow the seed in the flowering position and thin out the seedlings. A site in full sun or partial shade is ideal.

VIOLA* Pansy

This group of flowers includes both the viola and the garden pansy (*V. × wittrockiana*) which is still the most popular. A vast number of varieties are available but for me, it is the flowers with 'pansy faces' that have the greatest appeal; in fact I started my gardening at the age of six with a penny packet of pansy seed and I still love to see them smiling in the sunshine.

The superb strain of Swiss giant pansies called 'Roggli Giant' Mixed is well known and a packet of seed will have many colours. 'Tiara' Mixed, which has large flowers is a good variety as are 'Engelmann's Giants'. The lighter coloured faces of 'Love Duet' Mixed are simply charming. Amongst the faceless pansies, 'Azure Blue', which is a clear blue with a yellow eye, is excellent and 'Golden Champion' and 'Clear Crystal' Mixed also deserve a mention. However, these are only a few of the many good varieties.

Violas make compact plants with somewhat smaller flowers freely produced throughout the spring and summer in the most surprising colour combinations.

Viola, the smiling garden pansy

After the first flush of flowering of pansies it is wise to cut back the plants, spray them for aphids and give them a feed. Then you will be able to enjoy another longer flowering period. The best time to sow the seed of both pansies and violas is in June/July outside in shallow drills. Prick out the seedlings as soon as they are large enough to handle so they have room to grow into showy plants. Then transplant into their flowering positions in September/October. Propagation by soft cuttings taken in June or July is possible but they will need shading until rooted. This is a certain way of building up a stock of a pansy or viola of which you are particularly fond and do not wish to lose.

HARDY PERENNIALS

These are plants which once established in a border will go on growing and flowering for several seasons. Whilst most can be grown from seed it is usually better to start with young plants of named varieties. Before planting always make sure that the planting sites are free from perennial weed roots, otherwise an uncontrollable weed problem will develop.

ACHILLEA*
All varieties are members of the yarrow family, and they have aromatic fern-like foliage and round heads of clusters of small closely packed flowers. The plants do best in dry, sunny situations and they should be divided and replanted in the spring. If they are left undisturbed for several seasons, the flowers deteriorate.

The following are good varieties for the herbaceous border: 'Coronation Gold', which flowers in July/August, bearing golden yellow heads on slender stems clothed with silver grey foliage and grows 90 cm (3 ft) tall; 'Gold Plate' – a taller variety that can grow up to 1.2 metres (4 ft) tall and flowers from July through to September, bearing large golden yellow flowers heads on stiff stems clothed in grey-green foliage, and 'Moonshine' – a dwarf variety growing only 60 cm (2 ft) high and very useful for the front of the border. This is a new pale yellow hybrid with silver foliage. This is the variety to choose for the flower arranger's garden.

ALCHEMILLA*
Lady's Mantle
This well-loved plant, A. mollis, produces its clouds of tiny lime-green flowers in June. However, it is its pale green foliage that makes it so truly lovely. It is most useful for the flower arranger and has been recommended as a ground cover plant but I have not tried growing it this way. It is easily grown from seed, sown outside in spring, or by division in the spring, and will thence forward seed itself freely.

ALSTROEMERIA*
The Peruvian Lily, A. amaryllidaceae, is a species that varies considerably in hardiness, so to be on the safe side, plant the fleshy roots at least 15 cm (6 inches) deep. It is a good plan to raise your own plants from seed which should be very fresh or foil-packed. Sow very thinly in trays or pots in spring, and put these in a cool greenhouse. Germination time will vary greatly in relation to the freshness of the seed; it can be a month – it can be six months. When the seedlings are large enough to handle put them individually into 8 cm (3½ inch) pots, trying to disturb the roots as little as possible. When they are well established plant them outside about 30 cm (12 inches) apart in the warmest sheltered position possible, again with the minimum of root disturbance. They are happiest when the soil is deep, on the dry side with some sand in it and drains well.

One of the hardiest varieties is 'Aurantiaca' which grows to 90 cm (3 ft); its 4 cm (1½ inch) orange flowers are streaked red. The 'Ligtu' hybrids, which grow 60 cm (2 ft) tall, and are well known for their pale pink, pale lilac or whitish trumpet shaped flowers are also a good choice. Both flower from June to August and will provide excellent cut flower material.

ALYSSUM*
The commonly grown plant, A. saxatile, has grey foliage and light yellow clusters of flowers that appear in profusion in the spring. It grows to a height of about 30 cm (12 inches). Whilst it is not fussy about the soil, it does prefer to have as much of the sunshine as possible. The stems are lanky and unless the plants are cut back after flowering they soon become untidy looking. It is very easily propagated from cuttings taken after flowering.

ANCHUSA*
Anchusa azurea is listed as a perennial but with us it is a rather short-life plant so I treat it as a biennial. It does prefer somewhat drier and sunnier situations than we have. We grow our plants from seed sown outdoors in May/June in a seed bed. After a couple of months they are thinned and we plant them out in their flowering positions in October. If you grow them from rooted off-sets, do not take

these until the spring otherwise you will have winter losses. If you prefer to buy plants, April is the best time. 'Loddon Royalist' is a splendid, relatively new variety. Although it grows 90 cm (3 ft) tall, it has a bushy habit and should not require staking to keep its large royal blue flowers off the ground. 'Morning Glory', which grows to 1.2 metres (4 ft), has super gentian-blue flowers on tall stems which will need support. 'Royal Blue' also has pure gentian-blue flowers which, like other varieties, appear in June. It grows 90 – 120 cm (3-4 ft) high and needs staking, otherwise the plants will be untidy and you will lose much of their beauty. Even taller, growing to 1.2 – 1.5 metres (4 ft) is 'Azurea Dropmore', which has rich deep blue flowers that appear just a little bit later on in the summer.

AQUILEGIA* Columbine

Our native *Aquilegia vulgaris*, so charmingly known as Granny's Bonnet, has mainly blue or purple flowers with short spurs and is indeed inferior to some of the hybrids now available. Aquilegia seeds freely and we have found it necessary to ruthlessly eliminate seedlings from blue and purple flowers, otherwise these colours become dominant in the self-sown areas. Aquilegias appreciate some light shade in a situation where the soil is likely to be moist and cool. Ours grow happily in a shrub border.

The long-spurred hybrids are most attractive with their many combinations of col-

The graceful and dainty aquilegia with its delicate flowers

ours, from crimson through to the delicate shades of pink, yellows and white. The 'McKana Giant Hybrids' which grow 75-90 cm (2½ – 3 ft) tall are outstanding, and can be grown from seed sown outside or from plants purchased in the spring.

We have also grown *A. alpina* with its pretty blue and white flowers, but it does not always come true to colour when grown from seed. It grows 30 cm (12 inches) tall. We also have a great affection for *A. formosa* with its dainty brick-red flowers produced on slender stems. Growing to 90 cm (3 ft), it is so graceful and as a bonus it will come true from seed.

Do remember that greenfly unfortunately will simply adore your aquilegias.

ARABIS* Rock Cress

These trailing plants that grow no more than 15 cm (6 inches) high are especially suitable for rockeries and walls. Flowering commences early in the spring when it is a beautiful sight, but unfortunately it does not last very long. The plants are easily grown in ordinary soil; all they need is good drainage and tidying up after flowering.

Grown from seed sown either in a cold frame in March/April or outside in May/June. Seed in the separate colours – white, pink or rose-purple – is catalogued, as well as mixtures of the colours. All will give you mass displays of their tiny flowers.

ARMERIA* Thrift

Our native sea pink *Armeria maritima* will be found growing wild along much of our

The tiny flowers of rock cress, Arabis

Western coastline, where, in late spring and early summer, its masses of pink or pinkish-lilac rounded flower-heads borne on short stems produce beauty on a grand scale. We have found a place for a few plants we brought back from the west coast of Scotland, but it is 'Giant Pink' with its 45-60 cm (18-24 inches) stems which we grew from seeds, that gives us a great show without a break from early spring to autumn. Sow the seed in March/April outside in a seed bed to flower the following season.

'Vindictive' is an improved form of *A. maritima* which has rich rose-crimson rounded flowerheads. Early spring would be the time to order plants of named varieties.

ASTER* Michaelmas Daisy

If Michaelmas daisies, *A. novi-belgii*, are perhaps not quite as popular as they were some years ago, the decline could be traced to mildew. Happily, however, this can now be minimised by giving the plants a good start. It is old, over-crowded plants grown in dry soils, especially in the shade of trees, which suffer most from mildew. Michaelmas daisies will really thrive, flower well and have healthy growth if divided and replanted each March in a well-prepared rich moist soil. Putting bonemeal in the planting hole and watering early in any drought period will help greatly. As with so many diseases, it is the growing conditions and the weather that determine whether or not mildew is going to be a problem. If the weather is very dry, a timely spray with a fungicide may give control.

For autumn border displays, Michaelmas daisies are without equal, blooming first in September and going on right through October. As this is a time when autumn gales often occur, it is advisable to provide some support. A few twiggy sticks put around the plants early in the growing season is an answer without being unsightly.

There are many good named varieties with heights ranging from 60-120 cm (2-4 ft) in colours from crimson-red through to light pink and blue. A few I know well are: 'Ada Ballard' – which has lavender-blue flowers and grows 90 cm (3 ft) tall; 'Crimson Brocade', which has semi-double, rose crimson flowers and grows

90 cm (3 ft) tall; 'Ernest Ballard', which has very large semi-double rose crimson flowers and grows 90 cm (3 ft) tall, and 'Pride of Colwall', which has double violet-blue flowers and grows 75 cm (2½ ft) tall. New plants should be purchased from the nursery in March and planted straightaway for flowering the same year.

ASTILBE* False Goat's Beard
An easy-to-grow perennial provided there is plenty of moisture in the soil at all times of the year. The colourful plumes produced during the summer are most attractive. They are at their best in partial shade. Available in colours from white through pinks and lilacs to deepest red, good varieties included 'Bressingham Beauty' – rich pink; 'Deutschland' – intense white; 'Fanal' – deep red. Planting time: October – March. Prop-

agation is by division of the roots, March/April. For maximum flowering lift and divide the plants every third year.

AUBRIETA*
This low-growing plant is well known for its mass displays early in the spring. Ideal for dry sunny positions, plant it in a rock garden or in pockets in a dry wall and it will soon spread itself out into large mat-like plants. Do not be tempted to despise it because it is common; if you plant named varieties or grow your plants from seed, you can have a considerable range of colours.

Sow seeds in March in trays and put in the greenhouse. When the seedlings are large enough to handle prick them out into pots. They will be ready for planting in their final positions in October.

Of the named varieties, I can recommend the following: 'Barker's Double' – deep rosy

purple, 'Bressingham Pink', 'Dr. Mules' – violet purple, and 'Riverslea' – mauve pink. Do not be afraid to cut aubrietas back immediately after flowering; they will benefit.

BERGENIA*
These are plants of the saxifrage family and are excellent subjects for planting in dry borders, amongst shrubs or even conifers, as they are able to flourish in deep shade. They should certainly find a place in every flower arranger's garden. In March and April, the branching sprays of close set flowers produced on short fleshy stems are at their best. For the rest of the year, the foliage also has its value. In spring the young bold evergreen foliage is a green colour, but as it ages it takes on most attractive hues of red and

A clump of sea pink, Armeria maritima

bronze. The most popular species is B. cordifolia, which grows 45 cm (18 inches) high and finds favour as a plant for the border and for cutting for flower arrangements. Its pink flower heads are carried on long stems. B. cordifolia purpurea has the same growing habit but its flowers are a deeper rose-crimson. The lower growing B. delavayi is also popular. It grows to 30 cm (12 inches) high and has evergreen, crimson-backed foliage which turns dark, bronzy purple in the winter. Propagation is by division of plants in the spring. Plants can be grown from seed sown in the greenhouse but germination is rather unpredictable.

CAMPANULA* Bellflower

Within this group, there is great variety ranging from dwarf alpines to large herbaceous plants. None is particularly fussy about growing conditions but do best in cool, rich limestone soils where there are good moisture levels combined with adequate drainage. It is impossible to list more than a few, all of which make excellent subjects for the herbaceous border and which flower in June/July. They are: C. glomerata dahurica, which has violet-purple flowers and grows 45 cm (18 inches) tall; C. lactiflora 'Loddon Anna', which has lilac-pink flowers and grows 75 cm (2½ ft) tall; C. lactiflora 'Pritchard's Variety', which has pale violet-blue flowers and grows 90 cm (3 ft) tall; and C. macrantha which has foxglove-like spikes of amethyst-violet flowers and grows 105 cm (3½ ft) tall. At the other end of the scale,

there is C. lactiflora 'Pouffe', which at 23 cm (9 inches) is a real dwarf. It has lavender-blue starlike flowers, and along with some many others, is well worth considering.

Campanulas are easily propagated by division of the roots in the spring and that is also the time to plant new acquisitions from a nursery. If growing from seed, sow early in spring in seed compost, and protect the trays from the weather in either a cold frame or cold greenhouse. Plant out in their flowering positions in May/June.

CATANANCHE*
Cupid's Dart

A very suitable plant for the border, C. caerulea grows some 60 cm (2 ft) tall and has starlike purple-blue flowers that are not unlike cornflowers but with darker eyes. It is one of those 'cut-and-come again' plants and it will flower almost continuously from July till September if cut back after flowering. However, it does sometimes suffer from a desire to produce too many flowers at the end of the season, so reduce the number of flower buds in September to keep the plant in good condition for the following season. Anyone interested in flower arranging will find it very useful, not only as a summer flower but also for preserving.

It does well on light soils in sunny positions where the drainage is good, and it resents wet winter soil conditions. It is easy to propagate from root cuttings taken in the autumn or from spring-sown seed kept in a cold greenhouse to germinate.

CERASTIUM*
Snow in Summer

Cerastium tomentosum is a mat-forming plant, that grows only 15 cm (6 inches) high. It has lovely grey foliage which is covered with small white flowers in May and June. Very suitable for dry walls and sunny positions that need covering, it is really less suitable for the rockery as it is too invasive. It is easily grown from seed sown outside in April/May, either straight in its flowering position or in a seed bed.

CHRYSANTHEMUM*

For the herbaceous border, spray varieties of this popular flower are best. These require little attention during the growing season except for some support to prevent wind damage at flowering time. Keep a watchful eye open for greenfly and possible mildew signs and take appropriate action to prevent either of these causing damage (see p. 17). All chrysanthemums appreciate well prepared soils with good drainage in open situations.

We have derived enormous pleasure from growing the following garden varieties which all have double flowers: 'Pennine Bright Eyes' – pink, 'Pennine Crimson', 'Pennine Orange', 'Pennine Yellow' and 'Pennine White', as well as some of the single spray varieties such as 'Pennine Dream' – pink, 'Pennine Globe' – gold, and 'Pennine Tango' – a bronze. Most of these grow 90-120 cm (3-4 ft) tall. For the front of the border, 'Fairy' can be very colourful in late summer and early autumn. It is a dwarf pompom chrysanthemum with numerous round rosy-pink flowers. It grows to only 30 cm (1 ft).

To avoid winter losses of chrysanthemums, it is advisable to lift the stools (roots) in the autumn and house them in an airy cold frame. In spring take cuttings for rooting in the greenhouse. You will find new plants tend to flower more profusely than those grown from old roots.

Chrysanthemum maximum, (Shasta daisy), although quite a different flower, makes a good border plant. One of the best varieties is 'Esther Read' which grows 75 cm (2½ ft) tall. Its large golden-eyed white flowers appear on long stems from June until August and are good for cutting. Propagate by root division in spring.

COREOPSIS*

Appreciated for their long flowering season (July-September) as long as they are given a position in full sun, these plants, commonly known as tickweed, are not fussy about soil type, although it must be well drained. *Coreopsis grandiflora* is a robust species from the U.S.A. that grows 45 cm (18 inches) high. Its leaves are narrow and deeply toothed and its bright yellow flowers measuring up to 7 cm (2½ inches) across, carried on good stems are first class for flower arrangements. *C. grandiflora verticillata* produces smaller flowers but more of them. Other named varieties include 'Badengold' which grows to 90 cm (3 ft) high and has golden yellow flowers, 'Perry's Variety' which grows to 75 cm (2½ ft) high and has

The lovely blue flower spikes of delphinium

semi-double yellow flowers; 'Sunray' which grows 45 cm (18 inches) high and is very free flowering with double golden yellow flowers; 'Mayfield Giant' which grows 60 cm (2 ft) high and is a golden yellow and 'Sunburst' also (2 ft) high and a bright yellow, semi-double variety.

Flowers can be grown from seed sown in May/July outdoors for flowering the follow-ing season, but propagation is best by division in the spring.

DELPHINIUM**

These are the aristrocrats of the herbaceous border and they are not difficult to grow if you start them off well. The first requirement is a deeply dug, well prepared soil. I en-

The attractive flowers of bleeding heart, Dicentra spectabilis

sure this by digging the area in the winter, leaving the rough clods exposed to the elements. If the soil is inclined to be acid I apply a light dressing of garden lime before breaking down the clods in the spring. This winter exposure of the soil helps reduce the risk of subsequent slug damage to the dormant buds below ground. April/May is a good time to plant out but if the weather turns dry it will be necessary to water the plants until they are well established. Few garden plants grow faster than delphiniums and in consequence to get the finest blooms on healthy plants they need feeding and watering. I start by giving established plants an application of fertiliser towards the end of February – just about the time the new growth emerges. When the first flush of blooms has been cut down in July, I give a repeat application of fertiliser.

There are many named varieties of delphiniums and in making your choice, it is important to take note of the heights they will reach. Staking and tying the taller ones will generally be necessary, especially if the garden is exposed. The tallest variety we have grown is 'Royal Marines' which reaches 2.4 metres (8 ft) and is dark purply blue. Our favourite, however, grows to only half this height. Called 'Clack's Choice' it has flowers that are a real delphinium blue colour, and as its stems are strong, it needs no staking.

Raising delphiniums from fresh seed is easy but as the seed ages germination results deteriorate. Storing seed in the refrigerator helps to slow down the deterioration. Sow the fresh seed in a seed bed in spring. Propagation from new cuttings taken early in the season is simple and successful. Using a very sharp knife cut a 10 cm (4 inch) shoot from the plant with a hard heel of the root. Put this in a jam jar containing 5 cm (2 inches) of sand and add water to come about 2.5 cm (1 inch) above the sand. Keep in a shaded, frost-free place. In four to five weeks, roots will have developed and the cuttings can be potted into 7.5–10 cm (3-4 inch) pots for planting out into their flowering positions in April/May.

DIANTHUS*
Pinks, Border Carnations

Whilst pinks and border carnations are listed here as perennials, after two or three years they do become untidy, producing weaker growth and poorer quality flowers, so it is best to replace them every second or third year with fresh plants. This is not difficult since they are easy to root either from cuttings taken between June and early August or by layering them in July and August. Whichever way you choose, propagating from young plants will give the best results. From pegging a layer down to rooting takes roughly six weeks. It is then time to sever the link with the mother plant and wait a further four weeks before lifting the new plant for its final planting out. Pinks and border carnation seed is readily available and should be sown thinly in a pan or box. Put in an unheated greenhouse or cold frame to germinate.

The growing plants need a sunny position in soil that is well drained. They favour a chalky soil, but failing this give a light application of garden lime prior to planting.

My first garden pinks were 'White Ladies', which have a

double white flower, and 'Mrs. Sinkins Pink'. Both of these have a glorious perfume. Of all the border carnations I have grown, 'Robin Thain' with its white striped rosy-crimson, clove-scented flowers is outstanding. Another old favourite is 'Zebra' which has maize-yellow flowers that are striped crimson. Also worth mentioning is 'Salmon Clove' which has soft salmon pink flowers that are delightfully perfumed. Pinks grow to about 30 cm (1 ft) high and generally do not need support to keep their blooms off the ground, but the border carnations, at twice or more this height, certainly will.

In between the border pinks and carnations there are the perpetual flowering hybrids, *Dianthus × allwoodii* which make truly wonderful garden plants. A particular favourite is 'Doris', which is a salmon pink colour with red eyes.

DICENTRA* Bleeding Heart
Growing some 75 cm (2½ft)

high, *D. spectabilis* is a tall, graceful plant. The rows of rose-pink and white heart-shaped flowers dangle from arching stems and are at their best in May and June. They are equally attractive in the flower bed or in a flower arrangement, and they are plants for that shady sheltered corner, away from the wind and the spring frosts. They can be grown from seed sown in May/June in pans protected from the weather in a frame. Seedlings should be potted singly in pots and planted out in spring in a planting site that has good drainage and some well-rotted compost incorporated. They can be propagated also by dividing lifted roots in March.

ECHINOPS* Globe Thistle
The globe thistles, with their round, prickly, ball-shaped flowerheads and dramatic grey and green foliage are always majestic plants during July and August. This is the time to cut and dry the flowers

for winter use in flower arrangements. All varieties need plenty of space in a sunny well drained position. They can be grown from seed sown in April/July in open ground, or propagated by dividing the roots in October for over-wintering in a cold frame. Plant out in March.

'Veitch's Blue' is a good dwarf variety, growing 75 cm (2½ft) tall, and it has large deep blue flowerheads. 'Taplow Blue' produces steel-blue flowerheads which turn silvery with age. It grows 1.2 metres (4 ft) tall. *E. ritro*, growing to 1.35 metres (4½ft) is appreciated for its soft blue flowerheads.

ERIGERON* Fleabane
A wide range of garden hybrids is now available, all of which succeed well in sunny borders and are not greatly perturbed if the soil is poor. The mauve and violet

Brightly coloured fleabane, Erigeron

flowered varieties are hardy, but the pink ones may die out during cold winters especially if the soil is poorly drained. All have a long flowering season, starting in June and going on until the autumn. The daisy like flowers last well when cut for indoor decoration.

The hardiest varieties include 'Darkest of All', which grows 45 cm (18 inches) high and has deep violet flowers with golden eyes; 'Dignity' which grows 60 cm (2 ft) tall and has flowers that are deep blue turning mauve and 'Sincerity' which grows 75 cm (2½ ft) tall and has flowers that are lilac mauve with a clear yellow centre. Those in the pink-rosy-carmine colour range include 'Foersters Liebling', growing to 60 cm (2 ft) tall with semi-double, rosy-carmine flowers and 'Gaiety' which grows 75 cm (2½ ft) tall and has large pink flowers.

Plants can be grown from seed sown in April/May in a cold frame for planting out in October or March, or by dividing the roots in March.

EUPHORBIA* Spurge

This genus of about 2000 species is widely distributed throughout the world. For the flower garden however, we are only concerned with the hardy herbaceous or sub-shrubby members of the family. The flowers of euphorbia are small and insignificant; it is the surrounding petal-like bracts that create the beauty. At Clack's Farm we get the best results for these plants when grown in our poorest and driest soil areas and it doesn't matter whether they are in sun or partial shade.

The popular and colourful fuchsia

E. *Polychroma* is outstanding; growing to 45 cm (18 inches), it produces brilliant yellow bracts in early spring akin to a touch of sunlight. E. *Wulfenii* grows to 75 cm (2½ ft) and has glaucous foliage and yellowish-green spikes appearing in May. E. *Griffithii* 'Fireglow' grows to 45 cm (1½ ft) and has orange-red bracts and pinky foliage. It remains splendid from May/July. Euphorbia can be grown from seed sown in April/June in a cold frame or outdoors, for planting out in the following autumn. Alternatively, propagate by dividing the roots in March/April or by taking soft wood cuttings in April/June.

FUCHSIA**

This is probably among the most popular of all plants. Although it is seldom used as a hardy perennial, with some extra care several varieties can be left in the flower bed during the winter.

When starting to grow fuchsias obtain advice and plants from a good fuchsia nursery. Taking cuttings is easy and best done during May/June. These should be overwintered in a frost-free greenhouse so that they grow into healthy young plants. Plant these out at the end of May, putting them as deep as is practicable in the ground. This is the best protection you can give the plant against winter frost damage. Cut them back in November and put a layer of compost, and if need be, bracken or straw, on top to protect the plants further. With nearly all varieties, new growth will come from the roots in April/May and plants will start flowering from July/August. Regular feeding and watering during dry spells is essential for maintaining healthy and vigorous plants. They tolerate any soil as long as it is moisture retentive.

'Mrs. Popple' is one of the hardiest varieties together with 'Riccartonii' but many others such as 'Celia Smedley', 'Madame Cornelissen' and 'Tom Thumb' do well.

GAILLARDIA*
Blanket Flower
The garden hybrids are plants for hot sunny borders, but they do not have a long life, particularly when a cold wet winter intervenes. A well drained soil is essential and if it is light so much the better. Spring is the time to plant these flowers, certainly no later than early May. Propagation is by division of roots in March/April or by root cuttings taken in January and kept in a cold greenhouse or frame. Plants can also be grown from seed sown outdoors in May/June. The seedlings should be thinned and

left to grow into healthy plants ready for planting out the following March/April.

The following are a few of the colourful varieties that will flower from July till September: 'Burgundy' which grows 60 cm (2 ft) high and has red flowers; 'Mandarin' which grows 90 cm (3 ft) high and has bright rusty orange flowers that have no yellow eye and 'Wirral Flame' which grows 90 cm (3 ft) high and has flowers that are a deep rusty red with a yellow edge. It is advisable to provide twiggy supports around the plants early in the season otherwise the flower stems tend to flop over in the slightest wind.

Gentiana sino-ornata

GENTIANA**
This family of plants come from high altitude alpine regions where the winter snows cover and protect them from frost, where the peaty soils are moist during the growing season and where the air is always clean and the summer sunshine intensely bright. It is these factors that have to be considered if gentians are to be introduced successfully into our gardens, for failure to give them something akin to their natural environment is sure to produce poor and disappointing results. Having said that, it is possible to achieve success by preparing pockets of moist peaty or leaf mould soils amongst the stones in a sunny rock garden. As a substitute

for winter snow, a raised sheet of glass over each plant will prevent them suffering from root damage caused by winter water-logging.

My favourites are G. acaulis, the blue trumpet gentian which flowers in May/June, G. sino-ornata with its brilliant blue flowers in September/October, and the autumn-flowering G. × macaulayi.

Plants can be propagated either from root cuttings taken in April/May or by division of plants in March, G. acaulis should be divided in June).

Fresh seed sown in late summer and subjected to winter freezing in a cold frame generally germinates well.

GERANIUM* Cranesbill

This is a large family of hardy summer-flowering perennial plants which are very different from bedding geraniums. So varied are they in size and growth habits that some of the tall ones can be planted in herbaceous borders to advantage whilst other low growing varieties are more suitable for rock gardens. The whole family is happiest when the soil is well drained and not too rich. In such conditions the plants should be liberally smothered with blooms.

G. psilostemon, growing to 75 cm (2½ft) high has numerous magenta red flowers with black centres and veins. In addition it has beautifully coloured leaves in autumn. It likes a position in full sun. G. pratense, (the meadow geranium) grows 60 cm (2 ft) high and is available in several colours from white to violet blue; the one I particularly like is 'Flore Peano' with its double

blue flowers. G. macrorrhizum 'Ingwersen's' variety is shade tolerant and often used as ground cover as it only grows to 30 cm (1 ft) high. It has soft pink flowers and masses of aromatic leaves which colour beautifully in autumn. For the rock garden try the low-growing G. cinereum 'Ballerina' which reaches only 7.5–15 cm (3-6 inches) high and has pale rosy purple flowers deeply veined with crimson.

Propagation is by division of plants in March.

GEUM*

Given the right conditions – that is a fairly rich soil in full sun – geums make a colourful contribution to the flower garden for most of the summer. To keep them in good flowering health, it is advisable to lift and divide the roots every second or third year. Early spring is the best time either for planting or re-planting, and the plants like a little really well-rotted compost underneath them.

The varieties I have been pleased to grow are: 'Mrs. Bradshaw' which grows to 60 cm (2 ft) high, and with its double flaming brick red flowers, is an old favourite of mine; 'Lady Stratheden' which grows 60 cm (2 ft) high and has semi-double, warm yellow flowers and 'Fire Opal' which grows 75 cm (2 ft) high and also has semi-double flowers, that are orange-scarlet with purple stems.

Plants can be raised from seed sown in a cold frame from April to July for planting out the following spring or by division of the roots in March/April.

GYPSOPHILA*
Chalk Plant

This is planted in small numbers to supply material for cut flower arrangements, particularly to go with sweet peas and carnations in July/August. It is at this time that the delicate sprays of tiny flowers are quite beautiful and make every vase or bowl look a professional arrangement. The plants grow best in full sun on chalky soils; on other soil types an application of garden lime before planting is advisable. To get the best effect allow the plants adequate space to spread out their flowering branches without crowding. A free-standing plant in full bloom becomes a glorious hazy cloud of colour. Once planted they should not be disturbed.

'Bristol Fairy' which grows 1.2 metres (4ft) high is my favourite and is probably the best double white for cutting; it is also a good strong grower. The pale pink-flowered 'Rosy Veil' is a different type; growing only 45 cm (1½ft) high, it has a low spreading habit.

Propagation can be achieved by root cuttings taken in May/June and rooted in sand or a rooting bag. G. paniculata which grows 75 cm (2½ft) tall, can be grown from seed sown in the greenhouse in February/April. It should be kept at a temperature between 10°-15°C (50°-60°F).

HELENIUM* Sneezeweed

This could be described as one of our best herbaceous plants. It thrives in a poor soil and simply loves a hot summer. Under these conditions, the 90 cm (3 ft) stems are hard and strong and stand well without

support. By planting several varieties, the flowering season can cover the four months from July to October. In common with many other perennials, the flowering quality is maintained by lifting, dividing and replanting every other year.

To start the season we grow 'Moerheim Beauty' which flowers in July/August and reaches a height of 90 cm (3 ft). There is considerable warmth in its large crimson-red, daisy like flowers, which have a dark centre. Another for July/August flowering is 'Coppelia', which grows 90 cm (3 ft) high and has coppery-orange flowers. For flowering in August/September, 'Bruno' has really deep crimson-red flowers with a dark centre. It grows to 90 cm (3 ft). After that try 'Butterpat' which also grows 90 cm (3 ft) tall and has

bright yellow flowers that remain into October. The earlier flowering varieties, such as 'Moerheim Beauty' will sometimes produce a second flush of flowers in October if cut down immediately after the first crop is finished.

As always I prefer early spring planting. Propagation is by division of roots in early spring.

HELIANTHEMUM*
Rock Rose

For a display of colour in June and July plant these rock roses. They never fail to brighten up a flower garden, particularly if given the benefit of full sunshine and good drainage. They are most at home in a sunny rock garden, where they will quickly demand more and more space. After flowering therefore, it is wise to trim the plants back

Rosy clouds of pale pink-flowered Gypsophila 'Rosy Veil'

drastically. This annual pruning gives rise to the production of new vigorous growth for flowering again later in the season.

Some of the best named varieties are 'Ben Afflick', which has orange and buff flowers; 'Beech Park Scarlet' which, true to its name, is a crimson scarlet; 'Wisley Pink' – a delightful pink, and 'Wisley Primrose' – a soft yellow. Planting out time is September to March when the soil is not frosted.

Propagation is done by taking 7.5 cm (3 inch) cuttings of non-flowering growth with a heel from June to August. Overwinter newly rooted plants in a cold frame and plant out in March when it is getting warmer.

HELLEBORUS*
Christmas and Lenten Rose

It is surprising how few hellebores are needed to bring considerable life and joy to a flower garden in winter and early spring. It is such a thrill to have two or three Christmas Roses (*Helleborus niger*) as a centre piece on the dinner table at Christmas time, that it is worth all the trouble of using cloches and dealing with the slugs to get them in bloom for that special occasion. All our hellebores do fine in shade or semi-shade where the soil is moist. We leave them alone as much as possible so as to avoid the slightest disturbance of their roots, but give them a little fertiliser feed after flowering. By hand-weeding around the plants we get quite a few self-sown seedlings.

There are several forms of the Christmas Rose – some with very much larger flowers than others. We favour Potter's Wheel, which has pure white, broad petals with no pink flush on the back of them. If protected with a cloche against the weather and slugs, this variety will give perfect blooms for Christmas, but be prepared to wait a couple of years or so for the plant to settle down before it decides to produce flowers. *Helleborus orientalis*, the Lenten Rose, produces several large nodding flowers on each stem from February to April. It gives us so much pleasure, particularly as we now have numbers of seedlings, each with a different arrangement of colours, from deep purple to creamy white petals with or without spots inside. If, after cutting, you dip the flower

stalk ends in boiling water for a second or two and then stand the flowers up to their necks in water overnight, you will find that they keep so much longer in an arrangement. *Helleborus corsicus* grows to 60 cm (2 ft) and makes quite a large plant. Its strong stems carry creamy-green flower trusses from early February until May. Not only are the flower heads sought after by flower arrangers but the seed heads that follow are just as interesting for the same purpose. *Helleborus foetidus*, Stinking Hellebore, grows to 45 cm (18 inches). A native of this country, it produces its flower heads from February to April, followed again by attractive seed heads.

All hellebores are beloved by whitefly and greenfly so preventive spraying is essential. Best planting time is March. Propagation is by division of roots in March or seedlings planted out at that time.

HEMEROCALLIS*
Day Lily

These easily grown plants have a unique flower production system; during the flowering season a single flower on each stem opens in the morning and dies at night to be followed by a new fresh bloom on the same stem the next day. This flowering routine goes on without a break for six to eight weeks and by growing several varieties of the best garden hybrids it is possible to have these beautiful lily flowers from May until August. The plants do well in most soils, either in partial shade or sun.

To start the flowering season in May/June, plant 'Gold

Dust' which grows to 45 cm (18 inches) tall and has yellow flowers with a dark reverse. Follow with 'Tejas' which grows to 75 cm (2½ ft). Its bright coppery-crimson flowers appear in June/July. If you prefer a clear yellow flower plant 'Hyperion' instead; it grows to 90 cm (3 ft). For July/August, you could choose from 'Bonanza' which grows to 45 cm (18 inches) high and has flowers that are buff yellow with a dark brown throat or 'Mrs John Tigert', which grows 75 cm (2½ ft) tall and has coppery-red flowers with a dark centre. At the end of the flowering season cut the stems down to ground level.

Propagation is by division of roots between October and March. Once planted take care not to disturb the roots.

HOSTA* Plantain Lily

The bold, spade-shaped leaves in many shades of grey, green and sometimes almost blue or golden yellow, with or without contrasting margins, make hostas great plants not only for the flower gardener but also for those interested in flower arranging. These plants thrive particularly well in partial shade provided by close shrubs or trees, and where the soil is cool and moist; nearby the edge of a pool or pond is a good spot. In such conditions they will go on producing leaf up on leaf to make ever-enlarging plants from the time they wake up in the spring until late autumn. In addition to their magnificent foliage, they do grace the garden with upright spikes of delicate lilac, lily-like flowers. In shady conditions the foliage generally grows better, whereas if the plants are in full sun, there tends to be a better crop of flowers.

There are certainly too many varieties of hosta to list here, but two outstanding ones are: *Hosta fortunei* 'Albopicta' which has yellow leaves edged with pale green (in fact there are several *fortunei* varieties in different combinations of green and yellow) and *Hosta sieboldiana* with lovely blue-grey crinkled, and deeply veined leaves.

Propagation is by division of the clumps in spring; the divided plants must be replanted at once. When the weather is dry, water the newly planted plants regularly. Hosta can also be grown from

The Christmas rose, Helleborus niger

seed sown in April/May, but remember that each plant will be an individual and will probably not be the same as the parent plant.

IBERIS* Candytuft

These small, evergreen, 'no-trouble' plants are so easy to grow; they ask simply for ordinary soil and a dry sunny position. *Iberis saxalitis* reaches some 10-15 cm (4-6 inches) in height and is a spreading plant, well suited for a rock garden. The white flat flower heads make a good show in May/June. *Iberis sempervirens*, growing 15-23 cm (6-9 inches) is taller and makes a larger spreading plant, reaching anything up to 60 cm (2 ft) across. It is more suitable for planting on top of a dry wall or for general open situations. Two other good varieties are

'Little Gem' and 'Snow Flake' growing 15 cm (6 inches) and 23 cm (9 inches) tall respectively. Both have white flowers.

Propagation of named varieties is by heel cuttings taken after flowering.

IRIS* Bearded Iris

This is the June-flowering iris, commonly known as Flag Iris. For the best results, give them a position in full sunshine with good drainage. Any water-logging will be fatal. They are at their happiest on chalky soils; on other soil types additional garden lime is necessary. It is advisable to apply a general garden fertiliser at the beginning of the growing season. On all soils deficiencies of calcium and phosphates in the soil results in poor plant health and in extreme cases, death of the plants.

Although the flowering season of iris is short, whilst it lasts the display of colour and beauty will always be spectacular, especially if you select the varieties you grow carefully. There are so many varieties to choose from, that rather than name a few I suggest you consult a specialist's catalogue, or better still make a visit to a nearby nursery in June to see those that they have in flower. In addition to the taller varieties and hybrids there are many dwarf ones, some of which only grow to 10 cm (4 inches) high.

For all varieties the best planting time is October. Set the solid rhizome, (bought initially from a nursery) into the planting hole so that the upper side is exposed to the sun; deeper planting can result in the rhizome rotting. To propagate irises, divide established healthy rhizomes soon after flowering; select outer pieces which each have a good strong leaf fan and then clip the fan to half its size before planting, discarding the old centre. To maintain plant health and free-flowering, replant in this way every third year.

KNIPHOFIA*
Torch Lily, Red Hot Poker
These are plants that do best in full sunshine on well-drained soils. Shade reduces flowering and winter water-logging causes plant losses. To keep the plants in good flowering condition, apply an organic fertiliser around them in April. Continuity of flowering can be achieved by cutting the stems down close to the base when they have finished flowering. On heavy soils or in cold, wet areas, it is advisable to provide some protection against possible frost damage, such as covering the roots with straw or bracken. To reduce possible winter damage, I would always recommend planting in the spring rather than the autumn. When planting, do make sure that the planting hole is large enough for the roots to be well spread out.

Of the many varieties, 'Samuel's Sensation', which grows 1.5 metres (5 ft) high, is outstanding with its bright red-scarlet blooms. 'Bressingham Torch' growing to 90 cm (3 ft) is also spectacular and has orange-yellow spikes. Propagation is by division of established plants in April.

LAVANDULA* Lavender
It is difficult to imagine any flower garden without at least one or two well cared for lavender plants. On a summer day, their masses of perfumed flower spikes are glorious. To grow lavender well, an adequately drained soil is needed. If it is slightly chalky so much the better; for success, just plant in a full sunshine position. If the soil is light and inclined to be acid an annual application of garden lime is beneficial. Lavender is generally short lived, but trimming back and tidying up the plants, cutting away all the dead flower spikes each year in March or April, does tend to keep them in good health for longer.

The Old English Lavender (*Lavandula spica*), renowned for its fragrant essential oil, is still popular in spite of the fact that its height – it grows to 90 cm (3 ft) – means it needs plenty of space. Its blue-purple flower spikes bloom from July to September. The dwarf variety, 'Munstead', growing to 45 cm (18 inches) is my favourite with its deep mauve spikes of flowers, and it is undoubtedly good for an average-sized garden. 'Hidcote' is another compact variety and has dark violet flowers. If you want to dry stems of flowers, cut these when the flowers are just showing colour but not fully open. The fragrance is then retained at its best.

Propagation is easy; take 7.5 cm (3 inch) cuttings of ripe non-flowering shoots, and when rooted overwinter them in a cold frame. Plant out in March or April.

LUPINUS* Lupin
Apart from the tree lupin *Lupinus arboreus* – which incidentally is a plant well worth growing from seed – today's hybrid garden lupins are the result of dedicated breeding work. The world famous Russell strain are lupins with strong stems, plenty of vigour and clear colours in every flower, usually with two distinct colours in each one. One of the first lupins I grew was 'Elsie Waters', bright pink and cream with white edges, a sensation at that time. There are still many named varieties available.

Lupins are at their best in a light, lime-free soil with no manure added. All Russell lupins grow to about 105 cm (3½ ft) and flower in June/early July. If the dead flower spikes are removed before seed formation, flowering will resume in a limited way. Propagation of named varieties is done by cuttings taken with a heel in April. Alternatively sow mixed seeds in May/June in a frame for planting out in October. These plants will then flower the following summer.

MECONOPSIS**
Himalayan Poppy, Welsh Poppy

There are many species of these hardy perennials, all of which have poppy-like flowers. For me, the exciting ones are those with blue flowers that give us so much pleasure in June and July. To grow them successfully, provide them with the right conditions – a light rich, moist soil that is always moist but nevertheless well-drained in a spot that is sheltered and semi-shaded. In addition, they need plenty of water during the summer and – ideally – as little winter rain as possible. In wet districts it would be advisable to cover the roots with cloches immediately after cutting down the dead flower stems. Throughout late autumn and winter, the roots are completely dormant with no sign of life above ground.

Meconopsis betonicifolia (syn *M. Baileyi)*, the Himalayan blue poppy, is the one with those delightful sky blue flowers and bright yellow anthers, and it is well worth that extra bit of tender loving care demanded to grow it successfully. It reaches a height of 90 cm (3 ft). *M. grandis* produces its dark blue, almost purple with a tinge of red, flowers slightly earlier in May/June. The yel-

Russell lupins in full flower

low varieties, *M. cambrica* (Welsh poppy) and *M. integrifolia*, are attractive but can become a nuisance as they seed very freely. The seeds are easy to harvest but should then be sown immediately as they quickly lose their germination qualities. With fresh seed germination takes two to three weeks. When the seedlings can be handled, prick them out into trays and overwinter in a cold frame. The seedlings also go completely dormant; do not despair, they are not dead but just resting. In the spring, growth will recommence, at which time they can be planted outside. The plants can also be propagated by division in March/April.

NEPETA* Catmint
This attractive aromatic plant, with its blue-grey foliage and misty mauve flower spikes, is often used as an edging plant. It does well on light soils in full

The pretty, papery yellow flowers of the Welsh poppy, Meconopsis cambrica

sun but on heavy, cold, poorly drained soils, it tends to die out fairly quickly.

Nepeta mussinii, which grows to 45 cm (18 inches) high, is the species commonly grown, but the variety 'Six Hills Giant', which grows to 60 cm (2 ft) and has violet-blue flowers, makes a better and more positive display. However, it is sterile and therefore cannot be grown from seed.

Propagation is by division of roots in spring or by soft cuttings taken after flowering. *N. mussinii* can be grown from seed sown outside in May/June.

PAEONIA* Paeony
There are several different types of paeonies including the old-fashioned, cottage gar-

den types with their green foliage and scented double flowers. The double Chinese paeonies are now very popular; they have a greater range of delightful colours and the added virtue of being scented. There are also the single Japanese and Imperial paeonies, which have cupped blooms of five to ten petals, each with a cluster of yellow stamens. Unfortunately, however, all of these are somewhat weaker growers.

Paeonies need plenty of sunshine and well-prepared ground with some well-rotted compost or manure incorporated. Some of the better perfumed varieties are subject to spring frost damage which can spoil the opening flower buds, so if possible, plant them in such a position that they escape early morning spring sunshine. After planting paeonies in the spring considerable patience is needed as they may take several years before showing any sign of flowering. Established plants benefit considerably from an annual springtime mulch, again with the well-rotted compost or with manure.

Amongst the old cottage paeonies, (*P. officinalis*), which grow to 45 cm (18 inches) tall, there are 'Alba-plena' – a double white; 'Rosea-plena' – a double pink and 'Rubra-plena' – a double crimson. All flower in May/June. Among the many excellent double Chinese paeonies, all of which flower in June, are: 'Adolph Rousseau' – a crimson; 'Alex Fleming' – bright rose-pink; 'Kelway's Glorious' – pure white and 'President Wilson' – pale cream pink. Single bloom varieties include 'Globe of Light' – a pink with a large cream-yellow centre; 'Jan van Leeuwen' – pure white with a golden centre and 'Soshi' – rose with a yellow centre.

Propagation is done by division of roots in September or early October. Once planted, on no account disturb the roots. With no disturbance paeonies will live thirty years or more, progressively making larger roots and flowering more prolific.

PENSTEMON*

These graceful plants, with their 60-90 cm (2-3 ft) tall spikes of open-mouthed flowers appearing from July to September, are well worth a place in any garden. They are short lived, however, so frequent replacement is necessary, but being easy to grow this does not present any real problems. Plant in the spring, giving them a place in the sun where the soil is well-drained. 'Garnet' is just about the hardiest of the large-flowered penstemons. It makes a neat bushy plant and produces spikes of super crimson flowers. 'Firebird' has the same growth habit but its flowers are bright scarlet. Various seed mixtures are available such as 'Grandiflorum Excelsior' which grows to 75 cm (2½ ft), or 'Skyline' which has a more bushy growth habit. Both have a lovely mixture of colours.

Sow seed outside in a seed bed from June to August and transplant to flowering positions in October. The plants will flower the following season. Propagation can also be done by division in the spring.

PHLOX*

These are undoubtedly the plants to grow for a late summer colour display, although they need looking after. They need a rich, well-cultivated soil and one that is capable of holding its moisture during the growing season. Failing this, some artificial watering during dry periods is necessary. Eelworm in phlox can become a problem, especially if they have grown on the same ground for many years. Because of this, it is always wise to plant fresh healthy stock on ground where phlox have not been grown in recent years. If possible select a sunny or slightly shaded position, prepare the ground thoroughly with either well-rotted com-

A magnificent double white paeony

post or manure and then plant out in the spring. Replace with young healthy plants every three or four years. All phlox are prone to suffer from mildew but early spraying will control this.

My own choice of varieties include 'Cinderella' which has lilac-pink flowers with rose eyes and grows to 90 cm (3 ft) tall; 'Firefly' which grows to 75 cm (2½ ft) tall and has pink flowers with crimson eyes; 'Rembrandt' which is pure white and grows 90 cm (3 ft) tall and 'San Antonio' which is claret red and grows 75 cm (2½ ft) tall. The only variegated type, with pale mauve flowers, is 'Norah Leigh' and it grows 60 cm (2 ft) tall. It is a really bright choice for the border, although it is a slow grower.

Root cuttings taken in March and grown on will be ready for planting out the following spring, but only propagate from healthy plants.

PHYSALIS*
Chinese Lantern

These plants are usually grown for the ornamental calix which looks like an inflated orange balloon. If cut whilst the colour is still good, the stems of lanterns can be dried for winter indoor decoration, but remove the foliage first. Before the puffy green balloons change colour in late autumn, they can be used to advantage in flower arrangements.

Spring is the best time to plant these flowers; do so in a sunny or partially shady situation where the soil is well drained. Keep a careful eye on the plant as it grows; it is not

only invasive with its roots, but it also self-seeds freely.

Propagation is by division of the long fleshy roots or by seed sown from May to July in a cold frame. The resulting plants can be planted out in spring the following season.

POLYGONATUM*
Solomon's Seal

Solomon's Seal, *P. multiflorum*, is one of the easiest plants to grow in a border. Although it is not at all particular about the type of soil in which it grows, we have found that ours do well with their roots in the shade and their arching stems in semi-shade. In May and June, the white-waisted flowers in clusters of two or three, hang gracefully down almost along the full length of each stem. They are set off by a background of equi-spaced oblong mid-green leaves, which turn a lovely shade of yellow in the autumn.

Propagation is by division of rhizomes in March/April or from small rhizome eyes potted on and kept in a cold frame or greenhouse until large enough to be planted out.

PRIMULA*

From a vast number of species collected in the Southern hemisphere, there are fortunately some that have proved to be hardy enough to tolerate the varying conditions in our flower gardens. Generally speaking, they behave best when the soil is cool and moist throughout the whole year, which is why most of them are happier in the northern half of the country. Our native primrose (*P. vulgaris*) is still one of the finest garden plants; if you

can, give it a place on a heavy loam grassy bank in semi-shade and then leave it undisturbed to establish itself. The ever popular purple-red version, *P. vulgaris* 'Wanda' is far less fussy in its growing requirements. A recent introduction, *P. vulgaris* 'Sue Jervis', with shell-pink flowers, is also worth trying. All these flower in March/April.

Polyanthus, with their trusses of primrose-like flowers produced on stout stems, are all garden hybrids, well known and appreciated for their colourful displays in the spring. We have found 'Pacific Strain' particularly successful. For borders, members of the 'candelabra' group can be recommended. Most of these have whorls of flowers arranged on their elongated stems. Our choice includes 'Bullyana' – shades of orange; 'Japonica' hybrids – a mixture of crimson, rose and white, 'Pulverulenta' – rosy-purple – and one we particularly would not be without, 'Florindae', which was jokingly called by a visitor 'a cowslip on a stick'. All flower between May and July. *Primula denticulata* (drumstick primrose) is now available in several colours – varying from pale lilac to deep purple and rose pink to crimson, as well as pure white.

All primulas can be grown from seed, but this should be as fresh as possible. Sow from May to August in trays and cover with glass or plastic sheeting to prevent drying out. Keep in a fairly cool place; high temperatures impair germination. The plants can also be propagated by division of roots after flowering.

PULSATILLA*
Pasque Flower

Sometimes known as *Anemone pulsatilla*, it is difficult to believe that this exquisitely beautiful plant, *P. vulgaris*, was once a weed of our West Country pastures. Now it is regarded as one of the garden treasures. It has mid-green flower buds, which open to cup-shaped, pale lilac flowers. These are followed by glorious seed heads. We grow it in a

Physalis, the Chinese lantern

sunny position, where, during the autumn it dies down completely to come back to life in March. It does best on well-drained soils, especially if given a little garden lime.

As the plants are difficult to grow from division, it is best to start with seed which should be as fresh as possible. Sow this outdoors in August. Seed of hybrids in mixed colours is available, but bear in mind that some of the red hybrids are rather less vigorous than the original plant.

PYRETHRUM*

Excellent plants for a sunny border, these do best on light, well-drained soils where slugs are not a problem. Their large daisy-like flowers with golden 'button' centres, brighten up the garden continually from May until August. It is advisable to provide some support to prevent the slender flower stems being blown over; a few twigs pushed into the ground around each plant early in the spring will suffice. During drought periods watering will be necessary to maintain growth of foliage and flowers, but do start well before the plants show any signs of wilting.

There are numerous good varieties to choose from. I can recommend 'E.M. Robinson' – a pale pink, 'James Kelway' – a crimson red, and 'Marjorie Robinson' – a deep pink.

Propagation is by division of the roots in the spring and that is also the time for planting bought-in stock. Autumn planting can result in considerable losses. Large-flowered hybrids may be raised from seed sown in June/ July outside or in a cold frame.

RUDBECKIA* Cone Flower

These are invaluable plants for a late summer show of colour. They like a well-drained prepared soil with adequate drainage in an open sunny position. In exposed situations some form of support is advisable, or else the flower stems are inclined to get spread-eagled in high winds. Of the many available varieties, I would suggest 'Goldquelle', which, with its bushy habit, grows to 75 cm

(2½ ft) high and has large double yellow flowers that bloom from July to October; 'Goldsturm', which grows to 60 cm (2 ft) and has flowers with long deep golden yellow petals surrounding a black centre, appearing from July until September, and R. newmanii 'Speciosa' which is the original 'Black-Eyed Susan' having yellow flowers with black centres, appearing on branching stems from July until September.

Propagation is by division of the roots in spring and excellent plants can be raised from seed sown outside from March to May.

SALVIA* Sage

The hardy perennial sages are not what I would call exciting plants, but, nevertheless, some varieties are undoubtedly worthy of a place in a large border. Being relatively short-lived plants and untidy in old age, replacement is advisable every few years and they should also be trimmed back each autumn. All varieties do best when planted in an open sunny position.

Salvia haematodes grows to a height of 90 cm (3 ft) and has graceful branching spikes of lavender blue flowers. It is one of the most popular varieties for June/July flowering. Salvia superba grows to a height of 75 cm (2½ ft) and makes a bushy plant with violet-purple flowers that appear in July/August. Salvia superba 'Lubeco' at 45 cm (18 inches) tall is a shorter more compact plant. The foliage of all has an aromatic scent.

Propagation is by cuttings with a heel taken during the late summer and overwintered in a cold frame for planting out the following spring. Alternatively you can sow seed in August/September in the greenhouse.

SCABIOSA*
Scabious, Pincushion Flower
These really splendid plants for cut flowers all have a long flowering season – from June to September – if the dead heads are removed regularly. To grow them successfully a thoroughly prepared soil which has had an application of garden lime is needed. They will not do so well on acid soils. The ever popular 'Clive Greaves', which grows 90 cm (3 ft) high, produces a constant supply of large lavender blue flowers on long stems which do not require staking. 'Miss Wilmott' with its white flowers has similar growth habit and the relatively new 'Lucida' has pink flowers above dark green foliage.

Propagation is by division of roots in the spring or by cuttings taken with a heel after flowering. Planting out should always be done in the spring.

SEDUM*
Stone Crop, Ice Plant
These late-flowering semi-succulents S. spectabile, with glaucous green foliage are beloved by the butterflies and bees in the autumn. For the sake of both plants and butterflies, it is best to plant them in full sunshine. Being fairly rapid growers they need space to spread out so they can display their rosy-purple large flat flowerheads to their best.

The variety, 'Autumn Joy', is well named; its flowers open to a salmon pink and go on changing colour until the end of the season. It grows to a height of 60 cm (2 ft). The dwarf variety, 'September Ruby', growing only to 30 cm (1 ft), has deep rose-pink flowerheads.

Propagation is easy; stem cuttings taken in June/July will seldom fail.

SOLIDAGO* Golden Rod
These are so easy to grow that they are often neglected and as a result become poor plants. Being gross feeders they do need a feed of general fertiliser each spring to keep them in good trim. They undoubtedly do best in full sun, but will tolerate partial shade. The taller varieties may need staking to prevent them flopping over when fully grown. As with most perennials the old flower stems should be cut down in October/November.

Some of the newer varieties I would recommend are: 'Cloth of Gold', which grows to 45 cm (18 inches) and makes a robust plant with deep yellow flower heads; 'Crown of Rays', which grows to the same height and has attractive horizontal golden spikes; 'Golden Thumb', which grows to 30 cm (1 ft) and is a neat plant with yellow fluffy flowerheads, and the tall 'Mimosa', which grows 1.5 metres (5 ft) high and is a trouble-free plant with yellow flowerheads.

Propagation is by division of roots which should be done in March/April. Plants can also be grown from seed which you should sow in a cold frame in March.

VERBASCUM* Mullein

These rather short-lived plants always capture attention especially when they flower majestically as individual plants in a garden. They are so stately looking, often towering above their surrounding neighbours to show off their long, thick and sometimes woolly spires of flowers which appear in July/August. They really are a must for any flower garden, even if you only grow a single plants. They love the sun and are not deterred by drought.

'Cotswold Queen' grows 1.3 metres (4½ft) high and has branching stems and buff-orange flowers. 'Gainsborough' grows 1.2 metres (4ft) high and is the most beautiful of them all with its graceful, spikes of clear yellow flowers. Unfortunately it is beautiful of them all with its graceful spikes of clear yellow high and has branching stems to carry its pure white flowers above the felty green leaves.

Propagation of named varieties is by taking 7.5 cm (3 inch) long cuttings in March for rooting in a cold frame, or from root cuttings taken in December/January. To grow from seed, sow 'Choice' mixed in April/June outside for flowering the following year.

VERONICA* Speedwell

This is a useful and attractive border plant, which given a well-drained soil enriched with some well-rotted compost and a place in full sun or partial shade will be very happy. Veronica gentianoides grows 60 cm (2 ft) high and is sometimes planted for ground cover. It produces slender spikes of palest grey-blue flowers in April/May. Veronica incana 'Saraband' grows 45 cm (18 inches) high and has beautiful grey foliage followed by violet-blue flowers that appear from June to August. Veronica spicata 'Barcarolle', grows to 45 cm (18 inches) and makes a neat carpet of dark foliage punctuated with narrow spikes of deep rose-pink flowers in June/July. V. spicata 'Red Fox', grows to 37 cm (15 inches) and has red flowers

Veronica gentianoides, speedwell

from June to September.

All named varieties can be propagated from lateral cuttings taken in July/August. They should be rooted in a cold frame and potted on for planting out the following March.

Veronica teucrium 'Shirley Blue' can be grown from seed sown in May to July outside to flower the following season. It grows to 30 cm (1 ft).

ROSES

It is impossible for me to imagine a flower garden, however small or large without at least a few roses. Whatever variation the seasons may bring, roses never fail to greet the early summer days of June with the splendour of their glorious, colourful blooms. If a careful choice of varieties is made the delight of perfume will come as an extra bonus.

There are literally hundreds of varieties to choose from, but as their growth and flowering habits vary greatly the first thing to do is to decide on the type of rose plants you want to grow. Bush roses, for example are divided into two groups, Hybrid Teas (H.T.s) which produce large individual blooms on single stems, and Floribundas whose characteristic of many blooms produced in clusters or trusses has made them very popular for mass colour displays. Both Hybrid Teas and Floribundas can also be grown as standards; in this instance they flower on a 90 cm (3 ft) single stem which will need a strong stake for support.

For covering pergolas, walls or fences, roses with vigorous growth habits are needed. These are classified as climbing or rambling roses, of which the older varieties will flower only once during the summer. Some of the more recent additions, however, provide repeat displays of blooms throughout or later on in the season. Some of the modern shrub roses, too, have the same repeat-flowering qualities and merit consideration, not only as individual plants in a bed or border but also for planting as flowering hedges. Their useful deterrent of thorns against vandals – human or otherwise – make them particularly effective when grown as a hedge.

After several false starts, miniature roses which almost live up to their classification, have been produced. They can be expected to grow to about 45 cm (18 inches) high and produce miniature flowers in great quantity. Grown in small containers or pots, where their root growth is restricted, they can do extremely well. Provided they are watered and fed regularly, they prove good value for money. Amongst the miniatures, there are a few varieties with prostrate or semi-prostrate growth habits. These have been segregated

and termed 'Ground Cover Roses'. Whilst we have been delighted to have them at Clack's Farm, the term ground cover can be somewhat misleading. We found the weeds loved the shelter provided and because of the thorns on the roses, weeding has become fairly painful.

The first golden rule for success with roses will always be the preparation of the soil before planting. A heavy clay soil, which is the best type for growing roses, often lacks good drainage; digging in of home-made, well-rotted compost or a mixture of peat and sand will improve it. With lighter soils it is advisable to step up the water-holding capacity by digging in well-rotted compost or farmyard manure. If neither of these is available, use peat on its own.

Another golden rule is to plant your roses in the sunniest position possible; they will repay you royally for giving them the best place in the garden. Feed them regularly with a rose fertiliser, first in March, followed by a repeat application in early June. If you can get some farmyard manure to use as a top dressing early in March, your roses will be more than grateful. It will certainly give a lift to the overall health of the plants, improving the foliage and the quality of the blooms.

PRUNING ROSES

The pruning of roses is a controversial subject. Whilst the third week in March is often suggested as the correct time, I have for years pruned our bush roses before Christmas and, by so doing, have been able to contain the black spot problem simply because all the old dead infected foliage is then out of the way. I prune them down to two or three buds above the ground in late autumn; it is important to make a clean cut on a slant so that water cannot collect on the top of the stem causing it to rot. Then in early spring, I remove any wood that has died back. Make sure that your secateurs are really sharp so that you achieve a clean cut without crushing the wood. Bush roses should also be pruned just after their first flowering to encourage a second flush of blooms.

Climbing, rambling and shrub roses should be pruned at the end of their flowering season as they all flower on old wood. Climbers and ramblers should be pruned back to a framework of healthy wood; with shrub roses, it is wise to cut out all the thin straggly growth and cut the strong wood back by one-third.

PROPAGATING ROSES

You can propagate favourite roses by taking cuttings of them in August. Select strong shoots of the current season's growth and cut a 18-20 cm (7-8 inch) length of stem cleanly below a node at the base, and just above a node at the top. Carefully remove all the leaves without damaging the buds, then dip the bottom end of the cutting in a rooting powder or solution. These cuttings are now ready for planting in a prepared position outside. When doing so, make sure that only one-third of the cuttings are above ground, otherwise too much drying out will occur. Rooted cuttings will be ready for transplanting to their permanent positions in November the following year.

In compiling the following A-Z lists, I have limited them to the varieties we have grown with success at Clack's Farm and can therefore recommend.

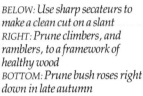

BELOW: Use sharp secateurs to make a clean cut on a slant
RIGHT: Prune climbers, and ramblers, to a framework of healthy wood
BOTTOM: Prune bush roses right down in late autumn

HYBRID TEA ROSES*

'Alec's Red': This is a sturdy medium-height grower, admirably suited to the smaller garden. The large, deep red blooms are well carried on strong upright stems and the claim that it has a sweet perfume is certainly true.

'Blessings': This great rose bred by Gregory of Nottingham, is very free flowering. We love its blooms of delicate coral salmon, which, when it decides to be generous, are produced in clusters. Being another upright grower, it is a never-fail rose for the small garden.

'Fragrant Cloud': A very popular rose that is well known for its perfume which is freely given off by its large coral-scarlet blooms. It is very free flowering and has vigorous qualities which mean it can be grown successfully on poorer soils. Its one weakness is that when the flowers age they turn dull and need dead-heading earlier than most.

'Grandpa Dickson': This is a great rose by any standard and was introduced in 1966. Its lemon-yellow blooms are often seen on the show bench but its real value is in the garden. A moderate grower, it needs a little extra attention to get the best from it and that includes its perfume.

'Josephine Bruce': For fragrance, this rose is still supreme, although it is relatively old (1949). It is well known, too, for its beautiful dark crimson velvet-like blooms, as well, unfortunately, for its susceptibility to mildew. Control the latter (see p.19) and you will love it.

'Just Joey': This is one of our favourites, and could really be called a 'poppet'. Really fragrant, especially when the air is warm, the coppery orange-red-veined blooms are beautiful. It is very free flowering and being an upright grower, easy to manage.

'Maestro': A 'hand-painted' masterpiece bred by Sam McGredy, we first saw this rose in New Zealand. The fully open blooms are an artistry of deep crimson edged with white, making it a very striking new rose. It is only a moderate grower so needs a regular feed to keep it 'on stream'.

'Mullard Jubilee': Here is a rose with robust vigour, so in consequence it needs a little more space than most. Its large rose-pink blooms are well shaped and prolific.

'National Trust': With us, this rose has never failed to go on and on producing its deep, crimson-scarlet, perfectly

'Just Joey', a beautiful bloom

shaped blooms. At all times during the growing season it remains a tidy, compact plant with strong healthy foliage. The coppery red colour of this when young adds greatly to its attraction.

'Peace': In spite of the fact that this is a variety that needs no introduction, it is still a great rose. Although its large, creamy-yellow edged and shaded pink blooms are never produced very freely, the three or four blooms produced per plant at a time still make a spectacular show. It is a vigorous grower.

'Piccadilly': This is a rose we have grown since its introduction in 1960, and with us it seems to have brushed aside such diseases as black spot and mildew. In addition it has always been generous with its scarlet and gold high-pointed buds which open to reveal the full beauty of this rose.

'Pink Favourite': One of the best bedding roses ever produced, this rose really has got everything; fragrance, large, well-shaped rose-pink blooms, plenty of healthy glossy foliage and an upright habit. It is also a good grower.

'Prima Ballerina': This is another of our favourites, bred by Tantau and introduced in 1957. A reliable grower, it makes a medium-height bush which from June onwards displays its very fragrant deep rose pink blooms. It is a good choice for a small garden.

'Whisky Mac': Another great rose from Tantau, which with us has always been a good healthy grower, never disappointing us. Its attractive deep gold blooms, with their bronze shading are perfumed and justly admired. It makes a compact bush covered with bronze-green foliage.

For growing as **standard roses** I would recommend any of the following: 'Alec's Red', 'Blessings', 'Fragrant Cloud', 'Just Joey', 'National Trust' or 'Piccadilly'.

FLORIBUNDAS*

'**Arthur Bell**': This is a rose that has done well with us since its introduction by Sam McGredy in 1965. Its rather large blooms, produced in trusses rather than clusters, are individually reminiscent of hybrid tea roses in their shape. These trusses of bright golden yellow roses are well perfumed and carried on strong upright stems. The dark green foliage has shown considerable resistance to disease.

'**Australian Gold**': We first planted this variety in 1980, since when it has proved to be a constant cropper of copious blooms with a colouring akin to ripe peaches. It is another upright grower of medium height with healthy looking dark green glossy foliage.

'**Bonfire Night**': A rose aptly named by Sam McGredy, as when in flower every stem carries clusters of blooms that glow with colours similar to the flames of a bonfire – a combination of orange tinged with yellow and scarlet. It is a really beautiful variety and makes a spectacular show when several are planted together.

'**City of Leeds**': Here is a rose introduced in 1966 by Sam McGredy which could be called a 'winner', either for mass planting or even as a single bush. With a more gla-

morous name, it may well have found the place it deserves in every rose garden. I planted 100 bushes at The Lenton Research Station in Nottingham in 1966 and every plant was still healthy and flowering well when I last saw the bed in 1981. Few new varieties have such staying powers; the delightful rich salmon blooms almost cover the plants for most of the summer.

'**Elizabeth of Glamis**': Right from its introduction in 1964, the name of this rose has made it extremely popular. That apart, however, it is a beautiful rose, sporting double flowers

The very popular 'Elizabeth of Glamis'

that are coral-salmon shaded with pink. On the debit side, it dislikes heavy cold clay soil situations and needs regular and careful spraying as it is less than usually resistant to disease. Lifted from the nursery with bare roots it sometimes fails to survive the transplanting. It is sensible, therefore to purchase it as a container grown plant.

'**Frensham**': This is the variety which will aways be associated with the advent of floribunda roses. It led the way

77

and became immensely popular immediately after its introduction in 1946. Its masses of deep crimson blooms and its vigorous growth has a compelling appeal, which has remained in spite of its susceptibility to mildew. This must be dealt with early in the season or the disfiguring disease will run riot (see p.19).

'Iceberg': One of the finest floribunda roses ever introduced, this truly great rose from Kordes (1958) is a fairly tall grower with a parading shrub-like habit. For mass planting it is without equal and its large decorative sprays of pure white make a continuously graceful display throughout the season. The slender stems are almost devoid of thorns making it a joy at pruning time.

'Kerryman': A rose that has given great pleasure at Clack's Farm, the clusters of large hybrid tea-shaped blooms produced in various shades of pink are simply delightful. It flowers freely throughout the season and is an excellent choice for the smaller garden.

'Lili Marlene': When introduced by Kordes in 1959, this rose was an immediate success, partly because of its name and partly because of its semi-double, crimson-scarlet blooms and its compact medium-growth habit. It is a good garden rose especially for planting towards the front of a rose bed. We have found it necessary to start spraying early in the season to keep it free from mildew throughout August and September.

'Koresia': With good yellow roses still something of a rarity this one stands out as su-

'Iceberg' is a superbly free-flowering rose

perb. Here is a variety that has charmed us with its fragrance and its golden yellow blooms that appear in clusters and are of the classical hybrid tea dimensions. They are produced in quantity on the plants which grow to medium height and good shape, thus making this the type of bush that always looks tidy.

'Mary Sumner': The double copper-vermilion blooms of this rose are freely produced in well shaped trusses, and seen against the background of glossy, truly healthy foliage, they make an immediate appeal. The rose was an intro-

duction from Sam McGredy (1975); we love it and would expect to be growing it for many years to come.

'Masquerade': This was the first multi-coloured floribunda introduced by Boemer in 1949. Its blooms (like Joseph's coat of many colours) were unique at its time of introduction and made it tremendously popular. Its bright yellow buds open to reveal anything from cream to pink, moving on to crimson in the open flowers. Its ability to flower freely, its neat growth habit and above all its cheerful appearance during the summer flowering season, helps it to retain its favoured place in many gardens.

'**Matangi**': We regard this as one of Sam McGredy's best introductions (1974). Right from the start, it has been a healthy grower with a medium height, bushy growth habit, making it well suited for planting either singly or in quantity. Its double blooms of orange-vermilion with silver shading at the base of each petal, repeated on the reverse, are delightfully fragrant. The glow of Matangi in full bloom reminds us of the New Zealand sunset colours.

'**News**': We regarded the introduction of this rose as great news in 1969. Coming from Norfolk it is a robust grower and very free flowering. The deep wine red buds are most attractive, and they open to blooms that become rich purple with golden anthers.

'**Regensburg**': A fascinating little rose which needs encouraging to make sufficient growth when planted in a bed. It is an ideal rose for planting in a container to brighten up a patio. The double white and pink blooms with their open eyes, are a just reward for Sam McGredy and his endeavour to introduce what almost seems to be hand painting of rose petals in his roses.

'**St Boniface**': Another low-growing variety named by Kordes (1980) in honour of a British saint. Its perfectly shaped blooms are always a bright and cheerful vermilion. When planting choose a place at the front of the bed so that it can be seen or, alternatively, plant it in a narrow raised bed.

'**Scarlet Queen Elizabeth**': Bred by Dickson and introduced in 1963, this rose is not quite as tall as the more famous pink Queen Elizabeth but it is nevertheless a strong robust grower. It produces bright scarlet, semi-double blooms and has most attractive healthy bronze-green foliage. Plant it at the back of the bed or as a hedge.

'**Sue Lawley**': This is another 'hand-painted' rose from Sam McGredy's vintage year, 1980. Like Regensburg, it also loves that extra handful of farmyard manure. The double rosy-pink blooms with their white eyes are delightfully edged with lighter pink and white which unfortunately do tend to bleach in bright sunlight.

'**Queen Elizabeth**': This well known and still very popular, tall-growing rose was introduced by Lammers in 1956. Few roses can compete with the clarity of colour in its blooms, the soft, clear pink of which has won it its place in so many gardens. Give it space where its height is an advantage or plant it as a hedge and it will be a real joy. Few roses have as good a health record, every leaf shines brightly.

'**Trumpeter**': A rose that has been an outstanding success. From the start to finish of each season it has produced its scarlet trusses of blooms so generously, it must merit the strongest possible recommendation. In addition its short compact growth habit makes it one of the best bedding roses available at this time. It can be termed a truly great garden rose.

Some floribundas are very good for growing as standard roses. Of those listed here I would suggest: 'Iceberg', 'Koresia', 'Mary Sumner', 'Matangi' and 'Trumpeter'.

'Trumpeter', a truly glorious colour

REPEAT-FLOWERING SHRUB ROSES*

These are a real asset to any garden but generally need more space than either hybrid teas or floribundas. In a smaller garden, a single specimen is acceptable but if the garden is on the large side these shrub roses look well planted in groups of three.

'Ballerina': Makes a 1.2 metre (4 ft) shrub which, in bloom, is covered with great clusters of small single pink flowers with white eyes. Introduced by Bentall in 1937, it is a very showy rose and one of the flower arranger's favourites as it lasts well after cutting.

'Dorothy Wheatcroft': A floribunda shrub rose introduced by Tantau in 1960 that is very vigorous. It will grow up to 1.5 metres (5 ft) high on good soil. The glowing bright red single blooms are carried in large trusses and tend to be so perfect that they are often seen on the show benches with red 1st prize winners cards.

'Kerdes Robusta': As a rose we were privileged to grow before its introduction in 1982, we cannot speak too highly of this one. Grown as an individual plant it needs space in order that it may be enjoyed to the full. With us it grows to 1.5-1.8 metres (5-6 ft) and is truly vigorous, with excellent dark green foliage and some mighty strong thorns. The latter make it a variety to grow as a hedge to keep away unwanted visitors; whilst the thorns may deter the vandals the single scarlet blooms with their outstandingly beautiful golden stamens are a joy to everyone. Flowering begins early and goes on until the autumn. It really is a great rose if you have space or want to make a flowering hedge.

'Louise Odier': One of the old Bourbon roses (1851), this is a firm favourite for the flower arranger's summer creations. It has a rich pink bloom, softly shaded with a tinge of lilac and a scent that pervades the garden. It is not too vigorous a grower.

'Westerland': The bright golden orange semi-double blooms of this shrub rose are a real joy. Whilst it is vigorous in habit, it can be contained with drastic pruning and could therefore be grown in a bed.

SUMMER-FLOWERING SHRUB ROSES*

There are many different types of roses that come under this heading; the damask, moss and rose species being some of them. Only a few can be mentioned here, but any good rose catalogue will give a more extensive list.

'Fritz Nobis': One of the so-called modern hybrids, we put this at the top of our list for beauty and performance. Early in June the long pointed salmon-pink buds appear, soon to be followed by the large semi-double blooms of soft creamy pink. It is a vigorous grower easily reaching up to 1.8 metres (6 ft) or more.

'Madam Hardy': One of the damask roses we like very much, it makes a vigorous bush of medium height. The pure white blooms give out that wonderful old fashioned fragrance.

'Nuits De Young': This is a beautiful moss rose with deep blackish-purple small blooms which, when fully open, show yellow stamens. It is not too vigorous, its maximum height

'Madame Hardy', a damask rose

being about 1.2 metres (4 ft) which makes it suitable for the small town garden.

Rosa × highdownensis: This is our first choice of the rose species, and it is a vigorous grower needing plenty of space. It has deep pink single flowers, but its main attraction is its flask-shaped hips.

Rosa rubrifolia: This is without doubt our second choice. It is a much more moderate grower with dark red stems and purple grey foliage. A variety for the flower arranger, the small pink flowers are followed by bright mahogany hips. Its growth habit is best suited to the smaller garden.

CLIMBING AND RAMBLING ROSES*

'Albertine': This wonderful summer flowering climbing rose, seen at its best in June-July, was introduced by Barbier in 1921. Few roses can claim to bloom more profusely, or be more beautiful or more fragrant than Albertine. Just a single plant will add another dimension to your flower garden. The deep coppery red buds open to soft salmon-pink flowers, so numerous that they simply smother the whole plant to make a magnificent display which lasts for fully a month.

Altissimo': This is a really vigorous climber which will make 4.5 metres (15 ft) or more growth without much encouragement. Its dark green foliage clearly displays its health and vigour and, given a chance, it will go on flowering throughout the whole season. Seen against a brickwork background the single large flowers with their golden stamens are indeed glorious.

'American Pillar': Still grown

'Albertine' is a prolific climber

and popular although introduced as long ago as 1902 by Van Fleet, this is a vigorous rambler appreciated for its bright cerise pink, white-centred flowers which are at their peak in June and July. It is a variety that is often planted and then forgotten, but it does so much better when it is given an occasional feed with a rose fertiliser.

'Danse Du Feu': This is a climber that can be grown against a north wall although it does somewhat better in more sunny situations. A vigorous grower – reaching up to 4.5 metres (15 ft) – it is capable of making a fine show throughout the season with its semi-double, bright orange-red blooms and glossy dark green foliage. It is a great rose for the front of the house.

'Dreaming Spires': This rose is a 1973 Mattock introduction of fairly vigorous habit. The bright golden blooms have a delightful fragrance and are shown up by its heavy dark green foliage. If given that extra dose of fertiliser, it will flower through the summer.

'Galway Bay': A climbing rose from Sam McGredy which was introduced in 1966, it has a growth habit which makes it suitable for training as a pillar rose rather than up against a wall. From June onwards it produces its cerise pink blooms generously.

'Golden Showers': A rose we love, this one will suffer all sorts of treatment and still come up with its bright yellow blooms in profusion throughout the whole season. As a climber it is excellent, even on a north wall, and it will go to a height of 1.8 metres (6 ft). Restrained by pruning and treated as a shrub, it is still happy if the soil is good.

'Handel': One of our finest climbers (Sam McGredy 1965), this rose grows up to 3 metres (10 ft). There can be few more beautiful sights in a garden than an established Handel in full bloom with its creamy-white suffused roses edged with bright rose-pink. The half open blooms are of medium size and near perfectly shaped. It is no wonder that it is so popular either as a climber or as a restricted growth shrub rose.

'Mermaid': Once established this rose is very vigorous but it may sulk for a year or two after planting before deciding it likes and will accept the position in your garden. Once settled in a spot with plenty of room, it produces large, single, pale sulphur yellow flowers with amber stamens that are unbelievably beautiful. No other climber has such glossy foliage.

'Park Direktor Riggers': A very clean, vigorous and large grower introduced by Kordes in 1957, this rose has plenty of strong wood to cover a house wall. It then adorns it with super brilliant crimson, semi-double blooms in large clusters, set off by beautiful glossy dark green foliage. I have never known anyone to be disappointed with it.

'Pink Perpetue': This is a variety greatly admired by visitors to Clack's Farm. Planted on the south-facing wall of our house it starts to flower to-

'Zephirine Drouhin' is a thornless climber

wards the end of May and goes on producing its bright rose pink with salmon-rose shades blooms until the autumn. Already our two plants have exceeded 3 metres (10 ft) and have every appearance of growing higher still.

'Wedding Day': This is a true summer flowering rambler, suitable for growing into trees and over tall archways. The buds are yellow but open to white flowers with a rich fragrance.

'Zephirine Drouhin': The thornless climber introduced way back in 1868 by Bizot, which was almost lost until seen on television growing in the Royal National Rose Society's trial grounds at St. Albans. Now it is a great favourite with those who know how to control its mildew problems. Its glorious carmine pink blooms are delightfully fragrant and it will flower continuously throughout the whole season.

All these climbers, ramblers and true shrub roses produce their flowers on the previous season's wood, so in consequ-

ence they are not likely to flower in their first year after planting. Do remember this when pruning; leave some new growth otherwise there will be few roses on the plants the following season.

MINIATURE ROSES*

Whilst some of the miniature roses are recommended for open ground planting, my own experience with them indicates that while they do produce charming miniature blooms, practically all exceed their catalogue heights even during their first year outdoors. However there is undoubtedly a place for them in containers or pots where root restriction has a considerable effect on the size of the plant. A patio or balcony is the obvious place for them.

'Baby Masquerade': A charming small bush with multi-coloured miniature yellow, pink and red flowers right through the summer.

'Dresden Doll': This is the star of them all with its miniature shell-pink moss roses. They start as tiny buds covered with

The miniature 'Baby Masquerade'

growth that looks like light green moss. Later they open into small, fully double blooms making it a most charming plant.

In this same category come the **ground cover roses**, so called because their spread is greater than their height.

'Nozomi': A dainty ground cover rose with small pale pink single flowers in large clusters. It will grow to a height of 30-45 cm (12-18 inches) and is very effective when grown in a tall container or where it has the opportunity to trail down.

'Snow Carpet': Bred by Sam McGredy (1980). We have found that after three years at Clack's Farm each plant covers almost a square metre (just over a square yard) but its height has continued to remain under 20 cm (8 inches). Its foliage is dark green throughout the season when much of the time the plants are covered with tiny snow-white double miniature roses.

PATIOS AND WINDOWBOXES

Patios, windowboxes and other containers offer an exciting extension to traditional gardening, especially for those with little garden space. Even the tiniest back garden can be turned into an attractive patio with a variety of plants. An empty balcony or a plain front porch can be transformed into a blaze of colour with hanging baskets, urns and tubs of contrasting flowering plants. Patios, of course, are not restricted to confined space gardens. An 'outdoor living area' is always appreciated in a large garden.

Windowboxes are the perfect way to brighten up the exterior of homes which have no garden. All town houses and flats have windows and that usually means window-ledges suitable for anchoring windowboxes to. There are various containers to suit all types of dwellings – from simple white plastic window-boxes for modern homes, to ornate terracotta containers for older properties. Better still, you can make your own wooden windowboxes to fit the available space – much cheaper and not difficult.

One of the main advantages of container gardening is the flexibility it offers. Special soil and moisture conditions can be provided in tubs, windowboxes and hanging baskets – extending the range of plants that can be grown. Colourful displays can be maintained all-year-round by replanting containers when the contents have passed their best. Winter boxes, filled with evergreens, can be under-planted with dwarf flowering bulbs to provide colour through the spring. The choice of plants to replace these for a summer display is endless, but fuchsias, pansies and impatiens are always popular.

Athough most container and patio plants are purely decorative, there are some exceptions. Herbs, of course, are traditionally grown. They are especially useful – either in a windowbox or in tubs just outside the back door – within easy reach of the kitchen. A raised herb bed on the patio also looks most attractive and has a wonderful aroma! A surprising range of fruit and vegetables can also be grown. Strawberries, cucumbers and tomatoes are suitable container plants; small fruit trees and soft fruit bushes can be planted directly into the soil on the patio.

A patio – large or small – adds a new dimension to outdoor living by extending the time normally spent in the garden. At different times it can be a place for entertaining, relaxing, for the children to play in, or a quiet spot to work in. A patio adjacent to the house can be treated as an additional room in summer, and furnished accordingly – with table and chairs. On a warm summer's evening, nothing is more enjoyable than a barbecue on the patio.

For the gardener with an eye for design, a patio offers plenty of scope. All sorts of containers can be used, from wooden hanging baskets and windowboxes to terracotta jars, stone troughs and wooden half-barrels. In addition, there are usually opportunities for planting some material directly into the soil. Small flowerbeds between paving stones are most effective.

Few patio sites are perfect. By virtue of its position the patio may have to house the dust-bin, an oil tank or ugly drain pipes, for example. But these unsightly objects can be hidden by positioning trees, raised beds or screens carefully, and climbers can make any wall or screen look attractive. The potential growing space on the walls of a small patio is often greater than the ground area and should never be wasted. Apart from the flowering climbers, such as clematis, cotoneasters and honeysuckles, many of the dwarf fruit trees can be fan-trained to splendid effect against a wall.

One of the most appealing aspects of patio and windowbox gardening is the comparatively small amount of effort required to create an attractive display. No strenuous digging, constant weeding or laborious mowing is involved. The key to success is careful planning – selecting suitable plants and positioning them for maximum effect. The chart on pages 74-77 provides at-a-glance information on growing requirements of patio and windowbox plants – especially useful when choosing plants to be grouped together. The A-Z section tells you how to look after each one.

CONTAINERS

WINDOWBOXES

A well-stocked windowbox can bring character to even the most ordinary house, or brighten the dreary facade of an office block in town. For the flat dweller without a garden, windowboxes are invaluable. With a little thought they can provide pleasure all year round. The choice of plants can vary with your likes and needs. In spring a colourful display can be created with bulbs planted the previous autumn – hyacinths, polyanthus, narcissi, low-growing tulips and dwarf irises all provide possibilities. These can then be changed for colourful summer bedding plants, such as pansies, fuchsias and stocks. A herb box is ideal for the kitchen window.

Windowboxes can be fitted to most windows – obviously taking great care that they are securely fixed to prevent them falling or sliding off. Most sash windows will take a box actually sitting on the sill, but casement windows that swing open have to have the box slung below the sill, and the plants must be low enough to allow the window clearance above them.

When fixing, remember that windowboxes are very heavy when filled with moist soil and plants. Be careful to check that all brackets and fixing screws are adequate for the job. If you are hanging a trough below a windowsill, make sure that the trough is strong enough to take the stress of being supported by a bracket at each end, otherwise the bottom might drop out together with the contents. The dimensions of the windowbox will obviously depend on the size of windowsill, but it should have a depth of 15-20 cm (6-8 inches) to give a good root-run for most plants. If the window is particularly wide it is better to have several short boxes rather than one long one as smaller boxes are more robust and rigid, and easier to handle.

The timber used for a windowbox should be at least 2.5 cm (1 inch) thick for the structure of the box. If you are using plywood make sure you use exterior or marine ply as this will withstand the weather and dampness. All nails and screws should be rust-proof and the glue should be waterproof. Treat timber with a wood preservative that will not affect plant life –

most manufacturers produce one that is formulated for this purpose. Some of the copper-based preservatives may leave the wood with a green tinge, but this can be painted over. If you prefer not to paint the outside of the windowbox, choose one that will leave the wood with a more natural colour.

All windowboxes should have adequate drainage in the base to allow excess water to drain away. If the box is hung below the sill, be sure that the holes are placed so that the water will not run down the wall and leave an unsightly stain. The holes should be placed near the front edge so that any drips fall free of the wall. When positioning the windowbox on the sill, place a removable drip tray underneath it to collect any excess water. As most sills slope to stop water standing on them, wedges should be placed under the windowboxes to keep them level and lift them clear of the ledge. This helps with drainage and aeration.

Some gardeners prefer to keep all their plants in individual pots and sink these into a peat,

A composite windowbox provides a colourful spring display – primulas, hyacinths, crocus and a dwarf juniper are an effective combination.

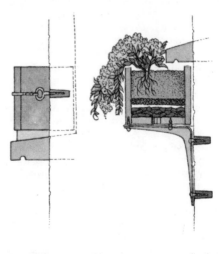

Iris, fuchsias and yellow alyssum – plants of different heights are combined to provide an attractive summer windowbox.

LEFT: *Above the sill, secure boxes with wall plugs and galvanised wire. Use a wedge to keep the box level.*
RIGHT: *Brackets, rustproof screws and wall plugs will hold a windowbox firmly beneath the sill.*

Plants can be potted individually and then inserted into a windowbox filled with peat or vermiculite. This makes transplanting and maintenance of individual plants easier.

vermiculite or perlite bed in the windowbox rather than planting directly into the box. This has the advantage that an ailing plant can be removed without disturbing the roots of the others. If the tops of the pots are filled with the same materials as the windowbox the pots become almost invisible. As an alternative, a board with holes, into which the pots can be dropped, can be fixed to the wall with brackets. If planted with trailing specimens the pots are concealed by the foliage.

By careful selection of plants, windowboxes can provide attractive all-year-round displays. For a colourful springtime show plant bulbs – daffodils, crocus and tulips – and interplant with evergreens. For a summer display, plant in May and choose from petunias, impatiens (busy Lizzie), asters, heliotropes, helianthemums and mesembryanthemums. Alternatively, opt for begonias, salvias and pansies which will flower all through summer and early autumn – until the first frosts appear.

Maintain windowboxes through the winter months by planting with evergreens; winter-flowering erica is a good choice. Some of the summer-flowering plants, such as santolina, offer attractive foliage in winter.

Pelargoniums (geraniums) are amongst the most popular windowbox plants because of their long flowering period. If you want flowers for cutting – to enhance the inside of your home as well as the outside – choose anemones, dahlias, tulips and iris. For fragrance, consider alyssums, antirrhinums and violas.

Composite arrangements can be most effective in windowboxes – providing contrast in shape, size and colour. For best results, make sure that the plants you group together can easily be grown in the same compost or soil, at the same temperature and in the same light situation. For example, wall-flowers, pansies and violas can be grown together in a lime-containing soil. Use the chart on pages 74-77 as a quick guide to plants which flourish under similar conditions.

HANGING BASKETS

Hanging baskets can brighten up plain walls, porches, doorways, basement areas, pergolas and archways, and they can bring colour and interest up off the ground to eye level or above. There are free-hanging baskets or half baskets to fit on to walls. They are made from wire, plastic, wood, or pottery. The wire models can be painted, galvanized, or dipped into plastic to make them weatherproof, while the plastic variety can be supplied with or without an integral reservoir for water.

Again the planted baskets can be quite heavy, so great care must be taken to check that the supporting brackets or hooks and chains are strong enough and firmly fixed to the wall. It is possible to obtain supporting hooks that allow the basket to be raised and lowered for watering and maintenance. This is particularly valuable where it would be difficult to water from a window above.

It is vital to provide a good heart to the basket to supply water and food for the roots of the plants. First line the basket with sphagnum moss or osmunda fibre, then fill it to within 4-5 cm (1½-2 inches) of the rim with a mixture of peat, to absorb moisture, and a suitable compost (see page 24). It is possible to use a plastic sheet in place of the moss to keep the moisture from evaporating too quickly, but as this can look unsightly it is best to place the plastic sheet between the peat and an outer lining of moss, so that the plastic is hidden. To prevent the

A cross section of a wire basket showing the centre core of moss peat, surrounded by peat-based compost. An outer layer of moss hides the plastic sheet lining. Small plants can be introduced through the sides of the basket.

The minimum of effort is required to grow flowering plants, such as these calceolarias and fuchsias, in a plastic hanging basket which has an integral reservoir of water in the base of the container.

moss then appearing dry, spray occasionally with water. If plastic sheeting is used, it must be pierced with holes for drainage. 'Foam' basket liners are also available.

The sides of hanging baskets can be planted as well as the top surface, provided this is done as the basket is being filled. Once the base of the basket has been lined with moss and the plastic sheet, some trailing plants can be inserted through the mesh, moss and plastic and their roots spread out and packed round with the peat mixture. Continue this procedure, gradually filling up the basket and completing it with the top planting.

When finished, the basket should be immersed in a container of water and allowed to soak for a couple of hours. Allow the basket to drain before hanging it in its final position. Flourishing baskets require regular watering, preferably by immersing the whole basket in a bucket of water about once a day, although this can be difficult if you have prolific trailing plants. Hanging baskets should also be fed at least weekly from July through to the frosts for the best results.

Suitable plants for hanging baskets include anemones, begonias (tuberous-rooted), campanulas, fuchsias, lobelias and pelargoniums. During the winter months baskets can be planted with suitable subjects such as dwarf junipers surrounded with hardy succulents, and small evergreen climbers, such as small-leaved ivies. If you use these as temporary

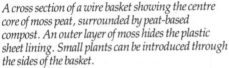

An easy way to water plants in a hanging basket is to immerse the entire basket in a box lined with plastic sheeting, and filled with water. The basket can be left to soak for a few hours.

fillers, keep them in pots rather than uproot them each time. Choose varieties that have varied leaf form and colour. Alternatively 'winter baskets' can be moved to the north side of the house and other baskets planted with spring-flowering plants and bulbs can be hung; these in turn can be replaced with summer-flowering baskets so that you have a colourful display throughout the year.

There are plenty of flowers that thrive in hanging baskets. The more exotic ones are tender and can only be used in the summer; they need the protection of a greenhouse or conservatory during the winter. There are other plants that can grow in baskets: for the gourmet, a basketful of strawberries grows very well, safe from the harmful attentions of slugs and other ground-based pests. Another basket planted with mint, chives and parsley can serve the cook, particularly if it is within easy reach of the kitchen window.

It is easy to be carried away with enthusiasm and overdo the number of plants squeezed into a hanging basket, but try to avoid this. It is better to keep to a simple colour scheme or to have a basic planting with variations in the flower colour. A basket full of one kind of plant, such as petunias, can provide a marvellous spectacle while a complicated planting can end up looking a mess.

TUBS AND URNS

Tubs and urns are the most common of the containers used for planting and can be used for a variety of purposes from brightening up a dull patch in the garden to adorning balconies, terraces or patios, or even decorating a doorway or a flight of steps. They are particularly useful for giving height to what would otherwise be a rather flat area.

Tubs fall into two categories – the round half-barrel and the Versailles square tub. The latter has a removable side so that maintenance of the soil and root pruning can be undertaken without lifting the plant out of the tub. Normally both kinds are made from wood, but you can now get plastic and glass-fibre tubs too. The advantage with these new types is that they do not rot. However, the cheaper models are not particularly rigid and can become distorted into strange shapes by the weight of the soil. The ideal choice is a tub made from hardwood that

A cross section of a large wooden tub showing (from top to bottom) the layers of pebbles, potting compost, peat, capillary matting and crocks.

has been pressure treated with preservative as this will last for many years.

Urns are usually constructed from stone, lead, or re-constituted stone. The latter is crushed stone that is mixed with cement and pressed into a mould to produce a replica urn with all the looks of the original stone but at a fraction of the cost.

Some tubs and urns are constructed without drainage holes, in which case sufficient holes must be bored before the container is used. This is a relatively easy task if the containers are made of timber and plastic, but if they are made of stone there is always the possibility of breaking or chipping the edge. It is wise to use a power drill and a small masonry bit to drill a guide hole right through the base of the container; then use a larger masonry bit – as large as your drill will take – and drill halfway from the inside and then complete the hole from the outside. In this way it is possible to avoid chipping the edges.

If a wooden tub is used it is advisable to lift it clear of the ground by positioning it on a few bricks. This allows air to pass freely underneath, keeping the timber dry to prevent rotting. It also makes the tub a less attractive proposition for unwanted insects.

A layer of crocks (broken clay pots) or stones should be spread over the base of the container, making sure that the drainage holes are not blocked. The depth of the crocks depends on the size of the tub or urn, but as a general rule you should allow not less than 25 cm (10 inches) above the crocks for soil, unless you are growing alpines or plants with very shallow roots. Spread a piece of capillary matting over the crocks. This will allow any surplus water to drain away but prevent the soil from seeping down and silting up the drainage holes. On top of the matting put a 5 cm (2 inch) layer of peat and then place the soil mixture on top of this. Use a potting compost with either a soil or peat base.

One of the advantages of containers is that they can be moved to a new site if required.

Once a tub or urn has been planted, however, moving such a weight can be quite a problem. One way to overcome this is to mount the containers on trolleys or castors and, provided the surface is fairly smooth, the container can then be trundled around without strain.

The siting of the containers needs to be considered carefully. Avoid placing them in cold and windy corners, otherwise the plants will be stunted. On the other hand a sheltered and warm arbour will encourage tender plants to thrive.

Should you wish to grow plants that will not normally flourish in the type of soil in your area – such as camellias in an alkaline or chalky soil – a container can provide the answer as it can be filled with a soil mixture that suits the individual plant's requirements.

RIGHT: Climbing plants, such as sweet peas, can be trained up a wig-wam of canes in a tub for a tall arrangement.

FAR RIGHT: A Versailles tub is an effective container for a clipped bay tree.

ABOVE: A small peach tree can be grown successfully in a half-barrel. An underplanting of helianthemums enhances the display.

FROM LEFT TO RIGHT
– A barrel cut lengthways is the perfect place to grow your favourite herbs.
– A tall chimney pot provides an ideal stand for a potted cistus.
– For a rustic look, cover a wooden box with lengths of split larch poles and fill with flowering plants, such as pelargoniums, lobelias and alyssum.
– An old kitchen sink can be turned into an attractive container by covering with a peat, sand and cement mixture.
– A simple wire frame can be fixed in a container to enable climbing plants, such as clematis, to be grown.

UNUSUAL CONTAINERS

Apart from the variety of tubs and urns available in garden centres there are many other sources for attractive and interesting containers that can make an individual contribution to your patio area. Drums, barrels, boxes, old pipes, sinks, baths, chimney pots, buckets, jars, washtubs – in fact almost anything that has been used as a container and is weatherproof is a potential holder for plants.

Before using any container that might have held a toxic substance, it must be washed out thoroughly. Timber that has been creosoted must be allowed to weather to neutralize the chemicals that will kill plant life. Plastic drums that have held corrosive substances may have to be treated chemically to make the container harmless. You will need to consult someone with a knowledge of the chemistry involved. Some metals can corrode and develop poisonous salts, and may need coating with protective paint or lining with plastic sheeting to isolate the plants from the metal; again you will need expert advice.

Often the container has to be cut, either in half or to have one end opened. Before doing this consider if it is the best way of using the receptacle. It may be possible to make two interesting plant holders by cutting halfway down the container rather than across. In this way you can get shapes that stack to give an attractive vertical arrangement. Such containers should be reinforced to strengthen the cut edges so that they do not collapse when filled with soil.

Pre-planted flower pots can look charming when placed in the end of old chimney pots and pipes and can easily be lifted out when the plants fade, to be replaced with fresh ones. The height of many chimney pots and pipes makes them vulnerable to being knocked over, so weight the bases to make them more stable.

Wooden boxes should be treated against rot and insect attack, and if they are on the flimsy side they can be reinforced by fixing additional timber on the outside. This can be made into a decorative feature if split larch poles with the bark still intact are used; or tongued and grooved timber, such as cedar, attached. The larch wood gives a rustic finish while the cedar can be treated or varnished to give a more sophisticated look.

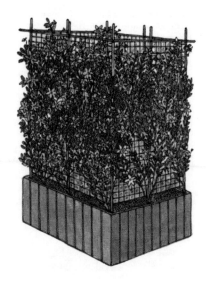

Metal boxes should be treated on the inside with a bitumen paint, and provided with adequate drainage holes. The exterior can be left if the finish is weatherproof, but if it is likely to rust to produce unsightly oxides then the metal should be protected; again you can use a bitumen paint if it is a ferrous metal, but use a lacquer on cleaned copper. When in doubt about the effect of the metal on plant life it is best to play safe and line the container with a plastic sheet to keep the soil away from the metal. Remember to pierce holes in the bottom of the sheet so that surplus water can drain through the holes in the metal.

Sinks and baths make excellent containers. The old-fashioned stone sinks are rare and in great demand, but modern white-glazed sinks are more common and can be disguised by painting a layer of PVA glue over the exterior and then spreading on a mixture of 2 parts peat, 1 part cement and 1 part sharp sand. This should be mixed with water and 50 ml (2½ fl oz) of PVA adhesive for each sink to make a thick, rough composition. The mixture is then spread over the outside of the sink to give an attractive rough, stone-like texture. When dry the sink can be filled with soil and planted.

Baths can be left unadorned if they are ancient and of interesting shape with fancy claw feet, but modern baths look best if they have a brick or stone wall built around them to form a raised bed.

Pipes come in a variety of widths and lengths and even pre-cast concrete drainage pipes that come in sections can be used as containers, although they should be regarded as permanent as they lack a base. The smaller ones of pottery, plastic, metal and concrete can be very useful for adding height and variety to the patio. Long pieces of pipe need to be filled to a good depth with crocks. For lightness, pieces of expanded polystyrene can be wedged in the pipes to allow for good drainage.

Whichever type of container is chosen, half the battle is positioning it correctly. Try the empty container in several places to make sure that you are happy with it. It is a good idea to place it on a join in the paving so that drainage water can seep away without leaving unsightly marks on the paving itself. Once you have decided on the best position the container can then be filled with soil and suitable plants.

93

PATIOS

WHERE TO SITE A PATIO

Patio was originally the Spanish word for an interior courtyard, but it is commonly used in this country to refer to a paved area adjoining the house for relaxing and entertaining. For most people a patio provides a convenient place to sit in the sun on every available opportunity, and, by careful positioning and screening, it is possible to keep the temperatures up and so extend the period of outdoor living. For the few days when clear blue skies in the summer make the heat rise, some shading is important, and this should be considered when looking at sites. Taking advantage of the shade offered by an already established tree is one idea for this.

A south-facing position is obviously the ideal choice for a patio, but if this is not possible choose a site that makes the most of the morning or evening sun. Consider what the patio will be used for – will it be for entertaining in the evening, or will you be needing a small private sun patch in the morning. Check that neighbouring trees and buildings do not cast shadows across the patio when you are most likely to want to use it, and that the area is not overlooked by a neighbour's window. Privacy is an important consideration and a shift of a few feet in siting your patio could make all the difference. It is vital to consider all these points carefully, for once the patio has been constructed and planted it is very expensive to move to another site.

When you have decided on the site, determine the shape and size you would like it to be. Peg out the area with canes and string so that you can see just how big it is going to be, and how it relates to the rest of the garden and the house. An alteration at this stage is easy and costs only a few moments of your time. When it is pegged out, place a chair within the area and sit there to make sure that it is right for the sun, and that shelter from the wind is provided. Consider whether you will need some cover from rain, protection for your garden furniture, and storage space for all those other indispensable items that make for relaxing in the sun.

It seems a contradiction to find a sunny site and then build a shady structure to keep the sun off, but if the design is right it should keep the sun off you when it is high in the sky, but allows it to shine underneath the canopy when it is lower, in the spring, autumn and winter. As an alternative consider a pergola and clothe it with plants that conveniently lose their leaves when the sun is needed and grow a filter of fresh ones when shade is required.

TYPES OF PATIOS AND USES

Patios can be rooms which have an open wall, or walls without a ceiling; they can be courtyards, terraces, or areas for relaxing, dining or other activities. The one thing that these all have in common is the floor, which is the most crucial part of any patio.

The material for the floor should have a smooth, even surface; this will prevent chairs 'rocking', and it will be easy to sweep clean and maintain. It should also have an attractive colour and texture. Choose a material that will not reflect the glare from the sun, that dries out reasonably quickly after the rain, and that has a non-slip surface.

Paving slabs are usually the first material to

Even the smallest area by the side of the house can be paved and used to enjoy the sun. Shade is provided by dwarf trees.

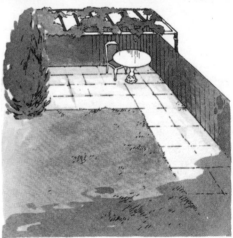

A larger patio offers more scope. A vine-covered pergola provides shelter for a barbecue, table and chairs. The fountain makes an attractive focal point.

The patio need not be adjacent to the house. A site at the end of the garden may make the most of sunny days – away from the shade of the house.

95

Break up a large expanse of paving by planting areas with trees and decorative grasses. Filling in areas with gravel also looks effective – and makes the paving stones go further.

Add interest to a large patio floorspace by laying concrete slabs and paving with a brick surround. A lightweight screen around the sides provides some protection and privacy.

spring to mind. They are easily obtained and laid, require little maintenance, and are fairly easy on the pocket. However a large paved area can look monotonous and needs to be broken up visually.

Other materials include: real York stone slabs (but these cost a small fortune); bricks, which can look very interesting if laid in patterns, but they need to be a hard, frost-resistant variety; tar-macadam, which will give a smooth surface but will become soft in really hot weather; gravel, which is cheap but uncomfortable to walk or lie on; sand, which is unstable and dusty but is rather like having your own beach; wood, which is very pleasant but needs to be installed properly and requires some maintenance; concrete, which has to be laid well with other materials otherwise it will look like a section of motorway; and tiles. A combination of surfaces is probably best on the eye, and the pocket. A large patio area will not dominate the garden if it is broken up visually with changes in colour and texture, but bear in mind how the plants will look against the various shades.

For entertaining, space should be provided for food and drink. A barbecue will provide a pleasing focal point but remember that a permanent structure takes up space while a mobile model can be brought out onto the patio just on the occasions when you need it.

Whether you have benches or tables and chairs depends on the style of eating and drinking that you want to provide – a formal dinner table can only cater for a chosen few, while the stand-up informal buffet can accommodate a whole crowd of people.

Depending on the proposed uses of the patio, various forms of screen wall can be considered. There are pierced concrete blocks that can be used to form a decorative wall; bricks, timber or open structures that can be covered by climbing plants. Some screen walls will need to be substantial as they have to take weight as well as the buffeting of the weather, others can be lighter if they have nothing to support and are only decorative in a sheltered corner. If positioned correctly, a screen can provide shelter from cool winds and give the patio more privacy. Overhead beams should be strong enough to support themselves as well as growing plants and supporting blinds if needed.

Permanent structures should really be made to last as long as the house. If in doubt about brick constructions and planning permission for a large undertaking, have a word with the local planning officer at the council offices. He will advise you on what you are allowed to erect and where, but for most paved areas and simple garden structures no permission is required.

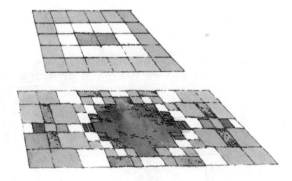

Different coloured paving stones can be combined to brighten up a square or rectangular patio. Formal and informal designs are both effective.

An attractive circular patio can be constructed with bricks or tiles. The area is screened by a low hedge and a timber frame for climbers.

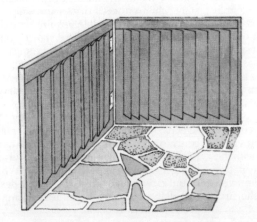

An angled timber screen provides a sheltered corner. Crazy paving is used for the patio floor.

PATIO DESIGN

If you are lucky enough to have lots of space you can design the patio area on a grand scale, using large paving slabs and creating areas for different functions. If, like most of us, you only have limited space and budget it takes a degree of ingenuity to make a worthwhile patio. Use moderately sized furnishings, small-scale building units, a brick or sett floor, raised planting to give height, and make the most of wall and overhead plants to create a sense of space.

Often it helps to make the patio look as if it is an extension to a room. Use similar materials, and keep the patio screens or walls the same proportions as the internal walls. This adds another living space to the house.

Patios can be square, rectangular, circular or free-form – the shape is immaterial provided the patio is functional and is in keeping with the rest of the garden and house style. Many patios are just a paved area that could be improved with some screening to add height, shelter and privacy, or simply extra plants.

Overhead screens keep out the rain – especially useful where the patio is used as a play area; corrugated plastic is ideal.

One idea is to make a list of the needs of your family when designing the patio area so that all possible requirements are considered. For instance children need a dry area on which to play on damp days, the elderly require a snug corner out of draughts and a short distance from shelter in case of rain. Families with young children may want an area to leave a baby safely... and adults need somewhere to relax after work.

By gradually working through these various demands and the natural limitations of the site, the shape of the patio will evolve. Walls, screens, overhead beams, blinds, planting, benches and decorative features such as pools, raised beds and built-in barbecues will all start filling in areas on or next to the patio. When the layout is complete, tidy up the whole design so that all the lines and shapes are pleasing to the eye as well as functional.

CONSTRUCTION

Having prepared the layout for the patio design you will want to know how to construct it. You need to be sure that when it rains the patio will not subside, or hold water, that frost will not crack the surface, walls will remain standing, and that a long life of trouble-free pleasure is ensured. By following time-tested practices and rules you should have a patio on which you can relax sure in the knowledge that there is a secure structure around you.

Areas to be paved need to have a firm foundation so that the paving stones will not crack or sink. Mark out the area for paving with pegs and string before excavating. Dig out the top soil to a depth of about 18 cm (7 inches) and remove to a safe place as it is invaluable for spreading over the rest of the garden. Level the bottom of the excavation and spread a 7.5 cm (3 inch) layer of hardcore or rubble over the area and compact well with a hand-rammer to form a firm base.

Over the hardcore, place 5 cm (2 inches) of builders' sand to fill in any gaps, then lay the paving on top of this, ensuring that the top surface of the paving is the same level as the surrounding ground.

If the paving needs to withstand some traffic of wheelbarrows, garden equipment, and plant containers, apply five spots of mortar to each 60 cm (2 feet) square paving slab. Smaller slabs and bricks should be laid on a 2.5 cm (1 inch) bed of mortar laid on top of the sand and tapped well down with a wooden mallet to form a firm and level surface. The surface itself should have a fall or slope towards the outer edge, away from the house to allow rain to run off freely. The slope should be at the rate of 5 cm (2 inches) for every 3 metres (10 feet). Where there is no suitable edge for the rain to run off, build a drain and soakaway in the centre and have the paving sloping towards the drain.

If you use gravel or sand as a patio surface the main problem is keeping the area weed-free. If you use capillary matting over a 7.5 cm (3 inch) layer of hardcore to prevent the sand or gravel being washed into the hardcore, a 7.5 cm (3 inch) layer of sand or gravel should keep deep-rooted weeds at bay. The annuals can be held in check by dosing the area with a long-lasting weedkiller. Of course the matting is not essential and a persistent weed killer will take care of any weeds if applied annually.

Timber used out of doors should be treated against rot and insect attack. Ensure that where it will be in close proximity to plants the pre-

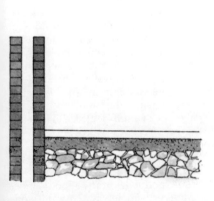

A cross section through a patio floor showing the lower layer of hardcore, the narrow layer of sand with the paving laid on top.

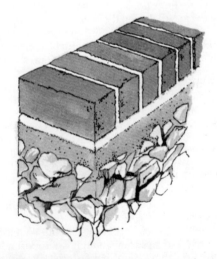

If bricks are used as the patio surface, they must be laid on a 2.5 cm (1 inch) bed of mortar on top of the sand and hardcore.

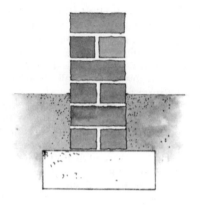

Where the patio has brick walls, foundations are necessary to distribute the weight of the wall and make it more stable. The concrete foundation should be twice the width of the wall and at least 15 cm (6 inches) beneath the soil.

servative is safe for them. The timber should be raised off the ground to allow air to flow underneath, keeping it dry. The most satisfactory method is to build concrete or brick piers on which the timber can rest. Always use rust-free nails and screws and be sure that the top surface of the timber is smooth and free from splinters, splits, or rough edges.

Where there is a large expanse of plain paving the gaps between the slabs can be left open and free from mortar. These crevices can then be filled with potting compost and planted with low creeping plants, such as thyme, to soften the look of the area.

If the patio design requires walls of brick, stone or blocks, it is important to have good foundations to spread the weight of the wall over a larger area so that it will not crack or lean. Most manufacturers of pre-cast blocks give recommended dimensions for foundations but as a general rule make the concrete strip twice the width of the wall and at least 15 cm (6 inches) thick. It should be 15 cm (6 inches) below the soil surface, more if the soil has been disturbed or built up.

Timber screens and beams should be fixed securely and be strong enough to support not only their own weight but also the weight of any plants that they are going to support. All fixings should be rust-proof and where adhesive is used, make sure that it is waterproof.

PLANTS ON THE PATIO

Large containers, such as tubs and urns, always look attractive on patios. Most types of patio also offer the opportunity of planting some material directly into the soil. Shrubs and small trees are suitable for direct planting and many of them thrive in even the poorest soil. *Betula pendula* is particularly tolerant of difficult soil. Rhododendrons and fruit bushes can be used to break up large paved areas, and climbing plants, such as grape vines, are most effective against a screen or wall.

If the soil on the patio is poor, it should be removed to a depth of at least 15 cm (6 inches). Check that drainage is adequate by pouring one or two buckets of water into the hole. If the water does not drain satisfactorily, break up the sub-soil by digging it thoroughly. Finally, replace the top soil with fresh, fertile soil or compost.

If there isn't an area readily available for direct planting it is usually possible to create one – simply by removing a few paving stones. Raised beds are another alternative. These are normally composed of stone, or paving stones held together with hardcore or concrete. They offer the opportunity of growing plants at waist height – particularly advantageous for fragrant herbs and flowers.

A POOL ON THE PATIO

One of the great joys of a patio is to be able to sit in the sunshine and listen to the sounds of nature. Water gives this pleasure an added dimension whether it is just the gentle drip of water, the gurgle of a waterfall, or the splash of a fountain. Visually, too, water enhances your enjoyment by bringing light and sparkle, reflections and movement to the patio.

Few patios are of a sufficient size to take in a pool in the real sense of the word, but constructions need not be large – some are just basins with or without a small fountain unit. Many models are available from garden centres, in a variety of sizes and styles from antique to modern. Some are very simple, say a large millstone with water bubbling through the centre, while others are complicated and have interconnecting pools. Small waterfalls can be introduced, or fountains that give a constantly changing water flow. These can be illuminated to provide an attractive evening display.

Whichever style appeals to you it must fit into your patio layout. Allow plenty of space around the feature, or if space is limited put your water feature in an alcove where it can give pleasure without being a nuisance.

The selection of aquatic plants ranges from simple tufts of reed to exotic and colourful water-lilies, as well as underwater plants that provide oxygen for fish and marginal plants that hug the edge of the pool. Some will have to be planted in baskets resting on the bottom of the pool and others will grow in pockets of soil round the water's edge.

The water can support fish provided the surface area and depth are sufficient. The most common are the goldfish, of which there are many different varieties. Fish can cost from a few pence to over £50 according to their breed, colour, and size. It is possible to purchase a balanced package of plants, fish, and water snails for different sized pools from specialist water garden nurseries.

Various different types of pool construction are available, ranging from cheap to expensive. At the bottom end of the market there is the

One of the least expensive ways of constructing a pool. A hollow is dug at the chosen site and lined with plastic sheeting. Heavy stones are used to anchor the edges of the plastic as the water is poured in. The weight of the water stretches the plastic and forces it to take up the contours of the hollow.

inexpensive plastic sheet that lines a hollow dug into the ground. Ordinary polythene has a life expectancy of only a few years, but better plastics – such as PVC – are available which are less affected by sunlight. Some even have a reinforcement of nylon and carry a 10-year guarantee.

The best material for a pool liner is butyl rubber – it is even used for reservoirs! It is very tough, rotproof, easily repaired if it should be pierced accidentally, and available in any size. It usually carries a 15-year guarantee although it could last for as long as 50 years.

Liners allow you to create a pool in whatever size and shape you wish, from a small formal pool to a large, irregular lake. The pre-formed plastic and glass-fibre pools, on the other hand, come in set sizes and shapes. The hole for these must be excavated to fine limits to prevent distortion when the pool is filled with water. There are some heavy-duty models that will provide years of good service.

The most expensive type of pool is the concrete one that needs plywood shuttering into which the wet concrete is poured and held until it has dried and set. This is labour-intensive but provides a solid structure which can be any shape or style you wish. The main problem is pouring in the concrete in one go to prevent joins that can leak. If leaks do appear the pool must be drained, the crack repaired and the pool painted with a waterproofing paint.

Concrete pools should last for many years provided they have been constructed correctly with good materials, and reinforced to prevent cracking. In practice, they tend to leak after a few years of exposure to severe frosts.

Remember to 'cure' new concrete pools before adding fish or plants, by painting on a special preparation available from water garden nurseries and some garden centres.

To increase the pleasure and use of the pool there are pumps that will power fountains and waterfalls, and lights that can be used for underwater lighting or for floating on the surface. All these items need electrical power, which must be installed by a qualified electrician if you are planning to run mains-voltage equipment outdoors. Some systems utilize transformers that step down the current to 12 or 24 volts, which is perfectly safe and should not cause any installation problems.

CARE OF PATIO AND CONTAINER PLANTS

Patio and container gardening is not difficult, but it is unnatural for the plants. Often they have to grow in a volume of soil or compost that gives them only a fraction of their normal root-run, and keeping them supplied with nutrients and moisture is always a problem.

Even where plants are grown in raised beds on the patio, or in areas between the paving, their sheltered position often means roots are drier than they would be in the open garden.

To help offset these handicaps, it makes sense to give plants the best possible start with well-prepared compost or soil. As ordinary garden soil rarely gives good results in small containers, such as windowboxes and hanging baskets, it is better to use a good compost. In large containers, and in flat or raised patio beds, where compost would be too expensive to use, improving the soil is the best alternative.

SOIL FOR PATIOS

Soil is a mixture of fine particles of rock or stone, with decayed vegetation – called humus – to bind it together. It is a home to millions of micro-organisms, most beneficial but some harmful. The humus-coated particles and the spaces between them act as a reservoir of nutrients and moisture. The size of the soil particles and the spaces between them largely dictate the structure of the soil. Soil can be categorized roughly as 'heavy' (clay), 'medium' (loam), or 'light' (sandy). It is not difficult to decide which type of soil you have to work with . . . which is the first step to improving it.

Clay soils have very small air spaces between very fine particles, and this results in a sticky soil through which little air can percolate. In winter a clay soil is heavy with moisture and in summer it bakes hard, the surface cracking open as it shrinks. To improve this type of soil it is advisable to add sharp sand (really quite large grains of rock) and plenty of humus in the form of compost, manure, peat, pulverized bark and other bulky organic materials. These should help to open up the soil, allowing better drainage, and air to reach the lower levels – encouraging plants to develop better root systems. In winter the soil will be less sticky and in

summer there should be less cracking on the surface. Of course this will not happen in a couple of days, but by constantly adding and feeding the soil it will improve over the years.

Sandy soils have large grains of stone often with little humus, which makes them light and easy to work. However rain will drain away rapidly from sandy soils and wash any goodness out of it. Sandy soils also dry out quickly in summer and are often acid. Sand is quick to germinate seeds as they warm up quickly, but the plants are poor in quality as they lack moisture and nutrients. To improve a sandy soil and encourage moisture retention, dig in plenty of organic matter, farmyard manure or garden compost. Liming will reduce the acidity of the soil so that it can support a wider range of plants (but use a soil-testing kit first to be sure that it really needs it).

Loamy soils come midway between the previous two and are the nearest to ideal for most plants. If you are blessed with this soil all you need to do is to keep it in good condition, free from weeds, and to replace the nutrients that are taken out by the plants by adding manure and fertilizers.

In some areas, particularly on soil overlying natural chalk or limestone, the soil may be very alkaline – which is fine for the plants that are naturally adapted to this, but will cause many other plants to make poor, sickly growth. If you suspect your soil may be too alkaline (or too acid) check it with a soil-testing kit or a meter.

To improve the moisture-retentiveness of any soil, you can add peat, and mulch well during spring and summer, using peat, pulverized tree bark or garden compost.

Soil at the base of south-facing brick or stone walls will soon face drought conditions when a dry period occurs. To prevent the wall from absorbing moisture from this soil it is necessary to dig the soil out along the wall to a depth of 45 cm (1½ feet), exposing the wall. This is then painted with a bitumen paint and the soil replaced when the paint has dried, adding a heavy quantity of peat or compost to the soil as it is put back. This should improve the moisture level provided it is well-watered initially.

MATCHING SOILS TO PLANTS

Plants vary considerably in their soil requirements. Bog plants need a high level of moisture, while some alpines are happy in near drought conditions; campanulas enjoy a high chalk or lime content, which may kill some summer-flowering heathers, camellias, rhododendrons, and magnolias. By changing the soil it is possible to provide the correct conditions for the plant. Relatively few need a special soil. The main problem is to achieve the correct acidity or alkalinity of the soil. You can check this by using a simple soil-testing kit or meter that will give you the answer in terms of a pH factor number: 7 is neutral, above 7 is alkaline, while below 7 is acid. As the figures increase or decrease so the soil is becoming more alkaline or acid. By adding lime to the soil the pH level is increased, making it more suitable for lime-loving plants; if acid peat or flowers of sulphur are added, the soil will become more acid. It will need to be rechecked every two or three years and re-balanced.

Alpines, rockery plants, and some herbs thrive in a poor soil as long as the drainage is good. This type of soil can be simulated by mixing in a quantity of stone chippings, either limestone (for lime-loving plants) or granite (for lime-haters). The surface should be covered with a layer of chips to keep the stem base dry and to deter slugs. By growing those herbs that need a dry sunny position in a poor, well-drained soil, you will find that the aroma of the herbs becomes stronger and so fewer leaves are needed to flavour food.

PLANTING MIXES FOR CONTAINERS

Ordinary garden soil is often full of weed seeds and potential diseases and pests, and it is quite likely to be deficient in certain nutrients. Although strong, vigorous plants can usually cope with such soil, the tender ones grown in small containers are likely to succumb to at least one of these hazards. It is far better to give a good start to plants by using compost that has been specially prepared with balanced foods, sterilized to kill weed seeds and unwanted pests and diseases, and has a good structure that holds moisture while still being free-draining and allowing air to penetrate.

There are many potting composts to choose from, and both loam-based and peat-based types have their uses. The best-known soil-based composts are those made to the John Innes formula. If properly prepared from good loam these are good, but quality does vary. Soil-less composts on the other hand, can be controlled far more accurately and the quality within a particular brand is likely to be the same whether you buy the compost in Scotland or in Cornwall.

A box filled with moist soil can be a considerable weight, and with windowboxes and some containers this could be a problem. The disadvantage of light-weight peat-based composts is that they do not provide much stability for tallish plants exposed to wind. You can improve this by mixing your own compost of one part peat-based compost, one part washed river sand (not soft builders' sand), and one part expanded clay granules of the type used for

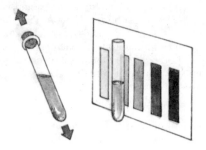

A simple soil testing kit enables you to determine whether the pH of your soil is acidic or alkaline – important to know when choosing which plants to grow.

For alpine plants, mixing stone chips into the soil helps to improve drainage. A layer of chips spread on the surface of the soil acts as a mulch and deters slugs.

hydroculture and on greenhouse benching.

It is very important that all containers have good drainage. Sufficient holes should be drilled in the base to allow surplus water to drain away freely. The base of the container should be covered with a good layer of crocks or pieces of stone, brick, tile, or pottery. Some experts spread a 2.5 cm (1 inch) layer of peat over the crocks to prevent the soil being washed down and clogging the drainage holes, but in time this too will break down and filter into the crock layer. A far better method is to use a piece of capillary matting. This acts as a filter to prevent soil silting up the crocks, and also absorbs and holds moisture.

Peat can be spread on top of the matting to act as an additional reservoir of moisture, and then the container can be topped up with the compost. This should be pressed down lightly, leaving the rim of the container standing proud by at least 2.5 cm (1 inch) which will allow a mulch of peat or a layer of stones to be spread over the surface to stop moisture from evaporating too quickly. In this way a good foundation for your plants is ensured.

For deep containers increase the depth of crocks to allow less compost, unless plants that need a deep root-run, such as fruit trees or deep rooted shrubs, are being planted.

It is much more convenient to buy ready-mixed compost, but if you do want to make your own it is possible. The recipe for John Innes potting compost is:

7 parts sterilized loam
3 parts peat
2 parts sharp sand

All parts are by volume. These components should be mixed with the following proportions of John Innes base fertilizer (which you can buy ready-mixed from a garden centre) and ground chalk or limestone: To every four 9-litre (2-gallon) buckets add:

For John Innes No 1
20 g (¾ oz) ground limestone or chalk
120 g (4 oz) John Innes base fertilizer

For John Innes No 2
40 g (1½ oz) ground limestone or chalk
240 g (8 oz) John Innes base fertilizer

For John Innes No 3
65 g (2¼ oz) ground limestone or chalk
350 g (12 oz) John Innes base fertilizer

Unless you can sterilize your loam properly it is best to buy ready-mixed compost. You really need a proper sterilizing unit, which is expensive to buy unless you need a lot of compost.

Mixing your own peat-based composts is not easy either. There are problems in getting the nutrient balance right, and many of the chemicals used in commercial composts are not available to amateurs. For this reason it is best to stick to one of the good proprietary composts, or kits which contain the necessary chemicals and instructions.

FEEDING

Plants need nitrogen, phosphorus and potassium for good growth. Other minerals are also necessary in smaller quantities, such as sulphur, calcium, and magnesium. Others are needed in even smaller amounts and are referred to as trace elements: these include iron, boron, copper, zinc, and molybdenum. These nutrients are present in soil, and they are gradually absorbed by the plants.

Different types of plants have different requirements – alpines need very little food, but rampant and greedy growers will require greater quantities of goodness from the soil.

A plant that is grown for its leaves is likely to require a high level of nitrogen. This is available in a variety of forms that can be processed by the plant: Nitro-chalk is suitable for plants that can tolerate lime, sulphate of ammonia can be used for other plants. If you spurn chemical compounds, make compost from grass cuttings and pea and bean roots, or fish meal, and this will supply nitrogen to the plant in a natural form.

For good root growth the plant should be supplied with phosphorus. This can take the form of superphosphate, as a chemical preparation, or for a natural product bonemeal should be used, but make sure that it has been sterilized as it can contain disease from the animal.

Flowers and seeds of a plant are improved if there is sufficient potassium in the soil. This can be increased by adding potassium sulphate (sulphate of potash) as a chemical product, or you can use fresh wood ash (old ash will have had most of the potash washed out of it by the weather).

Some plants will have sufficient food in the soil to supply their needs and only occasionally need a little extra food. Plants in containers, however, will almost always need supplementary feeding throughout the summer. Even if a good compost was used to start with the plants will gradually exhaust the food supply. Nutrients are also leached away by rain and drainage, and can become unavailable through chemical imbalances that neutralize or 'lock up' the chemicals. For all these reasons it is usually necessary to restore nutrient levels by adding fertilizers or manures.

Fertilizers are mainly – but not exclusively – man-made chemicals and can be in liquid, powder, solid, or granular form. Manures are bulky, organic natural wastes such as farmyard manure and well-rotted leaf and vegetable matter – in fact anything that is natural, bulky, and will decay into a crumbly texture.

Manures and composts can be used in spring for non-container plants. They will gradually break down and release nutrients into the soil.

With windowboxes and containers there is insufficient space to dig in a good quantity of manure or compost. Manure can be substituted for the peat in the original soil mix as it provides plenty of fibre, but as pots and containers need a continual supply of food this is best provided by fertilizers. Liquid fertilizers should preferably be reserved for use during the growing season.

WATERING
Watering should achieve a delicate balance. Too much water will wash the goodness out of the soil, too little will stunt or kill the plants.

Some plants require more water than others. Those with soft, sappy stems and thick lush leaves indicate a thirsty plant; a thin, woody stem and a dwarf stature suggests the plant can manage with less water.

When watering it is better to soak the soil thoroughly rather than sprinkle a little on the surface as this will encourage the fine roots to come up to the surface, by which time the water will have evaporated leaving the roots to dry out and die. Always use a fine rose on the watering-can or a fine spray on the hose otherwise large drops or jets will stir up the top layer of soil exposing the fine surface roots, which will then gradually dry out making the plant less stable and more susceptible to drought.

Always bear in mind the watering problem when deciding how many containers to have.

Look for the tell-tale signs of water and nutrient deficiencies and restore them quickly. A bonemeal mulch will supplement the phosphate in the soil.

Each will need watering at least once a day during the hot days of summer: a tedious task.

PLANTING
Sowing: It is preferable to sow seeds in boxes or pots, rather than directly into the final container. They will be easier to care for and you can be using the display containers for other plants while the young ones are maturing.

Fill the container almost to the top with a good seed compost. Gently firm and moisten compost before sowing the seeds. Transplant the seedlings as soon as they are large enough.

Transplanting: Seedlings should be transplanted into trays or pots of potting compost as soon as they have formed two or so true leaves (not the seed leaves) and can be handled. Tease the tiny plants out of the compost, trying not to damage their roots or leaves. Place in holes made with a small stick and gently firm the compost around them; don't leave air pockets.

Planting out: Once the seedlings are large enough, and the conditions are right outside, they can be planted out. If the plants are tender (likely to be damaged by frost), or vulnerable to drought and wind, make sure that the weather is mild enough before planting out. It is wise to bring the plants out in the open during the day and return them to a warm place at night when the temperature falls for a few days before you plant them.

Make a hole to take the root-ball of the plant and firm it in well, then water and keep the plant and soil moist.

Larger plants, such as small trees, are sometimes sold with bare roots. Make the hole large enough to accommodate the roots when spread out. Cover them with soil, and firm it down to avoid any air pockets around the roots. All plants will need regular watering until they are established.

PROTECTION
Choosing the right position is important if you want the best from your plants. Most will need to be protected against excessive heat, cold, and wind, but you should also consider individual preferences. It is a waste of time, for instance, to try to raise a sun-loving plant in deep shade.

However, we all want to try to grow plants in places where they are not ideally suited – so efforts have to be made to improve the conditions whenever possible. For moisture-loving plants a soil that dries out rapidly can be covered with a mulch of well-rotted manure or compost, which helps to hold the water in the soil. It also protects the roots from frost.

Protection from wind can be important. Wind can turn leaves brown and stunt growth, but a screen of canes or a plastic mesh can cut down the strength of the wind to acceptable levels. Plastic mesh comes in various grades that will cut down the wind in different proportions, so you can choose a mesh most likely to provide the necessary degree of protection.

Transplant seedlings by gently teasing them out of the compost with a small stick, taking care not to damage the roots or leaves.

Plants can be protected against too much heat by providing shade. This can be achieved by a permanent structure or planting, or by erecting a temporary screen to protect the plants until they are mature. Split-cane blinds and greenhouse blinds make excellent screens.

Frost is probably one of the most obvious problems for the gardener. It sometimes comes at unexpected times in late spring and early summer before tender plants have become established. Newspapers will give adequate protection during dry weather but soon become sodden in the rain. A plastic or glass cloche will give cover against a light frost, but a layer of straw or bracken can be very effective against a more severe one.

PESTS AND DISEASES

Pests and diseases are the bane of a gardener's life, creeping up on plants, often unseen, and perhaps infesting them beyond cure. With one or two plants to look after you can keep an eye out for trouble, but when you grow a lot of plants it becomes more difficult.

Both pests and diseases can be brought to the garden by air, in the soil, on plants, or even on seeds. Often they spread from weeds. Many pests and diseases can be controlled by chemical sprays or dusts, but do read the small print on the container to find out what restrictions there might be – whether it is safe for children and pets; whether you can pick and eat the plant the same day as treatment, and whether you have to use the chemical at a specific time of the day. Bear this in mind when using the charts on pages 30-34.

Pests can vary from birds that peck the emerging buds to slugs that thrive on young seedlings and lush growth, from aphids that cover a plant and wither it by sucking out the sap, to microscopic organisms such as gall mites and eelworms that bore into the plants. Nature will help to control many problems by providing predators and parasites – ladybirds will eat aphids; birds will eat snails, caterpillars, and leatherjackets; hedgehogs and toads will search out many unwanted insects. So by ensuring a natural balance the pests in the garden can be kept in check. Do not expect an immediate reduction in your pest population, however, as it takes time to work.

The most effective remedy for disease is hygiene; keep your tools clean, particularly secateurs, and your soil fresh and clean. After planting out seedlings they can be watered with a fungicide to reduce fungus attack.

When a plant's leaves wilt and die, turn yellow and blotchy with lighter or darker markings, or the flowers are small and fewer in number, the plant should be examined carefully for insects, both on the surface and underneath the leaves. Where there is no sign of insect attack look for mould, fine downy hair that is not part of the plant's normal structure, and see if there is any rotting tissue (black slimy areas on the stem is a sure indication of a

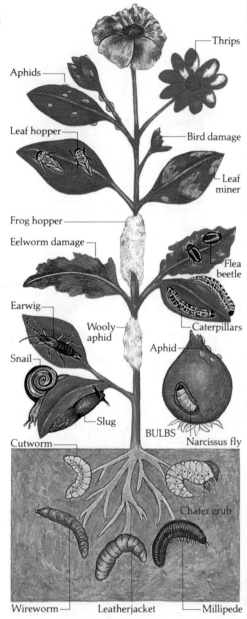

problem). If there is no sign of trouble above the ground the plant should be lifted so that the roots can be examined for swollen sections, rot, or insect attack. If there is no sign of either mould, rot or insects it could be a virus disease

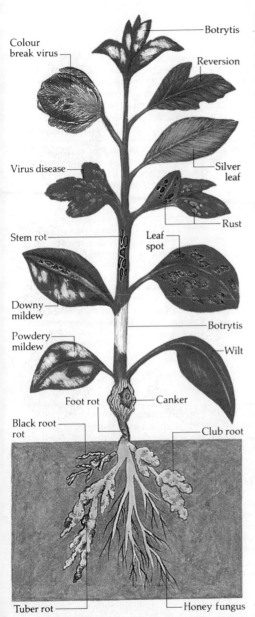

Colour break virus

Botrytis

Reversion

Virus disease

Silver leaf

Rust

Stem rot

Leaf spot

Downy mildew

Botrytis

Powdery mildew

Wilt

Foot rot

Canker

Black root rot

Club root

Tuber rot

Honey fungus

plant so can too much chemical treatment. Full instructions for use are always given on the container, and unless these are followed precisely, the plants can suffer. For those who have a healthy dislike for chemicals in the garden there are a number of other methods of control, such as picking caterpillars off the plant by hand, using greasebands for keeping crawling insects off trees and shrubs, mothballs as a soil fumigant to discourage insects and animals underground, and netting to keep birds away from buds and fruit.

Unhealthy plants may not necessarily be the result of pest or disease attack. The soil conditions may be wrong, or excesses of heat or cold could be the cause. Look for poor growth, leaves turning yellow, or failure to flower; this could be due to a deficiency in the soil. Feed the plant with a liquid fertilizer that contains trace elements as well as the basic foods, and within a few days there should be a marked change in its appearance. Frost and sun scorch can damage leaves and stems but unless the plant is tender it should recover and regrow.

Although some plants seem prone to attacks, there are still plenty that remain trouble-free. These are normally strong plants with a good compact growth, green leaves and a healthy root-ball, and this is the type to look for when buying plants. Avoid weak and spindly looking growth, and discard plants that have been forced in a greenhouse. Instead choose plants that have been hardened off. Look for those with no damaged stems or leaves but with plenty of growth buds, and where possible buy disease-resistant varieties.

USING THE CONTROL CHARTS
Often there are several chemicals – sometimes many – that will do the same job. Those mentioned in the following charts are not all the possibilities, but are representative and give you options from which to choose. There is no substitute for reading the label carefully – sometimes there is a minimal interval between treating edible crops and eating them (it can range from days to weeks); occasionally certain plants should not be treated because they will be damaged by the chemical.

For simplicity common chemical names are used in this book – you will find them on the containers sometimes in small print.

that is attacking the plant cells. If this is the case the plant should be destroyed to prevent the virus spreading to other plants. The key to pest and disease control is to act quickly.

Just as an excess of water can damage or kill a

PEST CONTROL CHART

Pest	Description	Control
Aphid (greenfly, blackfly)	The colour may vary, from green to black, but all are 1-5 mm long, soft-bodied, and with relatively long legs. They do not always have wings, in which case the plump body is conspicuous.	There are many greenfly killers, most of them very effective. Malathion is popular. Pirimicarb and permethrin are among the newer insecticides intended for aphids. There are many others, including dimethoate if you want a systematic insecticide.
Big bud mite	Only likely to affect blackcurrants. The buds become swollen – hence the common name. A tiny mite is responsible. Also known as black currant gall mite.	Chemical control is difficult. Pick off affected buds. Regular spraying with benomyl (actually a fungicide) seems to give some control.
Cabbage root fly	Although mainly a pest of cabbages, cauliflowers, and Brussels sprouts, cabbage root fly also attack wall-flowers. The plants wilt and become stunted. If lifted, the small maggots will be seen eating the roots.	Not much can be done once the plants have been attacked. As a precaution dust the soil with bromophos or diazinon when transplanting or thinning.
Capsid bug	You are most likely to see the symptoms before you see the pest. It leaves small ragged holes in the leaves, and flowers may be deformed. The insects are up to 6 mm long, but very active and are likely to drop to the ground when you look for them. The colour is usually green, but may be yellowish or brown.	A systemic insecticide such as dimethoate is particularly useful. For a non-systemic, try fenitrothion or malathion.
Caterpillars	Too well known and too diverse to warrant description. The appearance obviously depends on the species, but it makes little difference to control.	Bioresmethrin, malathion and trichlorphon will achieve control. Derris – as a spray or dust – is also effective. You can try gamma-HCH.
Codlin moth	A pest of apples. You are unlikely to notice the moths, but you will see the maggots inside the apples.	Spray with permethrin or fenitrothion just after the petals have dropped, and again three weeks later.
Earwig	Earwigs are usually about 2.5 cm (1 inch) long, brown in colour, and with 'pincers' at the end of the body. Suspect them if plants, such as dahlias (but also many others), have ragged holes torn in the leaves or petals.	Spray or dust with gamma-HCH, or use carbaryl dust. Traps should not be dismissed. An upturned flower pot on a cane, filled with straw, will attract them. You will have to empty the trap regularly and kill the earwigs.
Eelworm	Eelworms are microscopic – less than 2 mm, often smaller. There are many kinds, and symptoms vary. The ones mentioned in this book are mainly bulb and stem eelworms, affecting plants such as hyacinths and narcissi.	There is no effective cure available to amateurs. Lift and burn affected plants, and do not replant the same kind of plants in that piece of ground.

Pest	Description	Control
Eelworm (cont)	On these plants the neck of the bulb usually feels soft and if the bulb is cut across there will be dark rings of dead tissue. Growth is usually malformed or stunted.	
Flea beetle	Flea beetles make small, usually round, holes in the leaves of seedlings, and occasionally older plants. The beetles are about 3 mm long, and tend to jump.	Dust with derris or gamma-HCH.
Froghopper	It is not the froghopper insect that you are likely to notice first, but the frothy 'cuckoo spit' that appears on plants from May onwards. It protects pale coloured nymphs inside. The mature insects are up to 6 mm long, and jump when disturbed.	Malathion should give control. You may need to use a forceful spray to remove the protective froth.
Gooseberry sawfly caterpillar	Caterpillars up to 4 cm (1½) long, with black spots and head.	Spray with derris or malathion, repeating as necessary.
Leather-jackets	These greyish larvae are about 2.5 cm (1 inch) long, and are found feeding on the roots of plants, which may turn yellow and wilt, and even die.	Work bromophos or diazinon into the soil around susceptible plants.
Narcissus fly	The bulbs produce yellowish, distorted leaves, and usually fail to flower. The maggot will be found inside the rotting tissue of the bulb.	It is best to lift and burn affected bulbs.
Scab	Scab is common on apples. Greenish-brown blotches appear on the leaves; cracked, corky spots on the fruit.	Thiophanate-methyl or benomyl sprayed fortnightly from bud-burst onwards should achieve control.
Slugs and snails	Too well known to need description. There are several kinds of both slugs and snails to be found in the garden. All respond to the same treatment.	You can buy various traps, but these can have little affect on the total population. Slug pellets based on metaldehyde or methiocarb will protect plants reasonably well.
Whitefly	Small, white, rather triangular flies. Not normally a problem outdoors, but may attack the plants that you take indoors or into the greenhouse for the winter.	A systemic insecticide such as dimethoate is effective. You can spray with non-persistent insecticides such as malathion, bioresmethrin, or pyrethrum, but be prepared to repeat the application until control is achieved.

DISEASE CONTROL CHART

Disease	Description	Control
Botrytis (grey mould)	As the common name suggests, the main symptom of this disease is a grey mould – usually on dead flowers or on fruit, but it can occur on leaves or stems. A cloud of dust-like spores may be released when the affected part is moved.	Pick off any affected parts and destroy them. Then spray with benomyl or thiophanate-methyl, repeating at intervals if necessary.
Damping off	This is a disease (which can be caused by several fungi) of seedlings. The seedlings collapse where they have rotted at soil level.	Use sterilized compost as a preventative measure whenever possible. Cheshunt compound is the traditional remedy, but it is best watered into the soil before the disease has a chance to appear.
Dry rot	Dry rot can affect a number of plants with bulbs or corms, but gladioli are particularly vulnerable. The leaves turn brown and die; the corms show a number of small sunken lesions, or larger blackish areas.	Do not plant bulbs known to be infected; avoid replanting on infected ground. As a precaution soak the corms or bulbs in a solution of benomyl or thiophanate-methyl for about half an hour before planting.
Bacterial soft rot	Affects many different plants, including vegetables such as turnips and parsnips. Bulbs can become soft and slimy, with a bad smell.	There is a little to be done about the disease except to destroy affected plants, and to make sure you plant a similar crop on different ground next time.
Club-root	Although a problem of brassicas – such as cabbages and cauliflowers – it will also affect ornamentals such as wallflowers and stocks. Growth is poor and stunted, and the roots are enlarged, often with unsightly swellings.	If you are growing food crops it may be worth trying to achieve some control with root dips based on calomel or thiophanate-methyl when transplanting. For ornamental crops it is best to grow something different if you know the land is infected with club-root. Fortunately you can usually use compost for containers, so susceptible plants grown in these should be unaffected.
Leaf spot	There are several leaf spots. They may vary from small, fairly regularly shaped spots to larger, irregular blotches. The colours vary from brown to black.	Sometimes leaf spots are more disfiguring than dangerous to the plant. Spraying with benomyl or Bordeaux mixture is likely to achieve some control, but remove badly affected leaves, and be prepared to repeat the treatment.
Mildew, American gooseberry	The powdery white fungus coating on the shoots starts to appear in April. It can spread rapidly, but affects the stems more than the leaves, causing stunted growth.	Cut out badly infected shoots. Spray with benomyl or thiophanate-methyl, and be prepared to repeat the treatment.

Disease	Description	Control
Mildew, downy	The plant becomes covered with a whitish or somewhat purplish growth. Easy to confuse with powdery mildew. If you wipe the growth off with a finger, downy mildew tends to leave the plant beneath rather yellow.	Mancozeb should give some control. Not easily controlled.
Mildew, powdery	The plants – particularly leaves and shoot tips – become covered with a white, powdery-looking growth. Affected parts may become distorted.	Try a systemic fungicide, such as thiophanate-methyl, benomyl, or carbendazim. Be prepared to spray once a fortnight to achieve control. If this does not work, it may be downy mildew – in which case try mancozeb.
Peach leaf curl	This is a distinctive disease; affected plants produce distorted leaves with ugly reddish blisters.	Collect and burn affected leaves, as soon as you notice them. Spray with Bordeaux mixture after the leaves fall and again as the buds swell in late February or early March.
Rust	There are numerous rust diseases, but most produce brown or orange spots or pustules on the leaves.	Mancozeb should achieve some control, but you may have to persist with the treatment. Where rust-resistant varieties are available – as with antirrhinums, – choose these if you have had trouble in previous years.
Tomato blight	Brown blotches appear on the leaves, dark brown streaks on the stems. Fruit tends to rot.	Spray with mancozeb as a precaution in damp seasons, once the first fruit has set. Repeat at 10-day intervals.
Tulip fire	Leaves and shoots are distorted, and often withered. Flower buds usually fail to open.	Lift and destroy affected plants immediately. Do not plant suspect bulbs, and do not replant more tulips on infected land. If neighbouring tulip bulbs seem unaffected, soak them in a benomyl solution for half an hour before replanting, as a precaution.
Virus	There are many different viruses, and the symptoms vary with the disease and the plant. Suspect any plants that have distorted or stunted growth, or yellowish, mottled leaves that you cannot put down to another problem.	Virus diseases cannot be cured, and leaving the plants risks spreading the infection. Lift and burn any suspect plant.
Wilt	As the name suggests, the most common sign of wilt (there are several kinds) is wilting leaves on the plant – though they may recover at night. If the stem is cut through some distance above ground level the stem will be discoloured internally.	You can try drenching the soil with benomyl or thiophanate-methyl (made up as for a spray), and repeat the treatment. If this fails, uproot and burn the plant.

BULBS

The plants included in this chapter are grown from corms, rhizomes, and tubers, as well as true bulbs, but you can buy all of them from garden centres.

By careful selection of the different groups of 'bulbs' the patio or container gardener can obtain a colourful display of flowers all year round – late winter blooms of crocus followed by daffodils and narcissi, then hyacinths and tulips, which will run into the anemone flowering season, followed by the summer bulbs and the autumn-flowering crocus. With few gaps, that brings us back once again to the winter bulbs.

One problem with bulbs is what you do with them once they have flowered. The leaves often look untidy after flowering has finished, but you should not cut them off because they help to manufacture food that is then stored in the bulb to act as a reservoir for the following year. If you pull the leaves off too early, the bulbs will become smaller and the plants will flower less frequently.

If you want to replant the containers before the leaves have died naturally, you can lift the bulbs and replant in a convenient part of the garden to let nature take its course. Later you can lift them and store in a cool, dry place until the time comes to replant. However, if you have a garden where you can plant your old bulbs permanently, it makes sense to buy fresh bulbs each year for your container displays – at least you will be fairly sure of a good display where it matters.

You can increase your stock by separating and planting the offsets or small bulblets or cormlets that develop around the mother plant. Pick or rub off the offsets gently and plant in a separate area, known as a nursery bed, or a box of soil, until they are large enough to be planted out with mature bulbs and corms. This may take several years, and it is unwise to depend on these where your bulb display is important. Much, however, depends on the type of plant. Daffodils are relatively easy to propagate, tulips are much more unreliable.

ANEMONE*

Windflowers, as anemones are sometimes called, are ideal for patio or container cultivation. Most kinds require little attention once planted and, by successive planting, the florist's anemone (*Anemone coronaria*) can be in flower from January right through to December. However to achieve this you need to be able to offer protection and it does call for special skill.

There are two types of florist's anemone – De Caen are single, St. Brigid are double or semi-double. Both will grow up to 30 cm (1 ft) high with flowers 5 cm (2 inches) across, in white or vivid shades of red and blue.

For an early spring display,

the dwarf *Anemone blanda* is most striking. It grows up to 15 cm (6 inches) high and generally has blue flowers, although white, pink and mauve forms are available. Established clumps look best. The star-like blooms can be up to 2.5 cm (1 inch) across.

General Care: Grow anemones in a good, well-drained soil with plenty of humus. The corms of *Anemone blanda* should be planted 5 cm (2 inches) deep in the autumn 10-15 cm (4-6 inches) apart. Those of the florist's anemone can also be planted in spring for a summer display.

Propagation: Anemones can be grown easily from seed or from cormlets removed and replanted in late summer.

Pests and Diseases: Slugs and snails can be troublesome as the shoots emerge, and flea beetles may also make holes in the leaves. Mottled and distorted leaves suggest a virus infection. Affected plants should be destroyed to stop the disease being transmitted to other anemones.

CROCUS*

These hardy plants are ideally suited to containers and patio borders in full sun. There are many species, but the easily obtainable Dutch hybrids have large flowers in a wide variety of colours from white through the yellows to purple, including some with stripes, coloured bases and two-tone effects. Crocus will grow up to

Pests and Diseases: Leather-jackets sometimes attack the corms. If birds are a nuisance cover the plants with a net or use strands of black cotton. Dry rot causes the corms and leaves to shrivel; lift the diseased plants and destroy. Do not replant bulbs on the same ground.

HYACINTH*
These bulbous plants bear their familiar bell-shaped flowers on a spike in spring, when they appear from a rosette of strap-like green leaves. Ideal for containers and ordinary garden use, hyacinths have a beautiful strong perfume. They come in a variety of colours, including white, yellow, pink, red, blue and purple. Growing to about 23 cm (9 inches) in height, they are compact enough for most containers.

General Care: Plant the bulbs 10 cm (4 inches) deep in the autumn in a sunny or semi-shaded site. Keep the ground free from weeds and remove dead stalks and leaves at the end of the season.

Propagation: Hyacinths can be grown from seed, but it is best to purchase bulbs produced by a specialist grower.

Pests and Diseases: Leaves and stems are sometimes attacked by eelworms, which reveal themselves as yellow stripes to the leaves. Affected plants should be destroyed and healthy bulbs moved to a fresh site. Bulbs can also be affected by rots; infected bulbs should be dug up and destroyed. Do not replant bulbs on the same ground.

12 cm (5 inches) high. There are also autumn-flowering species which will bloom from September to November (but do not confuse these with colchicums, also known as autumn crocus).

General Care: Plant the bulbs in a well-drained soil and provide some protection from wind to encourage early flowering. Do not remove heads after flowering and wait for the leaves to turn yellow before pulling them off.

Propagation: The corms produce small cormlets which can be carefully removed and grown in a separate container, where they will not be lost among other plants. They will take about two years to reach flowering size.

Crocus can also be grown from seed, but take two to four years to flower. Young plants should be grown 7.5-10 cm (3-4 inches) apart.

Rhizome iris

with a liquid fertilizer after flowering. The rhizome irises can be planted at any time, but the most satisfactory time is just after flowering.

Propagation: The bulbous irises are increased by bulb offsets. Lift the plants carefully with a fork after the foliage has died down; allow the clumps to dry for a few weeks then clean off the soil and carefully divide into single bulbs. Replant in the autumn about 10 cm (4 inches) apart.

Pests and Diseases: Most bulbs are susceptible to moulds and rot, such as bacterial soft rot. Irregularly streaked or mottled leaves may be due to viruses.

NARCISSUS* AND DAFFODIL*

The most popular of the spring-flowering bulbs, there are over 8,000 named, cultivated narcissi varieties, most of which are well-suited to windowboxes, containers and beds. They have a variety of colour that ranges from white through yellow and pink to orange; there are single and double forms with short or long trumpets, and the flowers are borne singly or in clusters on each stem. They vary in height from about 10 cm (4 inches) to about 60 cm (2 ft).

General Care: Once planted, very little attention is needed. If they are in beds, keep the area weeded. Wherever the bulbs are situated, keep them well-watered in dry weather. Remove the dead flower heads so that the plant can build up strength for the following season.

IRIS*

There are two groups of iris, those with thick underground stems called rhizomes, and those that grow from bulbs. Most of the rhizome kind have sword-shaped leaves carried in a fan-like display. They grow from 25 cm (10 inches) up to about 90 cm (2½ ft).

For windowboxes, containers and small beds the smaller bulbous irises are best, as they take up less space and are more in scale with neighbouring plants. Some, such as *Iris reticulata*, will flower in the winter and spring, while others are summer-flowering. The florist's irises – Dutch, Spanish and English – are bulbous hybrids that are descended from *Iris xiphium;* they normally flower from June to July, and have a good colour range.

General Care: If grown on heavy soil, lift the bulbs after the foliage has died down and store in a dry, airy place ready for replanting in September. Bulbs can be left in the ground if grown in a lighter soil and space is not a problem. Feed

Propagation: Every three or four years the clump of bulbs should be lifted in the early summer, allowed to dry out and then split up. The bulbs can then be replanted singly, the small ones in a nursery bed where they can be weeded easily. When the bulbs are mature they can be planted out 10-20 (4-8 inches) apart.

Pests and Diseases: Narcissus fly can attack bulbs after the leaves die back. Pale stripes on the leaves and stunted plants indicate microscopic eelworms at work.

TULIP*

Tulips were brought to Holland from Turkey and other areas over 300 years ago, and began the Dutch bulb industry. The smooth, thin-skinned bulb usually produces a single flower stem normally with a deep, cup-shaped bloom. Some are double, some open out like stars, and some have petals with fringed edges. The blooms come in a wide variety of colours, from white to deep purple, including ranges of yellows, oranges, reds and mauves. If you include the small species and large-flowered kinds, their size varies from 10 cm (4 inches) to about 90 cm (3 ft).

General Care: Tulip bulbs should be planted in November, about 15 cm (6 inches) deep and not less than 10 cm (4 inches) apart. They prefer a rich soil and a reasonably sunny position. Remove the dead flower heads when the petals fall to encourage the chance of flowers the following year. Large-flowered tulips do not usually flower dependably the second year, but species and species hybrids are more reliable.

Propagation: Tulips can be grown from seed, but it is easier to use the offset bulbs found clustered round the parent bulb. Plant these at a depth of 5 cm (2 inches) in October or November; they take up to three years to reach flowering size.

Pests and Diseases: Streaked and distorted leaves suggest a virus infection. 'Scorched' specks and streaks, and distorted leaves and shoots, which occur soon after emerging, can be a serious fungal disease called tulip fire. Infected plants should be destroyed immediately. Any tulip bulbs showing signs of moulds or rots should also be destroyed.

Daffodils

ANNUALS

Plants that complete their life cycle within a year – from germinating to flowering and dying – are called annuals. They are usually easy to grow and can quickly fill a patio garden or a window-box with an enchanting display of colourful blooms.

Annuals are classified as either hardy or half-hardy. The hardy annuals can cope with the cold conditions of early spring, so they can be sown or planted out in their flowering positions even while there is a risk of frost. Half-hardy annuals are not so robust and the seeds or seedlings need to be protected from frost.

Many perennial plants are best grown as annuals – antirrhinums and impatiens are examples – either because they are not hardy or because they become less attractive with age. All these plants that are used to provide a temporary summer display are generally called bedding plants.

Most bedding plants are best raised in a greenhouse – although you can raise a few on a well-lit window ledge indoors.

As soon as the seedlings are large enough, prick them out into seed trays or small pots and keep them growing steadily in good light until ready to plant out in the open.

Before planting out, the young plants should be 'hardened off' to acclimatize them to the harsher conditions outdoors. Place the plants in a garden frame (an unheated box with a glass top would do) until they are tough enough to be planted out in the open.

Some annuals will flower for longer if you 'dead-head' them. This means cutting off the faded flower-heads to prevent seeding, which would sap the strength from the plant and result in fewer flowers.

ALYSSUM*

These hardy annuals flower throughout the summer. White is the most common flower colour, although there are pink, mauve and purple varieties. All of these are low-growing, up to 10 cm (4 inches) high, which makes them ideal for edging beds, for stone walls, and even between paving stones.

General Care: Alyssum will grow in ordinary well-drained soil in full sun. They should be dead-headed regularly with scissors to encourage further blooming.

Propagation: Sow seeds in March, transplant the seedlings into boxes and harden off before planting out, 20-30 cm (8-12 inches) apart, in their final position in April.

Alternatively the seeds can

Anthirrhinums (snapdragons)

be sown directly into the soil, thinned out, and then followed by another sowing in early May to increase the flowering season.

Pests and Diseases: Slugs are sometimes a problem with young plants. Powdery mildew is the most likely disease but is seldom a real problem.

ANTIRRHINUM*

These are the popular snapdragons. The smaller varieties can be grown in pots and borders. Some can be as low as 10 cm (4 inches). Tall varieties can grow up to 1.2 metres (4 ft). All produce spikes in a wide range of colours, in separate shades or mixtures. Some have ruffled or double flowers.

General Care: All types need a fertile well-drained soil, full sun, and regular feeding during the summer months. Pinch out the centre of the plant to make it bushy, and dead-head the flowers to prolong the flowering period.

Propagation: Sow the seeds in boxes in February or March and just cover with fine sand. Water the seeds gently, transplant and harden off before planting out at the end of May in a sunny position where they need little care. Plant intermediate varieties 45 cm (1½ ft) apart, half this distance for dwarf varieties.

Pests and Diseases: Damping-off may cause seedlings to collapse and break off at soil level. Aphids attack young plants.

Antirrhinums are particularly prone to rust, so it is worth selecting your plants from the range of rust-resistant hybrids if this has been a problem in the past.

ASTER*

The bedding plants grown as asters are really *Callistephus*, but you will nearly always find them described as 'asters'. For containers and patio beds the dwarf varieties are best. These generally grow about 15 cm (6 inches) high and are prolific, producing flowers in a wide range of vivid colours. They flower in late summer and autumn.

General Care: Grow asters in a good well-drained garden soil in a frost-free area, or provide protection from frost and cold winds. The plants should be dead-headed to encourage fresh blooms.

Asters (callistephus)

Propagation: Sow seeds in boxes in March or April, or directly into the soil from mid-April, just covering with some fine sand or compost. Protect from frost.

Pests and Diseases: Slugs may be a problem with young plants, but the major health problem is aster wilt. This turns the leaves brown and shrivelled, and the plants will die. They cannot be saved, so dig them up and burn them to prevent any spread of disease and further infection.

Powdery mildew can be disfiguring in some seasons.

Begonia semperflorens

BEGONIA SEMPERFLORENS*

This fibrous-rooted plant is perfect for patios and windowboxes. Although it can be kept indoors over the winter, it is best to buy fresh plants raised from seed each year.

There are many varieties – mainly pink or red flowers some with bronze foliage – but all are compact, seldom exceeding 15 cm (6 inches).

General Care: Plant in a sunny position, after all risk of frost has passed, and keep watered throughout the season.

Propagation: *Begonia semperflorens* is not particularly easy to raise from seed unless you have the experience and the facilities. The seed is very fine, and it needs the warmth of a propagator to germinate well. You can try raising a few plants on a warm sunny window ledge indoors. Sow in February and prick off into seed trays when they are large enough to handle.

Pests and Diseases: These plants are normally trouble-free, although aphids may occasionally call for action.

CALCEOLARIA**

The calceolaria suitable for bedding is *Calceolaria rugosa*. It has pouched yellow flowers, grows about 30 cm (1 ft) high, and will flower throughout the summer in a border or container.

General Care: Calceolaria like a well-drained soil with plenty of moisture, in a sunny position for good flowering, although they will tolerate partial shade.

Propagation: Sow the seeds in February or March on the surface of the compost, and shade from direct sun. They should germinate in two weeks.

Pests and Diseases: Aphids and slugs are potential hazards. Otherwise calceolaria are trouble-free.

CINERARIA**

Cineraria maritima, also known as *Senecio maritima*, is grown for its deeply-cut evergreen silver foliage, which provides a foil among the greener leaves of neighbouring plants. It grows to a height of 60 cm (2 ft) and has yellow flowers, 2.5 cm (1 inch) wide. The flowering period is from July to September.

General Care: Cineraria prefers a sunny position in ordinary soil. If the site is exposed, use twigs for extra support. This plant can sometimes survive winters out of doors, but is best treated as a half-hardy annual.

Propagation: Sow the seeds in trays in February or March. Transplant and harden off before planting out 30 cm (1 ft) apart at the end of May.

Pests and Diseases: Aphids may attack but cinerarias are normally disease-free.

GYPSOPHILA*

There are perennial gypsophilas for the herbaceous border and the rock garden, but the annual species usually grown is *Gypsophila elegans*. It grows about 45 cm (1½ ft) tall and bears a profusion of white or pink flowers.

General Care: These plants enjoy a sunny position in a well-drained neutral or alkaline soil. In an exposed position, it is wise to provide some protection by using twigs as an extra support.

Propagation: Sow direct into garden soil in September or March and then thin out seedlings to about 30 cm (1 ft) apart. Keep them free of weeds.

Pests and Diseases: Gypsophilas are usually trouble-free.

HELIOTROPE*

The heliotropes grown as summer bedding plants are semi-woody and form an attractive, bushy shape with clusters of tiny lavender, violet and purple flowers from June to October. They are pleasantly scented. The plant will grow up to 60 cm (2 ft) tall.

General Care: Heliotropes like a place in full sun with good, well-drained soil. It is wise to support the plants where they are exposed to high winds.

Propagation: Sow in February or March in seed trays. When the seedlings are large enough to handle, transplant into boxes. Pinch the tops out when the seedlings are 7.5 cm (3 inches) high to encourage bushiness. Harden them off before planting out 30 cm (1 ft) apart at the end of May.

Pests and Diseases: Heliotropes are generally trouble-free.

IMPATIENS*

The impatiens, popularly known as the busy Lizzie, is often regarded as a houseplant, but it also makes a superb patio and windowbox plant. Modern varieties produce compact plants with a spreading, but neat habit, and there is such a wide range of vivid colours in some of the mixtures that a bed of them is quite spectacular. In a windowbox they are most effective on their own.

There's a bonus in that these plants will grow in partial shade as well as full sun.

General Care: Do not plant impatiens out too early. They are tender and will make better plants if they can grow without a check. Do not let them become stressed through lack of water at any time.

Propagation: Unless you have a heated greenhouse or can raise a few plants indoors on a warm window ledge, it is best to buy the plants. Sow seeds in February or March and prick off into individual pots rather than boxes. It is best to raise fresh plants each year.

Pests and Diseases: Outdoors there are unlikely to be many problems, but in damp weather botrytis could set in around dead flowers.

LAVATERA**

Lavatera trimestris is a hardy annual, bushy in shape with prolific trumpet-like flowers 10 cm (4 inches) wide in deep pink and white. The flowering period is from July to September. The plants reach about 90 cm (3 feet) high, and have pale green leaves.

General Care: Lavatera prefer a sheltered, sunny position with a soil that is not over-rich. Where the plants are exposed to the wind, some cane support will be necessary.

Propagation: Sow the seed in March or April where the plants are to flower, and cover lightly with soil. In May, thin out seedlings to about 45 cm (1½ ft) apart.

Pests and Diseases: Lavatera are normally pest-free, but yellow-brown spots appearing on leaves are likely to be caused by leaf spot.

Impatiens (busy Lizzie)

Purple-flowering lobelias

LOBELIA**

The bedding lobelias are treated as half-hardy annuals and are excellent for patio borders or containers. The trailing varieties are popular for hanging baskets and for the fronts of windowboxes. The dark blue varieties are particularly popular, but pale blue can look very effective. If you want a really distinctive edging, you can buy one of the mixtures that will include pinks, reds and whites, as well as blues.

General Care: Lobelias like a rich, moist soil. They will grow in partial shade as well as full sun.

Propagation: Lobelias are easy to grow from seed. Sow the fine seeds in February or March under glass, and keep moist. Transplant in clumps of two or three as they are too small to separate easily. Keep the seedlings relatively cool. Harden off and plant out about 10–20 cm (4–8 inches) apart in late May or early June.

Pests and Diseases: Apart from the risk of seedlings damping off, lobelias should be trouble-free.

MARIGOLD*

There are three kinds of marigold: the English pot marigold (calendula), the French marigold (*Tagetes patula*), and the African marigold (*Tagetes erecta*). The first type is hardy and will even survive the winter months unprotected, from an autumn sowing, in favourable districts. The French marigolds have small flowers on dwarf plants, while African marigolds have much larger, ball-like flowers on taller bushier plants. There are also hybrids between the two – known as Afro-French marigolds, and these are excellent container plants, combining the best of both types.

Neither African nor French marigolds are hardy, but the pot marigold (calendula) is. If you want to grow this in containers, sow in peat pots and transplant when there is space, and be sure to grow a dwarf variety for containers.

All these marigolds have a particularly long flowering season, from early summer until the first frosts in the case of French marigolds.

General Care: All types of marigold enjoy an open, sunny place with well-drained soil. Dead-head the flowers to prolong blooming and increase flower size.

Propagation: With the tagetes sow seeds in late February or March under glass, just covering them with fine compost. Transplant the seedlings into boxes and harden off in a garden frame before planting out in their flowering positions in late May. Spacing will depend on variety – follow the advice on the seed packet.

Seeds of pot marigolds (*Calendula officinalis*) can be sown in the autumn for spring blooms if you can provide cloche protection, or sown directly into containers in March or April to provide summer flowers. If you prefer, sow in peat pots as already suggested.

Pests and Diseases: Calendulas are susceptible to mildew. African and French marigolds are prone to attack by slugs and snails when they are first planted out.

MESEMBRYANTHE-MUM*

The mesembryanthemum, used to provide a spectacular summer display from seed sown in the spring, is popularly known as the Livingstone daisy. It is a low-growing plant ideal for the edge of a border

Pot marigolds (calendulas)

or for those containers which occupy a position of full sun. The brilliantly coloured daisy-like flowers only open in bright sunlight.

The plants are only a few inches high, but can be covered with flowers up to 3.5 cm (1½ inches) across, from June to August... provided it's sunny!

General Care: Mesembryanthemums like a dry, sunny position and thrive in a light, sandy soil.

Propagation: Sow seeds in March under glass, prick out, and harden off before planting out in late May, about 23 cm (9 inches) apart.

Pests and Diseases: Mesembryanthemums are normally trouble-free, but downy mildew sometimes affects them.

NICOTIANA*

Nicotianas, commonly known as tobacco plants, range in height from 25 cm (9 inches) to about 90 cm (3 ft). They are grown for their flowers, which can be white, pink, red, maroon or green, and their delightful fragrance which perfumes the evening air from June to September. The white flowers of *Nicotiana affinis* are heavily scented but only open at dusk, while the varieties 'Daylight' and 'Dwarf White Bedder' stay open all day. The fragrant nature of the tobacco plant makes it an ideal candidate for the windowbox if you choose a very dwarf variety.

General Care: The taller varieties may require some staking to prevent them being blown over. All plants need to be dead-headed, to prolong flowering. They prefer a rich, well-drained soil in the sun.

Propagation: Plants can be raised from seed sown in a greenhouse from February to April. Plant out after hardening off, from late May onwards, when there is no significant risk of further frost.

Pests and Diseases: The young plants are quite often attacked by aphids.

PETUNIA*

Petunias have become so improved through breeding that the range of colours and forms available is very extensive. The funnel-shaped flowers are generally about 5 cm (2 inches) wide, but can be up to 12.5 cm (5 inches) across, and come in many colours, including striped blooms. The plants flower from June to the first frosts in autumn, and they are ideal for containers and windowboxes. They can also look good in hanging baskets.

Choose from Grandiflora varieties where you want large flowers, but for a massed dis-

Petunias (grandiflora variety)

play choose a Multiflora variety – it will have smaller flowers but is likely to be very prolific.

General Care: Wind and rain can damage plants, so choose weather-resistant varieties for areas that are prone to gales and storms. Grow in a sunny position, water freely, and feed regularly. Dead-head to prolong flowering.

Propagation: Sow the seeds in a heated greenhouse in March and transplant into boxes. Harden off the plants before planting out 30 cm (1 ft) apart at the end of May.

Pests and Diseases: Aphids attack young plants. Yellow-streaked and distorted leaves could be due to virus infection.

SALVIA*

Salvia splendens is the species grown for summer bedding. Although usually bright red, there are pinkish and purple shades too. Tall varieties grow to about 40 cm (16 inches), but dwarf kinds only grow to about 20 cm (8 inches).

General Care: Grow in any ordinary garden soil, preferably in a sunny position. The tips of the plants should be pinched out when they reach 7.5 cm (3 inches) high to encourage bushiness.

Propagation: Sow the seeds in trays of seed compost under glass in February or March and transplant seedlings into boxes or pots. If temperatures are too low the leaves may turn yellow and the plants become stunted. Keep protected when the weather turns chilly. Harden off salvias in a garden frame before planting out 23-38 cm (9-15 inches) apart at the end of May.

Pests and Diseases: Capsid bugs may be responsible for tattered leaves, but generally salvias are trouble-free.

STOCK*

The most popular stocks for bedding are the Ten Week type (so called because they can be brought into flower 10 weeks after sowing under glass). Normally there will always be a percentage of the less attractive single flowers, but 'selectable' types can be grown that enable you to decide at the pricking out stage which are likely to be doubles. Dwarf kinds grow to about 25 cm (10 inches), taller ones can reach 75 cm (2½ ft). The scented flowers come in a wide range of colours.

The night-scented stock, *Matthiola longipetula bicornis,* has rather dull, unexciting flowers that remain closed all day, but their lovely fragrance in the evening amply compensates for their lack of daytime interest.

General Care: Stocks enjoy full sun but will tolerate partial shade. They are best in a good garden soil that is slightly alkaline or chalky.

Propagation: Sow the seeds of Ten Week stocks under glass in February or March, then transplant into boxes and harden off before planting out in May. For later flowering the seed can be sown direct into its final position in April and the seedlings thinned out so they are about 30 cm (1 ft) apart.

Sow night-scented stocks from March to May, where they are to flower.

Pests and Diseases: Young plants can be attacked by flea beetles and aphids. Caterpillars occasionally eat the leaves of older plants. Club-root is a possibility (avoid planting stocks on infected ground).

SWEET PEA*

The container gardener will find all types of this hardy annual climber valuable. Perhaps the best varieties suited to container cultivation are the 'Knee-Hi' and 'Jet Set' groups, which grow to about 60 cm-1½ metres (2-4 ft) tall and require the minimum of support. There are also dwarf varieties that only grow 20 cm (8 inches) tall. They are robust plants producing hundreds of flowers in a wide range of single or mixed colours – from June to September. Most varieties are scented.

Sweet peas

General Care: An open, sunny position suits sweet peas best, but the plants should not be allowed to become dry, and liquid feeds are beneficial. Dead flowers should be removed to keep the peas flowering.

Propagation: Soak the seeds for 12 hours (most sweet pea seeds have a hard outer coat) before sowing in September or March under glass. Pot up the seedlings and pinch out the tips when they are 10 cm (4 inches) high. Harden off before planting out in April or May, about 15-25 cm (6-10 inches) apart.

Pests and Diseases: Young plants will probably need protecting from slugs and snails. Aphids are always a potential problem.

PERENNIALS AND BIENNIALS

A perennial plant is one that lives for several years. The term is often applied specifically to a non-woody plant that dies down in the winter and re-emerges in the spring (an herbaceous perennial), although trees and shrubs are perennials too. This chapter contains mainly herbaceous perennials, though a few shrubby plants, such as fuchsias, and 'evergreens' such as the succulent sempervivum, have been included too.

Biennials need two seasons to complete the cycle from seed to flowering, after which they die. Pansies, violas and wallflowers are amongst the most popular biennials.

Herbaceous perennials can often be increased by dividing the root with a garden fork or sharp knife. This is best done in autumn or early spring by lifting the whole root and dividing it into sections with some roots and some top growth or stalks.

AJUGA REPTANS*

This ground cover plant normally grows about 10 cm (4 inches) high, but it bears blue flowers on stems that shoot up to 30 cm (12 inches) in June and July. There are varieties with green, purple, bronze, and variegated leaves, and the plants have a spread of about 45 cm (1½ ft).

General Care: *Ajuga reptans* can be planted in any ordinary garden soil provided it is neither waterlogged nor frozen. Keep the area weeded until the plants have become established.

Propagation: The plant can be lifted and divided at any time when the soil is in an easily workable and moist state. Replant the pieces 30-45 cm (1-1½ ft) apart.

Pests and Diseases: *Ajuga reptans* is usually trouble-free.

AUBRIETA*

These low-growing, hardy plants thrive on dry walls and rocky banks. They grow to a height of 10 cm (4 inches), have a spread of up to 60 cm (2 ft), and produce a prolific display of purple to rose coloured flowers. These appear from March to June, and if the plants are trimmed right back after this flowering, they may flower again later, though more sparsely.

General Care: A sunny position is best, in ordinary garden soil. Trimming the plants after flowering will keep the shape compact.

Propagation: Aubrietas are easily grown from seed sown in February or March. Transplant to boxes, and transfer to pots when large enough to handle. Plant out in September or October.

Aubrietas can also be increased by cuttings or by division of established plants, in spring or autumn.

Pests and Diseases: Although generally pest-free, downy mildew may be seen on the undersides of the leaves.

Aubrieta

BEGONIA, TUBEROUS-ROOTED*

Begonias are particularly versatile plants and look attractive when grown in patio beds, troughs, hanging baskets, or windowboxes. The tuberous-rooted kinds used for summer bedding in sheltered places have magnificent double flowers throughout the summer. They grow 30-60 cm (1-2 ft) high and the flowers can have a diameter of 15 cm (6 inches). To make the most of hanging baskets, try the pendulous varieties. The fibrous-rooted begonias are quite different in appearance and best treated as annuals (see page 40).

Begonias can tolerate a partially shaded position and the brilliant colours of the flowers – yellow, pink, orange, and scarlet – can transform a dull corner into a blaze of colour.

General Care: Start the tubers off in boxes of moist peat in February or March. Pot on to medium sized pots of potting compost and harden off before planting out at the end of May or early June. Plant 45 cm (1½ ft) apart. A rich, moist soil is necessary, but it should also be well drained. Keep the tubers free from frost by lifting them in early October when the leaves are turning yellow, and store through winter in a box filled with dry peat and covered with newspapers.

Propagation: Old tubers can be divided into sections as they start into growth – but each piece must have a shoot. Dust the cut surfaces with sulphur powder.

Pests and Diseases: Mildew can be a problem, but begonias are generally trouble-free.

BERGENIA*

These plants form excellent ground cover as they are evergreen and low-growing, with a height of about 30 cm (12 inches) and a spread up to 60 cm (2 ft) wide. The leaves are large, glossy, and leather-like, while the flower spikes have bell-shaped blooms that shoot up in late winter and spring. One of the advantages of bergenias is that their leaves often change to shades of red in the autumn – a time when colour is usually in short supply.

These plants grow happily in wide-rimmed flat-bottomed containers.

Bergenia

General Care: Bergenias will grow in any garden soil even if it is alkaline, though they appreciate a sheltered site. Remove the flower stems after blooming and place a mulch round the plant in late spring. Leave undisturbed for as long as possible.

Propagation: Divide the plant, taking some root with each piece, and replant in the autumn or March, spacing them 30-38 cm (12-15 inches) apart.

Pests and Diseases: Bergenias are normally pest-free. Sometimes the leaves show brown patches as a result of leaf spot.

CAMPANULA*

There are over 300 species and hybrids of annual and perennial campanulas known. A favourite for windowboxes and hanging baskets is *Campanula isophylla*, sometimes known as star of Bethlehem or Italian bellflower. A dwarf perennial, its blue flowers appear among the heart-shaped leaves in July or August if used outdoors. *Campanula medium*, the Canterbury bell, is a tough upright plant, growing up to 1 metre (3 ft), with hairy foliage. The bell-shaped flowers appear from May to July.

General Care: Plant in a good garden soil that is well-drained, in a sunny or partially shaded position. The taller varieties may need support in exposed positions. Feed regularly and dead-head to encourage more flowers.

Campanula isophylla is really a greenhouse plant and must be kept indoors or in a heated greenhouse through winter.

Propagation: Divide *Campanula isophylla* in spring, or take cuttings in April or May. Canterbury bells (*Campanula medium*) are biennials and must be raised from seed each year. Sow in May or June, grow on in a nursery bed, and plant in flowering positions in the autumn.

Pests and Diseases: Slugs and snails should be kept at bay. Froghoppers are an occasional problem; their frothy 'cuckoo spit', which protects them, is the most obvious sign. Orange spots on the leaves are likely to be rust disease.

DAHLIA*

Dahlias fall into two broad groups: border dahlias (usually grown for their large blooms, and raised from cuttings) and bedding dahlias (usually with smaller, often single, flowers, and raised from seed).

The large-flowered kinds can make bushy plants 1.5 metres (5 ft) high, but the small bedding dahlias usually make compact plants little more than 30 cm (1 ft) tall.

The small-growing dahlias are suitable for container cultivation, but the bigger varieties are deep rooting and difficult to grow in shallow soil.

General Care: Dahlias like an open, sunny position with a rich, moist soil. Do not plant until risk of frost has passed. Avoid over-feeding, which will cause excessive leaf growth to the detriment of flowers, but water regularly. Remove flowers as soon as they fade. Lift the tubers once the foliage has been blackened by frost, and store in a frost-proof place once they have been dried off.

Propagation: Divide the tubers in spring, making sure each piece has an 'eye', and

Campanula isophylla

plant after the last frost. If you can start them off in a greenhouse, you can take cuttings from the developing shoots instead. Bedding dahlias are best grown from seed in March; harden off the plants before planting at the end of May or early June, 30-60 cm (1-2 ft) apart.

Pests and Diseases: Aphids are often a problem. Earwigs and capsid bugs will disfigure foliage and flowers. Dahlias can also be affected by virus diseases – plants with stunted growth, mottled leaves or yellowish spots are suspect. Destroy infected plants.

DELPHINIUM*

Delphiniums are imposing plants, with tall spikes of flowers in white, blue or purple. Most varieties grow 1.2-1.8 metres (4-6 ft) high, and need staking. Try to keep to dwarf varieties for patios.

General Care: Feed and mulch in spring, water in dry periods, and stake them before they become damaged by high winds. If you cut off the dead flower spikes, the plants may flower again later in the year.

Propagation: Lift the plants in the autumn or winter and split the crown of roots into several pieces, then replant. Delphiniums can alternatively be increased from cuttings taken in April.

Pests and Diseases: If the leaves and stems appear distorted and have yellow streaks or patterns, the plant probably has a virus infection. The plant should be lifted and destroyed. A powdery deposit on the leaves is likely to be powdery mildew.

Cascading fuchsia

FESTUCA*

An ornamental grass will usually add interest to a planting scheme, and *Festuca glauca* is particularly recommended for its blue-grey leaves which provide a change of colour among the greens of other foliage. This plant grows about 23 cm (9 inches) tall. Flower heads appear in the summer, but the main attraction of festuca is its foliage, which makes an ideal edging.

General Care: Plant in a sunny position in light, well-drained soil. If you want the best from the leaves, the flower heads should be removed; if left on, they should be cut off before seeding.

Propagation: Sow seeds in a light, sandy soil in April out of doors. Transplant into tufts of four or more when they are large enough to handle, then in the autumn plant out 15 cm (6 inches) apart in their final position. Established clumps can be divided in spring.

Pests and Diseases: Festuca is generally trouble-free.

FUCHSIA**

Fuchsias are particularly versatile plants and an ideal choice for the container gardener. They have been cross-bred to form the large variety of hardy and tender hybrids that are now available. Some fuchsias can grow over 1.8 metres (6 ft) high, while others grow less than 23 cm (9 inches) tall; some have a cascading habit that

Helianthemums

makes them perfect plants for hanging baskets and similar containers.

The distinctive flowers of most kinds hang down like a bell, with wing-like sepals, producing a characteristic appearance. Of the hundreds of named hybrids, many of the dwarf varieties are recommended for windowboxes and containers. Trailing kinds look marvellous in hanging baskets or on the edges of raised containers.

General Care: The tender varieties should be given a good moist soil and treated like a bedding plant, being put out in the open after the last frost and lifted before the first frost in the autumn. The hardy varieties should be cut back to the base and the roots protected with a layer of peat or straw during the winter. Some varieties are hardy enough to survive most winters outdoors but they are unable to withstand a very harsh winter.

Fuchsias grow well in full sun or light shade and require regular watering and occasional feeding.

Propagation: You can sow seeds in March or April, and then transplant into 9 cm (3½ inch) pots when large enough to handle. Later move them to 15 cm (6 inch) pots or directly to containers of mixed plants for a summer display.

However, it is more usual to take cuttings from non-flowering shoots in March. Insert 10 cm (4 inch) cuttings into a mixture of equal parts peat and sand, and keep at 16°C (61°F) until rooted.

Pests and Diseases: Aphids are a constant threat, but otherwise fuchsias are trouble-free.

HELIANTHEMUM*

Helianthemums are sun-loving plants normally grown in the rock garden, but they also make good container plants. They grow up to 23 cm (9 inches) tall and spread up to 60 cm (2 ft) across. The saucer-shaped flowers usually appear in June and July and are up to 2.5 cm (1 inch) wide. These flowers are commonly pink, yellow or white.

General Care: These vigorous plants can swamp neighbours, so plant with care. They thrive in ordinary garden soil, with some lime; they will even grow between paving stones. Choose an open, sunny position for planting. Trim back after flowering to maintain a neat shape.

Propagation: Either seeds or cuttings may be used. Sow seed in spring in trays or in the flowering position. For cuttings take a 5 cm (2 inch) non-flowering shoot with a heel of old wood in the summer, press into a pot containing a mixture of equal parts peat and sand, and place in a garden frame until rooted. Transplant to a potting compost and leave in the cold frame over winter, before planting out in the garden in April.

Pests and Diseases: Although helianthemums are normally pest-free, powdery mildew sometimes appears on these plants.

PANSY* AND VIOLA*

Although strictly perennials, pansies and violas can be treated as annuals – they will flower readily, the same summer, from a spring sowing – or as biennials. It is worth treating them as biennials for an early display. There are some winter-flowering varieties.

Most varieties reach about 23 cm (9 inches), but violas tend to have a more compact habit and smaller flowers.

General Care: Grow in a moist, well-drained soil in sun or semi-shade. Remove dead flower heads to keep the plants flowering throughout the season.

Propagation: To treat as a biennial, sow seeds in July out of doors, or in trays in a garden frame. Transplant the seedlings, placing them 10 cm (4 inches) apart. Finally re-plant 20-30 cm (8-12 inches) apart in their flowering positions in the autumn or early spring. Cuttings can also be taken in autumn or spring.

Pests and Diseases: Aphids may have to be controlled. These also spread virus diseases, which are likely to stunt or distort growth, and produce mottled leaves. Destroy affected plants.

Pansies

PELARGONIUM ('GERANIUM')*

The 'geraniums' generally used so effectively in containers outdoors are the zonal pelargoniums. The flower heads come mainly in bright shades of red, orange, or pink, and the plants seldom grow much more than 60 cm (2 ft) outdoors.

There are also trailing pelargoniums – ivy-leafed 'geraniums' – that make a spectacular display if planted where they can cascade effectively.

General Care: Do not plant out until risk of frost has passed. Pelargoniums love a sunny position. To make the plants bushy, pinch out the tips in spring. Keep fairly dry in winter and water moderately in summer, with occasional feeding.

Propagation: Sow seeds of suitable varieties in February, transplant into boxes and then into pots, or outside when there is no longer a risk of frost.

Alternatively, tip cuttings can be taken in March, July or September. The cuttings should be about 7.5 cm (3 inches) long, and inserted in a mixture of equal parts peat and sand. Keep shaded until they have rooted. Transplant into pots and, when the plants reach 15 cm (6 inches), pinch out the tops to make them bushy.

Pests and Diseases: Whitefly may attack pelargoniums while they are being kept in the greenhouse or indoors over winter.

POLYANTHUS* AND PRIMULA*

The primula family is diverse and includes the popular polyanthus. The polyanthus flowers, up to 4 cm (1½ inches) across, are carried in trusses on a stem about 20 cm (8 inches) tall. They are available in a wide range of colours from yellow, blue, red and pink to white. The primrose is another pretty plant, but it does not make such a bold display in the garden.

General Care: All primulas enjoy a rich, moist, fertile soil in sun or partial shade. Adding leaf mould or peat to the soil is beneficial, and regular liquid feeding during the growing months will usually help.

Propagation: A fresh supply of polyanthus is best raised from seed each year. Sow seed in trays in spring or early summer. Keep the compost moist and shade the seedlings from strong sunlight. Transplant into boxes and then set the young plants in their perma-

Trailing pelargoniums (ivy-leafed geraniums)

Saxifrages

nent positions in September for flowering the following spring.

Some primulas can be divided easily after flowering and then replanted.

Pests and Diseases: Aphids and slugs are the most likely pests. Among the possible diseases, leaf spot is sometimes troublesome. Virus diseases cause stunted plants, yellow mottled and distorted leaves, and poor flowering; remove and burn affected plants to prevent the virus spreading any further.

SAXIFRAGA*

This family covers a wide range of plants; some have close-growing rosettes of leaves, some are moss-like, and others have toothed leaves. Low-growing, few are higher than 30 cm (1 ft) and most are under 10 cm (4 inches). Flowers come in a variety of colours, including pink, white and yellow, but they are rarely more than 2.5 cm (1 inch) across.

General Care: All saxifrages prefer a sunny position, and a well-drained soil with some gravel and limestone mixed in, if possible.

Propagation Most saxifrages can be divided after flowering, then replanted; otherwise non-flowering rosettes can be cut off, the lower leaves removed, and the cuttings pressed into a pot containing a mixture of equal parts sand and peat. Keep just moist until spring, then water more freely and plant out in September 20-30 cm (8-12 inches) apart to form clumps, rather than a line.

Pests and Diseases: Generally free from pests, but rust disease is a possible problem (look for brown marks) on the encrusted varieties.

SEDUM*

The sedums, or stonecrops, are succulent plants, grown for the shape and colour of the leaf as much as their star-shaped flowers.

Some varieties will grow up to 90 cm (3 ft) tall, while others only reach 1 cm (½ inch). Colours of flowers include yellow, pink, and white.

One of the largest and most spectacular is *Sedum spectabile*, which has pale green, fleshy leaves. These set off the flat, pink flower heads which appear in early autumn. The flowers are usually carried on 45 cm (1½ ft) stems and attract butterflies in large numbers whenever the sun shines.

General Care: Sedums need a well-drained, loamy soil in a sunny position. Most will withstand dry periods. After flowering, the dead stems should be left on the plants until the spring, when they can be broken off.

Propagation: Sow the seeds in a tray in March or April. Transplant the seedlings into boxes, then later into 7.5 cm (3 inch) pots, which should be kept outside until October when the young plants can be planted out.

Clumps can also be divided and replanted during the winter months.

Stem cuttings can be taken in spring and pressed into a nursery bed out of doors. Plant the larger varieties 45 cm (1½ ft) apart, the smaller ones 15 cm (6 inches) apart.

Pests and Diseases: Slugs and snails are a threat to sedum, aphids a possibility. Provided the soil is free-draining, crown and root rot should be kept to a minimum.

SEMPERVIVUM*

Sempervivums (houseleeks) are hardy and half-hardy evergreen succulents, ideal for a hot dry site. They generally grow about 2.5 cm (1 inch) high, although the tight leaf rosettes push up a leafed flowering stem which can be as tall as 20 cm (8 inches) in the summer. Sempervivums look attractive growing in shallow pans, windowboxes, troughs, and sink gardens.

General Care: Provide a sunny site with well-drained soil. To prevent the plants from spreading out too far, you can remove the outer rosettes in autumn or spring.

Propagation: Sow seeds in March in trays, and keep in a cold frame. Transplant seedlings into boxes and then plant out in position in the autumn.

Alternatively, the offsets (rosettes round the edge of the parent plant) can be detached and replanted in spring.

Pests and Diseases: They are generally pest-free apart from occasional attacks by slugs and snails. Young plants can be uprooted by birds so it is wise to cover them with a net until established.

Rust disease can be seen as orange, cup-like dimples. Lift the affected plants and burn to prevent the rust spreading.

available – yellows, oranges, reds, purples and white. They are excellent as container plants, particularly in mixed colour schemes. The dwarf types, growing only about 23-30 cm (9-12 inches) high, are especially useful for windowboxes.

General Care: These plants will thrive in a well-drained soil that is neutral or slightly alkaline. They prefer a sunny position and young plants must be protected from cold winds. The tips of the plants should be pinched out when they reach 15 cm (6 inches) in height to encourage a bushy habit.

Propagation: Sow out of doors in May or June, and transplant the seedlings to a nursery bed 15 cm (6 inches) apart in rows. In October they can be moved to their flowering positions, where they can be planted about 30 cm (1 ft) apart.

Pests and Diseases: Cabbage root fly maggots are occasionally a problem; if the plants wilt, lift one and look at the roots for signs of maggots.

Club root can be a problem on infected land – the roots will be knobbly and swollen. Do not grow wallflowers on ground known to be infected.

Wallflowers

Sedums (stonecrops)

WALLFLOWER*

Although wallflowers are hardy perennials, they are normally treated as biennials. If kept over from one flowering to the next, the plants tend to get leggy and have few flowers. Flowering in late spring and early summer, wallflowers provide a useful bridge between early bulbs and summer bedding plants. They can grow up to a height of 60 cm (2 feet), but the dwarf bedding varieties are only half this height.

A wide range of fragrant flowers in warm colours is

TREES, SHRUBS AND CLIMBERS

No design for a patio garden is complete unless attention has been given to that vital backdrop provided by trees, shrubs, and climbing plants. These give height and depth to the overall scene, offer shelter to the other plants, and privacy to the people using the patio. Most of all, they bring a welcome sense of permanency to the garden.

Because these plants are long-lived, a great deal of thought should be given to selecting the right ones. Many of the shrubs and climbers will grow happily in large pots and tubs, provided that they are looked after properly. Often the restricted root-run encourages a profusion of flowers. As a general guide, a shrub that grows to about 1-1.5 metres (3-5 ft) will require a container that is about 1 metre (3 ft) wide and 45 cm (1½ ft) deep.

When choosing a tree, bear in mind its eventual height and width, its rate of growth, and the root room it will require. For small areas it is best to select slow-growing deciduous trees or dwarf evergreens.

Some of these plants will require pruning to maintain their shape and encourage new growth.

Good ground preparation is important for trees and shrubs at any time, but if you are growing them in containers, it is even more vital. It's well worth the cost of providing a good loam-based compost, such as John Innes No. 3 potting compost. If ordinary garden soil is used for large containers, add plenty of garden compost and peat.

Above all, make sure the compost never dries out completely – something that's always a risk with containers. Trees and shrubs are as vulnerable as other plants.

You do not have to plant in containers, of course. Why not lift a paving stone and plant directly into the ground? The plant will probably be much happier.

BETULA PENDULA*

This is the common silver birch, a fast-growing tree with small leaves but graceful habit. The ordinary species grows too rapidly and too tall for a small patio, but the small weeping birch, Betula pendula 'Youngii' is well worth growing. It will grow reasonably slowly to about 4 metres (12 ft) in height, and with a spread of about 2 metres (6 ft). Catkins appear in April or May, but the silvery bark and graceful habit are the main attractions.

General Care: Birches thrive in good garden loam, but they will also tolerate a light sandy or acid soil, though on shallow chalky soil they will not reach their full height. They will grow well either in sun or partial shade. No pruning is required.

Propagation: Because Betula pendula 'Youngii' is grafted, it is best to buy a young tree from a nursery.

Pests and Diseases: Birch polypore is a bracket fungus that enters through dead wood. All dead wood should be cut out and the tree wounds treated with protective paint.

BUDDLEIA*

There are two buddleias suitable for growing on a patio, both of them very attractive deciduous shrubs. Buddleia alternifolia can be trained as a small tree with a weeping habit. The flowers are carried in long, arching sprays.

Buddleia davidii is well-known for its attraction to butterflies. These love the large, pointed sprays of white, blue, purple, or violet flowers, carried from July to October. This buddleia will grow up to 3 metres (9 ft) tall with a similar spread if left unpruned; cutting it back quite severely each spring will keep it within about 2 metres (6 ft).

General Care: Buddleias prefer to be in full sun in a good loamy soil. Prune back Buddleia davidii in March to contain size and encourage large flowers. Buddleia alternifolia should be pruned after flowering to preserve a neat shape.

Propagation: Take cuttings about 10 cm (4 inches) long with a heel of old wood in July or August. Insert the cuttings into a mixture of equal parts peat and sand, and pot up into compost once they have rooted. Stand in a garden frame until the following spring, then transplant into a nursery bed. In the autumn plant the buddleias where they are to grow.

Pests and Diseases: Normally, buddleias are relatively pest-free. If the green leaves show a pale green or yellow spotting or mottling, cucumber mosaic virus is probably responsible. The plant should be dug up and destroyed to prevent the virus spreading.

CEANOTHUS**

There are evergreen and deciduous kinds; the evergreens need some protection, such as a sheltered wall, in most of the country, but the deciduous ones are hardy. They can grow up to 3 metres (10 ft) tall. The varieties usually grown have masses of small blue flowers – in April or May, or from July to October, depending on species.

General Care: Ceanothus prefer light soil, ideally on the acid side, and a position in full sun. The tender varieties should be grown against a south- or west-facing wall. Water liberally in dry weather.

Propagation: Cuttings 10 cm (4 inches) long with a heel of old wood can be inserted in a mixture of equal parts peat and sand in July. When the cuttings have rooted, pot them up into 7.5 cm (3 inch) pots and keep in a garden frame over the winter. Transplant to their final positions in the following autumn.

Pests and Diseases: Ceanothus are sometimes attacked by scale insects. Where plants are grown on chalk chlorosis may cause the leaves to turn yellow. This disease should be treated with chelated iron and heavy mulches of acid peat.

Ceanothus

CISTUS**

These evergreen shrubs can vary from only 30 cm (1 ft) high to upright plants 2.4 metres (8 ft) tall. The plants flower prolifically from May to July, with white, pink and crimson blooms, some with contrasting markings.

General Care: A position of full sun is ideal, and they do well on dry banks and chalky soil. Cistus will tolerate wind and salt air, but they may need some protection from frost. No pruning should be carried out, apart from removing dead wood and pinching out young growth occasionally to encourage bushiness.

Propagation: Sow seeds in March in trays, and transplant into pots when large enough to handle. Keep over winter in a garden frame and plant out in spring. Cistus can also be propagated by cuttings taken in July or August.

Pests and Diseases: Cistus are normally trouble-free but some dieback of shoots can occur as a result of frost damage. Dead wood should always be cut out.

manure should be put over the root area in spring.

Propagation: Stem cuttings of half-ripened wood can be taken in July. Make them about 10 cm (4 inches) long with two buds at the base. Insert them in a mixture of equal parts sand and peat, and provide some bottom heat. When rooted, transplant into pots and keep in a greenhouse over the winter. In the spring harden them off and plant out in the autumn.

Pests and Diseases: Slugs and snails have an appetite for the young shoots. Aphids and earwigs can also be troublesome. The most serious disease is clematis wilt, which causes shoots to die rapidly. Cut off affected shoots and spray with benomyl or throphanate-methyl, drenching the soil too. If repeated applications fail to control it, uproot and destroy the plant.

COTONEASTER*

There are many useful cotoneasters: some evergreen, others deciduous; some ground-hugging carpeters, some large shrubs.

Two very different but useful cotoneasters for a patio are *Cotoneaster horizontalis* and *C. hybridus* 'Pendulus'.

Cotoneaster horizontalis will carpet the ground or grow upright against a wall. Either way the herringbone-like branches are attractive, and the brilliant red berries in autumn impressive.

Cotoneaster hybridus 'Pendulus' is a small weeping tree, with cascading clusters of red berries in autumn.

CLEMATIS*

There are many clematis from which to choose, most of them large-flowered, but there are also some charming small-flowered species. The ones usually grown are climbers. Some will reach more than 9 metres (30 ft), but 3 metres (10 ft) is more usual for ordinary garden varieties. The large-flowered kinds have blooms up to 20 cm (8 inches) across, and there is a wide and vivid colour range.

General Care: Clematis prefer an alkaline soil in an open situation, but the base and roots should be shaded from direct sun. A cool root-run under paving is often recommended, but they are happy anywhere that their roots can be in shade and their flowers in the light.

You may have to tie in the young shoots initially, but once started they are self-supporting.

A mulch of well-rotted

General Care: Cotoneasters will grow in any ordinary garden soil but need a sunny position. No annual pruning is necessary, but strong-growing plants may need pruning to keep them in shape and stop them straggling. This can be done in late winter or early spring.

Propagation: Berries of *Cotoneaster horizontalis* can be collected in September or October, the seeds removed and sown in trays. Transplant the seedlings into boxes and later into a nursery bed. After growing for two years, transplant into their final position. Cotoneasters grown from seed will not necessarily be the same variety as the parent.

Alternatively, cuttings with a heel of old wood can be taken in August, rooted in a cutting compost, and grown on in a garden frame until ready to plant out.

Low-growing cotoneasters can also be layered. Nick a branch on the underside and press into the soil; keep weighted or pegged down. New roots should grow from the wound and the new plant can be severed after about a year.

Cotoneaster hybridus 'Pendulus' is grafted, so it is best to buy a plant rather than try to propagate it yourself.

Pests and Diseases: Aphids and scale insects are the most likely pests. Fireblight makes the flowers blacken and shrivel, the branches then die back with the leaves turning brown. This is a notifiable disease and the local branch of the Ministry of Agriculture should be told of any attack – they will advise on treatment.

ERICA*

There are literally hundreds of erica (heather) varieties, which together with the closely related callunas can provide flowers for most of the year. All are evergreens, and those usually grown in small gardens vary in height from about 5 cm (2 inches) to 60 cm (2 ft). Some form excellent ground cover, requiring little attention. They have bell-shaped flowers in white, or shades of pink or purple. The leaves can vary from green to yellow, orange, or red.

Consult a specialist catalogue for details of varieties – by careful choice they will provide year-round interest.

General Care: The winter-flowering species tolerate chalk, while the rest prefer an acid, sandy or peaty soil. They will need an open, sunny situation and require some moisture during periods of drought. Cut off dead flowers after they have bloomed. Trim leggy plants to preserve a neat shape.

Propagation: Take cuttings of young side shoots up to 5 cm (2 inches) long, inserting them to a depth of a third of their lengths into pots containing a mixture of 2 parts sand to 1 part peat. Keep moist and when rooted transplant into a nursery bed. Move them to their final position when they reach 7.5 cm (3 inches) tall.

Pests and Diseases: Ericas are normally pest-free. If fungus attacks the roots and collar parts, the diseased plants should be dug up and burned and the soil replaced before growing fresh plants.

Erica arborea

EUONYMUS*

A large family of deciduous and evergreen shrubs grown for their pink berries and bright leaf colour. The deciduous varieties are hardier than their evergreen relations and are better for growing in northern areas. One of the most useful of the bushy species is *Euonymus japonicus* 'Oratus Aureus', which has yellow variegation that provides year-round interest.

General Care: The young plants should be kept moist until established, and fed with a general fertilizer in spring and summer. Euonymus grows in most soils, but plant in an open situation, particularly the variegated varieties, to ensure good leaf colour.

Propagation: Take 10 cm (4 inch) cuttings with a heel of old wood and insert them into a cutting compost. Place in a garden frame to allow them to root. The following spring the young plants should be transplanted into nursery beds for two years, and then planted out in their final positions.

Pests and Diseases: Aphids and scale insects are possible pests. The diseases to watch out for are leaf spot and powdery mildew.

JUNIPERUS*

Junipers are evergreen conifers that vary in size from the prostrate varieties of 30 cm (1 ft) high, such as *Juniperus sabina*, through dwarf forms, such as *Juniperus communis*, to shrubs and trees that can reach up to over 7.5 metres (25 ft). The colour of the foliage varies from yellow, through green to blue and grey. Some, such as the variety *Juniperus virginiana* 'Skyrocket', are pencil-shaped and add height to a patio garden, without taking up much ground space.

Select juniper varieties according to the suitability of their growing characteristics for your garden.

General Care: Junipers will grow in ordinary garden soil that is well-drained. No annual pruning is required, except to trim the shape of prostrate varieties.

Propagation: Ripe seeds from the cones can be sown in the autumn and kept in a garden frame. Transplant the seedlings into a nursery bed and allow to grow for up to two years before planting out in their final positions. Coloured and named forms should be propagated from cuttings in the autumn. Take 10 cm (4 inch) cuttings with a heel of old wood and set in a cutting compost in a garden frame. Once rooted they can be treated as seedlings.

Pests and Diseases: Scale insects can attack junipers. Rust disease may leave brown or black spots on the foliage.

Lavandula and santolinas (front)

LAVANDULA*

Lavender is a hardy, aromatic evergreen shrub grown for its scent and for use in sachets and *pot-pourris*. It can grow up to 1.2 metres (4 ft), but height depends on species and variety. The striking grey-green foliage sets off the blue to purple flowers that appear from June to September.

Lavender grows well in containers and raised beds.

General Care: Lavender will grow in any well-drained soil, but thrives best in full sun. Cut back the flowers as they die, and replace the plants every five or six years as they become old and woody.

Propagation: Take 10 cm (4 inch) long cuttings of non-flowering shoots in August. Insert them into a mixture of equal parts peat and sand, and keep in a garden frame over the winter. In spring they should be transplanted into their final positions.

Pests and Diseases: Froghoppers attack lavender plants, – the frothy 'cuckoo spit' being an obvious sign. Leaf spot and grey mould can also be problems occasionally.

LONICERA*

There are shrubby loniceras – some are used for hedges – but the most popular species are the climbing loniceras, the honeysuckles. Honeysuckles produce their fragrant flowers from May to October, depending on variety. They can grow up to 6 metres (20 ft), and are marvellous for covering walls. Shrubby honeysuckles grow

Loniceras (honeysuckles)

well in large containers.

General Care: Honeysuckles thrive in a deep, rich soil that will keep moist in dry periods. This can be helped by mulching the root area to reduce evaporation. Feed with a general fertilizer in spring and summer.

Propagation: Take 10 cm (4 inch) stem cuttings in the summer, and insert into a mixture of equal parts sand and peat. Keep in a garden frame over the winter, then transplant into pots before planting out in the garden the following autumn.

Pests and Diseases: Pests are unlikely, but powdery mildew, rust, and leaf spot are possible diseases.

PHILADELPHUS*

There are several good philadephus (mock orange) species suitable for the garden. A small hybrid such as 'Avalanche', which grows up to 1.5 metres (5 ft) tall is particularly suited to a patio garden. The profusion of white flowers in midsummer have a delicious orange blossom scent.

General Care: On the whole, philadelphus require little attention. In very dry weather the plants will need watering, and it is worth applying a thick mulch in April or May to help reduce moisture loss in the summer.

Prune out old shoots but leave the young wood.

Propagation: Take 10 cm (4 inch) cuttings of half-ripe wood in summer, inserting them into a mixture of equal parts peat and sand. Place in a garden frame for the winter and transplant into nursery beds the following spring. By the following October they will be ready to plant in their flowering positions.

Pests and Diseases: Although philadelphus are generally pest-free, they are sometimes the victims of disfiguring leaf spot diseases.

SANTOLINA*

These hardy evergreen dwarf shrubs are grown for their feathery, aromatic, silver-grey foliage and small yellow button-like blooms that appear in July. They grow about 60 cm (2 ft) tall.

General Care: Santolinas grow well in a sunny site with well-drained, sandy soil. Trim off the dead flower-heads to encourage new growth. In April the plant can be cut hard

back or trimmed to make a more compact shape.

Propagation: Take 7.5 cm (3 inch) cuttings of half-ripe sideshoots in summer. Press them into a cutting compost in a garden frame. In April pot up the rooted cuttings for planting out in the following autumn.

Pests and Diseases: Santolinas are normally trouble-free.

SENECIO*

For the patio, the evergreen shrubs of the senecio family are most useful. *Senecio greyi* and *Senecio laxifolius* are of particular interest as they have most attractive grey felted foliage; they are compact, growing about 1.2 metres (4 ft) high. Their delightful yellow daisy-like flowers in early summer are a bonus.

General Care: Plant in full sun in a good, well-drained soil, but mulch the root area to help conserve moisture. Cut off the dead flowers and cut back straggly growth in the spring to keep a good shape.

Propagation: Take 10 cm (4 inch) half-ripe cuttings in September and insert them in a mixture of equal parts sand and peat. Place in a garden frame for the winter, transplant into a nursery bed in spring, then plant out the following autumn in their final positions.

Pests and Diseases: Senecios are generally trouble-free.

WISTERIA*

These ever-popular and attractive climbers produce large drooping clusters of blue, violet, or white flowers in May and June. They are hardy deciduous plants and

can easily reach 4.5 metres (15 ft), although they usually tend to spread sideways before this. They enjoy a rich soil. The species often grown is *Wisteria sinensis*.

General Care: Plant in a rich, deep soil against a warm wall in October or March. Mulch the root area in spring to help keep the soil moist during the

ing out in the final position.

Wisteria sinensis can easily be layered by taking a stem that can touch the ground and pegging it to the soil in spring or autumn, where it will grow roots. After a year it can be severed from the main plant and moved to a new site.

Pests and Diseases: Aphids may have to be controlled. Bud drop can be caused by dry soil. If the soil is too alkaline the leaves may turn yellow as a result of the iron deficiency. This is termed chlorosis and should be treated by feeding with chelated iron and a heavy mulch of acid peat.

YUCCA*

Yuccas have a dramatic appearance with swordlike leaves, growing up to 75 cm (2½ ft). They bear bold bell-shaped creamy flowers on 1.8 metre (6 ft) stems in the summer. These useful evergreen plants provide an interesting contrast to more convention-al-looking patio components.

General Care: Yuccas are tough plants and grow in ordinary, well-drained soil in beds or tubs. They only need watering in severe drought conditions. The plants do not need pruning. The species grown in gardens are normal-ly hardy.

Propagation: Remove the rooted suckers that grow up beside the parent plant in spring. If they are large enough, plant them straight into their permanent positions. If only small, the suckers should be planted in a nursery bed for a year and then moved to their flowering positions.

Pests and Diseases: Yuccas are normally trouble-free.

summer. Young plants should be fed in spring and summer to help them get established.

It is a good idea to restrict the growth of a mature plant by trimming new shoots back to two or three buds from the base in the winter, as this will encourage more flowers and less leaf growth.

Wisteria sinensis

Propagation: Take 10 cm (4 inch) cuttings with a heel of old wood in August, and root them in a cutting compost. Keep moist and provide bottom heat. When the cuttings have rooted, move them to a garden frame and then on to the nursery bed before plant-

FRUIT AND VEGETABLES

Most gardeners are surprised when they realize what a wide range of fruit and vegetables can be grown on balconies or patios, or even in windowboxes. The plants must be selected carefully, however, bearing in mind the limitations on root-run, space, light, and moisture.

FRUIT
Fruit crops are classified as top fruit (apples and cherries, for example) or soft fruits (such as strawberries, blackcurrants, and gooseberries). Both kinds can be grown to a restricted size if you buy the right varieties. In the case of top fruit such as apples, you also need to select a suitable rootstock.

VEGETABLES
With a little effort and ingenuity a small area can be used to produce a wide range of vegetables, although the quantity will obviously be limited. Almost any vegetable can be grown in a container or raised bed on a patio, but be sure to select the smaller varieties, as the root-run is obviously limited and space is at a premium. Growing bags can be particularly useful for vegetables on the patio.

APPLE*
The most popular fruit bush or tree, the apple, can be grown successfully on patios and in containers, but be sure to choose a variety that has been grafted on to a dwarfing rootstock such as M27 or M9. This will give a small plant that will be in scale with its neighbours.

There are various space-saving ways of training apple trees. They can take the form of a freestanding dwarf pyramid, but cordons and espaliers are worth considering. A cordon has a single stem grown at an oblique angle, an espalier has its horizontal branches trained to wires. Both espalier and fan-trained apples can be grown against a wall or framework of wires to form a screen.

You can also buy a 'family' tree which will have more than one variety grafted on to a single rootstock. Provided the vigour of each variety is carefully balanced, a 'family' tree is well worth considering if you only have enough space for one apple tree.

General Care: Apples grow in most well-drained soils, except those that are very alkaline. The centre of the tree should be pruned to keep it open and allow light in. The shape of the plant should also be controlled by pruning, and all dead and diseased wood should be removed. Apples need to be planted near a suitable pollinator if you want a good crop. If you buy a 'family' tree compatible varieties will have been chosen. Otherwise ask for advice when you buy them.

Propagation: Although apples can be grown from seed there is no guarantee of variety, so it is better to propagate by grafting. As this is a specialized job, and a suitable rootstock is essential, it is unwise to attempt this yourself.

Pests and Diseases: It is worth spraying with a winter tar-oil to control any pests which may remain on the plant through winter. Specific likely problems include codlin moth, aphids, capsid bugs, and scab.

BEANS, RUNNER*
The runner bean is a tender perennial but it is almost always grown as an annual. It can be grown as a climber against a wall or screen, or alternatively a 'wigwam' of canes can be made for the beans to grow up. This gives height to a patio, and the flowers are quite decorative – some are red, but most are white or pink.

General Care: Runner beans need moist, deep soil with plenty of humus. In periods of drought keep the soil moist by watering and mulching with a layer of peat or grass cuttings. Pick the pods before the seeds swell to encourage further cropping.

Propagation: Seeds can be planted outside in their permanent position after the danger of frost is passed at the end of May, or they can be sown in boxes under glass at the beginning of May for planting out at the end of the month. Plant at about 15 cm (6 inches) apart for best effect and heavy cropping.

Virus diseases cause stunted plants. To prevent a virus spreading to other plants dig up the affected plants and burn them.

BLACKCURRANT*

Blackcurrants, grown for their juicy, slightly acid fruit, are normally grown as bushes. They produce fruit on the previous year's growth. The plants can reach a height of 1.5 metres (5 ft) with a spread of 1.2 metres (4 ft) so you won't have room for many bushes on a patio! They are however self-fertile, so they can be grown as single bushes.

General Care: Most soils are suitable provided they are well-drained and moist. Mulch regularly with manure or compost, and apply a general fertilizer each spring. Prune new bushes to one bud above the ground, and on established plants cut out old wood before February to encourage young growth from the base.

Propagation: Insert 20 cm (8 inch) lengths of young shoots in open ground in October with only two buds showing above the soil. After a year transplant them to their fruiting site, allowing at least 1.5 metres (5 ft) between plants.

Pests and Diseases: Birds are one of the biggest problems as they can clear a good crop. The best deterrent is to cover the plant with a net. A tar-oil spray in the winter will deter aphids. Big bud is caused by a gall mite. If the cropping falls off it could be due to reversion virus, in which case the plant should be dug up and burnt. Leaf spot can be treated with a suitable fungicide.

Pests and Diseases: Slugs and snails can be a nuisance while the plants are becoming established. Aphids are a frequent problem throughout growth.

BLACKBERRY*

Although a native plant of the hedgerows, the blackberry is still worth a place in the garden. The wild blackberry bush is too well known to need description, but cultivated varieties have larger, more succulent berries – and some are even thornless!

General Care: A moist well-drained soil in sun or partial shade is best, but blackberry

Fan-trained apple tree

bushes will grow in a fairly poor soil. Cut out dead wood and train on a framework or up a wall to maintain a compact shape.

Propagation: In July, make a shallow hole in the ground and place the tip of a stem into it, then cover with soil or compost. By the following spring it will have grown roots and can be severed from the parent plant and moved to its final position.

Pests and Diseases: Raspberry beetle maggots and grey mould can spoil the fruit.

CHERRY*

There are two distinct kinds of cherry: the sweet and the acid. The acid cherry, 'Morello', is the best variety for the patio as it can be purchased as either a bush or as a fan-trained specimen for growing against a wall. However, it may still need a spread of 4.5 metres (15 ft) eventually. Unlike sweet cherries, a 'Morello' will grow well on a north-facing wall. It should flower profusely and produce deep red and black fruit in July and August.

General Care: Cherries will grow in most soils provided they are well-drained, but water regularly in dry weather to keep the soil moist. Each spring prune a few shoots to a growth bud on older wood to encourage fruiting growth.

Propagation: This is normally done by grafting or budding, and is best left to a professional. It is also advisable to purchase plants because these will probably have been partially trained.

Morello cherries

Pests and Diseases: Net the plant to stop birds eating the buds, and later the fruit. Aphids can also be a nuisance. Silver leaf disease is self-descriptive and is caused by a fungus. To treat diseased plants cut back stems and branches until clear untinted wood is found and then paint with a fungicidal paint.

CUCUMBER**

The long succulent fruits of the cucumber can provide an interesting feature in a patio garden. There are two main types of cucumber: the smooth-skinned greenhouse kind, that need to be grown with heat, and the prickly-skinned ridge varieties grown out of doors. For patios, ridge cucumbers are much more dependable.

General Care: Cucumbers need well-drained soil in full sun. Dig in plenty of well-rotted compost or manure and form a ridge, on top of which the seeds or plants can be placed. Pinch out the tips after six or seven leaves have formed. Keep the plants well watered.

Propagation: Seeds can be sown under glass at the beginning of May and the seedlings transplanted out of doors at the end of the month when the danger of a late frost is minimal. At the end of May seeds can be sown out of doors in their fruiting position.

Pests and Diseases: Although less of a problem outside than under glass, red spider mites can attack cucumbers. Spraying both sides of the leaves with water will help to deter them. Otherwise cucumbers should not be troubled by diseases outdoors, especially if grown in new growing bags.

FIG**

The fig is an almost hardy deciduous bush suitable for growing against a sunny wall. However, it is only likely to do well in favourable districts. The plant flowers one year and the fruit then takes two seasons to mature, but the large foliage is a bonus in the summer while you're waiting. Allow 4.5 metres (15 ft) for a fig to spread against a wall.

General Care: Figs will grow in good garden soil that has been fortified with bonemeal. Restrict the root-run by planting either in a well-like construction under the ground, or in a large 30 cm (12 inch) flower pot or container. Keep the roots trimmed as they tend to grow through the drainage holes.

Propagation: Branches can be layered by pegging them into the ground (roots should have formed after a year). Alternatively fig plants can be propagated from cuttings. However, you are unlikely to want more than one plant in your patio garden.

Pests and Diseases: Figs are normally pest-free. Coral spot or grey mould can cause the shoots to die back. In such cases cut off the diseased wood, then paint the wounds with fungicidal paint and spray with a systemic fungicide, such as benomyl or thiophanate-methyl.

GOOSEBERRY*

Gooseberries offer the first outdoor fresh fruit of the year – as early as May. Gooseberry plants can grow up to 1.5 metres (5 ft) tall, but most varieties produce bushes half this size.

General Care: A moist, well-drained good garden soil will suit most gooseberries. Plant in either full sun or partial shade. A mulch of well-rotted manure or compost should be applied in the spring to keep the moisture level high. Prune to keep the plant open; hard pruning of old bushes will improve the size of the fruit.

Propagation: Although gooseberries can be layered, it is more usual to take cuttings. These should be about 30 cm (1 ft) long, taken from young ripe wood. Insert them in open ground in the autumn after removing all but the top few buds. Allow to grow for a year and then transplant the healthy rooted cuttings in the winter.

Pests and Diseases: Cover the bushes with nets to prevent bird damage. Aphids and gooseberry sawfly caterpillars

can be major problems. Grey mould can kill off the stems; cut out the dead wood and paint the wounds with a fungicidal paint.

American gooseberry mildew attacks both fruits, which are coated with a felt-like growth, and stems, which are soon crippled. This disease must be dealt with immediately, by spraying the bushes with a suitable fungicide.

GRAPE**

This hardy deciduous climber is normally grown for its fruit, but its decorative maple-like leaves help to make it an attractive feature. The vines should be trained against a south-facing wall or over a pergola for the best effect in a patio area. The flowers are borne in May, and the grapes ripen in October. Make sure you choose a variety suitable for growing outdoors – these tend to be more suitable for wine-making than for eating as a dessert fruit.

Black grapes

General Care: Grapes grow best in a rich, well-drained soil. After the first year, cut off two-thirds of the main stems in September, and repeat this every year until the vine fills the area required. There are many ways to prune and train grape vines, but this is a simple rule where you want the vine as a decorative feature. In young plants pinch out shoots when they reach 60 cm (2 ft) long; in mature plants cut back to two leaves beyond the flowers. It is beneficial to mulch with well-rotted manure or compost every year.

Propagation: Take 5 cm (2 inch) sections of ripe stems with one bud each in February and bury the cuttings horizontally, except for the buds, in containers of potting compost. When the cuttings have rooted, move to larger pots and then plant out in October.

As an alternative take 30 cm (1 ft) hardwood cuttings and

Peaches

insert into the soil in their growing positions out of doors. Make sure you propagate from a suitable outdoor variety.

Pests and Diseases: Net the plants to protect against bird attack. Botrytis causes fruit to rot and powdery mildew can attack leaves, fruit and shoots.

PEACH** AND NECTARINE**

Peaches and nectarines are usually grouped together as the differences are little more than skin deep and they are treated in the same way. The peach has a furry skin while the nectarine is smooth.

For patios use either a fan-trained specimen and grow against a south-facing wall, or a dwarfing stock bush that can be grown in a large tub. Even

these are quite large bushes.

The fruit ripens from mid July to September.

General Care: Plant in a sheltered position. The early flowers need some protection against frost. A good rich garden soil that is well-drained will provide a good root-run and a generous mulching in spring with well-rotted manure or compost will help to keep the soil moist. Prune in February to maintain a good shape.

Propagation: Both peaches and nectarines can be grown from stones planted in pots. Crack the stone gently with nut-crackers to aid germination and plant it about 8-10 cm (3-4 inches) deep in a 9 cm (3½ inch) pot. Keep in a warm

place. Once the seedling is growing strongly, transplant into the garden.

Pests and Diseases: Aphids may be a problem. Peach leaf curl is an important disease on both peaches and nectarines.

PEAR*

The pear is a hardy deciduous tree that flowers in spring. The fruit ripens between September and December according to the variety. A pear tree will grow from 2.4 metres (8 ft) up to 6 metres (20 ft) depending on the rootstock and method of training. For the patio it is better to keep to a cordon, fan, espalier, or dwarf pyramid.

General Care: Plant in a warm site for frost protection (the tree will be hardy but the blossom can be vulnerable). Pear trees appreciate good soil; they do not like a high lime content. Mulch with well-rotted manure or compost each spring. Little pruning will be required other than to remove dead wood and maintain the shape of trained plants.

Propagation: Pears are budded or grafted on to rootstocks, which are usually quince. This is difficult as the two are often incompatible and an intermediate compatible variety has to be inserted between the two. For this reason, propagation is best left to the professional.

Pests and Diseases: Aphids and birds are likely problems. Bullfinches will strip the buds off a tree in late winter. Canker can attack pears and should be treated by cutting off the diseased section and painting the wound with a fungicidal paint. Scab may also be a problem.

STRAWBERRY*

Strawberries are the simplest crop to grow in containers. Suitable containers include troughs, barrels, wheelbarrows, pots – almost anything goes!

Outdoors, strawberries begin to crop in June. For the patio, strawberry barrels are particularly effective. The plants can be inserted through numerous apertures into good rich soil inside the barrel. A large crop is possible in very little space.

General Care: A rich soil with plenty of well-rotted manure will give good crops. Protect the flowers from late frost if possible and plant in full sun.

Propagation: The runners sent out in late summer can be rooted and then transplanted.

Pests and Diseases: Net the plants to protect them from birds and use slug bait to control slugs. Grey mould is a serious disease that will rot the fruit. If plants tend to die, the area should be cleared, the plants burnt and fresh soil used for new ones.

TOMATO**

Although tomatoes are tender you can expect a reasonable outdoor crop in the warmer counties of Britain. You should, however, choose a variety suitable for growing outdoors, and some of the 'bush' types are particularly useful. These do not need to have their sideshoots removed and growth is naturally bushy. You can grow them in large pots on a patio, but growing bags are likely to be more successful.

Plant tomatoes out at the end of May or in early June in a warm and sheltered position. You should be able to harvest outdoor tomatoes during August and September.

General Care: Plant in a good, deep moist soil with plenty of humus, if pots or growing bags are not used. The plants will need staking unless a bush variety is grown.

Once flower trusses have set, feed regularly with a tomato fertilizer (one high in potash). Keep well watered throughout the season.

Propagation: Sow seeds under glass or indoors on a windowsill in late March or April and transplant seedlings into pots where they should stay until planting outdoors after the risk of frost has gone.

Pests and Diseases: Aphids are occasionally a problem but diseases such as blight are far more serious.

Dark sunken areas at the end of the fruit are caused by erratic watering while the fruit was setting and is not a disease.

Strawberries

HERBS

Most herbs are undemanding and easy to grow. You must, however, choose a suitable site and make sure they receive the maximum amount of sunshine during the growing season. Protect them from cold winds, which often cause more damage than low temperatures.

Herbs are not only useful plants, they are also decorative. Mixed plantings of annuals and perennials, such as parsley, chives, dill and thyme, in sunken sinks, troughs, pots, windowboxes or hanging baskets, can make most attractive displays.

BAY*
The sweet bay (*Laurus nobilis*) or bay laurel as it is sometimes called, is a hardy evergreen shrub. If left unrestricted it can reach a height of 5.4 metres (18 ft), but when grown in a container (and it makes an ideal container plant) with a restricted root-run it can be kept to below 2 metres (6 ft). The bay can be grown as a bush or standard, clipped to shape, or left free. The shiny dark leaves are used for flavouring fish or meat, and mixed with other herbs to form a bouquet garni.

General Care: Plant bay trees in any normal garden soil in a sunny and sheltered position or in a container with a good potting compost. Normally no pruning is necessary, but when a shape is required use secateurs to trim, not shears (which will cut the leaves leaving a brown unsightly edge).

Propagation: Take cuttings 10 cm (4 inches) long with a heel of old wood in August or September. Push the cuttings into a mixture of equal parts peat and sand, then stand in a cold frame. In spring pot up the rooted cuttings and in the following autumn plant them out in nursery beds where

Bay tree planted with begonias

they should grow for a year or so before planting them out in the spring.

Pests and Diseases: Scale insects are a potential problem.

CHIVES*

Chives, members of the onion family, are hardy perennials with grass-like leaves. They make compact plants up to 25 cm (10 inches) tall and carry attractive pale mauve flowers in June and July. The leaves are used fresh for flavouring savoury dishes. They are easy to grow and increase rapidly.

General Care: Chives will grow well in most well-drained garden soils and also in windowboxes and other containers provided they are not allowed to dry out. The flower-heads are best pinched off when the plant is being used as a herb. In winter the chives die back, re-emerging in the spring, when they should receive a dressing of well-rotted manure or compost. If grown in containers, use a liquid feed.

Propagation: Chives can be grown from seeds sown in spring. Thin out the seedlings to 15 cm (6 inches) apart and transplant to their final position in May. They can also be increased by lifting the clump in spring or autumn and dividing it into smaller clumps of up to ten shoots.

Pests and Diseases: Chives are normally trouble-free.

DILL*

This is a fragrant, hardy annual growing up to 90 cm (3 ft) tall with a hollow stem and fine, needle-like leaves. It has small yellow flowers from June to August. The leaves are used to flavour vegetables and white meat, while the seeds have a stronger aniseed flavour and are used for pickling and flavouring sauces.

General Care: Dill grows well in most well-drained garden soils in a sunny position. Seeds are ready for collection at the end of the summer when they should be dried and stored in an airtight container.

Propagation: Sow seeds from March until July for a continual supply of fresh leaves, which are ready six to eight weeks from sowing. Thin the seedlings to 30 cm (1 ft) apart. Dill seeds itself and if allowed to do this will give good plants the following year.

Pests and Diseases: Dill is normally trouble-free.

Chives in flower

LEMON BALM*

This is a hardy perennial grown for its fragrant, lemon-scented green or yellow leaves. It grows to about 60 cm (2 ft) tall, with rather small, white flowers in June and July. The leaves and young shoots are used fresh for drinks and fruit salads, the dried leaves are mixed with other scented plants for pot-pourri.

General Care: Grow lemon balm in any well-drained soil in full sun. The richer the soil, the stronger the scent of the leaves. Plants with variegated leaves should be cut back in June to encourage new growth. In October cut back other varieties almost to ground level.

Propagation: Although easily grown from seed, it takes a long time to germinate. Sow seeds in their growing position at the end of April, thinning the seedlings to 30-45 cm (12-18 inches) apart. Alternatively, lift the root-ball in spring or autumn and divide into several pieces to replant.

Pests and Diseases: Lemon balm is normally trouble-free.

MINT*

The two mints most widely grown for herbal use are the common mint or spearmint and the apple or round-leaved mint. They are perennials growing up to 90 cm (3 ft) tall. The leaves are used to flavour lamb, tea, vegetables, iced drinks, and fruit salads. If mint is not grown in some kind of container, the roots can spread out of control.

General Care: Mints prefer a rich, moist soil but will grow in most soils as long as they have a sheltered shady position. Pick leaves or sprigs at any time until the plant dies down in the autumn to re-appear the following spring. Make a fresh bed every few years as the mint will drain the goodness out of the soil.

Propagation: Lift and divide the plants in spring. After they have been planted out give them plenty of water until they are established.

Pests and Diseases: Mints are normally pest-free. Mint rust causes the shoots to become swollen, distorted and covered with orange spores. Apart from using a fungicide, you may need to burn off the plant as it dies back in autumn to kill off any spores which could survive the winter.

PARSLEY**

All varieties of parsley are hardy biennials but are often treated as annuals to make the most of the young leaves. The curly leaves are used as a garnish and for flavouring salads, sauces, savoury dishes and stuffings. It grows up to 60 cm (2 ft) tall and has yellow flowers, which should be removed to keep the quality and flavour of the foliage. Parsley is a good plant for edging the herb garden and ideal for container growing.

General Care: Most well-drained soils will grow parsley, though it helps to incorporate some well-rotted manure or compost before sowing the seeds. Choose a sheltered position for planting and – to keep a supply going for the winter – protect from cold weather. The plants can be cut down in the autumn to encourage fresh growth.

Propagation: Sow the seeds out of doors between February and June. If the ground is cold it is better to sow the seeds in a seed tray and keep in gentle heat indoors or in a green-

Mint

house until the spring when the seedlings can be hardened off and planted out 23 cm (9 inches) apart.

Pests and Diseases: If the leaves turn yellow with orange and red tints, the plant is probably being attacked by carrot root fly. A soil insecticide such as bromophos, used when sowing and thinning, should solve the problem.

A virus disease also causes reddish leaves, but in addition the plants are very stunted. Burn any infected plants to reduce the risk of the disease spreading further.

ROSEMARY*

There are several forms of this hardy evergreen shrub, with long, narrow leaves that are aromatic and used for flavouring meats, poultry and fish. The shoots are sometimes distilled to make rosemary oil.

The rosemary plant can grow 1.8 metres (6 ft) high eventually, but it is slow-growing. There is a dwarf variety, only 45 cm (1½ ft) high that is ideal for container growing. The little blue flowers grow in clusters from March intermittently through until September.

General Care: Rosemary needs a sunny position and a well-drained garden soil. Dead growth should be cut out in the spring and long stems should be trimmed back to maintain a compact shape. Old bushes can be cut back by half in April.

Propagation: Take 10 cm (4 inch) cuttings of half-ripe wood in the summer and insert in a mixture of equal parts sand and peat in a garden frame. Put rooted cuttings into pots for the winter and keep in frost-free surroundings until the end of May when they can be planted out in the open.

Alternatively, take 20 cm (8 inch) cuttings of mature shoots in the autumn and insert directly into the soil. The rooted cuttings should be ready to plant the following spring and summer.

Pests and Diseases: Rosemary is normally trouble-free.

SAGE*

The leaves of this hardy evergreen sub-shrub are grey-green and aromatic, and are excellent for flavouring meat and poultry. They are a popular ingredient in stuffings. Sage grows to about 60 cm (2 ft) and has small, soft purple flowers in June and July.

General Care: Sage will grow in any soil provided it is well-drained and in a sunny place. Trim the plants back to the old wood in April to maintain a compact, bushy shape; cut off the dead flowers in the autumn.

Propagation: Sow seeds in trays in the spring, then transplant the seedlings into boxes. Move them into their final position in September. Cuttings can be taken using 10 cm (4 inch) lengths of shoots in August. Insert into a mixture of equal parts peat and sand in a garden frame. Put the rooted cuttings into pots and then plant out in the open the following March.

Pests and Diseases: Sage is normally trouble-free.

THYME*

The thymes are hardy, aromatic evergreen shrubs, growing no more than 30 cm (1 ft) tall. Some varieties grow considerably less and make attractive ground cover. Thyme also does well in containers. The shoots and small leaves are

Thyme in flower

used for flavouring meat and savoury stuffings. The flowers are normally red-mauve and attract large numbers of bees in June.

General Care: Thyme enjoys a sunny position in most well-drained soils. Plants should be replaced after several years as they become thin and lanky. The plants can be clipped back after flowering to maintain a trim shape.

Propagation: Clumps of thyme can be lifted and divided in the spring, then replanted. Alternatively, 5 cm (2 inch) cuttings can be taken with a heel of old wood in May or June. Insert these into a mixture of equal parts sand and peat, in a garden frame. Pot up the rooted cuttings, but leave in the frame until autumn, then transplant into their final position.

Pests and Diseases: Thyme is normally trouble-free.

GUIDE TO SELECTING PATIO AND WINDOWBOX PLANTS

Before choosing plants for any situation you must make sure that you can provide the right conditions. Some plants prefer a sunny position, others prefer partial shade; some cannot tolerate a soil rich in lime, others thrive in it. The following chart provides you with the growing requirements of each plant – relevant to selecting ones for your situation. All are suitable for planting directly in soil on the patio; where containers are suitable, these are suggested.

PLANT	SOIL					SUITABLE SITE		SIZE	SUITABLE CONTAINER			FLOWERING TIME
	Conditions Tolerated			Moisture Level Tolerated								
	Acid	Lime	Neutral	Moist	Fairly dry	Shade	Sun		Hanging basket	Tubs etc.	Windowbox	
	A	L	N	M	D	◑●	☼	SML	◒	🪣	▱	
Ajuga Reptans	A	L	N	M		●		S	◒	🪣	▱	June-July
Alyssum	A	L	N		D		☼	S	◒	🪣	▱	June-Sept
Anemone	A	L	N	M		◐	☼	S	◒	🪣	▱	Feb-Oct
Antirrhinum	A	L	N	M	D		☼	S/M	◒	🪣	▱	June-Sept
Apple		L	N	M	D	◐	☼	L		🪣		
Aster	A	L	N		D		☼	S/M	◒	🪣	▱	July – Oct
Aubrieta		L	N		D		☼	S	◒	🪣	▱	March-June
Balm, Lemon	A	L	N	M	D		☼	M	◒	🪣	▱	
Bay	A	L	N		D	◐	☼	L		🪣		
Beans-Runner	A	L	N	M			☼	L		🪣		
Begonia	A	L	N	M		◐	☼	S/M	◒	🪣	▱	June-Oct
Bergenia	A	L	N		D	◐	☼	S		🪣		March-May
Betula Pendula (Birch)	A	L	N	M	D	◐	☼	L		🪣		
Blackberry	A		N	M		◐	☼	L		🪣		
Blackcurrant	A	L	N	M			☼	L		🪣		
Buddleia	A	L	N	M	D	◐	☼	L		🪣		July-Aug
Calceolaria	A	L	N	M			☼	M	◒	🪣	▱	July-Aug
Campanula	A	L	N	M	D	◐	☼	S/L		🪣	▱	July-Aug

PLANT	Acid	Lime	Neutral	Moist	Fairly dry	Shade	Sun	SIZE	Hanging basket	Tubs etc.	Windowbox	FLOWERING TIME
	A	L	N	M	D	◐●	☀	SML	✓	✓	✓	
Ceanothus	A	L	N		D		☀	L		✓		April - May/July - Oct
Cherry		L	N		D		☀	L		✓		
Chives	A	L	N	M			☀	S	✓	✓	✓	
Cineraria	A	L	N	M	D		☀	M	✓	✓	✓	July - Sept
Cistus	A	L	N		D		☀	M/L		✓		June - July
Clematis		L	N	M		◐	☀	L		✓		May - June/Sept - Oct
Cotoneaster	A	L	N	M	D	◐	☀	L		✓		May - July
Crocus	A	L	N		D		☀	S	✓	✓	✓	March/Sept - Nov
Cucumber	A	L	N	M			☀	S/M		✓		
Daffodil	A	L	N		D	◐	☀	S/M	✓	✓	✓	March - May
Dahlia	A	L	N	M			☀	M	✓	✓	✓	July - Oct
Delphinium	A	L	N	M			☀	M/L		✓		June - Aug
Dill	A	L	N	M	D		☀	M/L	✓	✓	✓	
Erica	A			M	D		☀	S/M			✓	Nov - Dec/Jan - March/April
Euonymus	A	L	N		D	◐	☀	L		✓		June - July
Festuca	A	L	N		D		☀	S	✓	✓	✓	
Fig	A	L	N		D		☀	L		✓		
Fuchsia		L	N	M	D	◐	☀	S/L	✓	✓	✓	June - Oct
Gooseberry	A	L	N	M		◐	☀	M		✓		
Grape	A	L	N		D		☀	L		✓		
Gypsophila		L	N		D		☀	M/L		✓		June - July
Helianthemum	A	L	N		D		☀	S		✓	✓	June - Aug
Heliotrope	A	L	N		D		☀	S/M	✓	✓	✓	June - Oct

PLANT	SOIL					SUITABLE SITE		SIZE	SUITABLE CONTAINER			FLOWERING TIME
	Conditions Tolerated			Moisture Level Tolerated					Hanging basket	Tubs etc.	Window box	
	Acid	Lime	Neutral	Moist	Fairly dry	Shade	Sun					
	A	L	N	M	D	◐●	☀	SML	✓	✓	✓	
Hyacinth	A	L	N		D	◐	☀	S	✓	✓	✓	May
Impatiens	A	L	N	M		●◐	☀	S	✓	✓	✓	June - Oct
Iris	A	L	N	M	D		☀	S/M	✓	✓	✓	June - July
Juniperus	A	L	N	M	D	●◐	☀	S/L		✓	✓	
Lavatera	A	L	N		D		☀	M/L		✓		July - Sept
Lavandula (Lavender)	A	L	N		D		☀	L		✓	✓	July - Sept
Lobelia	A	L	N	M		◐		S	✓	✓	✓	May - Oct
Lonicera	A	L	N	M		◐	☀	L		✓		June - Aug
Marigold	A	L	N		D		☀	S/M	✓	✓	✓	June - Oct
Mesembryanthemum	A	L	N		D		☀	S	✓	✓	✓	June - Aug
Mint	A	L	N	M		●◐	☀	M	✓	✓	✓	
Narcissus	A	L	N		D	◐	☀	S/M	✓	✓	✓	March - May
Nectarine	A	L	N		D		☀	L		✓		
Nicotiana	A	L	N		D		☀	M	✓	✓	✓	June - Sept
Pansy	A	L	N		D	◐	☀	S	✓	✓	✓	April - Sept
Parsley	A	L	N	M			☀	S	✓	✓	✓	
Peach	A	L	N		D		☀	L		✓		
Pear	A		N	M			☀	L		✓		
Pelargonium (Geranium)	A	L	N		D		☀	S/M	✓	✓	✓	May - Sept
Petunia	A	L	N	M			☀	S/M	✓	✓	✓	June - Oct
Philadelphus	A	L	N		D	◐	☀	L		✓		June - July
Polyanthus	A	L	N	M		◐●	☀	S	✓	✓	✓	Jan - May
Primula	A	L	N	M		◐●	☀	S	✓	✓	✓	Jan - May

PLANT	SOIL					SUITABLE SITE		SIZE	SUITABLE CONTAINER			FLOWERING TIME
	Conditions Tolerated			Moisture Level Tolerated					Hanging basket	Tubs etc.	Window box	
	Acid	Lime	Neutral	Moist	Fairly dry	Shade	Sun					
	A	L	N	M	D	◐●	☼	SML	✓	✓	✓	
Rosemary	A	L	N		D		☼	M/L		✓	✓	
Sage	A	L	N		D		☼	M		✓	✓	
Salvia	A	L	N		D		☼	S/M	✓	✓	✓	July - Oct
Santolina	A	L	N		D		☼	M		✓	✓	July - Aug
Saxifraga	A	L	N		D	◐	☼	S	✓	✓	✓	May - June
Sedum	A	L	N		D		☼	S	✓	✓	✓	Aug - Oct
Sempervivum	A	L	N		D		☼	S		✓	✓	June - July
Senecio	A	L	N		D	◐	☼	S		✓		July - Aug
Stock		L	N		D	◐	☼	S/M	✓	✓	✓	July - Aug
Strawberry	A		N	M	D		☼	S	✓	✓	✓	
Sweet Pea	A	L	N	M			☼	L		✓		June - Sept
Thyme	A	L	N		D		☼	S	✓	✓	✓	June - Aug
Tomato	A	L	N	M			☼	M/L	✓	✓	✓	
Tulip	A	L	N		D	◐	☼	S/M	✓	✓	✓	April - May
Viola	A	L	N		D	◐	☼	S	✓	✓	✓	April - Sept
Wallflower		L	N		D		☼	S/M	✓	✓	✓	March - May
Wisteria	A	L	N	M	D		☼	L		✓		May - June
Yucca	A	L	N		D		☼	M		✓		July - Aug

THE HERB GARDEN

The owner of a herb garden can derive great satisfaction and pleasure from the special spot that he or she has set aside to grow colourful and fragrant plants which are both pleasing to the eye and useful in the home. Herb plants can be grown among flowers and shrubs in the border or in pots and containers when space is limited, but where possible, they are best cultivated in a patch on their own.

Herb plants have been used since ancient times for the health and well-being of man. For centuries they were an essential part of everyday life, not only providing both food and medicines, but also filling other functions. For example, while chemicals are now added to water to make it fit to drink, so years ago drinking water was sweetened and purified by adding the strongly aromatic plant pennyroyal, one of the dwarf-growing mints.

When food was scarce and had to be kept over a long period of time, strong herbs with antiseptic qualities such as rosemary, thyme and mugwort were used as preservatives. These herbs used on meat not only helped to preserve it but made the meat more digestible and disguised what must otherwise have often been an unpleasant flavour.

'Herb' was the name originally used to describe any soft-stemmed plant which was of use to man. Hyssop, rosemary, bay and similar shrubs and trees were therefore not regarded as herbs. Today, however, a herb means a fragrant plant which has a medicinal or culinary value in its leaves, stems, flowers, seeds or roots.

There is no doubt that herbs are some of the easiest plants to grow, which once established need remarkably little attention. Careful thought must be given to choosing your herbs before planning the herb garden because of the size of the plants and the amount of space each herb will require. Where you have little or no choice of site, select your herbs with even greater care, choosing plants which will thrive in that particular spot.

The growing chart on pages 68-77 may help to make your choice of herbs easier and may also assist you in planning the herb garden.

CHOOSING THE HERBS

The variety of herbs is so great that your first step towards a herb garden must be to choose the plants you want to grow by identifying the purposes for which you want to grow them.

It is usual to begin with a small bed of herbs useful for cooking. A larger bed could also contain other fragrant herbs to use in herb teas, for cosmetics and pot-pourris. The choice could include herbs to use as remedies for minor ailments or simply as ornamental plants.

Bear in mind when choosing the plants that many herbs overlap in their uses. Lemon balm, for example, is used for salads, stuffings and when cooking chicken. It also provides a soothing tea to help the digestion and the fresh leaves can be used to alleviate stings and bites. Its dried leaves can be added to pot-pourris and an infusion of the herb can be used as a lotion to soothe skin irritations or added to the bath water. This versatile herb is one of many; you will discover how adaptable herbs can be.

An important point to consider when choosing your herbs is the height to which they will eventually grow and the amount of room each herb will need when fully grown. If you intend to use fresh herbs throughout the season and perhaps harvest them for drying or freezing, it will be a long time before the plants reach their maximum height and width. Until that time, interplant with annual or biennial herbs.

HERBS FOR DIFFERENT USES

When making a choice of herbs it is useful to look upon them as falling into four specific groups. These are: herbs to use in the kitchen; herbs for teas and remedies; cosmetic and fragrant herbs for pot-pourris; and some herbs for an ornamental garden. The following suggestions provide a guide to help you to make a choice for your particular needs and your particular herb garden. For detailed information on the herbs consult the A-Z of herbs.

Herbs for cooking

The following list covers herbs for a compact kitchen bed. To supply the needs of a small family throughout the year these 12 would be sufficient.

Basil is a half-hardy annual and grows about 30 cm (1 ft) high. Whether you grow sweet basil or the smaller leaved bush basil, you will need two or three plants. These will enable you to freeze or dry some leaves for winter use as well as to pick them fresh throughout the summer months. Basil is particularly good with tomatoes, either raw in salads or sprinkled over cooked tomatoes.

Bay is a small evergreen tree which, after many years, grows quite tall. This handsome plant enhances any garden and is very useful among the kitchen herbs. One plant, once established, will give you sufficient leaves for cooking as many recipes call for only part of a leaf. Bay leaves are traditionally used for flavouring fish and meat dishes, and are delicious in a rice pudding.

Chives are a must in the kitchen herb bed. A perennial plant which dies down in winter, nevertheless it can be picked over a period of many months – from early in spring to late autumn. One clump of chives would provide plenty of leaves for cooking. Their slender lance-shaped leaves add a delicate onion flavour to green salads and many cooked dishes.

Dill is another annual for the cook to use. The small finely cut feathery leaves grow profusely on a single stem. Dill grows quickly and is soon ready for picking. Two plants would be sufficient in the herb bed if the leaves only are going to be used. To grow dill for seed you would need four to five plants. Dill combines well with cucumber in salad, sauce or soup and adds flavour to fish dishes.

Marjoram is a very useful herb to grow whether it is the annual variety or one of the perennials. The new perennial marjoram which combines the flavour of the annual sweet knotted marjoram with the growing habit of the perennial English wild marjoram is the best plant to grow in a small garden. The herb bears leaves throughout the year but they have little flavour until early spring. One plant is suggested for the kitchen bed. The small oval leaves provide a good flavour in salads and meat casseroles.

Mint is a good standby in the herb bed. This well-known creeping perennial is useful in

many ways. There are several mints to choose from, but spearmint and Bowles mint have the best flavour for cooking. One plant would be enough in a small herb bed for it quickly spreads in a season and would soon provide sufficient leaves for using fresh and for freezing or drying. The familiar flavour of mint adds liveliness to all salads and many sweet and savoury dishes.

Parsley is sometimes thought of as a rather ordinary herb, unimportant in the scheme of things. But it is an indispensably versatile plant and should be included in every kitchen herb bed. Though usually grown as a biennial, the plants will sometimes grow on for two to three years. Two plants are sufficient, producing lots of leaves for freezing, drying or using freshly picked.

Rosemary is a perennial shrub and a lovely herb to grow in any garden. One plant placed in an undisturbed spot in the herb bed will provide more than enough leaves for cooking. Since the flavour is strong, few leaves are required to add a distinctive flavour to meat dishes and salads based on pulses.

Sage is another perennial shrub, but it takes up less space in the herb bed than rosemary. That the fresh leaves can be picked throughout the year is a great help to the cook. One plant will suffice. Sage can be added to soups, sauces and meat dishes, as well as to stuffing.

Savory Summer savory is an annual plant; the neat attractive winter savory is a perennial. Two or three summer savory plants would be needed in the kitchen herb bed to give you enough leaves for picking, freezing or drying. One winter savory plant would be sufficient, as it is a larger plant and has many more leaves, which – despite the name – can be picked throughout the year. While summer savory has a more delicate flavour, both savories are good for seasoning bean dishes.

Tarragon is a perennial herb but dies down in winter. It is delicious for picking fresh through the summer months. One plant will provide plenty of leaves, but make sure you purchase a French tarragon plant as it has a far better flavour than the Russian tarragon. Use the leaves with savoury foods, sauces and salads.

Thyme is a small evergreen herb with leaves that can be picked all year round. One plant of garden thyme would suffice as it grows quickly. There are many varieties of thyme from which to choose, but those used in cooking are garden thyme, lemon thyme and wild thyme. The tiny leaves can be added to meat and fish dishes as well as to other savoury foods.

Herbs for teas and home remedies

A garden of 12 plants for teas and remedies can give a profusion of colour and fragrance.

Bergamot is a perennial herb with red, pink or mauve flowers according to variety. Two plants in a small garden will produce plenty of leaves to make a refreshing tea which is also soothing for sore throats. The flowers of the red variety can be eaten in salads.

Borage is a blue-flowered annual which grows rather untidily but is very pretty to look at. One plant will produce enough young leaves to make cooling summer drinks either on their own or added to wine cups and non-alcoholic drinks. Borage tea is a tonic and slightly laxative. Use the flowers to decorate the drinks or add them to green salads.

Chamomile is a feathery annual with a lovely scent and a great number of little white flowers.

Make sure it is the German chamomile when you buy the seed or a plant. To provide a good quantity of flowers grow as many plants as you can in the available space. Use the flower heads only to make a delicious tonic tea, good for the digestion and for sound sleep.

Fennel is a tall, elegant perennial herb with feathery leaves, similar in appearance to dill but with a stronger aniseed-like flavour. There are several varieties to choose from including an annual dwarf fennel, the base of which is eaten as a vegetable. Fennel grows quite quickly and one plant will provide ample leaves for picking as well as for freezing or drying. Use the leaves to make a pleasant tasting tea to settle the digestion. A strong solution of fennel makes an effective lotion for soothing tired eyes.

Lady's Mantle is an attractive perennial plant which, in mild areas, stays green throughout the winter. It is a low-growing herb and, until established in the garden, two or three plants would be needed to give sufficient leaves for picking. Lady's mantle is a medicinal and cosmetic herb. Juice from the leaves applied to the skin will help to cure acne.

Lemon Balm is a lemon-scented perennial. If the old stems are cut down in autumn, the plant will throw up new shoots providing leaves throughout the winter. One plant would be sufficient for picking, freezing or drying. Use the leaves to make a refreshing tea, soothing and calming, which can be drunk either hot or cold. Add fresh leaves to iced apple juice for a cool summer drink. Hot tea aids perspiration in feverish colds and is good for indigestion. Use crushed leaves in a poultice as a remedy for spots, boils and insect bites.

Marshmallow, once established, is a tall hardy perennial with pale rose flowers. The plant dies right down in winter. It has a place in the herb garden for its use as a remedy for minor ailments. Several plants would be needed for it is the root, when dried, which is used to make a cold soothing tea to be taken for diarrhoea and vomiting. A poultice made from the grated root helps to reduce inflammations.

Parsley is a herb mainly used in cooking but the leaves, especially those of the plain leaved variety, make a pleasant tea which is mildly laxative and an excellent remedy for haemorrhoids. It is well worth having one or two parsley plants of both the plain and curly leaved varieties to meet all the various requirements in the home.

Peppermint is a hardy creeping perennial with highly aromatic leaves. The leaves are a handsome blackish green colour and the pale mauve flowers are attractive. One plant will soon spread to provide sufficient leaves for picking to use fresh or for freezing or drying. The leaves make a fragrant tea, delicious hot or iced, which is good for the digestion and hiccups. Crushed peppermint leaves rubbed over the forehead and temples are cooling in hot weather and will cure an incipient headache.

Rosemary has so many uses that it is essential in any herb garden. It is an evergreen herb and one plant would give you enough leaves for most purposes. Rosemary tea is a pleasant drink to take as a remedy for headaches, colds and nervous depression.

Thyme is another evergreen perennial herb which makes an attractive plant in the garden and has countless uses. One plant of garden thyme would provide leaves for teas and remedies. Apart from its importance in the kitchen, an infusion of the leaves can be used as a gargle for a sore throat. Thyme tea is sedative and good for coughs. Inhalation of a hot infusion of thyme will help to ease bronchitis.

Verbascum is a tall perennial with a single stem growing out of a flat rosette of leaves. The flowers are a brilliant yellow. One or more plants would be needed to give enough flowers. It is the flowers only that are used to make a soothing tea which is taken for bronchitis and persistent coughs. This colourful tea, which must be carefully strained through muslin before drinking, is a most effective remedy.

Herbs for cosmetics and pot-pourris

Not many plants are needed to provide you with a sufficient quantity of each herb to make a wide variety of your own natural beauty preparations. The cosmetic herbs combine with herbs for pot-pourri – those fragrant plants, which when dried, hold their colour and scent to give sweet-smelling mixtures throughout the year. A list of 12 herbs is given here.

Caraway is a biennial plant which, in the second year, quickly goes to seed, and this is all to the good because it is the seeds only which are used in pot-pourris. Several plants will be necessary to provide enough. The seeds are dried then crushed or pounded before being added to the pot-pourri mixture. Caraway helps other dried herbs in the mixture to retain their scent.

Chamomile plants will be required in quantity to ensure a sufficient number of flowers to make cosmetic preparations. The dried flowers can also be added to pot-pourri mixtures. An infusion of chamomile is effective as a rinse for blonde hair, and can be used daily as a refreshing skin cleanser especially for oily skins. Use chamomile once a week in a facial steam as a deep cleanser. A hand cream made with chamomile has a softening quality, while its mild scent will stay on the skin for hours.

Fennel is an important plant to have in the cosmetic herb garden. One plant of this tall perennial will produce enough leaves and seeds for both cooking and cosmetic preparations. An infusion made with the leaves is a refreshing skin tonic and can be used on all types of skin. Fennel tea taken once a day is a natural aid in a slimming programme. A face pack of the leaves helps to smooth wrinkles and soften the complexion. Crushed fennel seed can be used as a substitute for the leaves during winter.

Lavender is a familiar shrubby perennial and an essential plant in any herb garden. Its long-lasting scent makes lavender an important ingredient in pot-pourri mixtures or even to have in bowls on its own. Two plants once established would provide enough flowers for drying. There are several varieties of lavender but the English lavender has the strongest scent. An infusion of lavender makes a sweet-smelling hair rinse and a strong decoction of the fresh flowers gives a delicious fragrance to bath water.

Lemon Balm, included among the herbs for teas and remedies, is another herb for the cosmetic garden. One plant will produce more than enough leaves for use. A strong decoction of fresh leaves, either with other herbs or on its own, adds a lovely fragrance to the bath water. A herb vinegar, made with plenty of lemon balm leaves, patted on to the skin is a refreshing way to ease a headache. An infusion of lemon balm soothes and softens irritations of the skin and smooths wrinkles.

Lemon Verbena is a handsome perennial shrub with fragrant leaves and flowers. One or two plants would suffice for, once established, they grow quite large. An infusion of the sweet-smelling leaves is a good skin lotion which can also be used for cleaning the teeth. Dried lemon verbena is lovely in pot-pourri mixtures.

Marigold Pot marigold is a colourful annual which flowers throughout the summer months. Marigold petals can be used in beauty preparations and pot-pourri mixtures. Five or six plants would be needed to give you enough

flowers for picking. Use an infusion of the petals to make a refreshing antiseptic lotion which is useful as a skin toner. Marigold petal ointment makes an efficient remedy for all skin blemishes, and soothes sunburn.

Mint is a fragrant herb to grow in the cosmetic garden and for pot-pourri mixtures. There are numerous different varieties to choose from of which the two most useful in this garden are peppermint and eau-de-Cologne mint. Two or three plants of each would suffice. Both mints can be used in a herbal bath and both, dried and crushed, give a lovely perfume to pot-pourris. Peppermint can be used to make toilet water and an infusion of peppermint leaves makes a soothing and refreshing foot bath for tired feet.

Orris is a perennial iris with handsome large white flowers. Several plants would be required and these must be allowed to mature before you use the rhizome, cleaned, dried and powdered, to add to pot-pourri mixtures. As the rhizome dries, it develops a strong scent of violets.

Rose Geranium is an unusual perennial plant normally grown in pots or containers. It can be transferred to the herb garden in the summer. Rose geranium provides strong rose-scented leaves which add a lovely perfume to pot-pourri mixtures.

Rosemary should not be omitted from any herb garden, because of its perennial shrubby growth and its leaves that can be used all the year round. It has a place in the cosmetic garden for its leaves make hair lotions and shampoos for dark hair, herbal baths and soothing baths for weary feet. An infusion of rosemary helps to lighten freckles and is used as a skin tonic. Dried leaves give a lasting perfume to pot-pourri mixtures.

Salad Burnet is a neat growing perennial of which is it worth having one or two plants. The leaves have astringent properties; when made into a lotion they help to refine the skin and close the pores. The lotion also cleanses the skin and is refreshing and beneficial to use on a hot summer's day.

165

Ornamental herbs

Because a collection of old fashioned herbs is decorative, it does not imply that you cannot use the plants. Lavender and rosemary are two herbs which have always been valued in gardens for their beauty. The six herbs suggested for this garden were all grown in the past for their medicinal properties, though modern methods of treatment have now overtaken them.

Camphor makes a showy plant in the decorative herb garden with a mass of tiny, white daisy-like flowers with brilliant yellow centres. The whole plant smells of camphor which is not unpleasant and it is useful for flower arrangements.

Hyssop is an attractive perennial well worth growing in the ornamental garden. The blue, pink or white flowers have a lovely scent which attracts bees and they have a long flowering period. A plant of each colour in the bed makes a colourful trio.

Jacob's Ladder is a neat growing perennial and highly decorative in the garden. There are two varieties, one with white and one with blue flowers. One or two plants take up little space in the herb bed. Originally the leaves were used for healing cuts.

Sage has several varieties which are most attractive and all are perennials. One plant each of pineapple sage and purple sage are suggested for the ornamental garden. The leaves of the former are sweetly fragrant and those of purple sage are a handsome colour.

Soapwort is a creeping perennial ornamental herb. One plant will soon increase sufficiently to give a mass of pale pink flowers in June. The flowers have little scent but are very showy. An infusion of soapwort was, and still is today, used for washing delicate fabrics.

Thyme amply justifies a place in the ornamental garden. Garden thyme produces highly decorative flowers and there are other variegated thymes which have colourful foliage continuing throughout the year. Five or six plants set together make a solid patch which is very fragrant and attracts bees.

RIGHT: The different greens of the herbs are attractive in this carefully planned bed

PLANNING AND PREPARATION

You will have success from the start if you remember a number of important points when choosing a site for your herb garden.

PLANNING THE SITE

First, the aspect must be carefully considered, as most herbs require some sunshine during the day. Many herbs originate from the warmer climate of those countries bordering the Mediterranean so the perfect position will be achieved if the herb bed can face south and west. Where the only possible place for your herbs is in partial shade, choose varieties that thrive in such a situation. Chervil, sweet cicely, bergamot, woodruff, angelica, chives and any one of the mints grow well in semi-shaded areas. A shady herb bed should have adequate protection from the north easterly winds. Ideally this protection should be in the form of a fence or wall rather than a hedge which, unless it is a useful herb, will be competing with the herbs for food, light and water. A hedge also harbours pests and diseases.

Herbs which are in frequent use need to be in a bed as near as possible to the house, so that they are convenient to reach when the weather is very wet.

The herb bed should consist of good garden soil (see also page 19) to encourage steady growth during the harvest season.

Size is another important consideration. When planning the herb garden allow 30-45 cm (12-18 inches) between the larger plants. Rosemary and sage, for example, need plenty of space when they are fully grown and it is better not to move them once they are established. While they are small you can plant annual or biennial herbs among them. Herbs of medium height need 30 cm (12 inches) between the plants; for small herbs 15-20 cm (6-8 inches) will be sufficient. Mint is a herb which can spread quickly in one season and may need to be contained.

Finally, you must be able to reach the herbs easily whatever the size of the bed. Plant to leave space for paths or stepping stones so that you can pick the herbs without treading on other plants or getting wet and muddy feet.

HERB GARDEN DESIGNS

Traditionally herbs were set out in a formal pattern, often of complicated design. Nowadays a simple arrangement of plants is easier to maintain and, if kept neat and tidy, can be a pleasure to look at as well as to use. To set the herbs too closely in a bed and allow them to grow unchecked would soon bring disappointment especially if you wished to use the herbs to any extent. Since the plants would all be

struggling upwards for light the lanky weak-looking herbs would have little flavour or scent.

The following suggestions for herb garden designs can easily be adapted to your own use.

In a large garden a semi-formal herb bed looks particularly effective. Curves, squares and rectangles can be combined in a definite pattern, criss-crossed with paths for easy access to the herbs.

The rather large country garden plan shows how a more formal design can be set out, which herbs to grow and where to place them. The taller perennials are set at the back of the bed where they can grow undisturbed. A low re-taining wall or a fence on the north side will help to protect the herbs from cold winds. One or two stepping stones placed at strategic points will make it easier for picking and tending the herbs.

1 SALAD BURNET, 2 WELSH ONION, 3 LAVENDER, 4 FRENCH TARRAGON, 5 LEMON THYME, 6 LEMON BALM, 7 BAY, 8 SAGE, 9 CARAWAY THYME, 10 ROSEMARY, 11 PENNYROYAL, 12 SWEET CICELY, 13 LOVAGE, 14 BORAGE, 15 CHERVIL, 16 PARSLEY, 17 APPLE MINT, 18 HYSSOP, 19 ENGLISH WILD MARJORAM, 20 MARIGOLD

The semi-circular herb bed lends itself well to the smaller town garden where it may be difficult to find a really sunny position for it. Bay could be replaced with lovage if the bed gets little sun. Chervil is a hardy bi-annual and could be replaced by bergamot making it an all-perennial bed of herbs. In place of tarragon, which prefers a sunny position, you could grow salad burnet. Flat stones are placed so you can easily reach all the herbs.

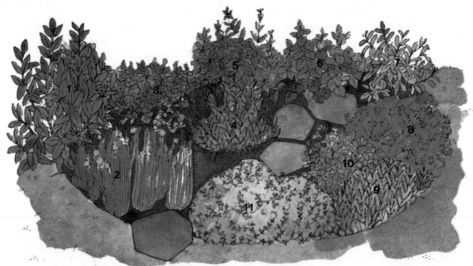

1 BAY, 2 CHIVES, 3 CHERVIL, 4 FRENCH TARRAGON, 5 MINT, 6 LEMON BALM, 7 SAGE, 8 PARSLEY, 9 WINTER SAVORY, 10 MARJORAM, 11 THYME

An easy herb bed in a cottage garden uses one wall of the house as the protected side of the bed and perhaps sites the bed adjacent to the kitchen door. A low hedge of lavender could be planted round one side to give further protection. Marigold and dill are the only annuals in this bed which could be replaced by others the following season.

1 SAGE, 2 MARJORAM, 3 FRENCH TARRAGON, 4 ROSEMARY, 5 DILL, 6 PARSLEY, 7 THYME, 8 WINTER SAVORY, 9 CHIVES, 10 MARIGOLD, 11 LAVENDER

Where space is very limited, a raised herb bed is a good idea. The plants get more light and you can provide them with a greater depth of soil. This will enable you to grow some of the taller herbs very successfully as well as the low growing ones.

Raise the bed to a depth of 60 cm (2 ft) with a south-facing wall. There is a wide choice of herbs for this type of bed. Nasturtium, an annual, will clamber all over the back wall and look very colourful. The raised bed full of aromatic herbs can be a pleasure to the disabled; those who are blind can enjoy the fragrance of the herbs.

1 ROSE GERANIUM, 2 MARJORAM, 3 BASIL, 4 THYME, 5 CHIVES, 6 HYSSOP, 7 CALAMINT, 8 NASTURTIUM

A very simple herb bed and one easy to maintain year after year can be made by using old roofing slates. These can be obtained from demolition yards. Set the slates on edge to form rectangles side by side. Placed along the side of a path the herbs are easy to reach. Fill the sections with small clumps of herbs such as chives, parsley, garden thyme and mint. Plant a few annuals also; try summer savory, sweet marjoram, marigold and dill.

1 CHIVES, 2 PARSLEY, 3 THYME, 4 MINT, 5 SWEET MARJORAM, 6 WINTER SAVORY

Herbs can be grown successfully on a sloping south-facing bank so long as the bank is not too steep or the soil so light that it will be washed away by a shower of rain. Where the soil is mostly clay it will retain moisture and be perfectly suitable for herbs; otherwise it is best to terrace the bed by building a low retaining wall. The herbs suggested for this bed are all perennials. Note that the mints are in the lowest part of the bank where they will get most moisture. If the bank is large and needs stepping stones make sure they are absolutely level.

There are, of course, many more ways in which you can set out your own herb garden bearing in mind the points set out above.

1 CHIVES, 2 FRENCH TARRAGON, 3 BERGAMOT, 4 FENNEL, 5 LEMON BALM, 6 SAGE, 7 LOVAGE, 8 ROSEMARY, 9 HYSSOP, 10 ORRIS, 11 EAU DE COLOGNE MINT, 12 SWEET CICELY, 13 SPEARMINT

Paths and edges

The importance of paths in providing essential access to every part of the herb garden cannot be overemphasized. Construct the paths of brick or paving slabs laid on to sand, or use concrete. All can look attractive as well as being functional. Do not lay grass paths as they are difficult to keep neat and trim.

A herb bed is easier to maintain if it has properly constructed edges, which can be of brick, concrete slabs or timber. An edging between lawn and herb bed will allow you to clip the lawn edge without the grass cuttings going over the herbs. A permanent edging also allows small creeping plants like pennyroyal and thyme to spill over the edge of the slabs.

A herb bed lends itself particularly well to being enclosed. A surrounding wall, fence or hedge, serves as a windbreak and reduces the danger of exposed plants being killed in winter. A wall is a permanent surround and can look attractive – one or more courses of brick or kerbstone create a neat edging. A low fence about 30 cm (12 inches) high constructed of wattle or strips of wood is less permanent but gives a softer outline. The traditional surround for a herb garden was the boxwood hedge but this takes goodness and moisture from the soil, to the detriment of the herbs. The most useful surround is a low hedge of lavender, germander, hyssop, thyme or sage. Lavender, sage and hyssop would need to be well trimmed.

PREPARATION OF THE HERB BED

Once you have decided on the site and chosen the herbs you wish to grow in your herb garden it is important to take trouble over the preparation of the bed. You should first peg out the dimensions and lay out paths and edges.

Preparing the soil

Soil which is a good medium for growing plants should be a balanced mixture of lime, sand, humus and clay. There should also be good drainage for easy working. This type of soil is easier to dig or fork over, and it warms up early in the spring giving a longer growing period. Soil conditions such as these are rarely found in the garden but with a little concentrated work applying compost, manure or rotted leaves, your soil will produce the right medium.

Drainage is most important where the soil is heavily compacted or consists largely of clay. If this is your problem, a drainage trench set in the lowest point in the garden must be provided. Dig a hole 60 cm (2 ft) wide by 60 cm (2 ft) deep and fill it to 45 cm (18 inches) with rubble or large stones, then replace the top soil.

Digging is important in the preparation of the herb bed. A heavy soil should be dug during the autumn to allow winter frosts to break it down. A sandy light soil can be dug during the winter or early spring but not in frosty weather.

A few weeks after digging is completed, sprinkle hydrated lime over the soil and leave it for the rain to wash in. Herbs require a well-limed soil, though if too much is added the leaves will turn yellow. A chalky soil will not need liming, but for all other soils lime is a good conditioner. It helps to bind together very sandy soil and breaks down heavy clay soil making it easier to work. Hydrated lime improves the soil and helps to keep the herbs free of pests, acting as a valuable natural insecticide. Lime neutralizes sour or acid soil, encouraging earthworms and useful bacteria to flourish which otherwise are absent in this type of soil. Lime is widely available from garden shops.

Once the herb bed is prepared, place any stepping stones required into position. Set flat stones on to well packed sand, making sure the stones are level and firm enough to stand on. Leave the herb bed to settle for two or three weeks before planting the herbs.

BELOW LEFT: Making a drainage hole
BELOW: Pegging out the herb bed

Preventing weeds

The simplest method of producing a weed-free herb bed is to lay suitable black polythene film over the soil with holes cut out for the plants. The sheeting can be bought from garden shops and centres and comes in varying widths. It offers several advantages: the polythene will last in the same place for two or three years, which helps the new herbs to become established without disturbance; it prevents any loss of water by evaporation; in a hot dry season it forms condensation which keeps the soil moist beneath the plastic, and it acts like a 'mulch' for the herbs, so that only occasionally do the herbs need watering. The black polythene smothers weeds by shutting out the light, allowing all the goodness in the soil to be available to the herbs.

Prepare the herb bed as described on page 19 and leave the earth to settle for two or three weeks before putting down the polythene. Cut sufficient film to cover the herb bed and stretch it down over the soil. The neatest way to anchor the outer edge is to bury it under a surround of narrow paving slabs. An alternative is to dig a trench to a depth of 5-7 cm (2-3 inches) along the edge of the bed and bury about 10 cm (4 inches) of the film. Fill in the trench with soil or pebbles. This is best done on a calm day as the plastic is light and easily caught by the wind.

When ready to start planting, first lay out the various herbs on top of the polythene in the position you have already planned for them. According to the type of herb, take a flower pot of appropriate diameter, stand it on the plastic and with a sharp knife cut a neat circle around the pot. Remove the disc and, using a trowel, plant the herb. For dwarf herbs and seedlings make a hole 6 cm (2½ inches) in diameter. For larger, container-grown herbs make a hole 10 cm (4 inches) in diameter. When the herbs are in place, hide the shiny black plastic by covering it with peat, gravel or sterilized soil.

HERBS IN CONTAINERS

You can successfully use containers both large and small to grow herbs. Wooden troughs, urns of stone or plastic, old sinks and large flower pots are all suitable. The containers can be put on a patio or terrace, or a narrow box full of herbs can be set against a wall. A collection of herbs can be grown in a hanging basket.

Herbs can be grown indoors in pots and containers. They need more care and attention as herbs naturally require a great deal of light to help them make good growth and produce flavour and scent. Herbs grown indoors also need more feeding and watering.

BELOW: Using black polythene to control weeds
RIGHT: A variety of herbs grown in containers

PLANTING AND ROUTINE CARE

Once you have chosen the herbs and prepared the bed, it is time to buy plants and seeds.

PURCHASING THE HERBS

Nowadays most garden centres sell a good selection of container-grown herbs, but there are nurseries specializing in herbs where you will find a wider variety of both the common herbs and their variegated species as well as the more unusual ones. At a herb nursery you will be able to see fully grown plants which will give you some idea of how your own herb garden will look when the plants are established.

Take with you to the herb nursery or garden centre a list of the herbs you want together with their Latin names. It is easy to get confused over the common names of herbs and it is important to purchase the correct ones.

When selecting herbs there are one or two points to remember. First, look for the fibrous root formation coming out of the base of the pot. This signifies that it is a well established plant which will have a greater chance of surviving. Second, choose sturdy plants in preference to tall ones with masses of growth, because the large herbs may have been too long in the pot and will take longer to establish themselves.

PLANTING HERB PLANTS

Give container-grown plants a good watering when you get them home, then leave them overnight. When planting remove the herbs carefully from the containers so as to disturb the root ball as little as possible. Plant out the herbs setting them in so that the soil comes just over the root ball. Woody stemmed herbs should be planted to the depth of the 'soil mark' on the stems. It is important not to crowd the roots, so make the planting hole sufficiently deep and wide to provide space for the roots which should be carefully spread out. Put a handful of compost in the bottom of the hole to give the herbs a good start and cover it thinly with soil. Once all the herbs are planted give them another good watering.

RAISING HERBS FROM SEED

At a herb nursery you will be able to find both

ABOVE AND LEFT: Planting container-grown herbs
ABOVE RIGHT: Planting woody stemmed herbs

annual and perennial container-grown herbs to give you a ready-made herb garden. This method is quick and easy but it can be costly. Many herbs can be grown cheaply and successfully from seed.

The annual herbs are easy to grow from seed and give you two added advantages. First, if you can sow the seed really early you will have plants that will be as good as, or better than, the container-grown herbs on sale in late spring. Second, you will be able to start picking and using the herbs earlier in the season. As early as February you can start sowing herbs indoors.

Herbs should be raised in well-scrubbed boxes. Add a small quantity of household disinfectant to the scrubbing water to reduce the risk of mildew and other diseases. Fill the boxes

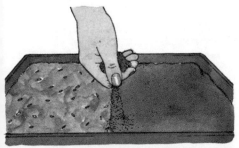

Sow seed sparingly (above) and cover seed boxes with glass and newspaper (below)

Remove covering once seedlings have germinated (above) and pot the herbs on when each has four leaves (below)

with a good seed compost. Water the compost and leave it for 24 hours before sowing the seed. Firm down the compost and sow the seed sparingly on top. Cover lightly with a little extra compost and firm down again. Cover the boxes with a piece of glass and then a layer of newspaper until the seed has germinated. Set the boxes in a greenhouse or warm place where the

temperature is more or less constant and not above 15°C (60°F). Once germination has occurred, remove glass and newspaper and leave the seedlings to grow until each one has four leaves. Pot the herbs on by setting them out 5 cm (2 inches) apart in boxes or in flower pots, filled with potting compost.

When the seedlings have 8-10 leaves, start hardening them off by carrying the boxes or pots outside during the day in warm weather. After a week to ten days, plant the herbs out.

Herb seed sown out of doors has to take its chance with the weather, so do not sow too early. Wait until all danger from frost is over, usually about May. Sow the seed directly into the herb bed and cover lightly with compost. Seed sown too deeply will not germinate. Once the seedlings are growing well, thin the plants to the recommended distance apart. If the weather is cloudy and cold put a cloche over the seeds to help them to germinate.

Perennial herbs can also be grown successfully from seed. Fennel, sage, lovage, hyssop and salad burnet are all easy to grow. Other herbs such as sweet cicely, parsley and some of the thymes take time to germinate. It is necessary to buy plants of the perennial French tarragon as it does not set seed. The slow-growing shrubby herbs rosemary, bay and lemon verbena are best bought as container-grown plants. An advantage in purchasing container-grown perennial herbs is that they can be planted out at any time of year provided the weather is warm and moist.

PLANTING IN CONTAINERS

To grow herbs in containers make sure the vessel is large enough to give all the requirements it needs when fully grown. Do not plant too many herbs in one pot. Different herbs can be set into a single container provided they each need the same amount of soil, light, air and watering. Set the containers, whether indoors or outside, in their permanent positions. Fill with a mixture of good soil and compost almost to the rim of the container and firm down the soil. If the container is too full of soil there will be no room for the extra soil which clings to the herb when planting. Leave space at the top of the container for watering and for adding extra plant food in later months. Water the soil well and leave for 24 hours before planting.

ROUTINE CARE

A simple programme of routine care, if carried out regularly, will provide you with a constant supply of lovely fragrant plants.

In the herb garden it is important to keep the ground free of weeds, which compete with the herbs for food and light. Hand-weed the bed when the plants are small so as not to disturb the roots. Hoe carefully between established herbs at regular intervals. This will help not only to keep down the weeds but will loosen the soil round the herbs so they get sufficient water. To prevent loss of water through evaporation, put peat round the plants, then hoe later in the season. In a long spell of dry weather water the plants in the evenings when the sun has gone down. If your herbs are set in black polythene film there should be few weeds and very little watering will be necessary.

Organic fertilizers such as bone meal, hoof and horn and dried blood can be applied in the spring to act throughout the growing season. Compost is valuable in supplying the soil with humus. After using it in the preparation of the herb bed, compost can be forked lightly into the top soil in summer or used as a mulch to retain moisture round the plants.

In an ornamental or decorative herb garden where the plants will not be subjected to continued cutting then the addition of bone meal or compost such as is given to a herbaceous bed is all that will be required. In a herb garden where a considerable amount of the herb plant will be harvested a more than average amount of nutrients must be added to the soil to allow the plants to recover before the winter.

Be on the lookout for pests or signs of disease in the herbs and deal with them promptly to keep the plants in good condition.

Once a fortnight in the growing season water the herbs with a liquid fertilizer, available from garden centres. This is necessary because if you are constantly picking the leaves the plants need extra food to ensure continued strong growth.

As they appear, cut off the flower heads of those herbs whose leaves you wish to gather so that the full flavour and scent will be concentrated there. Cut off the flowers of chamomile and verbascum for drying as soon as they are fully opened. This is a tedious task but one worth the effort as all the value of the plant goes

into the flowers and this disappears as the flower fades.

In early spring or in the autumn spread a small amount of organic plant food over the herb bed and gently fork it in. Do not give the herbs too much fertilizer or the plants will grow too quickly and have little scent or flavour as a result. Before winter sets in, take up the annuals. Cut off the dying stems at the base of those perennials which die down. Put in stakes for these plants, in case you forget where they are next year. Cut back a little of the year's growth on woody-stemmed herbs so that they will not straggle and break, but form strong bushy growth.

A number of herbs can be dug up and put into pots to keep indoors for the winter. Chives, mint, parsley and marjoram will overwinter happily inside a greenhouse, a frame or in the house. Other herbs such as pineapple sage and rose geranium will not survive the winter outside and have to be brought into warmth during the winter months.

Herbs kept indoors need a good supply of water and should never be allowed to dry out. In the winter, take care not to let the atmosphere become too dry – central heating can be a killer. A bowl of water next to the herbs will keep the air round the plants humid.

Make sure herbs in containers and those indoors are regularly supplied with plant food. With only a limited amount of soil in the containers it can soon become impoverished.

PROPAGATION

Once the herbs are established in the garden you can easily increase the number of plants yourself rather than buying in new ones. The simplest way, in late season, is to allow the flowers on one or two stems to go to seed. Leave the seeds to fall on the soil and new seedlings will soon appear. Angelica and lovage are best dealt with by this method, for their seed will only germinate when absolutely fresh. With other herbs, remove the seeds and sow them in spring in the usual manner. Treat annual herbs in this way.

There are a number of herbs which never or very rarely set seed. To increase your stock of these plants other methods have to be used. Provided you choose the right time of year to be sure of success, you can build up the number of herbs by taking stem or root cuttings, by root division or by layering shoots or branches.

Stem cuttings

These are best taken during the summer months from a well-established herb, as long as you do not take too many off one plant at any one time. Take the cutting from a new shoot and not from one which shows signs of flowering. Cut the stem 10-15 cm (4-6 inches) long just below a leaf bud and remove all leaves from the lower half of the cutting. Dip the cut end into water, shake off the drops, then dip it into rooting powder. Plant the cutting firmly into a pot filled with moist potting compost. Put the pot in the shade until you see signs of growth and keep the soil damp.

Another method is to put the cuttings into a shallow pot or seed box full of sharp sand. Rooting powder and sharp sand are available at garden shops. If you plan to take many cuttings set them in a shallow trench in the garden. Run a little sharp sand along the bottom of the trench, set in the cuttings and firm down the soil round them.

Some of the shrubby herbs such as rosemary or lemon verbena may take weeks to start growing, so give the cuttings plenty of time before you discard them. As soon as the cuttings have rooted, which will be evident from the appearance of new fresh leaves at the top, they can be planted in their permanent positions.

Root cuttings

Take these in the autumn from herbs such as angelica and marshmallow. The mints too can be increased in this way. When lifting the plant cut pieces of the root about 1 cm (¼ inch) thick and chop them in 5 cm (2 inch) lengths. Fill a seed box half full of potting compost and lay the roots on top. Cover the roots with about 1.5 cm (½ inch) more soil. Give the seed box a good watering and set it in the shade. Cover with a piece of glass and then a sheet of newspaper until signs of growth appear. Transplant the herbs into pots for planting out later.

BELOW: Take stem cuttings from a new shoot and remove bottom leaves

BELOW: Chop root cuttings into 5 cm (2 inch) lengths and set in a seed box to germinate.

Root division

This has to be done in early spring or in the autumn when the herb has either become too large for the bed or when it is going to be moved. If it has been a good growing season some herbs put on an enormous amount of growth, so dividing the plants is an easy method of increasing your stock.

Carefully dig up the whole herb and, using a spade, cut the plant into smaller clumps, or pull the roots apart if it is easier. Replant the divided roots into their new permanent positions and give them plenty of water until they are established.

Layering

An easy way to increase herbs, this can be done at any time of the year. Creeping species such as mints layer themselves, but others like rosemary and sage need help. Choose a strong growing branch close to the ground and, about 25 cm (10 inches) from the tip of the branch, make a small slanting cut. Moisten the cut with water and put some rooting powder on to it. Make a small hole in the soil and fill it with compost or sharp sand. Gently bend the branch down and bury the cut in the hole. Firm the soil

BELOW: Pull the roots apart to divide a small plant
BOTTOM: Make sure the branch to be layered is firmly secured in the ground

over the cut and secure it with a piece of bent wire stuck into the ground. Make sure the layered piece will not blow about otherwise the branch will bob up again. After about five to six weeks the branch should have taken root. Cut the rooted stem from the main plant and set it into its new position.

HARVESTING THE HERBS

In summer, herb leaves and flowers can be freshly picked as you require them. To ensure a good supply of your favourite herbs through the winter you can freeze them or, if no freezer is available, dry the herbs and store them in glass jars in a cupboard. Herbs gathered for preserving must be at their best for fragrance and flavour; the right time for this varies from herb to herb. As a rule cut the herb just before the plant comes into flower. Do not cut the whole plant; take only the best sprigs or leaves, otherwise the herb will not survive.

There are some exceptions to these general rules for harvesting herbs. Summer savory and thyme are gathered when the plant is in full flower. Bay leaves can be picked individually all the year round. Tarragon should be picked when it has grown about 30 cm (12 inches) high. When harvesting the bushy perennials lovage and fennel, cut back to about one third of their growth each time – they soon recover and produce plenty more fresh young leaves. Woody-stemmed perennial herbs can be preserved in small quantities during the summer months by cutting a few sprigs at a time. Otherwise have a grand freezing or drying session in the autumn after cutting the plants back to half the year's growth.

During the growing season annual herbs for preserving such as basil, chervil and dill can be cut down to within 15 cm (6 inches) of the base. In the autumn when you remove the plant altogether you can take another crop of leaves to freeze or dry.

Herbs are best gathered in the morning after dew has evaporated and before the heat of the sun is too great to affect the flavour. Try not to crush the leaves as you pick them. Wash the leaves gently in water if necessary and shake off the excess. No washing is necessary for flowers, petals or seeds. Roots which are dried need a good scrub to make sure all the soil is removed.

PRESERVING HERBS

It is of course very useful to be able to preserve your herbs and this can be done by freezing and by drying.

Freezing herbs

One of the simplest ways of preserving your herbs is to freeze them; indeed there are many which are better frozen than dried. Basil, mint, parsley and tarragon all freeze very well and retain their full flavour. The leaves for freezing should be clean and dry – discard any that are not perfect. Pick the leaves from the stems and place the individual herbs in small plastic bags or in plastic wrap. Freeze tarragon in sprigs rather than picking off the leaves. It is better to have a number of bags with a little herb in each as usually only a small quantity is needed in a recipe. You can mix two or three herbs together in one bag ready to add to a stew or casserole. Place all the bags in one large plastic bag so they do not get lost in the freezer. Chopped fresh herbs can be frozen by adding them to water in ice cube trays; when you want to use one, simply melt a cube.

Drying herbs

Herbs dried properly will remain green and retain all the flavour and scent of the plant. The process of cutting, drying and storing the herbs needs to be done as quickly as possible. Obviously thick fleshy leaves, flowers, petals and seeds will take longer to dry.

There are a number of points to remember when drying your herbs. With the exception of bay, use whole stems of leafy specimens rather than stripping off the leaves. Chives and Welsh onion tops should be washed and then chopped finely before drying. Spread the washed herbs out on sheets of greaseproof paper on wire cake trays. Do not pile the herb up high, but spread it out carefully – it will dry more quickly. Put the wire trays into a cool oven, or a warm airing cupboard. Leave the oven door slightly ajar so that the moisture evaporating from the leaves can escape. Always make sure that air can circulate around the trays. Never dry the leafy herbs next to chives as the strong flavour will permeate the milder herbs.

The length of drying time varies widely. Rosemary and sage take much longer than fennel or chervil. When fully dried the leaves should be crisp and friable and the stems can be discarded. Herbs should always be dried in the dark as light can affect the fragrance and flavour.

Flowers can be dried by laying them out on nylon netting stretched over a wooden frame in the airing cupboard. Small flowers and petals can be placed between sheets of newspaper and dried in a darkened airy room. Under the bed is a good place. Petals and flowers usually take from 10 to 14 days to dry and should be crisp and crackly when fully dry.

Seeds take a long time to dry. When the seed heads on the plant look dry and brown cut them off with a long stem attached. Tie the stems together carefully and lay them on newspaper so as not to lose any seeds in the process. Gently put the bunch of seed heads into a large brown paper bag and tie the bag loosely so that it does not fall off. Hang the bunch by the stems so the seed heads are upside down in the bag. As the seeds dry they will fall into the bag. After some weeks test the seeds. If the seeds smell at all musty or will easily snap in two, the seeds are not dry. Remove the seeds from the bag, spread them between sheets of brown paper and leave in an airy room for two or three weeks.

Roots and rhizomes for drying should be scrubbed until clean and cut into 5 cm (2 inch) lengths. Spread out the pieces on nylon netting so that air can circulate round them and set them in a warm dark place to dry. Both roots and rhizomes take a long time to dry, usually about six weeks, but this can vary.

Storing the herbs When the leafy herbs are dry, immediately rub the leaves from the stems by hand, crushing them into small pieces. Petals and flowers are left whole. Seeds are also stored whole – once ground they lose flavour much more rapidly.

To store your herbs for winter, place each in a screwtop jar and keep them in the dark. Do not mix herbs together in a jar unless you are making a special mixture when the quantity of each herb is carefully worked out beforehand. If you wish to store your herbs in tins, put the herb in a cotton bag before putting it into the tin. Direct contact with metal can affect the flavour. Label each jar and add the date. Dried herbs do not last forever and begin to lose their flavour after about a year. Petals, flowers and seeds can all be stored in the same manner.

PESTS AND DISEASES

Pests and diseases do not present a great problem in the herb garden because the strong aromatic oils contained in the leaves of most herbs keep the pests at bay. None will be found near camphor, thyme, lavender or juniper. Plants like these can help to control pests on more succulent herbs. Those pests which do attack the plants are fairly easy to control.

A certain amount of protection can be provided by planting the strongest smelling herbs among those that are more susceptible. It is most important that as far as possible natural organic products should be used. Chemicals might alter the flavour and scent of the herb and drive away the bees.

LEFT TO RIGHT: Caterpillar attacking young basil leaves; a snail on a young tarragon shoot; red spider mite on basil; powdery mildew on bergamot; mint rust; damping off disease on seedlings

PESTS

Caterpillars attack young leaves of basil, tarragon, sweet knotted marjoram and summer savory. The easiest solution is to remove the caterpillars by hand in a small herb bed but, if preferred, a light spray with derris powder will get rid of them. Derris powder is a perfectly safe organic insecticide and if sprayed on the herbs in the evening will not harm them for picking next day; wash the herbs before use.

Slugs and snails can be a nuisance when the weather is warm and wet; the young shoots of tarragon and bergamot are their particular favourites. A sprinkling of lime round the plants should help, or you can use slug pellets.

Another pest which in hot dry conditions might attack herbs is the red spider mite, a minute insect which attaches itself to the underside of the leaves by means of a fine web and feeds on the sap. The leaves turn a mottled

greyish brown. Usually the spider mite only appears on succulent herbs growing under glass. The remedy is to use a liquid derris spray.

DISEASES

Very few diseases are likely to appear in the herb garden. Powdery mildew does sometimes appear on bergamot, especially the pink-flowered variety, but this can be controlled by spraying with sulphur dust or a spray made from the dried stems and leaves of horsetail (*Equisetum arvense*). To make the spray use 25 g (1 oz) of horsetail to 2.75 litres (5 pints) of water. Bring to the boil and boil for 20 minutes. Allow the mixture to cool before straining and using as a spray. Use this mixture only on fully grown plants; if the process has to be repeated on the same plant, dilute the spray for the second application.

'Damping off' disease affects seedlings only. The base of the stem goes black and the plant withers. To prevent this happening do not sow the seeds too thickly in the box, do not use unsterilized compost and do not over-water.

Other ways to combat this disease are either to use a seed dressing at the outset or to water the seed boxes before sowing with a solution of Cheshunt compound, which is available at garden shops. This last process should be repeated when the seedlings appear and again when pricking them out. There are 'seed saver' preparations on the market; follow the manufacturer's instructions for use closely. If any seedlings are affected, remove and burn them, then water the remaining ones with the Cheshunt compound. Basil is particularly prone to 'damping off' disease.

Mint rust is a fungus disease which attacks all varieties of mint. The spores attack the roots then appear on the underside of the leaves and gradually spread up the stems. The only remedy is to remove the plant and burn it, then sterilize the soil with diluted Jeyes fluid.

A herb garden full of sturdy well-cared-for plants is the safest and best way to avoid pests and diseases. Keep the weeds down and water the plants in a dry spell and you will be rewarded with a trouble-free garden.

COMMON HERBS

ANGELICA*

Angelica archangelica biennial

A large handsome plant, angelica can grow to 1.8 m (6 ft) and is a lovely herb for the back of the garden in a partially shaded position where it can act as a windbreak for the more delicate herbs. The big spreading leaves are divided into three leaflets. Clusters of small greenish white flowers appear on the tops of the stems in the second year of growth.

Angelica is usually treated as a biennial, but if the flowerheads are cut off immediately the seeds set, the plant will continue to grow for a further few years. If the flowerheads are left to seed in the second year the plant will die. Angelica must be grown from seed that is absolutely fresh and must be subjected to winter frost before germination can be guaranteed. The seed which falls from the plant in the second year will germinate early the following spring to provide a mass of seedlings growing around the old plant. You can leave them quite happily to grow where they fall or you can transplant the seedlings into pots or a small trench in the garden.

It is easiest to buy your first angelica plant growing in a container. In spring set angelica into its permanent position. Once your new plant is established you can start to use the leaves although for the full flavour and scent you should wait until the second year.

Use: Angelica has a sweet scent and a pleasant but rather strong flavour. Candied angelica is well known as a cake decoration and can easily be made at home. Cut the young hollow stems into 5 cm (2 inch) lengths and boil them in a heavy sugar syrup until transparent and tender. Strain and allow the stems to dry completely before storing in screw-top jars. The candied stems impart a delicious flavour when cooked with rhubarb or gooseberries. Add young leaves to water when poaching fish and as a flavouring when making rhubarb jam. The midribs of the larger leaves can be eaten like celery. Cut them out and blanch them, by plunging them into boiling water then immediately into cold water.

Use the seeds infused in milk when making a custard. Make a herb tea using the chopped leaves to induce perspiration in a feverish cold. Add dried angelica leaves or seeds to pot-pourri mixtures.

BASIL***

Ocimum basilicum (sweet basil) half-hardy annual

Sweet basil and a smaller leaved variety known as bush basil are the two most commonly grown. Both basils grow about 30-60 cm (1-2 ft) tall. The sweet basil has broad dark green leaves with a strong spicy smell. The leaves of bush basil are a lighter green and though smaller are very much more profuse. The spikes of small white flowers appear early in the season.

Both basils are annuals and can be grown from your own seed year after year. A word of warning about sowing basil seed out of doors: it is difficult to grow from seed outside in temperate climates. The seed takes a long time to germinate and the seedlings will not thrive until the weather is really warm. This cuts down the length of its growing season and as a result there will be fewer leaves for picking.

In early spring sow basil seeds indoors in pots or seed boxes filled with compost. Cover them with a piece of glass and a sheet of newspaper. Once the seedlings appear, remove the glass and newspaper. Do not sow the seed too thickly in the boxes because of the danger of damping-off disease. Once they have germinated, do not overwater the seedlings. When they are large enough, plant them out about 15-20 cm (6-8 inches) apart in a sunny sheltered position. The leaves are ready for picking about six weeks after planting. Pinch out the flower heads as they appear to keep all the flavour in the leaves, allowing one plant or stem to flower and set seed for next year's plants. At the end of the season, pull up the plants and keep the seed dry in a brown paper bag.

Use: The strong peppery flavour of basil makes it an ideal seasoning herb in the kitchen; it is equally good fresh and dried. Add it to all tomato dishes to bring out their full flavour. Use with soups,

salads and sauces and for spaghetti dishes.

Use a small amount of the chopped fresh leaves in vegetable salads and tomato juice. Add basil to minced beef re-cipes and to sausagemeat for sausage rolls. A few finely chopped leaves can be added to egg dishes; they add a good flavour to omelettes. Add a tiny amount to butter sauces to

Angelica is a strikingly handsome plant with attractive flowers

accompany fish and sprinkle over cooked peas and boiled potatoes.

BAY***

Laurus nobilis evergreen tree

A slow-growing small evergreen tree, bay is a handsome formal herb to have in the garden. It can grow to 12 m (40 ft) but takes many years to reach that height. The glossy dark green leaves have a leathery texture and when fully grown are about 5-7.5 cm (2-3 inches) long. Small yellow flowers bloom in early summer and are followed by purplish black berries.

It is easiest to buy from a herb nursery a small bay plant which will already be one or two years old. Container-grown plants can be planted out at any time of the year but it is best to plant out all evergreens in showery weather between March and May.

BELOW: Bay, although slow-growing, is a handsome plant

Plant bay in a sunny sheltered position preferably facing south. Do not disturb the root ball when taking bay out of its pot. Dig a hole large enough to accommodate the roots. Put the plant in the hole and gently fill in with soil, firming it down as you go. Tread round the plant to make sure it will not shift in the wind. During the first winter, protect the bay tree by surrounding it with wire netting. Bay can easily be grown in a container which can be brought indoors in a severe winter.

Once bay is established, the fully matured leaves can be picked for use. In August or September stem cuttings can be taken from a strong growing plant but these take a long time to root.

Fragrant aromatic bay leaves are used in many recipes and are well known to all cooks. The leaves can be used fresh or dried. It is advisable to pick and dry some leaves during the growing season for winter use, rather than picking them from the bush all the year round.

Use: Bay leaves are used for flavouring beef or pork casseroles and are a must when poaching or boiling ham or fish. Add a crushed bay leaf to stuffings and made-up meat dishes. A bay leaf put into the water when boiling spaghetti or rice gives a good flavour. Use bay leaves when making pickles and chutneys. It is especially good for pickled beetroot. Bay is one of the herbs in a bouquet garni – the bunch of herbs added to soups, stews or stocks while they are cooking. A small piece of bay leaf can be placed in the dish when making a rice pudding.

BERGAMOT**

Monarda didyma hardy perennial

A strong-growing perennial, bergamot grows about 60 cm (2 ft) high with dark green mint-scented leaves and rather untidy-looking flowers in shades of bright soft red, pink, mauve or white. The red bergamot provides a lovely splash of colour in the herb garden. It flowers over a long period and is a well-known bee plant.

Buy in your first bergamot from the herb nursery in whichever colour you like. From then on you can renew your stock by gathering seed. The seed will come true to

RIGHT: Bergamot flowers provide a welcome splash of colour

form. Sow seed in early spring where plants are to flower and pinch out any unwanted seedlings to leave the plants 30-45 cm (12-18 inches) apart.

Plant bergamot in the autumn in a sunny moist spot in the herb garden. The shallow, fibrous roots soon spread and every two to three years the clump should be lifted and divided. Perform this task in spring as plants divided in the autumn may die completely in the winter. When replanting, use only the newer outside roots. Cut leafy stems and remove the leaves for use to keep the plant trim.

After planting, put peat or leaf mould round the plants to keep the roots moist. The plants die down in winter so use a stake to mark their position. In early spring watch for caterpillars and snails which attack the new leaves.

Bergamot is a useful plant

for flower arrangements. To obtain bigger and better flowers for display, cut off all the flowerheads in the first season. The following year there will be a lovely show of much larger flowers.

Use: Bergamot leaves and flowers dry well, retaining their minty scent and flavour. The leaves and flowers can be added to pot-pourri mixtures and used to make a sweet-scented tea. A few dried crushed leaves mixed in with Indian tea adds a delicate flavour.

Bergamot tea is refreshing and soothes a sore throat. Fresh leaves and flowers give a pleasant flavour to summer fruit drinks. Make a sugar syrup adding bergamot, both leaves and flowers. If the flowers are red this gives an attractive colour to the syrup which can be added to fresh fruit salads.

Borage

BORAGE*
Borago officinalis hardy annual
A very colourful herb which grows up to 90 cm (3 ft) high, borage is not recommended for the small herb garden. It self seeds freely and unless it is kept in check you will find borage seedlings coming up all over the garden. The thick stems and rough-textured leaves are covered with hairs. Throughout the summer borage is a mass of lovely clear blue star-shaped flowers. It looks its best grown on a bank or in a raised bed where the drooping flowers can be seen from below.

In early April borage seed can be sown outside where it is to flower. This is important as borage does not transplant well. The seed germinates easily and quickly. Choose a position in full sun and poor light soil. Thin out the seedlings to about 25-30 cm (10-12 inches) apart. In a windy spot it is best to stake the plant because the many-branched fleshy stems become top heavy and after a downpour of rain or high winds will be found lying on the ground.

Borage leaves are always used freshly picked but the flowers, gathered just as they have opened, dry beautifully and retain their pure blue colour. Mix them with other dried herbs in pot-pourri mixtures. Before using the flowers make sure you have removed all but the petals and stamens. **Use:** Borage leaves have a pleasant refreshing taste rather like cucumber. Pick only the young tender leaves with a few fresh flowers and add them to green salads. When greens are scarce, cook and eat borage leaves like spinach with a knob of butter and some freshly ground black pepper. Sprinkle finely chopped leaves over cut tomatoes before baking them and add leaves to cream cheese for stuffed cucumbers. Use some leaves to bring out the full flavour in cucumber soup or sauce and especially when making cucumber chutney.

For a cooling summer drink make a herb tea using both leaves and flowers; leave it to cool then strain it. Mix with lemon juice and sugar to taste and serve well chilled. Add a sprig of borage to cider, apple juice or chilled white wine.

Hot borage tea can be taken as a gentle laxative.

Candied borage flowers make a pretty decoration on cakes and ice creams and floating in a fruit salad. Dip the flowers first in beaten egg white, making sure they are completely covered, then into fine sugar. Leave the flowers to dry and harden on a nylon sieve. Candied in this way the flowers are for immediate use only.

CHAMOMILE*

Matricaria chamomilla (German chamomile) hardy annual
Anthemis nobilis (English chamomile) perennial
Both chamomiles are fragrant feathery-leaved herbs with small daisy-like white flowers, but their growing habits are completely different. The evergreen perennial English chamomile is a low-growing creeping herb mostly used as ground cover or to make a sweet-smelling lawn. It is also a useful edging plant. A variety of the English chamomile called 'Treneague' is non-flowering and cannot therefore cross pollinate with the annual chamomile. This avoids any confusion that might arise because German chamomile is the only variety that you can use in the home.

German chamomile is a charming annual growing up to 30 cm (12 inches) high and very easy to cultivate. Because it self-sows freely the first packet of seed is the only one you're likely to buy. The plants will continue to come up year after year. Each one produces many flowers, the only part of the herb which is used.

German chamomile seed can be sown either in the autumn or early spring. Sow seed in its final growing position in a moist sunny spot and thin out the seedlings to 15 cm (6 inches) apart. Sow English chamomile in seed boxes and transfer seedlings, when large enough, to the open ground. Increase the number of plants by layering the runners or else by dividing the roots in the autumn.

Pick the flowers of German chamomile as soon as they open. Because there will be a continuous supply, it will be a lengthy but well worthwhile task to pick them at this stage when the flowers are at the peak of their fragrance. Dry the flowers on nylon netting in an airing cupboard and store them in glass screwtop jars or add them to your pot-pourri mixture.
Use: The sweet-smelling flowers can be used fresh or dried. The dried flowers keep their lovely scent for a long time. Chamomile tea is a fragrant drink which is both pleasant to take and good for the digestion. An infusion of the flowers used as a rinse on blonde hair will help to keep it a good colour, soft and shiny. To clear the skin and as an effective remedy for a congestive cold make up a strong infusion in a bowl and inhale by covering the head and bowl with a towel, and breathing in the warm fragrance for about five to ten minutes. A strong decoction can be added to the bath water or a small muslin bag full of flowers placed under the running hot water tap, to perfume the water and provide a refreshing bath which is also good for the skin. Use the infusion for a gargle or mouthwash to sweeten the breath and as a remedy for sore gums.

CHERVIL*

Anthriscus cerefolium bi-annual

So simple and rewarding is it to grow, that chervil must be included in every herb garden. With lacy foliage and clusters of little white flowers, it reaches a height of about 30-45 cm (12-18 inches).

Chervil is a seasoning herb with a mild, delicious flavour. Large amounts can be added to most savoury dishes.

Chervil is raised from seed and, as the plants are small, it is important to provide yourself with a good succession of plants. In the early autumn sow some seed in a sunny position in time for the seedlings to get established before the winter. The plants die down in winter but will come up very early in spring, long before many other herbs appear. When they are large enough, thin the seedlings to 20 cm (8 inches) apart.

In early spring, sow chervil seed in partial shade as the hot summer sun is liable to scorch and discolour the leaves. Always sow chervil where the plants are to grow as seedlings do not transplant well. Successive sowings can be made through the summer months. If the flowers on some of the plants are left to go to seed, chervil will self sow quite happily. Alternatively, gather the seed for the autumn sowing and sow them in a different spot in the herb garden.

Chervil leaves dry well and it is useful to have them through the winter to use on their own or in herb mixtures. They combine well with other herbs.

Use: Chervil makes an excellent herb soup which is delicious served hot in winter. In the summer make a slightly thicker soup and serve it chilled with a little chopped mint sprinkled on top. Use chopped chervil leaves in salad dressings and in green or vegetable salads. Add chervil to sauces accompanying fish or chicken. Chervil soufflé is a light tasty dish and chopped leaves go well in other egg dishes.

Chervil does not have an overpowering taste so you can safely experiment with it, adding chopped leaves to your own savoury recipes.

Chervil is widely used in French cooking. It is added to vinaigrette, bearnaise and ravigote sauces and is one of the herbs in *fines herbes* – a mixture of delicately flavoured herbs used in many dishes.

CHIVES*

Allium schoenoprasum

perennial

Attractive little plants with thin tubular leaves, chives grow about 25 cm (10 inches) high. A clump of chives is essential in the herb garden. Their delicate onion flavour enhances savoury dishes.

The neat growing habit of chives makes them good edging plants in the herb bed. If one or two clumps are left to bloom, their bright mauve pompom flowers provide a gay splash of colour.

Since chives are slow to grow from seed it is easier to start by buying a small plant. Thereafter you can gather your own seed for sowing in the usual way. Clumps which get too big can, in early spring, be dug up and carefully divided. Divide the clumps every two or three years and make sure the new plants are well established before picking the leaves. The whole plant dies down in winter so put in a stake to mark their positions if you are likely to forget where they are.

Plant the chives in sun or partial shade in good soil, spacing the plants about 15 cm (6 inches) apart. At intervals during the growing season feed them with a liquid fertilizer, especially when you see the tips of the leaves going brown. Towards the autumn you can dig up a small clump and transfer it to a container to take indoors for the winter. It will continue growing in the warmth and so give you fresh chives to cut all the year round. In spring the exhausted plant can be thrown out.

Chives can very easily be dried in the oven but remember to dry them on their own or their strong smell will permeate other herbs. Leaves for drying can be cut at any time, but do not cut too many from a single clump at once, unless you feed the soil afterwards. The plant will not survive too severe a cutting.

Use: Chives chopped finely are used to flavour soups, sauces and salad dressings. Add chives to soft cheeses and mashed potatoes. Mix them with parsley to make a herb butter to garnish steak or chops. It is a good flavouring for fish and all egg dishes where only a touch of onion flavour is needed. There are countless ways of using chives and you will find there are many recipes of your own to which you can add them.

DILL*

Anethum graveolens annual
A decorative herb, dill looks at its best when a number of plants are clumped together in the herb bed. The delicate feathery leaves give an almost filmy effect to the plants and the greenish yellow flowers add soft colour. The whole plant grows 60-90 cm (2-3 ft) high.

Dill seed is best sown directly into its growing position as seedlings do not transplant well. In the spring, when danger from frost is over, sow the seed thinly in a sheltered sunny spot and cover the seed with a light sprinkling of soil. When the seedlings appear thin the plants to 25 cm (10 inches) apart. Plants need to be protected from the wind but if a sheltered position is impossible to find in your gar-den, stake the individual plants when they reach 45 cm (18 inches) high. Keep the soil round the young plants free of weeds that compete with the herb for nourishment. Fork the soil over lightly to keep it aerated.

Cut off the flowers of some of the plants as they appear so you can pick and use the leaves. Other plants can be left to go to seed. Once the seeds have formed and are starting to ripen the seed heads should be covered to stop the birds eating them. Tie pieces of muslin or fine netting over the seed heads. The light and warmth will continue the ripening process and you will be sure of a full harvest.

Dill leaves take only a short time to dry and are useful to have in the kitchen during the winter. Seeds take much lon-

Chervil is an easy plant to grow and has pretty, delicate foliage

ger to dry. The method for drying seeds is explained on page 27.
Use: Dill leaves have a delicate flavour which combines well with cucumber. You can add fresh or dried leaves to cucumber soup, sauce and chutney. Use the leaves in potato salad, in cream sauces to accompany fish or chicken and sprinkled over grilled lamb chops.

Dill seed, which has a much stronger flavour, is just as useful as the leaf. Add it to apple pie, bread or cooked cabbage and carrots. Use the seed in spiced beetroot or pickled baby cucumbers. Dill seed tea is very calming, is good for the digestion and will also help you to sleep.

Fennel

FENNEL*
Foeniculum vulgare perennial

A tall handsome herb, fennel grows 1.2-1.5 m (4-5 ft) high. The plant is a mist of feathery bright green leaves and has large flat topped clusters of yellow flowers. It is familiar to those who live near the sea where fennel grows wild along the lanes and clifftops not far from the shore.

A variety of fennel known as bronze fennel because of the colour of its leaves is an elegant plant to use in the background of an ornamental herb garden. Its growing habit is the same as common fennel. Another form of the common plant is the annual, Florence fennel, which grows about 30 cm (12 inches) high and produces fat bulbous leaf stems at the base of the plant. The leaves can be used in the same way as other fennels. The thick turnip-like base is dug up before the plant flowers and eaten as a vegetable. To keep the base white and to make it grow bigger, earth up the bottom when it is the size of a hen's egg. After about ten days to a fortnight the swollen root should be ready to dig up.

Fennel is easily grown from seed and thrives in a sunny sheltered position. In February sow seed indoors in gentle heat so that young plants can be set out into the herb garden in late April. Otherwise sow seeds in April directly into their growing position and pinch out unwanted seedlings. Leave some flowers on the plants to go to seed.

Both leaves and seeds are used in the kitchen; the seeds have a stronger fuller flavour than the leaves. Both can easily be dried for winter use.

Use: Fennel leaves and seeds have a very pleasant liquorice-like flavour. Florence fennel can be eaten either grated raw in salads or cooked and garnished with a butter sauce. Use fennel leaves when cooking all kinds of poached or grilled fish. Add chopped leaves to cheese sauce in macaroni cheese; a few freshly picked leaves add an unusual flavour to a green salad.

Use fennel seed in seed cake and herb breads, and in pasta dishes.

Fennel tea, made with leaves or seeds, is good for the digestion and helps you to sleep. Taken daily first thing in the morning its digestive properties are helpful in a slimming programme. A strong decoction of fennel seed added to yogurt makes a good face pack for toning the skin. A pack made of the leaves alone helps to smooth out premature wrinkles.

FEVERFEW*
Chrysanthemum parthenium
perennial

Feverfew bears small daisy-like white flowers which grow in profusion throughout the summer months. The yellowy green leaves have a pungent scent which is somewhat like chamomile. Feverfew is a bushy plant growing up to 60 cm (2 ft) high and takes up little space in the herb bed. Another variety of feverfew has bright yellow flowers and there is one with a very pretty double white flowerhead known as 'Silver ball'.

Feverfew is easily raised from seed. In early spring sow the seed out of doors where it is to flower and it will bloom in the first summer. The seed takes about three weeks to germinate but once the seedlings appear they grow very quickly. Feverfew prefers a sunny position in the herb bed but will flourish equally well in some shade. Pinch out unwanted seedlings, leaving the plants 20-25 cm (8-10 inches) apart.

Feverfew self seeds very readily, and by the second year you will find seedlings coming up all round the parent plant. It follows that you will have no problem increasing your stock of plants, but to ensure that they come true to form, you can take cuttings from the base of the plant in the summer. Make sure the cutting has a heel of the main plant.

Its many tiny flowers make feverfew a useful plant for flower arrangements; it lasts well in water. Both leaves and flowers can be dried successfully for winter use but should be dried separately as the flowers take much longer to dry than the leaves.

Use: As its name implies, feverfew is a medicinal herb, and was originally taken to bring down a fever. Fresh or dried flowers and leaves can be used to make an infusion which is a good remedy for headaches and which, taken over a period of time, is believed to be good for migraine. An infusion of the flowers is helpful for rheumatism.

Feverfew

GARLIC*
Allium sativum annual

A very distinctive strongly flavoured herb, garlic has flat
narrow tubular leaves rising
from a bulb and it produces
tiny bulblets at the top of the
single stem. These should be
removed so that all the plant's
energy goes into the bulb
growing in the ground. All the
flavour of garlic is contained in
that bulb, which is made up of
a cluster of bulblets known as
cloves. Each garlic bulb is
made up of about 9-10 cloves
which are held together inside
a silvery skin. Garlic is an ac-
quired taste but for those who
like it, it is well worthwhile
growing a few garlic plants.
They take up little space in the
herb bed and are a better flavour when used fresh.

Early in spring plant the tiny
bulblets or cloves from a mature garlic bulb. Put them in a
sunny spot in good garden
soil, spaced 15 cm (6 inches)
apart. In mild winters plant
garlic in December or January
so that the bulbs will mature
much earlier.

When the tops of the stems
begin to wilt and bend downwards the garlic bulbs are
ready to be harvested. Dig or
pull up the entire plant – do
not remove any of the green
tops at this stage. Lay the
whole herb on wire cake trays
and leave to dry in an airy
room. Gradually the skin
covering the bulb becomes
papery and crackles to the
touch. Finally remove the tops
and save for next year's seed.
Leave the bulbs out for a further two or three days then store
them in a cool place.

The strong flavour of garlic
is not to everyone's taste but,

used sparingly, it brings out
the flavours in many dishes.
Use: Garlic is a useful seasoning herb and in small
amounts, finely chopped, it
can be used in many savoury
dishes – especially with meat
and in casseroles, with chick-
en and added to sauces. A little
garlic juice can be added to
salad dressings. Garlic butter
is made by mixing a crushed
garlic clove with butter.
Spread the butter on to slices
of French bread, wrap the
bread in foil and leave in a hot
oven for 10 minutes. This is
delicious eaten with soups,
salads and cold meats.

HYSSOP*
Hyssopus officinalis perennial

Hysop is neat in appearance,
woody-stemmed, and grows
about 60 cm (2 ft) high. The
small narrow leaves are a dark
glossy green with a strong but
pleasant scent. The little flowers grow in spikes at the top of
the stems and are blue, pink or
white depending on the variety. A clump of the three different coloured hyssops looks
very well in the herb garden
and flowers continually from
July to October. Hyssop is well
known as a bee plant.

In mild areas hyssop re-
mains green throughout the
winter. It is useful grown as a
low hedge.

Hyssop grows well in full
sun and a light soil. It can easily be grown from seed sown in
spring out of doors in its
permanent position. Thin the
seedlings to about 25 cm (10
inches) apart. If only one plant
is required it is best to buy it
from a herb nursery.

Alchemilla

with a piece of glass and a sheet of newspaper to encourage germination. As soon as the seedlings appear remove the glass and paper. In July the seedlings can be planted out in their permanent positions. If you want a single plant, buy it from a herb nursery or garden centre. In spring you can increase stock by lifting and dividing the plants.

Both leaves and flowers can be dried successfully. The flowers should be dried separately and can be added to a pot-pourri mixture. After the leaves are dried store them in screwtop jars for use during the winter or add them to the pot-pourri.

Lady's mantle is a lovely plant for flower arrangements of soft hues, used especially with yellow and white. It is chiefly grown as an ornamental plant.

Use: Nowadays lady's mantle is little used in medicine but is still useful as a cosmetic herb. Together with other herbs it makes an effective skin cleanser either in a facial steam or as a lotion. For the lotion, make a strong infusion of the leaves, and leave to cool. Strain and smooth over the skin with cotton wool pads. This is a good cleanser for oily skins. For spots or acne, extract juice from the leaves. Wash them gently, then place them in a clean muslin cloth and twist the ends in alternate directions. Dab on to spots.

Lady's mantle tea is a remedy for diarrhoea and is also helpful to women with menstrual troubles.

You can increase the number of plants by taking stem cuttings in the summer; they soon take root. Hyssop also reseeds itself and the seedlings come true to form. After three or four years the plants become too woody and need replacing. Cut hyssop back after the flowers have died to keep the plant from growing untidily.

A good herb to grow in containers, hyssop can also be grown indoors. Its aromatic leaves have a pleasant scent and it will stay green throughout the winter.

Use: Hyssop is a useful plant for flower arrangements and lasts well in water. Both the flowers and leaves dry well. Remove the tiny flowers from the stems and dry them separately. Add the flowers and leaves to pot-pourri mixtures where they blend well with other dried herbs.

LADY'S MANTLE*
Alchemilla vulgaris perennial
A very attractive herb, lady's mantle can grow up to 45 cm (18 inches) high. Its flat rounded leaves are pale yellowy green and the clusters of tiny flowers, which bloom throughout the summer, are almost the same colour. The plant is a good foil for other herbs in the garden. In some areas lady's mantle will stay green all winter.

Lady's mantle thrives in an open sunny position as long as it is not too dry, and can be easily raised from seed. Sow seed in spring in a garden frame or seed box filled with compost and cover the box

LAVENDER**

Lavendula spica perennial

Such a fragrant plant as lavender deserves a place in every herb garden. An evergreen woody-stemmed herb, it grows up to 60-90 cm (2-3 ft) high. The spiky narrow leaves are greyish green. The flowers are beautifully scented and vary in colour from a brilliant blue to pale mauve, pink and white. All parts of the plant are scented. There is a dwarf form of lavender with the Latin name *Lavendula stoechas* which is a good choice to grow in a container or as a low hedge plant.

Lavender thrives in a sunny sheltered spot in well-drained soil. Buy your plants from a herb nursery or garden centre, because lavender is slow to grow from seed. Evergreens are planted early in spring to give them a full growing season in which to become established. Plant lavender in ordinary garden soil without adding any compost at planting time, and firm the plant down well. To increase the number of plants, take stem cuttings in August from plants which are one or two years old.

Harvest lavender for drying when the flowers are almost fully opened. Cut long stems, tie them loosely together and hang them upside down to dry in the airing cupboard. Place a piece of paper underneath to catch any stray flowers. When fully dried, rub the flowers gently off the stems and store in a screwtop jar.

Use: Add lavender to a potpourri mixture or place a bowl on its own to scent the whole room. Small cotton bags filled with lavender give a lovely fragrance when laid between handkerchiefs or among the linen. Lavender is a good moth deterrent. Added to the bath water it is most refreshing. Tie the dried flowers in a piece of muslin and hang it beneath the running hot tap.

An infusion of lavender flowers dabbed on to the forehead and temples is cooling in hot weather and soothes headaches. You can also use lavender water as an effective skin tonic for a tired dull-looking skin to bring back the colour to your cheeks; be careful not to get it near the eyes. The fragrance clings to the skin for a long time.

Lavender

LEMON BALM*

Melissa officinalis perennial

A hardy plant, lemon balm is a lovely bushy herb for the herb garden with fragrant lemon-scented leaves. Small rather insignificant flowers of white or yellow appear here and there along the stems throughout the summer. The whole plant can grow as high as 90 cm (3 ft) and, unless cut back occasionally will spread over a large patch of ground. Lemon balm dies down during the winter but in some areas after the autumn cutting, new shoots will appear to give leaves through the winter months.

Lemon balm can be raised from seed sown in autumn to make sure of getting good strong plants the following year. The seed takes a long time to germinate so to avoid disappointment buy your first plant from a herb nursery or garden centre. In October or March plant lemon balm in a warm sunny position where the herb will soon become established. Increase the number of plants by taking stem cuttings in the summer or, in the autumn, lift the plant and gently divide the roots. Set out the plants about 25-30 cm (10-12 inches) apart. Lemon balm is a vigorous growing herb and will soon recover after being disturbed.

In the autumn cut back the stems for freezing or drying. The dried leaves retain their lemony scent throughout the winter.

Use: A versatile herb, lemon balm is mainly used in cooking, but it is also a cosmetic and medicinal herb. The chopped leaves, fresh or dried, can be used in recipes wherever a hint of lemon is called for; in chicken or egg dishes, in stews, soups or sauces, added to salads and salad dressings and mixed into cooling summer drinks, especially apple juice. 'Melissa' tea made with the crushed leaves is a refreshing drink sweetened with a little honey and taken hot or cold. It helps to settle the digestion and is a soothing drink taken last thing at night.

An infusion of lemon balm leaves soothes skin irritations and helps to smooth wrinkles. Made up as a herb vinegar, lemon balm dabbed on to the forehead is good for a headache, and the juice from the leaves is a remedy for insect bites and spots.

Add dried lemon balm leaves to a pot-pourri mixture to give it the scent of lemons.

Lemon Balm

LOVAGE* *Levisticum officinalis* perennial

A large handsome herb, lovage is a good background plant for the garden. A clump of strong thick stems grows up to 1.8 m (6 ft) high. The deep green leaves are much divided and the yellow flowers grow in flat topped clusters much higher than the foliage. The whole plant looks and smells rather like celery, all on a much bigger scale.

Lovage grows well in a moist soil in either a sunny or shady position. It can be raised from seed sown in September in pots or seed boxes filled with compost. Cover the boxes with wire netting to stop the birds eating the seed, and leave the boxes in a sheltered place. In the spring plant out the seedlings 60 cm (2 ft) apart. In a good year lovage will seed itself and in spring the seedlings appear near the parent plant. When starting a new herb garden, it is easiest to buy a container-grown plant.

During the summer, when leaves are needed for cooking, freezing and drying, keep cutting off the flowerheads as they appear. Towards the end of the season leave one or two flowers to go to seed. These can be planted as soon as they are ripe, or dried and used in cooking. In the late autumn lovage dies right down and the old stems should be cut off at the base of the plant.

Lovage leaves freeze and dry well.

Use: The flavour of lovage strongly resembles celery. It is good for seasoning, but should be used somewhat sparingly at first. Lovage soup is delicious and can be made from fresh or dried leaves. Chopped fresh leaves, young stalks or lovage seeds can be added to meat stews in place of celery. Use lovage leaves with boiled ham, in salads and with haricot beans.

A strong decoction of the leaves added to the bath water acts as a skin deodorant.

MARIGOLD*

Calendula officinalis (Pot marigold) hardy annual
Well-known for its bright orange flowers, marigold has a well-earned place in the herb garden. It is an important cosmetic herb and for remedies for minor ailments; marigold can also be used in the kitchen.

It is essential when buying seed that you ask for pot mari-

Marigold

gold – make a note of the Latin name as there are many different species.

Marigold is grown in the herb garden for its petals so you will need a good number of plants to provide you with sufficient flowers. Use them for edging plants; they grow up to 30 cm (12 inches) high and provide a wonderful splash of colour.

Marigold grows well in sun or shade. In March or April sow the seed where the plants are to flower. Thin the seedlings to 15 cm (6 inches) apart. Marigold self-seeds readily so you will have no problem in providing yourself with plants year after year. Once the seedlings appear you can move them without risk. Alternatively you can collect your own seed and sow it in the spring in

the usual way. Marigold is a good plant to grow in containers or hanging baskets and requires very little attention.

Petals for drying should be gathered when the flowers are fully opened and perfect. They are as vivid when dry as when in full bloom.

Use: Marigold flowers have a strong sweet scent and a delicate flavour. Dried marigold petals can be added to a pot-pourri mixture or used in cooking in place of saffron, to add a soft colour and flavour to rice dishes. Fresh petals bring colour to green salads and can be added to the mixture when making buns or biscuits. Add a few petals to clear soups.

Marigold is a remarkably efficient remedy for minor

skin problems. An infusion of the petals is a refreshing skin toner and helps to keep the skin free of blemishes if used every day. An ointment made with the petals is an effective remedy for sunburn and can be used for acne and skin inflammations. A cool compress using a strong decoction of fresh or dried petals laid over a bruise or contusion will give immediate relief. Marigold oil, made by soaking the flowers in a good vegetable oil for two to three weeks is healing and soothing – excellent for spots and tired feet.

MARJORAM*

Origanum vulgare (wild marjoram) perennial
Origanum onites (pot marjoram) perennial
Origanum marjorana (sweet knotted marjoram) annual
Origanum marjorana var. 'Daphe ffiske' (new perennial marjoram)

The fragrant perennial or annual marjorams should have a place in every herb garden. There is also a perennial golden marjoram to add colour in the ornamental herb bed all the year round. Wild marjoram with its strong spicy taste has small oval shaped leaves and pale pinky-lilac flowers, and grows up to 75 cm (2 ft 6 inches).

Pot marjoram is a handsome herb with deep pink flowers and grows to about 60 cm (2 ft), spreading at least 60 cm (2 ft) across when fully matured. The flavour is not so pronounced as in other marjorams. The sweetest flavour comes from the annual sweet knotted marjoram which grows to about 20 cm (8 inches) and has greeny white flowers like little knots.

Combining the flavour of the two best marjorams is the new perennial marjoram which is a cross between the wild perennial marjoram and the sweet knotted annual. It grows up to 75 cm (2 ft 6 inches) high. The result is the best flavour with the growing habits of the perennial. It is obtainable at specialist herb nurseries as a container-grown herb. All other marjorams can be raised from seed, though some are rather slow to germinate. In early spring, sow sweet knotted marjoram seed under glass and plant out the seedlings in a sunny position when large enough to handle, spacing them 20-25 cm (8-10 inches) apart.

Perennial marjorams can be sown directly into their flowering position and the seedlings thinned to 25-30 cm (10-12 inches) apart.

To increase stock, take stem cuttings from a mature plant in summer. To keep the flavour concentrated in the leaves cut off the flowerheads.

Sweet knotted or the new perennial marjorams are good plants for growing in containers either outside or indoors where they can be in the sun.

Marjoram leaves can be easily dried and sprigs should be gathered just before the flowers appear. Marjoram has a sweet spicy flavour.

Use: The annual or the new perennial marjorams can be used sparingly in meat dishes and in green, leafy or vegetable salads. Make marjoram vinegar to use in salad dressings. Marjoram adds a good flavour to potatoes, dried beans and other bland vegetables. Wild marjoram has a stronger flavour and should be used with care.

Marjoram tea made with sweet knotted marjoram is a soothing drink and a remedy for nervous headaches. A strong infusion of wild marjoram makes an excellent mouthwash.

Pot marjoram

MINT*

Mentha spicata (spearmint)
perennial
Mentha rotundifolia (Bowles mint) perennial
Mentha piperita (peppermint) perennial
Mentha citrata
(Eau-de-Cologne mint) perennial

There are many different types of mint to choose from, each one with highly aromatic leaves and a distinctive scent. Only a few of the best-known mints are mentioned here but you will discover others when you visit the herb nursery.

Spearmint and Bowles mint provide the best flavours for cooking. Peppermint is a medicinal herb as well as being decorative and useful in the kitchen. Eau-de-Cologne mint, sometimes called bergamot mint, is highly scented and decorative. All are handsome plants in the herb garden.

Spearmint grows up to 30 cm (12 inches) tall with narrow pointed leaves and pale lilac-coloured flowers. Bowles mint has rounded woolly leaves, grows up to 60-75 cm (2-2 ft 6 inches) and is a vigorous plant with an excellent flavour. Peppermint has very dark purplish green leaves and grows up to 40 cm (16 inches) high. All mints have a creeping rootstock. There are two prostrate creeping varieties, pennyroyal (*Mentha pulegium*) and Corsican mint (*M. requienii*), which are lovely as edging plants and stay green right through the winter.

All the mints are easy to grow in any position in the herb garden; their chief requirement is plenty of moisture. Mints are invasive growers and in a small herb bed the plants can be restricted by surrounding them with old roofing slates sunk into the ground to a depth of 15-20 cm (6-8 inches). If the space becomes too crowded pull up some of the runners. Mint can be raised from seed or you can buy your first plants from a herb nursery or garden centre.

In spring, sow mint seed in pots or boxes filled with compost and cover them with a piece of glass and newspaper until the seeds germinate. When the seedlings are large enough, set them out in the herb bed 15 cm (6 inches) apart. Mint takes a lot of goodness out of the soil which should be replaced during the growing season, by applying a liquid fertilizer.

Increasing the stock of plants is no problem: simply cut off some of the runners and replant them. Small pieces of root can be laid in a seed box half filled with compost and more compost firmed on top. Keep it moist and new shoots will appear.

A mint bed should be renewed after three or four years to avoid 'rust' disease.

All the mints dry well, though spearmint loses some of its flavour and is best mixed with Bowles mint; both mints can be frozen successfully. Always dry peppermint on its own as it is very strong.

Use: There are countless ways in which you can use the mints, either fresh, frozen or dried. Spearmint and Bowles mint go well in salads, sauces, meat and poultry dishes and in cool summer drinks. Peppermint is delicious in fruit salads and as a syrup poured over ice cream. Sprinkle chopped leaves on to pea soup.

Make peppermint tea for indigestion and add dried leaves to pot-pourri mixtures.

Bowles mint

Dry Eau-de-Cologne mint for pot-pourri mixtures or place in small bags on its own to keep among your clothes and linen.

NASTURTIUM*

Tropaeolum majus hardy annual climber

A strong peppery-flavoured hardy annual, nasturtium adds a blaze of colour to the herb garden. Set at the back of the bed where it can clamber freely over a hedge, wall or fence, it looks very attractive. There is a dwarf variety – *Tropaeolum minus* – which is more compact and grows to about 40cm (16 inches). This is just as colourful as the climber and better suited to a small bed.

Nasturtium has round flat bright green leaves and colourful trumpet-shaped flowers which range in colour from a red-brown through red, orange and yellow to a creamy white. They bloom from July to October.

Nasturtium

Nasturtiums are perennial plants but are usually treated as hardy annuals, fresh seed being sown each year. They grow well in a sunny position in sandy soil. In April sow nasturtium seed where plants are to grow. They grow and bloom quite quickly and often re-seed themselves in the same season. To prolong the flowering period cut off the seed pods as they form.

Nasturtium plants are particularly vulnerable to attack from greenfly; as soon as they appear, spray with soapy water. As a preventive try putting mothballs round the plants when they are small.

Nasturtiums grow well in containers both indoors and outside on the patio or trailing from hanging baskets.

Nasturtium leaves can be dried for winter use; the flowers, if successfully dried, add colour to pot-pourri mixtures. Pick leaves for drying just before the plant flowers, and pick flowers once opened.

Nasturtium leaves and flowers have a hot peppery flavour and a high vitamin C content which is at its highest in the leaves just before the plant comes into flower.

Use: Nasturtium has medicinal as well as culinary properties. The fresh chopped leaves eaten in a sandwich are a remedy for a cold, though they are good to eat at any time. Juice extracted from the leaves helps to relieve itching.

Chopped nasturtium leaves and flowers can be added to green or vegetable salads, and at the last minute, stirred into a salad dressing. Add a small amount of chopped leaves to cream cheese for a dip or in sandwiches. Make nasturtium vinegar to keep and use for winter salad dressings. Pickle the seed pods while they are young and green and use them in place of capers.

201

Parsley

PARSLEY**
Petroselinum crispum hardy biennial

A deservedly popular herb, parsley has vivid green curly leaves which are particularly attractive in the herb garden as an edging plant. The variety of parsley which is plain-leaved is less eye-catching but has much more flavour. The curly-leaved parsley is useful as a garnish for many different dishes. The variety known as 'Hamburg' or 'parsnip-rooted' parsley is grown for its edible roots.

Though parsley is a hardy biennial, flowering in the second year of growth, it is usually treated as an annual and new seed is sown every year. Plants will sometimes grow on for two to three years – especially the plain-leaved variety which is much hardier than that with curly leaves. Parsley grows up to 30 cm (12 inches) high. If you start by buying a parsley plant pick a small sturdy one which will more readily transplant than a larger parsley. Parsley very quickly puts down a long tap root which will not survive a move.

To grow parsley from seed, first soak the seed in boiling water to help it to germinate; otherwise this can take weeks. In spring or autumn choose a shady spot for the plants and sow the seed there. Pinch out unwanted seedlings to leave 15 cm (6 inches) between the plants. To ensure a long life for the plants cut off all flowering heads in the second year.

Since this herb dries and freezes well, it makes sense to keep some for winter use. Harvest the leaves early in the second year before the plants flower. If flowers are allowed to form the leaves often begin to taste bitter.

Use: Apart from its traditional use as a garnish, fresh chopped parsley is a good seasoning herb to add to meats, casseroles, soups, vegetables, stuffings, salads and with eggs. Parsley not only makes food look appealing but raises its nutritional value as it is full of vitamins. Parsley is essential in herb mixtures as it combines so well with nearly all other herbs.

Parsley tea is an excellent remedy for piles and is believed to help ease rheumatism. A strong infusion of leaves, if used regularly, can help to fade freckles.

ROSEMARY**
Rosmarinus officinalis evergreen shrub

One of the most fragrant herbs to grow in the garden, rosemary is a lovely evergreen shrub which eventually grows up to 1.2 m (4 ft) high. Beautiful soft blue flowers appear in spring, covering the bush with a mist of colour. The flowering period lasts for 6-8 weeks, after which the plant throws up new shoots of its spiky grey-green leaves.

There are several varieties of rosemary. 'Miss Jessup's Upright' is useful as a hedging plant; *Rosmarinus prostratus* is good for ground cover but is rather tender.

It is a slow process to produce rosemary from seed; it is best to start by buying a plant from a herb nursery or garden centre. In April, set the plant in a dry sunny sheltered spot towards the back of the herb garden. Although it is a slow-growing shrub, once the plant is established you can begin to use the leaves. Late summer is the best time to harvest rosemary for drying. In the autumn, cut back half the year's growth on a mature plant. Young rosemary plants need protection during the winter as frost kills the roots. Put a good layer of straw or leaves around the plant and surround it with wire netting. Alternatively, if the plant is not too big, bring it indoors for the winter months.

To increase the stock of plants take stem cuttings or layer one of the branches growing nearest the ground. Summer is a good time to take stem cuttings, so that they can overwinter in a cold frame or greenhouse. Layering can be done at any time during the growing season.

Rosemary dries very well; it retains its strong scent but takes longer to dry than the soft-stemmed plants. Cut off whole sprigs for drying and strip them of leaves after they have dried.

Use: Dried rosemary can be added to pot-pourri mixtures or made up into little bags on its own to lay among your clothes and act as a moth deterrent.

Rosemary has a strong spicy sweet flavour which combines well in both sweet and savoury dishes. Add rosemary, fresh or dried, to roast lamb and to beef or chicken casserole. Sprinkle it over potatoes when roasting and use it with other vegetables. Use it to flavour fruit salads and cool summer drinks.

Make an infusion of rosemary to add to the bath water or to use as a rinse for dark hair. Drink rosemary tea for indigestion; rosemary steeped in oil is a helpful remedy for rheumatism when gently rubbed into the affected part.

Rosemary

SAGE*

Salvia officinalis evergreen shrub

A strongly aromatic herb, sage is a useful plant in the herb garden. There are a number of different sages; the best one for cooking is the narrow leaved garden variety. The flavour is strong but with no hint of bitterness. Sage grows up to 60 cm (2 ft) high, and a mature plant can spread up to 60-90 cm (2-3 ft) in diameter. The coarse grey-green leaves curl inwards when young. Brilliant violet flowers grow out of the bush on tall spikes. Other varieties worth knowing about are: broad leaved sage, which resembles the narrow leaved herb in size and habit but does not flower; purple or red sage, which is mainly ornamental, though the coloured leaves can be used in cooking; golden sage, with a golden variegated leaf, and 'Tricolour' sage which has variegated leaves of white, green and purple-red and is also ornamental.

All the sages can be bought as container-grown plants and planted in spring or autumn in a dry sunny position. In the first year, cut off the tips of the shoots to encourage good bushy growth.

Sage is very easy to raise from seed. In spring or autumn, sow seed in pots or seed boxes filled with compost or out of doors in a seed bed. Transplant the seedlings when they are large enough to their permanent positions. To increase the stock of plants, take stem cuttings in August or layer one or two of the low-growing branches. When layering a branch make sure you cover the cut in the ground with at least 1 cm (½ inch) of soil. Stem cuttings or layering of side shoots are the only ways to increase the number of purple sage plants because its seed does not grow true to form but reverts to the green-leaved sages. Because sage plants become very woody over the seasons they should be renewed every three or four years.

The narrow and broad leaved sages freeze or dry well and retain their full flavour.

Use: Fresh or dried leaves of garden sage should be used sparingly in stuffings, with lamb, pork, poultry and in sausages. Sage adds a pleasant flavour when cooking onions and dried beans. Try adding a few chopped fresh sage leaves to apple juice and cool summer drinks.

Sage tea is a warming drink in the winter and is good for colds and 'flu. An infusion of sage is a good rinse for dark hair, making it shine.

SALAD BURNET**

Sanguisorba minor perennial

A dainty herb, salad burnet is a bushy plant with thin lacy leaves. The small round red flowerheads grow out of a rosette of leaves to a height of 30-40 cm (12-16 inches). The leaves often stay green through the winter months. It has a refreshing cucumber flavour and is both a cosmetic and culinary herb. Salad burnet takes up little space, provides an abundance of leaves for use and is good value in your herb garden. You can buy the first plant from a herb nursery or grow salad burnet from seed. Set your plant in a sunny spot and renew the herb every year, as the full flavour is in the tender young leaves.

In February or March, sow salad burnet seed in boxes filled with a mixture of sand and compost. When the seedlings are large enough, prick them out into pots or seed boxes. Gradually harden off the plants and in late spring set them in their flowering positions 30 cm (12 inches) apart. Salad burnet self-sows freely. To ensure that all the value of the herb goes into the leaves, cut off the flowering heads as they appear.

Salad burnet will grow well in pots or other containers; put them out of doors in summer and bring them in for winter.

Since the leaves continue to appear throughout the winter it is not always necessary to freeze or dry the leaves, but they both dry and freeze well and retain their full flavour.

Use: Salad burnet is principally used as a salad herb providing a cucumber flavour when fresh cucumbers are not available. Salad burnet vinegar is a good base for salad dressings. Use chopped leaves in mayonnaise and with other herbs in a sauce for fish. It adds a refreshing flavour to cool summer drinks. Salad burnet tea drunk hot or cold is a tonic to the system.

An infusion of salad burnet is excellent for the skin when added to the bath water. A strong infusion, used cold, tones and refines the skin. It is refreshing and cooling.

Mixed sages with bronze-leaved fennel, bay, rosemary and young fennel

SAVORY**
Satureia hortensis (summer savory) annual
Satureia montana (winter savory) perennial

Two of the most delightful herbs to grow, summer and winter savory are useful and fragrant plants. Their flavours are similar but their growing habits are different. The annual summer savory grows up to 40 cm (16 inches) high with roundish aromatic leaves and tiny pinky-white flowers. It is a bushy robust little plant, sweet-smelling and quite hardy. Its sturdier relative winter savory is a hardy perennial and grows up to 30 cm (12 inches). The leaves are narrow and lighter in colour than summer savory and the flowers are white. Winter savory grows slowly but neatly into a little mound and in some areas is green through the winter. Both savories make good container plants.

In April or May sow summer savory seed in a sunny position in the herb bed where it is to flower. When the seedlings are large enough, pinch out those not required to leave about 15 cm (6 inches) between the plants.

Buy your winter savory plant from a herb nursery, because the seed is slow to germinate. In autumn or spring plant out winter savory in a sunny spot in light sandy soil. To increase plants, take stem cuttings in August or layer the low-growing shoots. In autumn plants can be lifted and divided.

Summer savory can be grown in pots indoors on a sunny windowsill. Winter savory can be brought indoors for the winter months.

For an annual, summer savory has a surprisingly strong peppery flavour. The flavour

Summer savory

of winter savory is not so strong but is nevertheless delicious.

Use: Both savories are best used when fresh but summer savory dries well and the plant should be harvested for drying when it is in full flower. Often called the 'bean' herb summer savory is particularly good with broad or runner beans. The savories add a good flavour to stuffings for poultry and in meat dishes. Sprinkle a little chopped savory into scrambled eggs. Use winter savory in herb mixtures when making soups and stews.

SWEET CICELY*
Myrrhis odorata perennial

The soft, downy, fern-like leaves of sweet cicely are among the first to appear in the garden in spring. It grows about 60-75 cm (2-2 ft 6 inches) high, but a fully matured plant will spread up to 90 cm (3 ft) in diameter. The flowers form clusters of tiny creamy white blossoms which quickly go to seed. The seeds are large and black when fully ripe. Sweet cicely self-seeds very readily if the flowerheads are not cut off, so once you have purchased your first plant you will have no problem in increasing the number. It is easier to begin with a container-grown plant as seed bought in a packet can be slow to germinate if it is not absolutely fresh. In the autumn seed can be sown for seedlings to appear in the following spring.

In October or March plant sweet cicely in an open sunny position; it also grows quite well in a shady bed – indeed in a very hot dry summer the

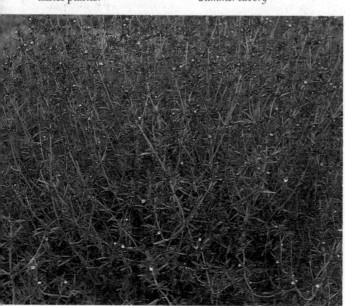

leaves are in danger of being scorched. Because the roots of sweet cicely grow very large it is not suitable for container growing. For the same reason, the mature herb, once over a year old, can never be successfully moved to another part of the garden.

In the autumn cut the large stems off at the base of the plant and leave the herb to die right down.

Sweet cicely has a pleasant, sweet, anise flavour and both leaves and seeds dry well. Gather the leaves throughout the summer months and collect the seeds as they ripen.

Use: Sweet cicely is the ideal herb to add to tart fruits like rhubarb and gooseberries; it reduces the acidity, softens the flavours and makes it possible to use less sugar. Add leaves to fresh fruit salads, plums and summer drinks. Sweet cicely is a mild herb and can be used fairly generously mixed with other herbs in salads and salad dressings and when making herb butter. It adds a delicious flavour when cooked with vegetables, particularly cabbage, parsnip and swedes.

An infusion of sweet cicely taken after meals is good for the digestion.

TARRAGON**

Artemisia dracunculus (French tarragon) perennial
A graceful looking plant with narrow pointed leaves and many branching stems, French tarragon is highly aromatic. It grows up to 60 cm (2 ft) high and dies right down during the winter; the tiny greenish white flowers rarely appear and are not known to set seed in this country.

When buying a tarragon plant make certain you get French rather than Russian tarragon. French tarragon has a far better flavour than the Russian which, though it grows into a vigorous spreading plant, seems to lose its flavour as it grows.

In October or March plant tarragon in dry sandy soil in a

Sweet cicely

sunny position. Good drainage is important, because tarragon will not survive the winter on wet or heavy soils. Once the plant is established, leaves can be picked for use in the kitchen. In September, cut the plant down and freeze or dry the leaves for use during the

Tarragon

winter. In winter protect the herb by covering it with some straw and securing it in place with a piece of wire netting. Remove this in the spring when danger from frost is over. Tarragon will flourish in the same position for some years but, every three or four years, it should be transplanted to another spot in the herb bed to keep it growing vigorously and to prevent any risk of disease. When lifting the plant you can increase your stock by carefully dividing the roots by hand. Set the new plants 20 cm (8 inches) apart. If you lift the plant in October try setting small pieces of root into a pot full of compost and bringing it indoors for the winter. Cuttings of side shoots can be taken in July and placed under a cloche for planting out in the spring. The cuttings may take some weeks to root.

Tarragon leaves freeze or dry quite well but the fresh herb has a superior flavour.

Use: Tarragon is a savoury herb with a strong but delicious flavour. It should be used sparingly in mixtures with other herbs so that they blend well together. Tarragon is an essential ingredient of Béarnaise sauce, and is good in a sauce for fish and a cream dressing for salads. Add chopped tarragon leaves to a leafy green salad and sprinkle them over grilled chops and steak.

Make tarragon vinegar to use in sauces and salad dressing, pickles and chutneys.

THYME**

Thymus vulgaris (common thyme) perennial
Thymus citriodorus (lemon thyme) perennial
Thymus 'Herba barona' (caraway thyme) perennial
There are a large number of different thymes that can be grown for their scent and as decorative plants, but for cooking the best flavours come from the common or garden thyme and the lemon thyme. There is an English wild thyme, still fragrant but with a less pronounced flavour. Caraway-scented thyme or *'Herba barona'*, as it is usually called, is mainly grown as an ornamental plant. Caraway thyme is of matlike growth and is a good ground-cover herb or to use for a path. It bears a mass of lovely, tiny, deep pink flowers and the whole plant has a beautiful scent which is released when the herb is crushed and walked on. There is another ornamental thyme with golden leaves which makes an extremely attractive edging plant.

Common thyme is a small shrubby fragrant perennial growing 15-20 cm (6-8 inches) high with small rounded leaves and pale lilac flowers. Over the seasons it can spread up to 45 cm (18 inches) in diameter. Lemon thyme sometimes grows up to 40 cm (16 inches) high; its leaves, rather darker than common thyme, have a delicate lemon flavour and scent.

All the thymes grow best in a warm dry sunny spot; they can be purchased as container grown plants from the herb nursery, or can be raised from seed. In April sow seed in their flowering positions and pinch out the seedlings to 10 cm (4 inches) apart. Common thyme grows easily from seed; the other thymes are best bought as plants.

The thymes tend to self-layering; to increase your stock of plants in March or April cut off the rooted stems, set them into pots or into the garden and when growing well plant them into their final positions. Every three or four years replant thyme to ensure continued vigorous growth. If the centre of a thyme plant starts to look dead, cover it with soil or compost to encourage new growth.

Harvest thyme for drying when it is in full flower.

Use: Thyme is an evergreen perennial but all varieties, particularly lemon thyme, dry well and are a useful standby in winter. Thyme has a strong delightful scent that blends well in a pot-pourri mixture. It is used in herb mixtures added to soup, stock and stews. Use a little fresh chopped or dried thyme in stuffings and cheese sauces, with potatoes, carrots and beetroot. Add a little lemon thyme to fresh fruit salads.

A tea made from common or lemon thyme is a fragrant drink good for indigestion or a persistent cough. It is also good for insomnia, added to other herbs for a sleep pillow.

VERBASCUM*

Verbascum thapsus (great mullein) biennial

A tall strikingly handsome biennial, verbascum grows to a height of 1.8 m (6 ft). The large grey-green woolly leaves grow in a flat rosette out of which rises a single flowering stem. The stem carries a mass of small golden-yellow flowers early in the second year of growth and flowers over a long period. Verbascum needs too much space to be useful in a small garden, but in a large herb garden it is well worth growing this attractive and useful medicinal herb.

Verbascum grows well in a sunny spot as a background plant. In April sow seed out of doors where the seedlings will get plenty of sun. When they are large enough, thin or transplant the seedlings to 15 cm (6 inches) apart. In April the following year set out the verbascum plants where they are to flower. Leave a few flowers on the herb at the end of the season, for the plant seeds itself very readily. After the second year you can remove the old plants and transplant their seedlings so you will have a constant succession of plants.

Verbascum flowers are the only part of the herb which is used. They can be used fresh or dried for, if carefully dried, they will retain their bright yellow colour. Pick flowers for drying when fully opened and absolutely dry; discard any that are not quite perfect.

Use: An infusion of verbascum flowers provides an effective remedy for chest complaints and in particular a persistent cough. The infusion should be a strong yellow colour by the time you drink it. Once the infusion is made carefully strain the liquid through a piece of fine muslin or cotton to ensure that none of the flowers goes into the drink. For a chesty cold or cough take several cups a day.

Thyme

UNUSUAL HERBS

ANISE* *Pimpinella anisum*
hardy annual
A mildly scented herb, anise is best known for its spicy seeds. It has feathery leaves and clusters of tiny white rather insignificant flowers. The plant grows rather slowly, to a mature height of about 60 cm (2 ft).

Anise is raised from seed which should be absolutely fresh. Germination is likely to be disappointing if old seed is used. In spring, as soon as the ground warms up and the danger of frost is over, sow anise seed where it is to grow, in light well-drained soil and a sunny position. Thin the seedlings to 15-20 cm (6-8 inches) apart. If you cannot sow the seeds directly into their flowering position, sow the seed in pots or boxes and transplant the seedlings when young and before the tap root gets to any size. Once established it is not possible to transplant anise with success. It is also because of its long tap root that anise is not a good plant for container growing. While anise is growing it is important to keep the soil round the plant free of weeds.

All parts of the plant have a pleasant flavour rather like liquorice. The leaves can be used fresh in the kitchen, but anise is principally grown for its seeds so all the flowerheads are left on the plant to go to seed. In mid to late summer gather the heads when the seeds are fully ripe. Choose a dry day to harvest the seeds and take them indoors to complete the drying process.
Use: The flavour of the fresh leaves is rather strong so use them sparingly at first. Add chopped leaves to curries of meat or poultry, or try a pinch in a savoury pizza topping.

The seeds have a pungent sweet flavour and are delicious used in cakes, bread and pastries as well as in soups and stews. Anise biscuits make an unusual accompaniment to ice cream.

Medicinally, anise seed tea is good for indigestion and for hiccups. It will also help to loosen a dry cough.

APOTHECARY'S ROSE**
Rosa gallica officinalis perennial
One of the earliest roses to have been grown in Europe, the apothecary's rose was so called because the dried petals were widely used in medicines and sold by the apothecary, a chemist who prescribed medicines as well as making them up.

This lovely old-fashioned rose is a beautiful sweet smelling plant for the ornamental herb garden. It is a shrubby perennial growing slowly to reach a height of 60 cm-1.2 m (2-4 ft) when fully matured. The flowers are a deep pink, sometimes mottled, with a delightful perfume and bloom throughout July and August.

The apothecary's rose thrives in a sunny position in any type of soil, and is an extremely hardy plant. Do not, however, take advantage of its accommodating nature by putting a new rose where a rose has been growing before.

Between November and March buy your rose from a specialist or garden centre and plant out in the herb garden when the weather is suitable. Do not plant when there is frost or snow on the ground. The apothecary's rose needs little or no attention but in the autumn any very long shoots should be cut back to keep the plant a neat shape and to prevent too much buffeting by the wind. Apothecary's rose will do well in a wooden tub on the patio or terrace.

Rose petals retain their lovely scent very well when dried. Gather petals for drying when the flowers have fully opened and take only the perfect ones. Dry them in the usual way between sheets of newspaper in a dark airy room.

Dried petals of the apothecary's rose keep their perfume for a long time; enjoy their fragrance either on their own or in pot-pourri mixtures.
Use: You can make your own rosewater using fresh or dried petals. Pour boiling water on to the petals, cover them and leave the mixture to infuse until quite cold. Rose petal water is a refreshing skin toner.

Use candied rose petals to decorate cakes and puddings. Dip dry, perfect petals into beaten egg white and then into sieved icing sugar or caster sugar. Leave them to dry and harden. Jams and jellies made with rose petals have a delicious flavour and rose petal tea, taken hot, is a remedy for chest complaints.

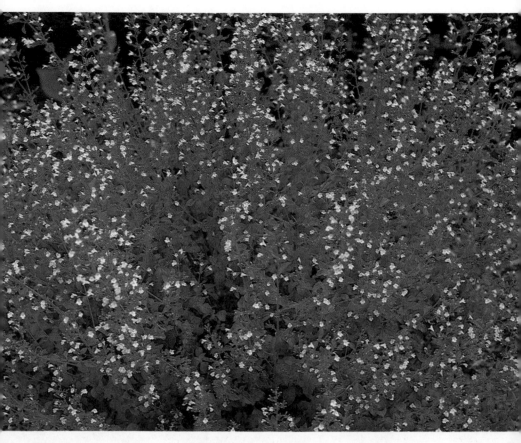

CALAMINT*

Calamintha ascendens perennial
A sweet-smelling, hairy-leaved perennial, calamint is a neat plant that makes a good edging for the herb garden. It grows about 25-30 cm (10-12 inches) tall with small bright mauve flowers which bloom from July to September. The flowers are pretty and colourful but calamint's chief claim to popularity is the lovely minty scent of its leaves.

Buy your first plant from a herb nursery or garden centre, and in the autumn or spring plant it in an open sunny position in the herb bed.

To increase your stock, take stem cuttings in the summer and place them in sharp sand in shallow pots or boxes either in a cold frame or outside and under a cloche. The following spring set them out in the herb garden spacing the plants 15 cm (6 inches) apart. Once the calamint is established it will need a sprinkling of lime round the plant once or twice in the growing season to encourage sturdy growth.
Use: Calamint leaves can be dried for adding to pot-pourri mixtures. Calamint syrup is a useful home remedy for coughs and colds.

Calamint

CAMPHOR*

Balsamita vulgaris perennial
A decorative addition to the ornamental garden, the camphor plant grows up to 75-90 cm (2ft 6 inches-3 ft) high. Its leaves are soft grey-green, its stems stout and square; tiny white daisy-like flowers bloom in great profusion from July to October. Though the whole plant smells strongly of camphor it is not related to the camphor tree which is grown on a large scale in China to produce camphor on a commercial scale.

Buy a camphor plant from a herb nursery in March or October and plant it out in a warm spot in the herb garden.

In summer you can easily increase your stock of plants by pulling off rooted pieces at the base of the plant and setting them elsewhere in the garden, or into pots, to be transplanted later.

The camphor plant grows too large for indoor cultivation, but can be grown successfully in a tub outside.

Once the flowers have opened cut off the plant's long stems. Tie them together loosely and hang the bunches of flowers upside down in a dark dry cupboard until dry and crackly.

Camphor

Use: Strip the leaves off some of the stems and put them into small bags for placing among clothes as an effective moth deterrent.

The camphor plant is excellent for both fresh and dried flower arrangements; it retains its scent when dried.

CARAWAY*
Carum carvi biennial

A hardy biennial, caraway has a bushy growth of feathery leaves and, in the second year, produces clusters of greenish white flowers. The mature plant reaches a height of 60 cm (2 ft) and takes up little room in the herb garden. Caraway is grown for the warm and spicy flavour of its fresh ripe seed.

Caraway thrives in a sunny position in dry light soil. Raise caraway plants from seed sown in autumn or spring where they are to grow. Thin the seedlings to 25 cm (10 inches) apart. If sown in the autumn, caraway plants will be sturdier and produce a crop of seeds the following summer. Thereafter if some seed is left to fall on the ground you will have a continuous crop of caraway each year.

Once the seed heads have formed keep a close watch to see when the seeds are ripe. To make sure no seeds are lost cover the seed heads with fine muslin secured lightly round the stem. This protects the seeds from birds while allowing sunshine and light to finish off the ripening of the seeds. When fully ripe, cut off the seed heads with long

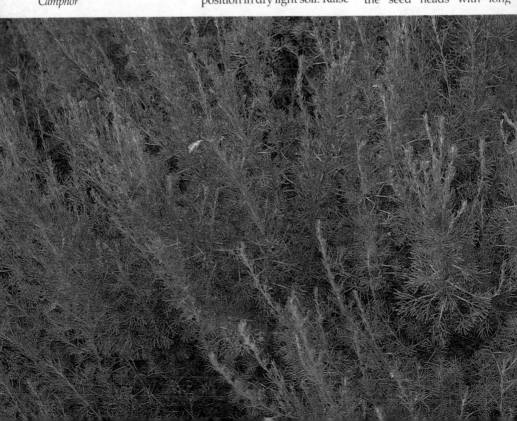

stems, tie the stems together and place the heads in a paper bag. Hang the bunches upside down so that when fully dried the seeds will fall into the bag. **Use:** Caraway seed can be used in meat dishes, soups, with cauliflower, cabbage and beetroot and added to cakes, breads, biscuits and cheese. It adds a delicious flavour to baked apples and apple pie.

Sugar-coated caraway seed is a tasty way of settling the stomach after a heavy meal. Caraway is often combined with other seeds such as anise and fennel to make a remedy for indigestion.

CORIANDER*

Coriandrum sativum annual

An unusual annual plant to grow in the herb garden, coriander somewhat resembles plain-leaved parsley in appearance. It is a single-stemmed plant with a long tap root and grows to about 30-45 cm (12-18 inches) high. Small pinky white flowers grow in clusters at the top of the stems and bloom in early summer. In hot countries coriander is grown for its leaves as well as its seed; the fresh leaves, with their sharp distinctive flavour, are sold in the shops as Chinese parsley.

Coriander grows well in a fairly sunny position and a light soil. As an annual, coriander seed is normally sown in April to flower the same summer, but seed sown in the autumn rather than in the spring will produce much sturdier plants. Always sow coriander seed where plants are to flower in the herb bed and pinch out unwanted seedlings leaving plants 25 cm

Coriander

(10 inches) apart. Because of their delicate root system coriander plants will not transplant. Coriander is a pretty herb but until the seed ripens the whole plant has a rather unpleasant smell.

As soon as the seed is ripe, and before it has a chance to scatter, tie pieces of muslin loosely round the seed heads. During July or August when the weather is dry remove the seed heads with long stems attached.

Put the seed heads into a large paper bag securing it so that it does not fall off. Tie the stems together and hang them upside down in a warm dry place. As the seed dries it falls into the bag. After some

weeks the seed should be completely dry and can be stored in screwtop jars.

Use: Fresh young leaves can be used in place of parsley, but go cautiously at first as the sharp rather strong flavour is not to everyone's taste. The chopped leaves are mainly added to hot spicy dishes and sauces.

Dried coriander seed is aromatic and has a distinctive but not sharp flavour. Use it in meat stews and pies, with game and in stuffings for poultry. Add ground coriander seed when baking gingerbread, biscuits and with stewed or baked apples.

CUMIN*

Cuminum cyminum annual
A slender growing annual, cumin is not often seen in the herb garden. It is quite small and inconspicuous with finely cut blackish green leaves and clusters of small dainty pink flowers which provide colour in the herb bed early in the season. Each plant produces a single branching stem and grows up to 30 cm (12 inches) high. A group of cumin plants set together in the herb bed look most attractive. Cumin seed has many culinary uses.

Cumin is raised from seed sown under glass in early spring. Use flower pots filled with compost rather than a shallow seed box as cumin seed needs a good depth of soil in which to grow. Once the seed has germinated and the seedlings are 20-25 cm (8-10 inches) high you can start to harden off the plants, setting them outside on a warm day or putting them into a cold frame. Finally, in early summer, plant out the seedlings in a warm sheltered position.

In a good summer cumin plants go to seed after three months. As soon as the seed is fully ripe, cut down the stems. Tie them together, place the seed heads upside down in a paper bag and tie it loosely in place. Hang the bunch upside down in a dry warm cupboard and the seed, when dried, will fall into the paper bag. After a few weeks check that the seed is well and truly dry then store in the usual way.
Use: Cumin seed has a pleasant spicy flavour and can be used whole or freshly ground. Add cumin to leek soup, meat stews, curries, pickles and chutneys. Use it sparingly in the mixture when baking cakes and biscuits.

GERMANDER*

Teucrium chamaedrys (wall germander) perennial
A very attractive old-fashioned herb, germander was once widely cultivated for use as a remedy for gout. Germander grows 15-30 cm (6-12 inches) high and has creeping roots. The dark green leaves are narrow and pointed; the pretty rose-coloured flowers bloom in June and July. Though the whole plant dies down in the winter, wall germander makes an usual edging plant for the herb garden. Clumps of germander in the front of an ornamental bed look striking when in flower. It is a bitter-tasting herb and the leaves when rubbed have a strong pungent smell rather like sage.

You can buy a wall germander plant from a specialist nursery or raise plants from seed. In early spring, sow seed where the plants are to flower in a sunny spot in the herb bed. The seed can take as long as a month to germinate so mark the place where it has been sown. When the seedlings appear, pinch out those not required to leave about 25-30 cm (10-12 inches) between the plants. The roots spread during the growing season and send up new shoots. In spring or summer take stem cuttings to increase the number of plants.
Use: Originally a medicinal plant, wall germander is now grown as an ornamental plant. The flowers are useful in flower arrangements.

GOAT'S RUE*

Galega officinalis perennial
A lovely herb to grace the back of the ornamental garden, goat's rue is a colourful old-fashioned plant. It grows up to 90 cm (3 ft) high with leaves divided into lance-shaped leaflets. All through the summer goat's rue produces long spikes with masses of little dark blue flowers; there is one variety with white flowers and another with pale blue flowers. Goat's rue can easily be raised from seed or you can buy in one plant of each colour

Jacob's ladder

JACOB'S LADDER**
Polemoneum coeruleum hardy
perennial

A showy plant for the decorative herb bed, Jacob's ladder grows 75-90 cm (2 ft 6 inches-3 ft) high. The bright green leaves consist of double rows of leaflets like 'ladders' along the midrib. Numerous flowers of a lovely deep blue bloom continuously throughout the summer. Jacob's ladder is sometimes called 'Greek valerian' in gardening catalogues, but other than in the shape of the leaf it bears no resemblance to the true valerians.

Jacob's ladder can be bought at a herb nursery or garden centre as a container-grown plant. Several varieties are commonly available. There is a very handsome one with variegated leaves and white flowers, and two others which only reach 30 cm (12 inches) in height. One has pale pink flowers and the other has flowers of pale blue.

Plant Jacob's ladder in autumn or spring. An open sunny position is best though it will grow very well in the shade. Once the flowers are over, cut off the flowering stems. In spring give the plants a top dressing of compost or leaf mould. Sometimes the plants will seed themselves, naturally increasing your stock of the herb. Alternatively in the autumn you can lift and divide the plant.
Use: The flowering stems of Jacob's ladder are useful in flower arrangements. The flowers also dry well and add colour to pot-pourri mixtures.

from the herb nursery.

In autumn or spring sow seed in an open sunny position in the herb bed where it is to flower and where the soil is not too dry. Once germinated, remove seedlings not required to leave 30 cm (12 inches) between each plant. An autumn sowing will produce much hardier plants. Set out container-grown plants any time from October to March, provided there is no frost.

In the autumn, when the flowers have died down, cut back the flower stems to the base of the plant. Once goat's rue is established in a good position where it has plenty of moisture, it will continue to bloom for a number of years producing a great show of flowers each summer. The plants may need renewing after three or four years.

Goat's rue leaves have no scent until they are bruised when they give off a rather unpleasant smell.
Use: The only use remaining for goat's rue nowadays is as an infusion of the leaves for bathing tired sore feet.

JUNIPER**

Juniperus communis evergreen shrub

Sharply aromatic, juniper is a lovely plant for the ornamental herb garden. Since a number of different forms are available, both small and large gardens can find room for a specimen. A slow-growing juniper with blue-grey foliage and a spread of 30 cm (12 inches), growing 60-75 cm (2-2 ft 6 inches) high is a most striking plant for a small garden. Taking up more space is a juniper with lush green foliage which again grows slowly but when mature has a spread of 3 m (10 ft) and is only for the large garden.

Juniper thrives in an open sunny position in soil where lime is present. Buy a plant from a garden centre and in early spring set it in the herb bed. No pruning is necessary for junipers. If the tips of the branches go brown sprinkle a dusting of lime around the base of the plant.

In late summer take cuttings of newly growing shoots to increase your stock of plants, putting them into a pot or box filled with sand.

Male and female flowers appear on different plants so to gather juniper berries it is necessary to buy two plants. The berries take two years to mature. In the first year the berries are green; in the second they turn blue-black, ready in the autumn for gathering and drying. They should never be used before they are fully ripe. Juniper berries are gathered singly and can be dried either on nylon netting in a dark warm place or between sheets of newspaper. The berries when dried have a coarse grained texture and a

Juniper

warm spicy flavour. They should always be dried before being used in cooking.

Use: Juniper berries are used to give gin its characteristic taste. In the kitchen the spicy flavour of the berries blends well in beef dishes and with game.

MARSHMALLOW**

Althea officinalis perennial

Tall and stately, marshmallow has soft, velvety, grey-green leaves and small rose-coloured flowers. It grows 90 cm-1.2 m (3-4ft) high and has a spread of 60-90 cm (2-3 ft). This makes it a good choice for the back of an ornamental herb bed where it can protect more tender herbs. Years ago marshmallow was widely used for its medicinal properties and was a common plant in the garden.

Marshmallow is raised from seed sown as soon as it is ripe,

but it is easier to buy in a plant from a specialist nursery. It will thrive in any position in the herb garden, though if set in a moist spot it grows very large. Once established marshmallow is a hardy plant which dies down in winter.

To increase your stock of plants sow ripe seed in autumn in a cold frame or seed bed and protect the seedlings through the winter. In the spring set the plants out 45-60 cm (18 inches-2 ft) apart where they are to flower. In the following autumn the plant can be lifted and the roots carefully divided.

Use: Years ago marshmallow root was the part of the herb used, dried and ground, in the making of sweets. A decoction of the root was given to those with chest complaints. It was used as a remedy for diarrhoea. Clean and peel the root before using it fresh or for drying. Marshmallow tea made from the flowers and leaves is still a useful remedy for coughs and colds.

ORRIS*

Iris florentina perennial
An attractive bearded iris, orris is a handsome herb for the decorative herb garden. You can also use the root of the plant in pot-pourri mixtures. Growing 45-60 cm (18 inches-2 ft) high, the light green spear-shaped leaves set off well the fragrant creamy-white flowers that bloom in May.

Orris is easy to grow and thrives in a sunny spot in a limed soil. In July, October or March set out orris plants 20-25 cm (8-10 inches) apart, making sure the rhizomes are near the surface of the soil and

Marshmallow

pointing south.

Over the seasons the plant will gradually take up more space as the rhizomes multiply; if you want to use the herb for pot-pourri carefully take up part of the plant. If this is done immediately after flowering you can divide the plant at the same time, replanting those rhizomes not required for drying.

Orris can also be raised from seed. As soon as the seed is

ripe sow it in sandy soil in a cold frame and set out plants in their flowering position the following spring.

Use: To dry the rhizomes, first scrub them well, making sure thay are free of soil, and cut them into smaller pieces for drying in the usual manner. As the orris dries the scent of violet becomes quite strong, and when the process is complete the pieces can be ground to a powder. Orris acts as a fixative for other scents in a pot-pourri mixture as well as adding its own fragrance.

PINEAPPLE SAGE**
Salvia rutilans half hardy
perennial

A lovely shrubby plant, pineapple sage grows up to 90 cm (3 ft) high. It is a tender perennial but well worth growing in the herb garden. The leaves are a deep reddish green and have the sweet smell of fresh pineapple when bruised – the finest scent of all the sages. The flowers, which do not bloom until late autumn, are long drooping spikes of rich red and make a brilliant splash of colour. Unfortunately as the flowers appear so late in the season, in our climate they are caught by frost before they bloom, unless the whole plant is removed indoors for the winter.

During the winter pineapple sage dies down; if it has to be left out of doors it must be protected by covering it with straw held in place with a piece of wire netting pegged down over the top.

Buy your first pineapple sage container-grown from a herb nursery or garden centre. Pineapple sage thrives in a limed sandy soil in a sunny sheltered position. Plant out the herb in spring when all danger from frost is over. In the autumn, either protect the plant for the winter or bring it indoors in a container.

In summer you can increase your stock of pineapple sage plants by taking stem cuttings.

Pineapple sage has no scent whatsoever when dried.

Use: Fresh pineapple sage leaves can be added to fruit salads and mixed into drinks.

ROSE GERANIUM**
Pelargonium graveolens
perennial

The rose-scented geranium is

Pineapple sage

one of the most fragrant of all the sweet-smelling pelargoniums. The dark green leaves are heart shaped and slightly hairy. The flowers, which grow in clusters of five to ten are rather small, purplish-white in colour with dark veins, and the whole plant will grow to approximately 60 cm (2 ft) tall.

Rose geranium is usually grown in containers but can be planted in a warm sunny position in the herb bed for the summer months when danger from frost is over. Before the cold nights of autumn the plant should be brought indoors, potted up in the usual way. Rose geranium is the ideal plant for the small garden or flat dweller because it is a very easy plant to look after and needs very little attention.

Buy your rose geranium from a garden centre and transplant it into a container whether it be wooden trough, tub or flower pot, or keep it in a sunny well drained spot in the herb bed. Geraniums in containers need to be set in good potting compost and once or twice during the growing season should be treated with a liquid fertilizer to keep them healthy and growing strongly.

Rose geraniums can be grown from seed sown in early spring in a pot filled with sandy soil and kept warm. Transfer the seedlings to larger pots when they are big enough. Keep them moist but not too wet.

In August or September, to increase your stock of plants, take stem cuttings, setting them singly in small flower pots of good potting compost. Keep them indoors or in a cold greenhouse until spring – somewhere that is frost free and not too cold. Make sure the cuttings do not dry out completely during this period. In late spring when they are well rooted, transfer the plants to their final containers.

For a winter flowering rose geranium take stem cuttings in early spring and follow the procedure set out above. Stand the flower pots containing the cuttings in a sunny cold frame until September. Transfer the well-rooted cuttings into larger pots and stand the pots where they are to flower on a sunny windowsill.

Rose geranium flowers and leaves can be dried successfully. They retain their lovely rose scent, and can be added to pot-pourri mixtures.

Use: Fresh or dried rose geranium leaves can be used in the kitchen to flavour jams, jellies, cakes, baked custard and ice cream. Rose geranium tea is a refreshing fragrant drink served hot, and is very pleasant served iced on a summer's day.

SOAPWORT*

Saponaria officinalis perennial
Stout-stemmed and colourful, soapwort is an unusual but useful plant for the herb garden. It grows 60-75 cm (2-2 ft 6 inches) high with many very heavily veined leaves. The herb has no scent but is a mass of pale pink flowers from July to September; a number of plants grouped together make a lovely show.

Because soapwort has creeping roots, once it is established plants come up all over the herb-bed, so there is no problem when you want to increase your stock of plants. When the plants become too invasive some of them can be pulled up by hand or sliced off with a spade.

Buy a soapwort plant from a herb nursery or garden centre in October and plant it into the herb bed in any position. Soapwort can also be raised from seed. The easiest method is to sow seed out of doors in April in a seed bed, transplanting the seedlings in June or July to their final growing position 15 cm (6 inches) apart. Soapwort needs watering in a dry hot spell. In the autumn the plant dies down and disappears. It is a good idea to mark the spot in case you forget where your soapwort is located.

Use: Soapwort is a cosmetic and household herb. A decoction of soapwort leaves cooled and strained into a screwtop jar is an effective cleanser for all skin types.

A strong decoction of soapwort leaves is a good shampoo. Strain the decoction and scent the shampoo with a little rose or lavender water. The shampoo makes the hair soft and acts as a conditioner.

To make a strong decoction use both leaves and stems. Strain off the herb and use the liquid diluted with warm water for washing delicate fabrics, lace and tapestries.

VALERIAN*

Valeriana officinalis perennial
Handsome and stately, the rich dark green leaves of valerian grow thickly at the base of the herb. One flower stem per plant, which often takes several years to appear, rises 90 cm-1.2 m (3-4 ft) above the foliage and produces clusters of creamy pink flowers. The flowers, which bloom from June to September, have a powerful smell which is most apparent on a hot summer's day. Since early times valerian has been used as a remedy for many complaints and earned itself the country name of All Heal.

Valerian grows well in sun or shade and in a heavy moisture-retentive soil. Plants can be purchased from a herb nursery or raised from seed sown when the seed is fresh from the plant. Sow ripe seed in a cold frame and transplant when the seedlings are large enough to their flowering position. In April sow seed out of doors where they are to grow, pinching out those seedlings not required. Leave

45-60 cm (18 inches-2 ft) between the plants.

Valerian's creeping roots make it easy to increase your stock of plants. In spring or autumn, lift the plant and carefully divide the roots. Set them into their new flowering position and water the plants well until established. If you lift the plant before it flowers the roots, which are the part of the herb used medicinally, are of a much better quality than the roots of older plants.

Clean the roots and grate them into large flakes before drying them in the usual way. Because of its strong smell, it is best to dry valerian away from other herbs.

Use: The lovely shape of valerian leaves make it a favourite with flower arrangers.

Valerian is an effective remedy for sleeplessness. A tea

Valerian

made by soaking the dried root flakes in cold water for twelve hours, is taken about an hour before going to bed.

VERBENA***
Lippia citriodora (Lemon verbena) shrub

A tender deciduous shrub, lemon verbena is a graceful and fragrant herb for the larger garden. The sweet-scented leaves are long and narrow and do not appear until late spring. In August, masses of tiny lilac-coloured flowers bloom at the end of the shoots.

Lemon verbena must be grown in a well-drained sheltered position in full sun. In the right position it will achieve a height of up to 1.8 m (6 ft). Lemon verbena plants too large to be transplanted

into a pot, should be protected out of doors in winter from frost by putting straw or peat round the base and surrounding it with wire netting. Lemon verbena is not a hardy shrub and, where possible, should be potted up and taken indoors for the winter months. After putting the plant in a pot cut back some of the longer stalks and only water it occasionally. These stalks can be planted as stem cuttings in sharp sand, to give you more plants for the following season.

Lemon verbena looks very well in a tub or similar container on the terrace or patio. In winter wrap sacks round the container to keep out the frost.

The beautiful scent and graceful growing habit of lemon verbena make it useful for flower arrangements.

Use: The leaves and flowers dry extremely well and add a lovely perfume to a pot-pourri mixture or put into small cotton bags to hang among clothes and bed linen.

Lemon verbena tea made with fresh or dried leaves is a fragrant drink and a remedy for sleeplessness. Fresh young leaves can be added to fruit salads and cooling summer drinks.

WOAD**
Isatis tinctoria biennial

Woad has attractive long narrow blue green leaves which grow in a flat rosette on the ground in the first year of growth. In the second year the flowering stems grow up to 105 cm (3 ft 6 inches) high, branching at the top and producing a mass of small brilliant yellow flowers. From June to September woad is in bloom and the flowers are followed by long blue black seeds. The whole plant is tall, sturdy and conspicuous and is best grown at the back of the bed. Both flowers and seeds make unusual flower arrangements.

Woad was traditionally used for its blue dye which was prepared from the leaves and stems. Nowadays it is grown commercially on a small scale.

A hardy biennial, woad will readily seed itself. Once established in the garden you will have a lovely clump of woad year after year.

Woad thrives in a sunny position in good garden soil. Buy in your first plant from a herb nursery or raise the plants from seed. Woad seed is sown in August where the

plants are to flower. Pinch out those seedlings not required to leave the plants about 25 cm (10 inches) apart.

WOODRUFF**
Asperula odorata (sweet woodruff) perennial

A very attractive ground cover plant for shady areas, sweet woodruff has narrow deep green leaves set in rosettes up the stem. The tiny star-shaped flowers are white and sweet-scented, and bloom in May and June. The whole plant is very dainty and does not grow higher than 20-25 cm (8-10 inches). Woodruff will grow quite happily in the shade of a larger plant such as sage or bay tree in the herb garden.

Sweet woodruff can be raised from seed sown in July or August but germination is exceedingly slow and the seed needs to be absolutely fresh. It is easier to buy in your first few

plants in the spring from a herb nursery and set them into the herb bed 15-20 cm (6-8 inches) apart. During the early summer, just after flowering, you can increase your stock of plants by lifting and dividing the roots. Thereafter the creeping roots of sweet woodruff will gradually spread over the ground providing a dense high mat. Sweet woodruff leaves have no scent when fresh but smell like new-mown hay when dried.

Use: The leaves of sweet woodruff dry well and can be used in small bags laid among clothes to keep away moths. Dried or wilted sweet woodruff can be added to Rhine wine to make a delightful exhilarating drink. Sweet woodruff tea made with dried leaves is a soothing, calming drink and a remedy for headaches.

Woodruff

HERB GROWING THROUGH THE SEASONS

A = Annual – a plant which grows from seed, comes to maturity and dies within one year
B = Biennial – a plant which vegetates one year and flowers, fruits and dies in the second
P = Perennial – a plant that lives more than two years

HERB	A B P Ba E	SPRING	SUMMER
ANGELICA *Angelica archangelica*	B 1.8m (6 ft)	Plant container-grown herb in partial shade at back of bed. Transplant seedlings growing around parent plant.	Cut off flowerheads as they appear. Leave one or two to set seed. Sow ripe seed in Aug. in seed bed or boxes out of doors.
ANISE *Pimpinella anisum*	A 60 cm (2 ft)	Sow seeds where plants are to flower in sunny position. Thin seedlings 15-20 cm (6-8 in) apart.	Keep soil round plants free of weeds. Gather seed when fully ripe in late summer.
APOTHECARY'S ROSE *Rosa gallica officinalis*	P 60 cm- 1.2 m (2-4 ft)	In March plant rose in sunny position or in a container on terrace.	Pick petals for drying throughout summer.
BASIL *Ocimum basilicum*	Half hardy A 30-60 cm (1-2 ft)	Sow seed in gentle heat. Prick out seedlings into pots. Keep pots in greenhouse or indoors.	Plant seedlings 15-20 cm (6-8 in) apart in sunny sheltered position. Pinch out flowers as they appear until end of season. Leave some to set seed.
BAY *Laurus nobilis*	E tree up to 12 m (40 ft)	Between March and May plant container-grown bay in sunny sheltered position in herb bed, or plant in tub or pot for terrace.	Pick leaves from established plants.
BERGAMOT *Monarda didyma*	P 60 cm (2 ft)	Sow seed where plants are to flower. Thin seedlings to 30-45 cm (12-18 in) apart. Lift and divide mature plants.	Put peat or leaf mould round plants to keep roots moist.
BORAGE *Borago officinalis*	A 90 cm (3 ft)	In April sow seed where plants are to flower in sunny position.	Thin seedlings to 20 cm (10 in) apart. Harvest flowers.
CALAMINT *Calamintha ascendens*	P 25-30 cm (10-12 in)	In March buy plant and set in open sunny position. Plant out last year's cuttings 15 cm (6 in) apart.	Sprinkle lime round base of plant. Take stem cuttings and set them in boxes of sharp sand. Leave in cold frame or outside.
CAMPHOR *Balsamita vulgaris*	P 75 cm (2 ft 6 in)	In March buy container-grown herb. Set in sunny position.	Flowers in bloom. When fully open cut off long stems for drying. Take rooted pieces from base of plant to increase stock.

Ba = Bi-annual – a plant that flowers and fruits twice in one year
E = Evergreen – a plant in leaf throughout the year

AUTUMN	WINTER	USES
Clear away old flowering stems and dead leaves.	Plant dies right down. In 2nd winter, after flowering, plant dies.	Candied young stems as flavouring. Young leaves in poached fish and rhubarb jam. Seeds to flavour custard. Tea for feverish cold.
Once seed is harvested remove old plants.		Seed in soups and stews, cakes, bread and pastries. Seed tea for indigestion and dry cough.
Cut back long shoots to neaten the shape.	Rose may also be planted in November (see 'Spring').	Make rose water from petals fresh or dried. Candied rose petals for cakes and puddings. Rose petal jam. Rose petal tea, remedy for chest complaints.
In late Autumn pull up plants and keep any seed for next year's plants.		Leaves in tomato dishes, with minced beef and sausages. Small amount in butter sauces on peas and boiled potatoes.
Aug-Sept take stem cuttings.	Bay in pots or tubs can be brought indoors for winter.	Leaves in meat casseroles and in stuffings. Add to water when boiling rice or spaghetti. In pickles and chutneys, bouquet garni, rice pudding.
Plant container-grown bergamot in sunny moist position.	Plants die down. Mark site with stake.	Flower arrangements. Dried in pot-pourri. Bergamot syrup in summer fruit salads. Tea for sore throat. Bee plant.
Continue harvesting flowers.	Dig up old plants.	Young leaves and flowers in salads, summer drinks. Leaves with tomatoes, cucumber. Candied flowers as cake decoration.
Cover cuttings with cloche.	Cut back flowering stems.	Edging plant. Dried leaves in pot-pourri. Syrup for coughs.
In October buy container-grown herb and set in sunny position.	Dies right down. Cut back old woody stems.	Fresh or dried in flower arrangements. Dried leaves are moth deterrent.

HERB	A B P Ba E	SPRING	SUMMER
CARAWAY *Carum carvi*	B 60 cm (2 ft)	Sow seed where plants are to grow in a sunny position. Thin seedlings to 25 cm (10 in) apart.	Cover seed heads with muslin.
CHAMOMILE German *Matricaria chamomilla* English *Anthemis nobilis*	A 30 cm (12 in) P	In early spring sow annual seed where it is to flower in sunny position. Sow perennial seed in boxes.	Thin seedlings to 15 cm (6 in) apart. Transplant perennial seedlings to open ground. Pick flowers of annual when open.
CHERVIL *Anthriscus cerefolium*	Ba	Sow seed in partial shade.	Make successive sowings throughout summer. Leave flowers on some plants to set seed and self sow.
CHIVES *Allium schoenoprasum*	P 25 cm (10 in)	Buy herb and plant bulbs 15 cm (6 in) apart in sun or partial shade. Lift and divide established clumps.	Cut off flowerheads. Cut leaves for drying. Feed clumps with liquid fertilizer.
CORIANDER *Coriandrum sativum*	A 30-45 cm (12-18 in)	In April sow seed where plants are to grow. Thin seedlings to 25 cm (10 in) apart.	Tie pieces of muslin over seed heads.
CUMIN *Cuminum cyminum*	A 30 cm (12 in)	In early spring sow seed under glass. Harden off seedlings when 20-25 cm (8-10 in) high.	Set plants in warm sheltered position. When seeds are ripe cut down stems for drying.
DILL *Anethum graveolens*	A 60 cm (2 ft)	Sow seed in sunny sheltered position.	Thin seedlings to 25 cm (10 in) apart. Keep plants weed free. Cut off flowerheads. Leave some to set seed.
FENNEL *Foeniculum vulgare*	P 1.2m (4 ft)	In April sow seed in permanent position in sun at back of herb bed.	Thin seedlings to 30 cm (12 in) apart. Cut off flowers. Earth up bulbous fennel. Harvest as required.
FEVERFEW *Chrysanthemum parthenium*	P 60 cm (2 ft)	In early spring sow seed outdoors in sunny spot. Thin seedlings 20 cm (8 in) apart.	Take cuttings from base of plant.
GARLIC *Allium sativum*	A	Plant bulblets (cloves) from mature herb in sunny position. Space 15 cm (6 in) apart.	
GERMANDER *Teucrium chamaedrys*	P 15-30 cm (6-12 in)	Buy plant and set in sunny position. In early spring sow seed where plants are to grow.	Thin seedlings to 25 cm (10 in) apart. Take stem cuttings.
GOAT'S RUE *Galega officinalis*	P 90 cm (3 ft)	Buy plants and set in sunny position at back of herb bed. Sow seed where it is to flower.	Thin seedlings to 30 cm (12 in) apart.

AUTUMN	WINTER	USES
Sow seed where plants are to grow in a sunny position. Gather seed heads for drying.	Dry seeds.	Seed in soups with meat, cabbage, cauliflower, beetroot. Add to cakes, biscuits, apple pie. Seed tea for indigestion.
Annual seed can be sown in growing position and seedlings thinned to 15 cm (6 in) apart. Layer runners or divide roots of perennial plants.	Remove dead annual plants.	Dried flowers in pot-pourri. Tea for indigestion. Infusion as rinse for blonde hair, to clear the skin, for colds.
Early autumn sow seed in sunny position. Thin seedlings to 20 cm (8 in) apart.	Remove all dead plants.	Dried leaves in herb soup. Fresh or dried leaves in salad dressings, salads, soufflé, sauces.
Pot up a clump to take indoors.	Plants die down. Mark positions.	Fresh or dried leaves in soups, sauces, salads, herb butter, soft cheese, mashed potato, egg and fish dishes.
Remove seed heads for drying. Sow seed where plants are to grow. Thin seedlings to 25 cm (10 in) apart.	Leave seeds to continue drying.	Chopped fresh leaves in hot spiced sauces. Dried seed in meat stews, pies, in stuffings; ground seed in biscuits, ginger bread.
Remove old plants.	Dry seeds.	Dried seed in leek soup, meat stews, curries, pickles, chutneys. Ground seed in cakes and biscuits.
Early autumn tie muslin over seed heads to protect from birds.	Dry seeds.	Fresh or dried leaves in salads, cucumber sauce, cream sauces. Seeds in apple pie, spiced beetroot, with cabbage, carrot.
Leave one or two flowerheads to set seed. Harvest bulbous fennel as required.	In February sow seed in gentle heat.	Eat bulbous fennel as vegetable. Fresh or dried leaves with fish, cheese, in salads. Tea for digestion. Seed for toning skin.
Dry flowers and leaves for winter. Plant self-seeds freely.		Flower arrangements. Infusion of leaves and flowers for headache, migraine. Infusion of flowers for rheumatism.
Dig up whole plant to harvest bulbs when stems wilt.	Remove tops. Leave bulbs to dry a few more days.	Sparingly in savoury dishes, meat, chicken, sauces. Juice in salad dressings. Garlic bread.
	Plant dies down.	Ornamental; edging plant.
Sow seed where plant is to flower. Thin seedlings to 30 cm (12 in) apart.	Cut back flowering stems to base of plant. Plant dies down.	Ornamental. Infusion of leaves for tired feet.

HERB	A B P Ba E	SPRING	SUMMER
HYSSOP *Hyssopus officinalis*	P 60 cm (2 ft)	Sow seed outdoors in sunny position, or buy plant.	Thin seedlings to 25 cm (10 in) apart. Take stem cuttings from established plant.
JACOB'S LADDER *Polemoneum coeruleum*	P 75 cm (2 ft 6 in)	Buy plant and set in sunny or shady position. Top dress established plants with compost.	
JUNIPER *Juniperus communis*	E 75 cm (2 ft 6 in) or 3 m (10 ft)	Buy plant, set in open sunny position. Buy male and female plants for berries.	Take cuttings of new shoots.
LADY'S MANTLE *Alchemilla vulgaris*	P 45 cm (18 in)	Buy plant and set in sunny spot. Sow seed in cold frame. Lift and divide established plants.	In July plant seedlings 25 cm (10 in) apart in sunny position.
LAVENDER *Lavendula spica*	E 60 cm (2 ft)	Buy plants and set in sunny sheltered position. Can be grown as hedge plant or in containers on terrace.	In August take stem cuttings from 2-year-old plants.
LEMON BALM *Melissa officinalis*	P 90 cm (3 ft)	In March buy plant and set in sunny position.	Take stem cuttings.
LOVAGE *Levisticum officinalis*	P 1.8 m (6 ft)	Plant seedlings from autumn sowing in sunny spot 60 cm (2 ft) apart, or buy plant.	Cut off flowerheads as they appear.
MARIGOLD *Calendula officinalis*	A 30 cm (12 in)	Sow seed in permanent position in sun or shade. Thin seedlings 15 cm (6 in) apart. Plant in tubs and containers.	Good edging plant. Self-seeds freely.
MARJORAMS *Origanum* spp.	A/P 20 cm (8 in)	Buy perennial marjoram plants and set in sunny position 25 cm (10 in) apart. Sow annual seed under glass.	Plant out seedlings 20 cm (8 in) apart. Take stem cuttings from mature plants.
MARSHMALLOW *Althea offiicinalis*	P 90 cm (3 ft)	Buy plant and set at back of herb bed. Set out plants 45 cm (18 in) apart where they are to flower.	Keep well watered.

AUTUMN	WINTER	USES
After flowering cut back the plant to one third of year's growth. Reseeds itself.	In mild areas stays green all winter.	Ornamental. Flower arrangements. Dried flowers and leaves in pot-pourri. Bee plant.
Buy plant and set in sunny or shady position. Lift and divide mature plants to increase stock.		Ornamental. Flower arrangements. Dried flowers in pot-pourri. Bee plant.
Sprinkle lime round plant when tips of branches are brown.	Dry berries.	Ornamental. Dried berries in beef dishes, with game.
Cut off flowering stems.	In some areas stays green all winter.	Ornamental. Flower arrangements. Fresh or dried leaves as skin cleanser. Juice for spots and acne. Dried flowers in pot-pourri.
Trim back stems at end of flowering period.	Protect 1-year-old plants with straw and wire netting.	Ornamental. Dried flowers in pot-pourri, in lavender bags. Lavender water as skin tonic. Infusion dabbed on for headaches.
Cut back stems to base of plant. Sow seed outdoors in sunny position. Thin seedlings 25 cm (10 in) apart. Lift and divide roots to increase stock.	Dies down in winter. In mild winter new shoots appear.	Fresh or dried leaves with chicken, in soups, sauces, salads. In cooling drinks. 'Melissa' tea for indigestion. Juice of leaves for bites. Dried leaves in pot-pourri.
In September, sow fresh seed in pots or boxes. Cover with wire netting. Leave outside in sheltered place.	Plant dies down in winter. Remove old flowering stems and dead leaves.	Fresh or dried leaves as herb soup. Add to meat dishes in salads, with haricot beans, baked or boiled ham.
Clear away dead plants.	Keep self-sown seedlings free of weeds.	Dried petals in pot-pourri. Fresh or dried petals in place of saffron. Infusion as skin toner. Ointment for skin complaints, sunburn.
Cut back flowering stems. Pull out annuals.	Divide perennial plants.	Fresh or dried leaves in meat dishes, vegetable salads, stuffings. Add to potatoes, dried bean dishes. Marjoram vinegar in salad dressings. Tea for headaches.
Sow seed in cold frame or seed bed. Lift and divide established plants.	Protect seedlings through winter.	Dried root as flavouring. Decoction of root for chest complaints. Tea of flower and leaves for coughs and colds.

HERB	A B P Ba E	SPRING	SUMMER
MINT *Mentha* spp.	P 30-60 cm (12-24 in)	Buy plants and set in moist shady spot. Sow seed in pots.	Plant seedlings 15 cm (6 in) apart in moist shady position. Water plants with liquid fertilizer.
NASTURTIUM *Tropaeolum majus*	hardy A climber	Sow seed in permanent position in full sun. Good container plants.	Plants reseed themselves.
ORRIS *Iris florentina*	P 45 cm (18 in)	In March buy plants out 20 cm (8 in) apart in sunny position. Set out plants sown in previous autumn.	After flowering lift and divide plants. Keep some rhizomes for drying.
PARSLEY *Petroselinum crispum*	B 30 cm (12 in)	Buy plant. Soak seed in boiling water and sow in shady spot. Thin seedlings to 15 cm (6 in) apart.	Cut off flowers in second year to prolong life of plant.
PINEAPPLE SAGE *Salvia rutilans*	P 90 cm (3 ft)	Buy plant and set in sunny sheltered position. Suitable for pots or tubs.	Take stem cuttings to increase stock.
ROSE GERANIUM *Pelargonium graveolens*	P 60 cm (2 ft)	Buy plant and set into tub or other container. Sow seed in sandy soil in gentle heat.	Set out plant in sunny position. Give pot plants liquid fertilizer.
ROSEMARY *Rosmarinus officinalis*	E 1.2 m (4 ft) shrub	Buy plant in April and set in sunny sheltered spot at back of herb bed.	Layer low-growing branches of mature plants. Take stem cuttings of new shoots – overwinter in cold frame or greenhouse.
SAGE *Salvia officinalis*	E shrub 60 cm (2 ft)	Buy plant and set in dry sunny position. Sow seed in pots. Set out seedlings 45 cm (18 in) apart.	Cut off tips of shoots in 1st year to encourage bushy growth. Take stem cuttings or layer low-growing side shoots of mature plants.
SALAD BURNET *Sanguisorba minor*	P 30 cm (12 in)	Buy plant and set in sunny position. Sow seed in boxes, harden off plants. Good plant for tubs.	Transplant seedlings to permanent position 30 cm (12 in) apart. Self-sows freely if left to flower.
SAVORY Summer savory *Satureia hortensis* Winter savory *Satureia montana*	A 40 cm (16 in) P 30 cm (12 in)	Buy plant, set in sunny position. Annual savory in pot on sunny windowsill.	Sow annual seed in sunny position. Thin seedlings to 15 cm (6 in). Take stem cuttings of perennial plant.

AUTUMN	WINTER	USES
Remove old flowering stems. Remove runners and plant in boxes to increase stock for next year.	Plants die down in winter.	Fresh or dried leaves in sauces, salads, meat, poultry; with fruit, ice cream. Dried leaves in pot-pourri.
Remove old plants.		Full of vitamin C. Fresh leaves in sandwiches, green and vegetable salads. Nasturtium vinegar for salad dressings.
Buy plants and set in sunny position. Sow seed when ripe in cold frame.		Dried rhizome ground in pot-pourri.
Soak seed in boiling water, then sow in permanent position in shady spot. Thin seedlings to 15 cm (6 in) apart.	Plants die down.	Fresh or dried leaves in all savoury dishes. Full of vitamins. Parsley tea for piles. Infusion for freckles.
Where possible bring plants indoors.	Indoor plants flower in November. Protect outdoor plants with straw and wire netting.	Ornamental. Fresh leaves in fruit salads and fruit drinks.
Take stem cuttings. Keep indoors until early summer.	Keep plants in frost-free place.	Dried flowers and leaves in pot-pourri. Fresh or dried leaves in jams, jellies, cakes, custards. Tea as refreshing drink.
Cut back half the year's growth on established plants. Bring small plants indoors if possible.	Protect young plants with straw and wire netting.	Add fresh or dried leaves to meat dishes, vegetables and fruit salads. Infusion as rinse for dark hair. Tea for indigestion. Rosemary oil for rheumatism.
Renew sage plants after about 4 years when very woody. Cut back half the year's growth.		Fresh or dried leaves in meat dishes, poultry, dried beans. Fresh leaves in apple juice. Sage tea for colds and 'flu'. Infusion as rinse for dark hair.
Cut back flowering stems	Plant outdoors. Stays green through winter.	A salad herb. Vinegar in salad dressings. In herb mixtures. With fish, cool summer drinks. Infusion as skin tonic.
Buy plant and set in sunny position. To increase stock lift and divide perennial plants.	In some areas perennial stays green through winter. Pot of perennial can be brought indoors.	The 'bean' herb – add fresh or dried savory to all bean dishes. Use in stuffings and herb mixtures.

HERB	A B P Ba E	SPRING	SUMMER
SOAPWORT *Saponaria* *officinalis*	P 60 cm (2 ft)	In April sow seed in seed bed.	In June transplant seedlings 15 cm (6 in) apart, any position. Water in dry spell.
SWEET CICELY *Myrrhis odorata*	P 60 cm (2 ft)	Buy plant and set in open sunny position. Transplant seedlings from autumn sowing 45 cm (18 in) apart.	Self-seeds freely if left to flower.
TARRAGON *Artemisia* *dracunculus*	P 60 cm (2 ft)	Buy plant in March. Set in dry sunny spot.	Take cuttings of side shoots, keep under cloche for planting out in spring.
THYME *Thymus* spp.	P 20-45 cm (8-18 in)	In March cut off rooted stems of mature plants. Buy plants and set in warm dry sunny spot. Sow common thyme seed in April.	Thin seedlings 10 cm (4 in) apart. Keep weeds down round tiny plants. Harvest for drying when in flower.
VALERIAN *Valeriana* *officinalis*	P 90 cm (3 ft)	Buy herb; plant in sun or shade. In April sow seed in flowering position. Lift and divide mature plants.	Thin seedlings to 45 cm (18 in) apart.
VERBASCUM *Verbascum* *thapsus*	B 1.8 m (6 ft)	Sow seed in April in sunny spot. Thin seedlings 15 cm (6 in) apart. Following April set in permanent position 30 cm (12 in) apart.	Harvest flowers every morning.
VERBENA Lemon verbena *Lippia citriodora*	P shrub 1.8 m (6 ft)	Buy plant and set in sunny sheltered position.	Harvest leaves.
WOAD *Isatis tinctoria*	B 105 cm (3 ft 6 in)	Buy herb and set in sunny position.	In August sow seed in permanent position. Thin seedlings 25 cm (10 in) apart.
WOODRUFF *Asperula odorata*	P 20 cm (8 in)	Buy plants and set 15 cm (6 in) apart in shade of larger herb or shrub.	To increase stock of plants, lift and divide roots. In July or August sow seed, thin to 15 cm (6 in) apart. Harvest flowering stems.

AUTUMN	WINTER	USES
In October buy plant and set in any position.	Plant dies right down. Mark spot with stake.	Decoction of leaves as skin cleanser, shampoo. Decoction of whole plant for washing delicate fabrics.
Cut back flowering stems and dead leaves. Sow fresh seed in boxes. Leave outdoors in sheltered spot.	Plant dies down.	Cuts acidity when added to tart fruits such as rhubarb or gooseberry. Leaves in fruit salads, with plums, in salads and salad dressings.
Buy plant in October, set in dry sunny spot. Lift and divide old plants and set 20 cm (8 in) apart.	Protect plant from frost by covering with straw and wire netting.	Savoury herb. Use in sauces and salads; sprinkle over grilled chops and steak. Tarragon vinegar in salad dressings, pickles, chutneys.
Thymes are self-layering. Trim plant if it becomes straggly.	Cover dead-looking centres of old plants with soil or compost to encourage new growth in spring.	Fresh or dried leaves in soups, stews, stuffings, with cheese and vegetables. Thyme tea for cough. Lemon thyme to fresh fruit salads, in pot-pourri.
Sow ripe seed in cold frame. Lift and divide mature plants. Keep some roots for drying. Transplant seedlings 45 cm (18 in) apart.	Plant dies down.	Flower arrangements. Tea for sleeplessness.
Leave some flowers on plant to self-seed.	At end of 2nd year remove old plants.	Fresh or dried flowers remedy for coughs. Dried flowers in pot-pourri.
Take stem cuttings and overwinter in greenhouse or indoors. Take plant indoors for winter – cut back long stems.	Wrap sack round containers standing on terrace to keep out frost. Protect outdoor plants with straw and wire netting.	Flower arrangements. Dried leaves and flowers in pot-pourri, in bags to hang among clothes. Fresh leaves in fruit salads.
Mark position of plant.		Ornamental. A dye plant.
Cut back dead flowerheads.	Dies down in winter.	Dried leaves among clothes to deter moth. Dried or wilted leaves in Rhine wine. Tea soothes headaches.

CHOOSING A GREENHOUSE

A greenhouse can open up a whole new world of gardening to anyone interested in plants, and it is an investment that will provide years of pleasure. You do not have to spend a fortune heating it either – even an unheated greenhouse can provide lots of interest, and just keeping it frost-free will widen the possibilities enormously.

A heated greenhouse will enable you to grow a whole range of plants that you would not be able to cultivate in the open – not just the 'exotics' but also many 'houseplants' as well as some fruit and vegetables. It can also be used to protect plants throughout the winter that are too delicate to stay outside.

There is also the possibility of raising your own bedding plants, and you can give vegetables like sweet corn and runner beans an early start.

Once you decide to buy a greenhouse, it is important to consider where to site it. Obviously much depends on the size and shape of your garden, but the following considerations should be taken into account:

- The position must receive the maximum amount of light. If possible it should run from north to south so that each side catches the sun, although with the narrow glazing bars of most modern greenhouses this is not too important, and opinions differ as to the best aspect.
- Make sure the site is not shaded by overhanging branches of trees or tall fences.
- Avoid a windy site. Shelter is essential as wind has a serious cooling effect.
- If you want to have mains water or electricity laid on, you should choose a place close to a source. It will reduce the cost of installation.
- A greenhouse should never dominate a garden, nor interfere with its ease of upkeep. Make sure it does not create awkward little corners that are difficult to look after.
- To reduce breakages, avoid a site anywhere near an area where children are likely to play ball games.
- The site should be level so that the greenhouse is easy to erect. This also ensures that water and cold air do not collect at one end.

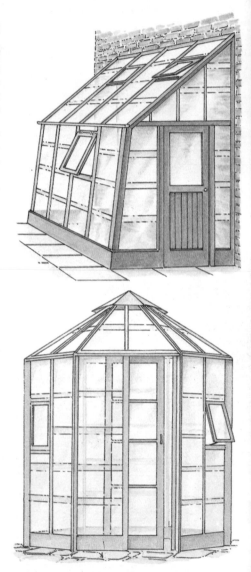

Lean-to (top) and circular (bottom) greenhouses are very useful in small gardens. The lean-to uses less material than a standard type and is frequently warmer; a circular greenhouse is convenient to work in and it can hold more plants than a conventional greenhouse.

FREE-STANDING OR LEAN-TO?

Although a free-standing greenhouse is likely to give you more growing space, you might like to consider a lean-to. These have many advantages: they are usually close to a water and electricity supply; heat 'stored' in the house wall reduces heating costs; the greenhouse has the convenience of being close at hand (you can even have a door directly into it from the house). Their main disadvantage is the limited choice that you have in positioning them, and the possibility that they will not face in the best direction for catching the sun.

In any case, there will not be as much light for the plants as in a free-standing model.

SIZE AND SHAPE

Deciding how large the greenhouse should be is never easy, but you should try to buy the largest you can afford, bearing in mind the other factors and the cost of heating. Most gardeners grow far more plants than their greenhouse will comfortably hold, so the larger it is the less likely you are to be frustrated.

Shape is usually of less importance. In theory, the nearer a greenhouse is to circular, the better the light admission, but making your own fixtures and fittings for it is very tricky unless you are a master-carpenter or a metal-worker. Rectangular greenhouses with straight sides make best use of benching and shelving, while those with sloping sides are claimed to admit more light.

WOOD OR METAL?

Probably the most vexed question of all is the initial choice between a wooden greenhouse and a metal one.

Wood is a soft material into which screws, nails, hooks, and so on, can easily be driven. This makes it simple to fix training wires, polythene linings and anything else that you might want to (although you can buy attachments that make all these things possible in most metal greenhouses). Wood is also a 'warmer' material than metal, and wooden greenhouses may retain a little more heat than metal-framed ones.

Whether stained or painted, a wooden greenhouse normally looks more in keeping with a garden. This may, at first, seem a small point but since everything in a garden should contribute to its attractiveness, it is important to consider the appearance of the greenhouse. The greater weight of a wooden structure adds to its stability in storms and gales.

There are, however, disadvantages to wooden greenhouses. They require much more maintenance than their metal counterparts to prevent deterioration. Wooden greenhouses are also flammable – a point not to be overlooked, especially if you intend to use a paraffin heater.

Metal-framed greenhouses have narrower glazing bars, and this admits more light. Very little maintenance is required in comparison with wood, and metal has a longer life, even if not looked after.

As regards the types of metal used for making greenhouses, aluminium alloy is an infinitely better material than steel. Steel is extremely heavy and its hardness makes the installation of any extras a major operation.

HOW EASY TO ERECT?

It is, of course, also necessary to consider the ease with which the greenhouse can be put up. The types and sizes that most gardeners buy come in various stages of pre-construction; some metal ones look like giant Meccano sets, whereas wooden ones are often delivered by the manufacturer with the two roof sections, the sides, and the ends already assembled. These wooden ones are fairly easy to put up, but the glazing, which has to be done with putty, takes a lot longer than it does with metal greenhouses. In these the individual sheets of glass are usually held in place by clips. From start to finish, however, the two sorts probably take about the same time to erect.

GLAZING MATERIALS

Except where breakages are likely to be frequent, glass is still the best value for money. Even in an unheated greenhouse, it can keep out something like 5°C (10°F) of frost. It has excellent light admission and, within limits, its strength is good. It is also relatively cheap. There are several rigid or semi-rigid plastics on the market but, for one reason or another (usually cost), they fail to match up to glass except in strength. Polythene is becoming a popular glazing material and is certainly cheaper than glass, but heat is not retained so well

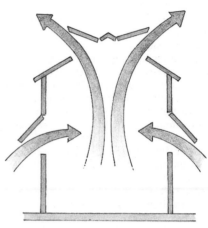

Good ventilation is essential in a greenhouse if the plants are to flourish. Not only does it help to keep them cool in the summer, it also encourages good air circulation, a vital part of pest and disease control. For maximum efficiency, ventilators should be fully adjustable and open as widely as possible. To ensure thorough air circulation, ventilators should be fitted in the sides of the greenhouse, as well as the roof.

and it has to be replaced every one to three years. If you do use polythene, make sure it is a heavy (thick) gauge and treated with an ultra-violet light inhibitor (often called UVI polythene).

Under normal conditions, glass is the best material. For greenhouse purposes it is usually 3 mm thick (⅛ inch). Do make sure that the system for replacing broken panes is straight-forward, for breakages inevitably occur.

VENTILATORS
Ventilation is essential to the efficient working of the greenhouse, yet it is rarely given sufficient thought at the planning stage. All too many greenhouses are simply equipped with a ridge ventilator on each side of the roof. This is fine from the point of view of letting hot air escape and for preventing the temperature from rising too high, but it does little to keep the plants themselves cool; the only fresh air in the

greenhouse is that which flows from one ventilator to the other.

The best way of overcoming this so that there is fresh air amongst the plants is to make sure that the greenhouse has side ventilators at about bench height. This will also give you far greater control over the temperature inside the greenhouse. At the same time it is important to avoid draughts, as these can be detrimental to many plants.

It is well worth considering louvre vents for the side of the greenhouse.

GUTTERS
Gutters are not essential, particularly if you are trying to keep the price down, but they are useful. Convenient though they may be for collecting rainwater, the amount you can save off a small greenhouse roof is never likely to be enough for watering the plants throughout the summer so its main job is to prevent drips outside the house. Judge for yourself how necessary this is.

SHOPPING AROUND
The key points to consider have been outlined in this chapter, but it must be emphasized that the only sensible way to decide is to inspect and compare as many models as you can. Only then can you select one that suits your requirements.

EQUIPPING THE GREENHOUSE

Once you become the proud owner of a greenhouse the obvious question arises as to how much and what equipment you should install. This chapter steers you through the many greenhouse accessories so that you can decide which are important to you and which are nice to have but by no means essential if you cannot afford them yet.

BENCHES AND SHELVING

Sometimes benching is included in the price of the greenhouse, but often it is an optional extra. This, of course, should be taken into account when comparing prices.

A greenhouse should have benching on one side at least. The other side can be used for tomatoes, cucumbers, and other large plants. On the other hand if you want to concentrate on pot plants you will probably need benches on both sides.

The decision is not one that need be made when buying the greenhouse – there are several types of benching or 'staging' that can be bought 'off the peg', later. These can be adapted to the size of your greenhouse and can be put up and taken down as required. It is also perfectly possible and quite easy, with a few tools, to make your own.

The choice of materials is between wood

and metal again, and the pros and cons are similar to those already mentioned for the greenhouse itself. If you are making your own, however, wood is much easier to work.

You may consider having a corrugated asbestos top to the benching. This is fine provided you get the kind with narrow corrugations; if it has wide ones, you will run into trouble with small pots tipping over, although this can always be prevented by spreading fine shingle over the asbestos. Something else worth doing is drilling holes in the 'troughs' to allow surplus water to drain away. *Caution:* wear protective clothing and a face mask when drilling into asbestos as the dust may be harmful, especially if inhaled.

In the spring, you may want to erect temporary shelving to house all the pots and boxes of seedlings. These will greatly increase the capacity of the greenhouse at a time when space is at a premium.

If planks are used for the shelves, they should be about 18 cm (7 inches) wide and 2 cm (¾ inch) thick. These shelves will comfortably hold two 9 cm (3½ inch) pots across as well as seed trays and will be amply strong provided they are supported by metal brackets every 60 cm (2 ft) or so, though the exact measurement will depend on the distance between the glazing bars.

You can, of course, buy aluminium shelves that are easily fixed to most aluminium alloy greenhouses with the special nuts and bolts provided.

If the top shelf is positioned about 7 cm (3 inches) below the eaves, it can be left in place and used as an anchor point for strings to support tomatoes and cucumbers when the staging underneath has been removed. Alternatively, a strong wire can be run from one end of the greenhouse to the other, with several fixing points in between, and the support strings tied to this.

Careful planning and tidiness are essential if your greenhouse is to be used efficiently. A clean, tidy interior also discourages pests and diseases.

FLOORS

This may sound rather an elementary subject but a greenhouse should always have a proper 'floor' – rather than packed mud with a profusion of weeds growing in it! The ideal material is properly laid concrete, as it is firm to walk on, can easily be scrubbed when it threatens to become slippery with green algae, and it is weed free. Paving slabs are also good, provided they are laid evenly on a bed of sand.

At a pinch, duck-boards can be used but they have the serious disadvantage that they can harbour pests and diseases, whilst the soil beneath them is often thick with weeds. Also, their life is apt to be short unless they are treated with a preservative at least once a year. This must not be creosote, whose fumes would damage or even kill the plants, but a copper-based preservative safe for use near plants.

The extent of the flooring need not be great; a walkway down the centre of the greenhouse between the two sets of staging is enough. Under the staging, the ground should be kept weed-free either by spreading shingle over it or by an occasional hoeing. Where appropriate, you could even grow tender ground cover plants in it; they would need very little attention as all their water and food would probably come as drainage water from above (but not if you use a capillary watering system).

It is a good idea to have a path leading into the greenhouse as well as a floor inside, as this will stop mud from being walked in.

INSULATION

With the ever-increasing cost of heating, anything that can be done to cut down the heat loss in winter is likely to pay for itself in the first season or two. As in the home, some form of double glazing is the answer, coupled with the careful control of heating.

You can buy a fully double-glazed greenhouse that uses glass. Both full-span and lean-to models are available, and the larger ones can have two compartments, either or both of which can be double glazed. Although excellent value for money, these are towards the top end of the market and most gardeners will be looking for something that they can do relatively cheaply themselves. Plastic insulating materials can easily be fixed to wooden greenhouses, and to aluminium alloy greenhouses

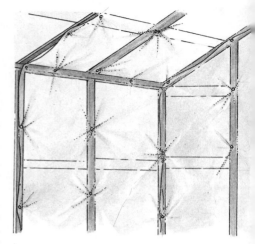

with special fixings that are readily available.

The cheapest form of double glazing is polythene sheeting fixed to the inside of the greenhouse (with drawing pins in a timber-framed greenhouse). The ventilators must be done separately otherwise you will not be able to open them.

Any kind of polythene lining will encourage condensation, but careful use of the ventilators and sensible watering should keep it to a minimum. The trouble with condensation is that it frequently drips onto the plants at a time when the foliage should be kept dry to reduce the risk of fungus diseases.

A more recent material that has much better insulating properties and is not so prone to condensation is 'bubble plastic'. This was originally designed as a packaging material instead of wood shavings but has since been developed as an insulator with larger bubbles. Although double skinned, the light admission is still good.

There is no specific time during which a polythene lining should be in place but it is usual to insulate the greenhouse from October or November to March or April.

VENTILATION

Ventilators are designed to control the heat within a greenhouse, so clearly they should be opened when a certain temperature is reached and closed again when it drops below that temperature. To do this manually would be a full-time job.

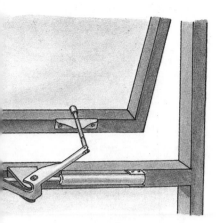

To overcome this problem, there are now automatic ventilator openers. These are completely self-contained, and no electricity is needed to work them: a fluid in a cylinder expands and contracts with changes in the temperature to move the operating arm. The whole system can be adjusted to open and close at any reasonable temperature. The more of these automatic openers that you fit to the greenhouse, the greater your control over the temperature, but most gardeners achieve reasonable control with just one.

An automatic ventilator will stop the temperature rising too high early on a summer's morning before you are up and about, and it will also close the greenhouse down in the late evening.

Of all the equipment that can be bought for a greenhouse, this is probably the most worthwhile as it saves a lot of work and worry, and is certainly beneficial for the plants.

SHADING

Along with the correct use of ventilators, shading is another means of controlling the temperature in a greenhouse.

The simplest and cheapest form comes in a tin or bottle and you paint it on like whitewash. The major drawback to this is that, once put on in the spring, it is there come rain or shine until you wash or rub it off in the autumn. It will certainly cut down the amount of sunlight that enters the greenhouse on a bright day, and this will keep the temperature down and prevent scorch. This disadvantage is that it also restricts

Although polythene lining (left) conserves a great deal of heat in the winter, keeping the plants cool in summer is just as important. Automatic ventilators (middle) and roller blinds (right) make this simple.

the light admission on dull days.

Whilst this 'liquid shading' is perfectly adequate for many gardeners, something rather more versatile and sophisticated is obviously better. Many types of blind can be bought, from the wooden slat kind to a simple small-mesh netting. Provided that the blinds cut out about a third of the direct sunlight, the real choice rests on how much you are prepared to pay and how easy to work you want the system to be.

The slatted kind is usually fitted with cords and pulleys to make raising and lowering it easy, whereas the netting comes in rolls from which you cut out panels of the correct size. With a bit of ingenuity, you can easily devise a way of operating this type, with wooden battens at the top and bottom of the netting.

HEATING

Even if you start off without any form of heating, the time will soon come when its advantages become apparent. If you want to get the most out of your greenhouse, however, there is much to be said for heating it right from the start. The actual choice of system depends on many things, such as the amount of heat required, the type of fuel and the cost of the heater – including how much it might cost to install and how much it will cost to run.

In the past, a coal- or coke-burning boiler feeding 10 cm (4 inch) hot-water pipes was the standard way of heating a greenhouse. Today, the vast majority of heaters warm the air directly rather than indirectly. These systems are far cheaper to install and their effect is more instant as there is little 'warming up' period.

The basic choice is between electricity, propane gas and paraffin.

Electrical heaters are the most expensive to buy, but they are clean to handle, are completely free of fumes, and are almost always fitted with a thermostat – which gives a more even temperature and avoids wasting fuel. Tubular heaters are very effective, and give a surprisingly even distribution of heat. You may, however, prefer a fan heater as these respond quickly and can be used to keep cold air moving in summer. For both types you will, of course, need an electricity supply in the greenhouse. A disadvantage of electric heaters is their vulnerability to power cuts, and unfortunately these are most likely to occur during the crucial winter months. There are many models and types of electrical heaters, so it pays to look at several before you decide on which one to buy.

Propane gas heaters can be run quite cheaply, and will provide a wide range of heat with little risk of harmful fumes, although water vapour is produced as with paraffin, and again some ventilation is generally advisable. The drawback of butane heaters is that they are cumbersome, and unless a pressure gauge is fitted they can run out of gas before you realize it. Also the replacement cylinders are heavy to carry. Many butane heaters include a thermostat.

Paraffin heaters are the cheapest to buy and can cost relatively little to run if you are just trying to keep the greenhouse frost-free. Against this is the fairly frequent filling they need, the messiness of paraffin, and the risk of damaging

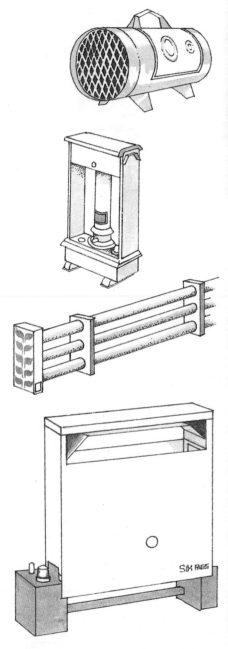

Types of greenhouse heater available: electric fan heater, paraffin heater, tubular electric heater, propane gas heater.

fumes if the wick is badly set. It is possible to buy a paraffin heater with a thermostat, but these models are not widely available.

Paraffin heaters produce water vapour that leads to increased condensation, and wherever combustible fuels are used, some ventilation should be provided to enable fresh air to enter the greenhouse. For safety's sake these heaters must be used carefully.

In summary: Electrical heaters are the most convenient but the most expensive to run. Paraffin heaters are cheap to buy and are usually adequate for a small greenhouse. Propane heaters are efficient but are apt to be bulky.

Size of heater: Having decided on the type of heater you prefer, the important thing is that you buy one powerful enough to heat your greenhouse to the sort of temperature you need. If you settle for one that will have to work flat out the whole time to maintain the temperature, there will be nothing in reserve if the outside temperature drops to the kind of level that it did in the winter of 1981-82. On the other hand, a heater that is capable of producing far more heat than is required will not only be more expensive to buy than a smaller and more appropriate one but it will generally be harder to keep the temperature down to a reasonable level. It is important to try to maintain an even winter temperature, especially if plants are in a dormant state.

PROPAGATORS

These are extremely handy if you want to raise a lot of plants from cuttings; and they are also useful for germinating seeds at any time of the year when the temperature within the greenhouse is too low.

Most propagators consist of a container very similar to a seed tray that is fitted with a transparent plastic lid. The tray is normally filled with a peat and sand mixture in which the cuttings are rooted, and the lid is put in place to maintain the temperature and a humid atmosphere.

Although many cuttings can be rooted without a propagator, it will greatly increase the chances of success and the range of 'rootable' plants. In addition, it will avoid the need to heat the whole greenhouse to the temperature required for rooting or germination, which means a considerable saving in fuel.

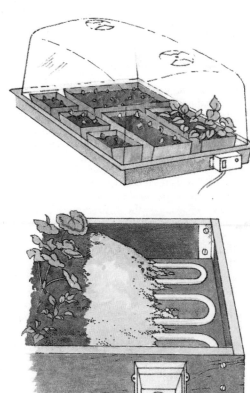

Readymade propagators with electrical soil warming cables are available (top). Alternatively you can make your own (bottom).

Propagators are available in many sizes and are made of several kinds of plastic as well as aluminium. However, they are usually one of two types: electrical ones that contain a heating element, and plain, unheated ones. You can, however, buy one that sits over a paraffin heater. Obviously heated propagators have a big advantage over the others and, if you can afford one and put it to good use, it is well worth the cost: it provides you with a mini greenhouse within the main one.

Most propagators are fitted with adjustable vents in the lid. Although these are certainly an advantage they are not essential. It is important to choose a fairly robust model because the cheaper ones tend to break all too easily.

You can, of course, make your own propagator, or even a heated bench. These can be heated with soil-warming cables buried in the peat and sand in the bottom. They are not difficult to use, and are fairly cheap to run.

WATERING DEVICES

The final 'extra' you might like to consider is automatic or semi-automatic watering.

A number of systems are available that work on the 'drip' principle in which a separate tube is led into each pot or tray from a larger pipe connected to a tap or reservoir in the greenhouse. This is a very efficient method if you have a lot of plants that all need the same amount of water at the same time. If you are growing a mixed collection, which is far more likely, it needs a certain amount of adapting otherwise some plants get flooded whilst others are still too dry.

A more practical system involves the use of capillary matting. This is a sort of blanket, which you keep saturated with water and on which the pots and trays are stood so that each one can soak up as much water as it needs. Not only does this eliminate hand watering but it also encourages far better plants, as they have as much water as they need without ever becoming waterlogged. Liquid feeding is best done by hand every so often but this is a small penalty to pay for the convenience. You can introduce the feed into the water supply, but there are drawbacks to this. The snag with capillary watering is that the plants might be too wet in winter.

When setting up a capillary system, the first essential is to have a waterproof base on which to lay the matting. This can be watered by hand when required, or you can set up a system of wicks leading to it from a basin of water. However, the basin should never be higher than the matting or a syphoning action will be set up which empties the basin and floods the matting. Or it can be fed from a special reservoir that you can buy.

Another way is to fill a gallon cider jar, invert it quickly and put the open end on a corner of the matting. As the matting dries, air gets into the jar and water glugs out until the matting is saturated again. Provided these systems are set up carefully, they can be very efficient, but as hand watering the matting takes so little time

their main benefit is only apparent if you have to leave the greenhouse unattended.

The forerunner of capillary matting, the sand bench, can also be made fully automatic. Fine sand is laid down in the same way as the matting and a level pipe is led into it from a cistern attached to the end of the bench. The cistern is linked to the mains through a ball-cock (or you can use a hand-filled reservoir) and as the level of water in the sand drops, more flows in. The art here is to place the cistern and adjust the valve so that the water level in the sand is exactly the same as that in the tank.

With any form of capillary watering, the three essentials are a completely level bench, a watertight base, and good contact between the matting or sand and the compost in the pot (which means that no crocks should be put in the bottom of pots).

MAINS WATER AND ELECTRICITY

Soil-warming cables, fan heaters, and propagators need a power supply, and some automatic watering systems need a mains water connection. Installing an electricity and water supply can be expensive, but they are not jobs to be economized on by doing them yourself. If there are any faults with wiring or fittings, the results could be fatal. Always enlist the help of a professional. *You have been warned!*

OTHER EQUIPMENT

Although various other gadgets, such as mist propagators, are available, those dealt with here are the ones that are most likely to be of use when you first buy a greenhouse; the others will come later as you build up experience and want to branch out. Above all, stay clear of equipment that is unlikely to justify its expense. Only buy those things that are going to be genuinely useful.

Although a wide variety of gadgets is available, it is perfectly possible to equip a greenhouse with simple, inexpensive items. Whether you use a fully automatic or a semi-automatic watering system, or simply a can, always aim to provide the plants with as much water as they need, but no more.

POTS AND COMPOSTS

Besides all the other little things that you will be using in the greenhouse, such as a dibber, watering-can, a presser board for firming the compost in pots and seed trays, a sprayer, plant labels, and split-canes for supporting tall plants, the most important items are likely to be pots and seed trays. As there are many types it pays to know what to look for when you buy them.

Pots were traditionally made from clay and seed trays from wood, but these have both been challenged by plastics. Which is best depends partly on what you want to grow and partly on personal preferences. Trial and error will probably determine which is the best for you, but the following pros and cons should alert you to the strengths and weaknesses of each.

CLAY POTS

Being porous, clay pots make it less likely that you will overwater the plants, and because of thickness, they also have a greater buffering effect against changes in temperature. They are also relatively heavy so that tall plants are less likely to topple over. They are often preferred simply for their appearance, which is usually more pleasing than plastic.

Against this has to be considered their greater weight when handling them in quantity and the fact that they take up much more room in storage. Some people regard them as more easily broken and, whilst this is undoubtedly true if you drop them, in other respects they are just as strong as plastic, and often stronger. A possible disadvantage of their porosity is that the compost in them will dry out quicker, but this depends on the method of watering you adopt; in the winter, drying out is certainly no problem. They are more difficult to scrub clean than plastic.

PLASTIC POTS

The thing to remember about plastic pots is that they vary enormously in quality, depending on the type of plastic from which they are made. The best sort is almost certainly polypropylene as it combines strength with semi-rigidity. So often you find pots that are either floppy or brittle; both are equally useless and are priced accordingly. Plastic pots are easy to handle in bulk and well-designed ones take up very little room when stacked. Good plastic pots are almost indestructible and are unaffected by extremes of temperature. They are frequently available in colours other than terra-cotta.

The main disadvantages of plastic pots are that tall plants are often top-heavy in them, and that you have to water the plants more carefully in the winter as the compost does not dry out so readily.

PEAT POTS AND BLOCKS

For seedlings that are to be planted outdoors or in the greenhouse border later, you can use peat pots or blocks. Most peat pots – and pots made from other materials that will allow the roots to grow through – are difficult to keep moist in the small sizes, but have the merit of causing

Peat blocks are most useful for growing seedlings, such as tomatoes and bedding plants, that are to be planted into the greenhouse border or into larger pots or growing bags later. A peat block compressor or 'blocking tool' is used to press out blocks from a special peat compost.

little root disturbance when the seedlings are eventually planted out. An alternative to peat pots are peat blocks, which you press out from a special peat compost using a 'blocking' tool. These blocks take up little room on the bench, and make transplanting easy. However, you really need to use a capillary watering system otherwise the blocks are likely to dry out and check the growth of the seedlings.

You can use small expandable peat 'pellets' to sow pot-plant seedlings into. These can then be potted up into an ordinary pot without the root disturbance caused by pricking out.

SEED TRAYS

To say that there is a choice of materials is somewhat misleading, as wooden ones have all but disappeared. They are certainly not as long-lasting as good plastic trays, and they take up a lot more storage room. But they do have the big advantage that they are rigid. This may not seem important but it does mean that they can be moved about with plants in them without twisting. The factors concerning the different types of plastic are the same as for pots.

COMPOSTS

The compost that interests the greenhouse gardener has nothing to do with the garden compost heap. Potting compost should always be made carefully from special ingredients.

Composts can be divided into three types: seed or sowing compost, potting compost, and all-purpose compost. The first is for raising young plants from seeds or cuttings; potting compost is for growing on plants of any age that already have an established root system; all-purpose compost can be used for raising plants and for growing them on.

The reason for having different composts for sowing and growing is that plant foods are required in varying amounts by seedlings (or rooted cuttings) and older plants. All-purpose composts are something of a compromise, but are perfectly suitable for the vast majority of gardeners; all-purpose composts are likely to be peat-based.

Soil-less composts can be made from peat alone, but usually include sand, vermiculite or perlite. Loam-based composts, such as the John Innes range, depend on soil as the key consti-tuent. Soil-less composts are certainly lighter to carry and handle, and because all the ingre-dients are naturally sterile there is little risk of plant diseases being carried by them. The majority are mass-produced. This, and the fact that there is very little variation in the raw materials, more or less guarantees that, for a given brand, the compost is going to be the same wherever and whenever you buy it. Against this are the drawbacks: peat-based composts are more difficult to 'manage' (they are more easily over- or underwatered) and they soon run out of nutrients, so you will probably have to feed your plants sooner than you would with a loam-based compost.

If you want to use a loam-based compost, one made to the John Innes formula (it is not a brand) is almost certainly your best choice – although quality can vary. John Innes composts are less susceptible to under-feeding as there is always a certain reservoir of nutrients in the

loam. They are also better for permanent large plants as their extra weight and density add stability and reduce the likelihood of top-heaviness.

The shortage of suitable loam can tempt some manufacturers to take short cuts, which result in an inferior compost. This has to some extent been overcome by the setting up of the John Innes Manufacturers' Association – their bags carry a seal of approval. Members of the association are bound by a code of conduct to stick to the original specifications – though even this is no absolute guarantee of quality. There have been improvements in fertilizer technology, however, and slow-release fertilizers are sometimes used (normally the compost can deteriorate after a few weeks because of chemical reactions). Alternatively it is possible to buy a compost to which you add the fertilizer provided before use.

There are four basic 'grades' of John Innes compost: one for seeds (seed compost) and three for potting (potting composts 1, 2, 3). No. 2 contains twice as much fertilizer as No. 1 and No. 3 contains three times as much. There are special mixes for lime-hating plants.

HOME-MADE COMPOSTS
Although ready-made composts are by no means cheap, it is folly to run the risk of failure by making your own special 'brew'; you will very likely be throwing away the cost of the seeds as well. Provided you buy a reliable brand of compost, you have the assurance that you are getting something of high quality that will do the job it is intended for.

It is, however, possible to buy a proprietary DIY compost kit that provides the necessary ingredients. This might be worth trying as there is no guesswork on your part – the right amount of fertilizer will be provided – but follow any instructions carefully.

It is most unwise to try to make your own compost using unsterilized loam, because pests and diseases can easily be introduced by doing so.

LOAM-BASED OR SOIL-LESS?
Both types of compost have their advantages and disadvantages, but either is suitable for the vast majority of plants. On the whole, however, the soil-less ones probably have more advantages, though they do need more careful handling. Once they are mastered, the plants grown in them are frequently better.

Another development of soil-less composts has, over the last seven or eight years, been introduced to the gardening public in the shape of growing bags. These have several advantages over traditional ways of growing many greenhouse crops as well as being equally suitable for use outdoors.

One of the big problems with using the greenhouse border for crops year after year is that, to be safe from soil-borne pests and diseases, the soil has to be changed or sterilized at least every other year, and preferably annually. Growing bags avoid the need for this as the plants in them are completely isolated from whatever lies underneath. They are quite expensive, but very convenient, and you will probably end up producing much better crops.

PLANNING WHAT TO GROW

Important though equipment and aids are, greenhouse gardening is about growing plants – and few decisions can be as important as which plants to grow. The A-Z of greenhouse plants in this book will show you what you can reasonably expect to succeed with, but you also need to take into account space and timing as well as things like the temperature you can maintain.

Space can be at a premium at any time, but particularly so in spring when you will be raising a lot of plants that are to go outside later on when the risk of frosts is over. For this reason alone, early sowing is not always a good thing as the situation will arise when there are too many plants or they are too large for the greenhouse yet it will still not be safe to plant them outdoors.

Likewise, when any plants are at the correct stage for planting out in the greenhouse, it must be possible to do so. Here, though, we find one of the advantages of growing bags as these can be planted up and put in a temporary position in the greenhouse until the proper position becomes vacant.

Along with making sure that the greenhouse is never overcrowded comes the necessity of ensuring that it is always being used to the full.

When crops such as tomatoes, cucumbers, or melons are taking up one side, you will probably be using staging on the other to accommodate a succession of pot-plants for the home. These can start in the early spring with hardy annuals overwintered in pots, and carry right on through the primula species, calceolarias and cinerarias, ending up in the winter with cyclamen.

Never waste space. Chicory can easily be forced under the staging in winter.

GARDENING YEAR IN THE GREENHOU[SE]

January	February	March	Apri[l]
Keep cacti & succulents cool and dry			
Grow on bulbs until flowering finished			
		Sow calceolarias, celosi[a], solanum, streptocarpus	
Keep foliage, flowering climbing plants on dry side			
Germinate outside vegetable plants from seed			
Germinate bedding plants from seed			
Keep apricots, grapes & peaches, cool and dry			Keep apri[cots] as require[d]
Sow aubergines, peppers & tomatoes			Pla[nt]
	Sow cucumbers		Pla[nt]
Sow melons			Pla[nt]
Grow and crop winter lettuces			
		Grow and crop spring & summe[r]	
Force rhubarb			
Grow strawberries in growing bags until they h[ave]			

At some point in the year, time should also be set aside for moving out existing plants and cleaning the whole greenhouse thoroughly. The most convenient time for this is when the tomatoes, for example, have finished and very little is being propagated.

Winter is a time when greenhouses are more or less empty. Whilst this is quite normal, if you have to heat the greenhouse for some plants it is more economical to have as much growing as possible. Apart from the usual pot-plants, the space under the staging should be used for forcing crops like rhubarb and chicory. These are unlikely to interfere with anything else, even when the time comes for sowing in the spring.

Bulbs are always welcome and many of the smaller species of crocuses and narcissi can be grown in pots without any heat at all.

There are a great many different uses to which the greenhouse can be put. It is best to decide on the most important vegetable and decorative plants first, then fit the others in as time allows. The greenhouse planner (below) provides a valuable year-round guide to using your greenhouse.

May	June	July	August	September	October	November	December
...ep cacti & succulents warmer, and water and feed						Keep cacti & succulents cool and dry	
					Plant spring bulbs		Grow on bulbs
...ed foliage, flowering & climbing plants and pot up ...necessary						Keep foliage, flowering & climbing plants on dry side	
...opagate foliage, flowering & climbing plants as ...quired							
...es & peaches warmer; water more frequently and feed						Keep apricots, grapes & peaches cool and dry	
...l feed aubergines, peppers & tomatoes as required							
...l feed cucumbers as required							
...l feed melons as required							
					Grow and crop winter lettuces		
...ettuce							
...ow mustard and cress as required at any time of the year							
							Force rhubarb
...hed fruiting							

ROUTINE CARE

This chapter covers the routines that will help you to raise strong and healthy plants. As advice on individual plants will be found in the A-Z sections, this chapter deals mainly with principles.

PROPAGATION

Plants can be propagated in many ways – from seeds, from cuttings of various kinds, by division, or from plantlets for instance. Many plants are easy to propagate, but some need coaxing. If you follow the advice below you should not find much difficulty with most plants that you are likely to grow.

Before you try your hand at propagation, be warned: you will have some failures among your successes. Do not let this deter you.

New plants from seeds: This is by far the most common way of raising new plants, and in many cases it is Nature's way. There are three essentials for success:

- The seed must be viable (alive).
- It must be kept constantly damp, though not waterlogged or it will rot.
- It must have warmth, though the amount will vary with the species involved.

Once the seeds have germinated, they will also need light if they are to make good plants.

All you need for seed sowing is a suitable container and some seed compost. If there are a lot of seeds to sow, a seed tray will be needed, but a half-tray or even a pot will be sufficient if there are not many in the packet. When using a clay pot in conjunction with John Innes seed compost, place a piece of crock (broken pot) over the drainage hole to stop the compost running out, but it is not normally necessary with seed trays or plastic pots, nor if you use a soil-less compost.

Half fill with compost, lightly firm it and then carry on filling until the container is overfull. Strike the surface off level with the rim and press the compost down gently with a presser board.

When sowing very small seeds, like begonias, the best plan is to water the compost before you actually sow, but with larger seeds it need not be done until afterwards.

TOP: *To encourage even seed germination, fill the container with suitable compost and firm it lightly to give a level surface.*

BOTTOM: *After sowing the seeds thinly and evenly, sieve some more compost over them so that they are just buried.*

Sow the seeds thinly and evenly over the whole surface of the compost. Using a sieve, cover the seeds with compost until they are buried to about their own depth; very small seeds should not be covered at all. The pot or seed tray should be thoroughly wetted either by standing it in a dish of water until it shows moist at the surface, or by using a fine-rosed watering-can. Put some glass or polythene over the container and a sheet of newspaper on top of that, to keep the moisture in and reduce the chance of overheating. Place the pot or tray somewhere warm for the seeds to germinate.

Check it daily, and the moment you see signs of growth take off the newspaper; the glass or polythene can stay on until the seedlings are almost touching it. The seedlings must then be given full light to prevent straggly growth.

Cuttings: The parts of a plant normally used to provide cuttings include the top of the growing shoot (a stem cutting), sections of a shoot that include at least one leaf (a leaf-bud cutting), and with some plants the leaf itself (a leaf cutting). The conditions needed for a cutting to produce roots are similar to those required for seeds to germinate (warmth and moisture) but they also need plenty of light.

Stem cuttings should be 2.5-7.5 cm (1-3 inches) long, according to the species of plant, and are better if taken from non-flowering shoots. In the vast majority of cases the base of the cutting should be trimmed off neatly immediately below a leaf or pair of leaves (which are then removed). The bottom of the cutting may be dipped in hormone rooting powder or liquid to hasten rooting and then inserted into the compost as described later. Most of the common plants can be propagated in this way.

Leaf-bud cuttings are used primarily for climbers like ivy and are prepared by cutting a growing shoot into sections so that each section contains a leaf with a bud at its base. It is from this bud that the new plant will develop. So that there is a 'handle' for inserting the cutting and a 'peg' for holding it firmly in the compost, leave about 1 cm (½ inch) of stem above and below the leaf. The bottom half can then be dipped in hormone rooting powder and the cutting inserted so that the leaf-bud is just covered.

Leaf cuttings of plants like the African violet can, in fact, be rooted in water but they are often tricky to establish when finally put in potting

TOP: *Propagation by tip cuttings. A stem cutting with several leaves attached is taken from the top of a mature plant.*
CENTRE: *Cuttings are inserted into half-pots.*
BOTTOM: *Begonia rex can be propagated from leaf cuttings. A whole leaf is used.*

ABOVE: Chlorophytum (the spider plant) is particularly easy to propagate. Simply peg down the plantlets into their own pot of compost.

ABOVE: When growing plants from seed, they should be pricked out into fresh compost as soon as they are large enough to handle.

compost, so rooting them conventionally is usually better in the long run. With African violets, a whole mature leaf and leaf stalk is cut from the plant and inserted at an angle so that there is a small space between the blade and the compost.

A different technique is used for *Begonia rex*; a mature leaf is laid on the compost and pinned down. Each main vein is cut through and after a while, each of these areas will root and produce a new plant. Streptocarpus leaf cuttings are taken by cutting the leaf into sections, each about 2.5 cm (1 inch) wide. The bottom of each section is then gently pushed into the compost and the new plant develops from the buried portion of mid-rib.

When rooting cuttings, it helps to have a propagator for keeping them warm and moist, but you can use something like a gallon ice-cream tub with a transparent lid, putting a small amount of compost in the bottom, inserting the cuttings, and then putting on the lid. Alternatively, use an ordinary flower-pot and put the whole thing in a polythene bag after inserting the cuttings.

The compost you use is a matter of personal preference. You can root the cuttings in a seed compost, or you could try a mixture of 1 part peat and 1 part sharp sand.

When choosing part of a plant for cuttings, do make sure that it is healthy. Cuttings should be gently firmed in and then given a good watering before you enclose them.

The time taken to root will vary enormously, but is usually between two and four weeks for most plants. When they have rooted new growth will start to appear; this is the time when care is needed, as the rooted cuttings will have to be weaned gently to the less protected atmosphere of the rest of the greenhouse. This is done by gradually exposing them to more and more fresh air over a period of three or four days. At the end of this time, they should be ready for potting up.

Division: This method of propagation is used solely for plants that grow in clumps (like African violets). The plant is removed from its pot in the spring or early summer and gently teased apart into a number of smaller clumps. Each of these can be potted up. Many of the ferns are dealt with in this way, and it is a good way to propagate the yellow and green striped form of mother-in-law's tongue, as the yellow edge is lost if you take leaf cuttings.

Plantlets: Some houseplants increase their numbers naturally by producing mini-plants either on the end of flowering stems (notably the spider plant) or around the edges of the leaves (some bryophyllums). Once a plantlet is developing roots of its own, it can be parted from the parent, potted up in potting compost and kept in a close atmosphere for a few days until it is established.

Pricking out and potting up: As soon as seedlings are large enough to handle and cuttings have rooted, they must be removed into fresh

ABOVE: *When first potting larger plants, pour the compost in evenly around the roots.*

ABOVE: *Peat pots are best for larger seedlings; smaller ones can be put straight into a tray.*

compost. This can be of the all-purpose type or a specific soil-less or John Innes potting mixture. In the John Innes range, either No. 1 or No. 2 should be used for seedlings and No. 2 for rooted cuttings. No. 3 is for mature plants needing a rich mixture.

Seedlings are usually 'pricked out' (moved) into seed trays, where they are spaced so that each has plenty of room to grow. When dealing with tomatoes and the larger type of seedling, it is much better to put them directly into small

pots. If you use a peat pot it can be planted along with the plant when the time comes; this avoids any check to the plants which might result from root disturbance.

Before you prick out into trays, fill them in exactly the same way as for sowing. A small hole should then be made with a dibber and the roots of the seedling fed into it before being gently firmed into place. Once the tray is full (five rows of seven plants is convenient), the seedlings should be given a good soaking and put back on a shelf or on the staging where there is plenty of light.

If pots are used instead, exactly the same routine is followed except for rooted cuttings and seedlings with a large root system. With these, a little compost is best placed in the pot and gently firmed, then the young plant held in the pot and compost poured around the roots. When the pot is full, the compost can be lightly firmed around the plant and then watered.

POTTING ON

This is the term applied to the job of moving any plant from one pot into a larger one. The stage at which you should pot on can easily be judged by tipping the plant out of its pot and examining the roots; if they are congested and hardly any compost can be seen, the plant needs a larger pot. If, however, there is still plenty of room for growth, leave well alone and have another look in a couple of weeks or so. Plants should only be moved into larger pots during the growing season, never in the late autumn or during the winter.

When selecting a larger pot, choose a size that will accommodate the plant for at least another month, but avoid one too big otherwise much of the fertilizer will have drained from the compost before the roots have made use of it. As a rule, go for a size that will leave a gap of about 1 cm (½ inch) all round between the inside and the root-ball of the plant. In practice, this will mean moving a plant from a 7.5 cm (3 inch) pot into a 10 cm (4 inch) one or from a 9 cm (3½ inch) one into a 13 cm (5 inch).

If the plant has a crock in the bottom of the root-ball, remove this before potting on, otherwise root growth could be impeded. When placing compost around the roots in the new pot, firm it gently as you proceed so that no air spaces are left; gentle firming is particularly important with soil-less composts, since they can easily become too compacted.

WATERING

Incorrect watering almost certainly causes more losses amongst plants than any other single reason.

During the growing season (about March to September in the greenhouse), plants will use an enormous amount of water and this should be freely available. Something like 90 per cent is transpired through the leaves to help keep the plant cool. Semi-automatic systems are, of course, particularly useful during this period as they ensure that the plants have all they need, at the same time maintaining a moist atmosphere around them. Even cacti and succulents like plenty of water; it is just that they have adapted to doing without it.

However, this need for water has to be considered with the equally important need for air around the roots – which is why drainage should always be good. If it is not, the air will be forced out of the compost and waterlogging will occur, which often results in the plant dying.

A completely different situation exists in the winter. Because there is much less natural light and a considerably lower temperature, plants should be encouraged to 'rest'. This will reduce their water needs to a minimum, and giving

A plant is ready for a larger pot when the roots are becoming crowded.

them summer quantities is asking for trouble. As with all aspects of gardening there are exceptions, but normally the compost in the pots should be kept only just short of dry; just aim to keep the plants from wilting. They will be far healthier if kept like this.

The most common symptom of overwatering in winter is the yellowing, wilting and perhaps loss, of the lower leaves.

FEEDING

This section deals with decorative plants only. Advice on feeding fruits and vegetables will be found in the relative entry in the A-Z sections.

In many respects feeding is closely allied to watering, and is essentially a spring and summer job. You should only feed plants when they are growing; it is then that they will be able to use nutrients.

It is not possible to say exactly when feeding should start in the spring, but the normal time is when you see the plants show signs of beginning to grow again. At that point, watering can be increased a little and fertilizer should be given to ensure that growth is strong and healthy. The frequency of feeding should be in line with the manufacturer's instructions on whichever make you buy. By September or October feeding should be gradually decreased and then stopped altogether until spring.

There are many different brands of fertilizer suitable for greenhouse plants, but all leading makes are likely to be completely satisfactory. They do, however, come in several different forms. The most common is the concentrated liquid type that has to be diluted before use, but you can also buy crystals that have to be dissolved. Some liquid concentrates can be applied direct to the compost a drop or two at a time, and there are granular fertilizers that are sprinkled on to the surface of the compost, fertilizer spikes which are pushed into it, and even pills that you bury amongst the roots. All of them work, and it is really a question of personal preference as to which you buy. Slow-release spikes and granules mean less frequent – but probably more expensive – feeding.

Plants grown for their foliage do best with a fertilizer with more nitrogen than potash in it; so do young flowering plants. However, once the latter start to develop flower buds, they respond better to a feed higher in potash, such as a tomato fertilizer. The composition of every fertilizer will be found on the label or carton.

PEST AND DISEASE CONTROL

One of the most disheartening things in gardening is to spend time and effort in growing plants only to find that they fall victim to some dreadful pest or disease.

A lot can be done to counteract this by growing strong plants, by being very careful not to import any 'nasties' with new plants, and by keeping a neat and clean greenhouse with no dead leaves lying about or weeds growing under the staging. Pick dead leaves or flowers off plants, and generally try to keep the greenhouse clean.

In spite of every precaution, trouble is more

A smoke cone is one effective control method.

or less bound to strike eventually, but you can usually control the problem by prompt action:
● Always be on the look-out for the first signs of pests and diseases.
● Take action as soon as you see any.
● Identify the trouble.
● Use the correct treatment.
● Be ready to treat again if one application is insufficient.

The first two steps are straightforward enough but it may not always be easy to identify the pest or disease – this is where some of the charts produced by chemical manufacturers can be of great value. Correct identification is important for appropriate treatment.

Along with using the right material comes the need to choose the correct formulation (spray, dust, aerosol, or smoke) because some are more effective than others. In a greenhouse, fumigation with smoke or a proper greenhouse aerosol is usually best as the smoke or vapour is carried into every nook and cranny and amongst all the plants, thus ensuring that nothing remains untreated.

To control difficult pests, such as whitefly, you must be prepared to repeat the treatment.

The chart opposite will tell you which chemical to use. These are the common chemical names, which will always be on the container, but sometimes in small print.

The chemicals mentioned do not form a complete list of those that will do the job. A longer list might give you more choice, but not necessarily control the pest or disease any better. The choice of chemical is always a personal one.

PEST AND DISEASE CONTROL CHART

Pest	Common chemical name	Formulation
Ants	borax sodium tetraborate	liquid liquid
Aphids (greenfly, blackfly)	dimethoate gamma-HCH malathion permethrin and heptenophos pirimiphos-methyl and synergized pyrethrins	spray smoke aerosol spray aerosol
Aphids, root	malathion	spray, used as drench
Caterpillars	permethrin permethrin and heptenophos	spray spray
Earwigs	permethrin and heptenophos gamma-HCH	spray dust
Leaf miners	gamma-HCH permethrin and heptenophos pirimiphos-methyl	smoke or spray spray spray
Mealy bugs	dimethoate permethrin and heptenophos pirimiphos-methyl	spray spray spray
Mealy bugs, root	dimethoate malathion	spray, used as drench spray, used as drench
Red spider mites	dimethoate pirimiphos-methyl	spray smoke or spray
Scale insects	dimethoate permethrin and heptenophos	spray spray
Sciarid (fungus gnat)	malathion pirimiphos-methyl	aerosol, or spray used as drench smoke
Thrips	gamma-HCH malathion pyrethrum and resmethrin	smoke or spray spray spray
Whitefly	bioresmethrin permethrin	aerosol or spray smoke or spray
Botrytis (grey mould)	benomyl tecnazene*	spray smoke
Damping off (in seedlings)	copper compound copper sulphate and ammonium carbonate (Cheshunt compound)	spray, used as drench spray, used as drench
Leaf spot	benomyl mancozeb	spray spray
Mildew	benomyl bupirimate and triforine thiophanate-methyl	spray spray spray

*sold in a formulation containing
gamma-HCH insecticide

FOLIAGE PLANTS

Most foliage plants require warmth during the winter months. For this reason large formal collections of foliage plants are more frequently grown within homes, rather than in greenhouses.

The choice of varieties that will tolerate low temperatures without any artificial heat is unfortunately very limited. If you are keen to grow a range of foliage plants in the greenhouse but wish to avoid fuel costs, then a good compromise might be to supplement your collection with more interesting varieties as the weather improves.

However, should you choose to heat the greenhouse during winter, foliage plants will enable you to make full use of all available space. Some plants such as ferns and palms prefer much lower light intensities than others and, in this respect, can be grown under the staging. Remember that even if your greenhouse is heated over the winter it is advisable to raise the plants up from the ground, where temperatures are likely to be quite a bit lower than on the staging.

Unless you intend to specialize in foliage plants and are prepared to heat the greenhouse through the colder months of the year, you may well decide to use your greenhouse for other types of plants which are more economical to grow.

AGAVE*

If you have a large greenhouse, an agave can make a useful addition. It is a succulent with sharp pointed tips to its leaves. *Agave americana*, the species usually grown, can reach a height of 1.2 metres (4 ft) with a similar spread. There are several varieties with plain green or variegated leaves.

General Care: One of the great things about agaves is that they are quite hardy, tolerating high and low temperatures. They do however need lots of light. Grow them in 25-30 cm (10-12 inch) pots of John Innes No. 2 potting compost. Water agaves reasonably often during the summer, allowing the compost to become dry between waterings. During the winter, keep them quite dry. Most species can tolerate temperatures as low as 4°C (40°F).

Although grown primarily for their leaves, agaves also produce tall spikes of yellow-green flowers from the centre of the rosette of leaves in late summer. After flowering, the plant then produces offsets around the base and usually dies.

Propagation: When the mother plant has produced offsets, carefully remove them in spring or summer, potting them up singly in a 13 cm (5 inch) pot in John Innes No. 2 potting compost.

Plants can also be propagated from seeds. Sow them in April, at about 20°C (68°F), in a mixture of 4 parts seed compost to 1 part fine sand.

Pests and Diseases: Mealy bugs and root mealy bugs occasionally trouble the plant but are easily dealt with.

ALOE*

Aloes are attractive succulents with different leaf patterns formed on a rosette of leaves in an overlapping arrangement. They form flower spikes in spring. Although the flowers are not very large, they are none the less attractive and vary in colour from yellow to orange, pink and red.

One of the most hardy and successful varieties that can be grown under glass is the popular *Aloe variegata* or partridge-breasted aloe, which has green-and-white-striped fleshy leaves and produces pinkish-orange flowers on 30 cm (12 inch) flower spikes.

General Care: Aloes are relatively hardy and adaptable and, although they prefer a well-lit situation, they can tolerate a slightly shaded position. During the spring and summer, water regularly, but not excessively, allowing the plant to dry out in between waterings. In the winter, however, the plant must be kept on the dry side, when it will tolerate temperatures down to around 4°C (40°F). Grow in John Innes No. 2 potting compost and in suitable sized pots up to 30 cm (12

Agave americana marginata

2 metres (5-6½ ft) with a diameter of about 1 metre (3 ft). Although it is related to the monkey puzzle tree which is grown outside in the garden, *Auraucaria excelsa* will not tolerate frost.

General Care: The araucaria adapts to a wide range of conditions from shade to full sun and at temperatures down to 10°C (50°F). During the spring and summer, try to allow the plant to dry out in between waterings and in the winter water infrequently, keeping the compost on the dry side. Grow it in John Innes No. 2 potting compost in 20-25 cm (8-10 inch) pots.

Propagation: The Norfolk Island pine should be propagated from seed sown in March in half or dwarf pots filled with John Innes No. 1 potting compost. Sprinkle the seed on the compost and lightly cover with more compost. Then keep the compost moist and warm at around 20°C (68°F) until the seeds have germinated. Grow on in the pots until large enough to handle then pot them up singly in 9 cm (3½ inch) pots filled with John Innes No. 2 potting compost.

Araucaria may also be propagated from cuttings in spring. Take 7.5 cm (3 inches) shoots and insert in a mixture of equal parts of peat and sand at a temperature of 13-16°C (55-61°F). When rooted, pot up as for seedlings.

Pests and Diseases: Usually trouble-free, but occasionally araucaria is troubled by mealy bugs and root mealy bugs.

inches) as the plant gets larger.
Propagation: It is quite easy to propagate aloes. They can be grown from offsets separated carefully from the mother plant in summer and potted up singly in 9 cm (3½ inch) pots containing a peat and sand potting compost.

Aloes can also be raised from seed sown in March in a medium of 4 parts seed compost to 1 part fine sand and kept at around 20°C (68°F). When the seedlings are large enough to handle, prick out and pot them up separately in a similar mixture.

Pests and Diseases: Mealy bugs and root mealy bugs are the most usual pests.

ARAUCARIA*

The variety commonly grown is *Araucaria excelsa*, the Norfolk Island pine, which resembles a soft feathery Christmas tree with radiating branches of dark green 'needles'. It grows to a height of around 1.5-

ASPIDISTRA*

Aspidistras, with their broad dark green or variegated leaves, take up little room in a greenhouse because of their erect habit. They reach a height of 30 cm (12 inches) and, although not outstandingly attractive, can complement a collection of foliage plants grown under glass.

General Care: Aspidistras should not be grown in direct sunlight as this can scorch the leaves. They are best in a slightly shaded situation in a corner or perhaps even under the staging in the greenhouse. A humid environment is appreciated and for this reason, aspidistras often thrive better under glass than when grown indoors.

Do not overwater and allow the compost to get on the dry side in between waterings. In winter, it is essential to avoid overwatering, because aspidistras will rot if kept too wet at low temperatures: aim for a minimum temperature of around 10°C (50°F). Grow in 15-25 cm (6-10 inch) pots of John Innes No. 2 potting compost. Feed monthly during summer with a diluted liquid fertilizer.

Propagation: The best way to propagate aspidistra is to divide the plant carefully in spring or summer. Moisten the compost and then use a sharp knife to separate the plant into the appropriate number of pieces, potting each up singly in 13 cm (5 inch) pots of potting compost.

Pests and Diseases: Red spider mites, mealy bugs and root mealy bugs will attack aspidistras. Red spider mite can be a particular nuisance.

ASPARAGUS FERN*

There are several different plants known as asparagus fern, but none of them is a true fern. Two varieties in particular are usually grown as pot plants under glass – *Asparagus plumosus* and *Asparagus sprengeri*.

General Care: Asparagus fern is very easy to grow. It should be kept in a well-lit position, but shaded from direct sunlight in summer. Grow it in 13 cm (5 inch) pots of John Innes No. 3 potting compost or a soil-less compost, and water frequently in summer. Conversely, keep it on the dry side in winter, and aim for a minimum temperature of about 10°C (50°F).

Asparagus fern can be grown on the staging or under it, in the border, or in a hanging basket if you are short of

Asparagus sprengeri (asparagus fern)

space. Whichever way you grow it, this plant will provide you with feathery foliage that can be used in floral arrangements. It will be necessary to feed with a high nitrogen fertilizer if the foliage is cut frequently.

Propagation: This is very easy – the plants are simply divided in spring. Moisten the compost well and gently tease apart the root, using a knife to cut through some of the fibrous root growth. Pot up each division into a pot filled with potting compost and grow on.

Pests and Diseases: Asparagus ferns can sometimes be attacked by mealy bugs and root mealy bugs, and occasionally by scale insects.

ASPLENIUM*

Commonly known as the bird's nest fern, the *Asplenium nidus avis* is a fairly tough fern with broad fronds that lack the usual finely cut appearance of other ferns. The fronds are shiny and are bright green in colour, growing up to about 1 metre (3 ft) on mature specimens.

General Care: In common with other ferns, aspleniums are happiest when out of direct sunlight as it bleaches the fronds. Probably one of the best places to grow them is under the staging, where they will thrive particularly if planted directly into the greenhouse border. Keep the compost relatively moist all through the year, but in the winter keep it slightly drier. If possible avoid overhead watering. During the winter, aspleniums will happily tolerate temperatures down to around 10°C (50°F) and sometimes even lower. Grow them in 13 cm (5 inch) pots of peat-based compost.

Propagation: As the plants get older, they will produce dark brown, gill-like growths on the underside of some of the fronds. The spores produced from these can be collected by tapping the particular fronds over a sheet of paper. The spores appear as brown dust and these can be sown in summer on to the surface of a half pot filled with a mixture of equal parts peat and a loam-based seed compost, or a peat-based seed compost. This should be kept moist and covered with a polythene bag to conserve humidity until the spores germinate. When the plantlets are large enough to handle, gently prick out and pot up singly in potting compost in 9 cm (3½ inch) pots.

Pests and Diseases: Scale insects are a particular nuisance to asplenium, and will attack both upper and lower surfaces of the fronds.

BEGONIA REX**

Begonia rex is one of the most beautiful foliage begonias, having roughly heart-shaped leaves in a wide range of colours and patterns.

General Care: This begonia likes a well-lit position away from strong direct sun. It will grow quite happily beneath the staging. The plant is fairly

Aspidistra

General Care: Chlorophytums are equally happy in pots, hanging baskets or troughs, but look particularly effective growing in hanging baskets. During the spring and summer, keep them in full light and water frequently, but avoid allowing the plants to become too wet. In the winter keep them on the dry side, and they will quite happily tolerate temperatures down to around 10°C (50°F) or lower. When the roots really fill the pot, pot on until they are in 20 cm (8 inch) pots, and feed weekly in summer with liquid fertilizer. Use either a John Innes or a soilless compost.

Propagation: The plant produces its characteristic flowering trails in spring and summer and you can propagate from the little plantlets when they have grown a little and you can see the roots starting to form. Either place them lightly in 9 cm (3½ inch) pots filled with potting compost whilst still attached to the trails or, if you are feeling bold, cut them off and take a chance! Although the former almost guarantees success, the latter rarely fails. Once you have separated the plantlets from the mother plant, trim back the trails to keep the main plant looking tidy.

Pests and Diseases: Aphids can attack chlorophytum during the spring and summer. Mealy bugs and root mealy bugs are sometimes troublesome.

tolerant of a warm, dry environment and prefers a temperature of about 18°C (65°F), though a winter temperature of 10°C (50°F) is adequate if the compost is kept fairly dry.

Propagation: Select a well-formed, mature (not old) leaf, lay it face down and cut it into postage-stamp squares using a sharp knife. Lightly dip the underside of the leaf cuttings in hormone rooting powder and gently lay right-side up on the surface of a seed tray or half pot filled with moistened seed compost. Cover with a polythene bag and keep at about 21°C (70°F). Remove any cuttings that wither or rot and take off the polythene when the little plantlets start to grow. When they are large enough to handle, gently prick them out and pot up.

Pests and Diseases: Mildew and grey mould (botrytis) may occasionally infect the plant. Mealy bugs also sometimes attack begonias.

CHLOROPHYTUM*

The spider plant, *Chlorophytum comosum*, also called the St Bernard lily, is one of the most common plants grown, with its green and white variegated leaves and long trailing runners. Although the chlorophytum grows reasonably well as a houseplant, it is happier in a greenhouse, where, with the advantage of better conditions, its habit and colour really excel.

COLEUS*

Coleus, commonly called flame nettles, are super little plants to raise and grow under glass. They are available in a

very wide range of highly coloured leaf forms. Apart from
providing a wealth of colour in
the greenhouse, they can also
be used as summer bedding
plants or as houseplants. They
are only likely to succeed as
bedding plants in a sheltered
position in favourable areas.
General Care: Coleus should
be allowed as much light as
possible; lack of light will
cause the growth to stretch
and lose its colour. As the
plant grows, pinch out the top
shoot or shoots from time to
time to encourage a compact
and well-shaped plant. Insignificant flowers will be produced and these can be
pinched out to maintain the
plant's vigour.

Water coleus freely in summer, but keep on the dry side
in winter. Feed mature plants
regularly. A temperature of
about 10°C (50°F) should be
sufficient to see the plants
through winter, although
they do tend to become rather

straggly if kept too long. Grow
coleus in 13 cm (5 inch) pots of
John Innes No. 3 potting compost, or a soil-less compost.
Propagation: Coleus can be
propagated from seed in early
spring. Sow seeds in half pots,
dwarf pots or seed trays filled
with seed compost, and keep
at around 18°C (65°F). When
large enough to handle, prick
out the seedlings and pot up
singly in 9 cm (3½ inch) pots of
potting compost.

Coleus can also be prop-
agated from cuttings taken
during July, August and even
into September. These cuttings can be obtained when
you trim the plant to encourage a bushy shape. Dip the
cuttings in hormone rooting
powder and insert, one to a
pot, in 9 cm (3½ inch) pots of
John Innes No. 1 potting compost, keeping them moist and
at a temperature of about 18°C
(65°F) until rooted.
Pests and Diseases: Coleus
may be attacked by aphids.

CYPERUS*
Cyperus alternifolius is a delicate
looking reed-like plant with
slender shoots up to 1 metre
(3 ft) high and umbrella-like
'fronds' at the top. The attractive bright green foliage makes
the plant a useful foil to a
mixed plant display.
General Care: Cyperus are
surprisingly easy to grow and
break the watering rules of
plant care. Unlike other plants
that should be allowed to dry
out a little before re-watering,
cyperus prefer to be kept moist
all the time. In fact, they are
happiest when allowed to sit
in a saucer of water con-
tinuously. During the winter,
it is best not to expose the plant
to temperatures below 10°C
(50°F); aim for an optimum of
between 13°C (55°F) and 16°C
(60°F). Cyperus are fairly
adaptable to the degree of light
that they are exposed to,
although you will achieve the
best results by placing them in
a lightly shaded situation.
Propagation: The best way to
propagate cyperus is by division. During the spring or
summer, when the plant is
most tolerant of any disturbance, divide the roots with a
sharp knife, potting up each
piece in a suitably sized pot
filled with John Innes No. 2
potting compost. Pot on into
13 cm (5 inch) pots of John
Innes No. 3 potting compost,
or good garden soil.
Pests and Diseases: Mealy
bugs and aphids sometimes
attack cyperus but can easily
be dealt with.

LEFT: Coleus
*OPPOSITE PAGE: Chlorophytum
(spider plant)*

ECHEVERIA*

There are many different echeveria with attractive rosettes of leaves and sprays of flowers ranging from white to yellow, orange and red. Some can be used to add a little extra interest to summer bedding with their unusual form. They are mostly only 7.5 cm (3 inches) high and often have a waxy bloom to the leaves. Flowers are produced on short stems in summer.

General Care: Echeveria are quite tough, and, as they are succulents, care should be taken not to overwater them. Care should also be taken not to splash the foliage as this will leave marks. During the spring and summer allow the plants to dry out in between waterings, and in winter keep them on the dry side. They will then be tolerant of temperatures down to around 4°C (40°F). Although fairly adaptable, they are happiest when allowed to grow in a situation of full light.

Propagation: The easiest way to propagate echeveria is gently to remove the fleshy leaves and to insert them in a mixture of seed compost and sand in a 4:1 ratio. The compost should be kept barely moist until the plants have rooted, otherwise the leaf pads may rot off.

Echeverias can also be germinated from seed in the same compost as that used for the cuttings. Fill a half pot with the compost and sow the seed on the surface. Lightly cover the seed with fine sand and keep at 20°C (68°F) until it has germinated. Grow the seedlings on until large enough to handle and, as with the young plants raised from

leaves, pot up in 9 cm (3½ inch) pots of John Innes No. 2 potting compost.

Pests and Diseases: Mealy bugs and root mealy bugs occasionally attack echeveria.

EUONYMUS*

The most common species of this plant, *Euonymus radicans*, is usually grown as a houseplant but it can alternatively be grown as a greenhouse shrub that requires no heat at all during the winter. The brightly coloured variegated forms can easily be grown outside, although the growth under glass is usually much more lush and vigorous.

Fatshedera lizei

General Care: Euonymus are very easy to grow. Avoid overwatering, and try to ensure that the plants dry out in between waterings. Although these plants are very adaptable, they should be grown in a situation of full light for the brightest variegation of the foliage. There is no need to worry about low winter temperatures, euonymus will even tolerate frost.

Grow in John Innes No. 2 potting compost in 13-25 cm (5-10 inch) pots, or until they become too large for your greenhouse. You can then plant them out in a sheltered part of the garden.

Propagation: Euonymus can easily be propagated from shoot cuttings, about 7.5 cm (3 inches) long, in August. Dip the cutting into hormone rooting powder and insert approximately three cuttings in a 9 cm (3½ inch) pot of seed compost. Cover them with a polythene bag to conserve moisture and avoid leaf dehydration. When the cuttings have rooted, remove the polythene bag and grow on.

Pests and Diseases: Aphids, mealy bugs, caterpillars and red spider mites will attack the plant, particularly during the spring and summer.

FATSHEDERA*

The deep green 'five-fingered' leaves of the *fatshedera lizei* provide an interesting shape in a foliage greenhouse plant collection. The plant climbs readily and will reach a height of 1.2-2.4 metres (4-8 ft).

General Care: Fatshedera is quite tough and capable of withstanding temperatures down to around 7°C (45°F) over winter. It should, however, be kept on the dry side and watered infrequently. During the summer, give the plant a slightly shaded situation away from direct sunlight, otherwise the leaves tend to lose their deep green colour. It should be allowed to dry out in between waterings, as it is sometimes prone to root rot. Grow it in 15-20 cm (6-8 inch) pots of John Innes No. 2 potting compost.

Propagation: Fatshedera can be propagated in July and August from tip cuttings, about 7.5 cm (3 inches) long, or stem cuttings with a leaf and a section of stem about 1 cm (½ inch) above the leaf and about 2.5 cm (1 inch) below. In either case, dip the bottom of the stem into hormone rooting powder and insert three cuttings in a 9 cm (3½ inch) pot of potting compost. Cover with a polythene bag to reduce water loss from the leaves; remove this when the cuttings have rooted and leave them to grow on in the same pot.

Pests and Diseases: Fatshedera is occasionally subject to attack by red spider mites, aphids, mealy bugs and root mealy bugs.

FICUS PUMILA*

The diminutive *Ficus pumila* or creeping fig is an ideal plant to grow under the staging in a greenhouse, either in pots, in a basket suspended from the staging or any other type of container placed out of direct light. The trailing or climbing habit of the plant is enhanced by its small, heart-shaped leaves that quickly hide any support canes. It reaches a height of 15-20 cm (6-8 inches).

General Care: Provided you do not allow *Ficus pumila* to dry out, you should have no problems in successfully growing the plant. As well as keeping the compost moist, take care to ensure that the plant is kept out of sunlight. Damping down the greenhouse is helpful in summer.

During the winter months, *Ficus pumila* will happily tolerate temperatures down to 10°C (50°F). Grow it in 10 cm (4 inch) pots of John Innes No. 2 potting compost, or a soilless compost. Pot on into larger pots as necessary.

Propagation: As the plant grows, it will become necessary to trim it. From April to June, you can use the trimmings for cuttings. Cut the lengths into pieces about

Ficus pumila

7.5 cm (3 inches) long and dip into hormone rooting powder, then insert about five of them into a 9 cm (3½ inch) pot filled with seed compost. To avoid leaf dehydration, cover the pot with a polythene bag and then keep at around 18°C (65°F) until the cuttings have rooted. Grow on in the pot, removing the polythene bag when the plants appear to be growing.

Pests and Diseases: *Ficus pumila* is occasionally subject to attack by aphids, mealy bugs and root mealy bugs.

FICUS ELASTICA*

The rubber plant will happily grow in your greenhouse provided you can give it enough head-room. Under such ideal conditions, the bold, oval-leaved plant may eventually grow so well that you will have to prune it each year to keep it in check.

General Care: The rubber plant is very hardy and adaptable and, although it prefers a lightly shaded situation, it will grow well in full light. Try to allow the compost to dry out between waterings. In winter, the *Ficus elastica* will tolerate temperatures down to around 10°C (50°F), provided the compost is on the dry side, but it prefers temperatures in the region of 16-18°C (61-65°F). Start in 10 cm (4 inch) pots of John Innes No. 2 potting compost or a soil-less compost. Pot on in April until the plant is in a 30 cm (12 inch) pot.

Propagation: *Ficus elastica* is a very difficult plant to propagate from cuttings, but is

worth a try next time you decide to trim back the plant in late spring. Cut up the stem into pieces about 5 cm (2 inches) long with a leaf in the middle. Dip the bottom 2.5 cm (1 inch) of the stem into hormone rooting powder and insert in a 9 cm (3½ inch) pot of seed compost, rolling the leaf loosely around a cane for support and placing a rubber band around the leaf and cane to secure it. Keep the cutting at a temperature of 27°C (80°F) until rooted, which may be six to eight weeks.

You can also take ordinary stem cuttings, which you may find easier. This method is usually more successful, unless you are trying to propagate a large number of new plants.

Pests and Diseases: Aphids, mealy bugs and scale insects can cause problems.

GYNURA*

Gynura, or the velvet nettle, is a low-growing trailing plant with fleshy foliage, which has a violet-coloured sheen.

General Care: Gynuras like a fairly well-lit situation as this helps to brighten the coloration of the leaves, but they also need to be shaded from hot sun in summer. Grow in 13 cm

Ficus elastica (rubber plant)

(5 inch) pots of John Innes potting compost No. 2, or a soil-less compost. To avoid overwatering the plants in summer allow the compost to become slightly dry before re-watering, but keep the atmosphere moist by damping down the greenhouse. During the winter, do not allow the temperature to drop below 10°C (50°F) and keep the compost a little drier to avoid root rot.

Although they are by nature trailing plants, gynuras can also climb to about 1 metre (3 ft) if given the support of a cane – but do not expect too much of them!

To keep the leaf colour, it helps to pinch out the orange-yellow tiny dandelion-like flowers. Don't be tempted to leave the flowers until they open, as they might look interesting, but smell horrid!

Propagation: Gynuras are easy to propagate in spring. Simply pinch off pieces, about 7.5 cm (3 inches) long, and dip the bottom of each stem into hormone rooting powder before inserting about three cuttings into a 9 cm (3½ inch) pot containing a mixture of equal parts peat and sand. When rooted, pot up singly in 9 cm (3½ inch) pots of John Innes No. 1 potting compost. Gynuras are best propagated afresh every two years.

Pests and Diseases: Mealy bugs, root mealy bugs and aphids may attack gynura from to time.

MONSTERA*

Monstera deliciosa, the Swiss cheese plant, can make a useful greenhouse plant, if you can accommodate it, for it

Monstera (Swiss cheese plant)

grows up to 2 metres (6½ ft) high, and its large leaves, with their characteristic holes and slits, may soon swamp the other plants in your collection. It has numerous aerial roots which can be trained down into the pot or left to dangle from the stems.

General Care: Monstera prefers a lightly shaded situation with a minimum winter temperature of about 10°C (50°F). During the spring and summer, the plant should be kept reasonably moist, but in winter it is preferable to keep the compost on the dry side to avoid the roots rotting. Grow it in John Innes No. 3 potting compost, and pot on annually until in 30 cm (12 inch) pots. Feed every two weeks in summer with weak liquid fertilizer. Fortunately, the usual humid conditions of a greenhouse help to maintain the

characteristic slits in the leaves, unlike the normal household environment where the leaves sometimes revert to plain heart-shape.

Propagation: *Monstera deliciosa* can be propagated from side shoots that are teased away from the mother plant when they are about 15 cm (6 inches) tall and potted up on their own in a 13 cm (5 inch) pot of John Innes No. 3 potting compost. However, the best way to raise monstera is from seed. If you can obtain seeds, sow in a pot of seed compost at about 21°C (70°F), potting the seedlings up singly in potting compost when large enough to handle.

Pests and Diseases: Monstera is sometimes attacked by aphids, mealy bugs, root mealy bugs and scale insects, but is generally free from pests.

Peperomia magnoliaefolia

PEPEROMIA MAGNOLIAEFOLIA*

This plant, more commonly known as the desert privet, is a tough plant to include in your collection of greenhouse plants. It has brightly variegated yellow and green fleshy round leaves, and grows to a height of 15 cm (6 inches).

General Care: *Peperomia magnoliaefolia* is very easy to grow in a well-lit position in the greenhouse. It takes up little space when grown on the staging and can also grow well in a hanging basket. Keep it in small pots up to 9 cm (3½ inches), using John Innes No. 1 potting compost, or a soil-less compost. Keep the plant on the dry side, watering infrequently during the winter as the plant is more likely to survive the lower temperatures if it is dry at the roots. Even so, avoid temperatures below 10°C (50°F).

Propagation: When the desert privet becomes rather straggly, it is a good time to think about propagating it. In summer, cut off the top growth in pieces about 7.5 cm (3 inches) long and, after dipping in hormone rooting powder, insert about three cuttings into a 9 cm (3½ inch) pot of seed compost. Covering the pot with polythene is unnecessary and can cause the cuttings to rot. Pot up the rooted cuttings singly.

Pests and Diseases: Aphids and red spider mites sometimes attack, especially during spring and summer.

PHILODENDRON SCANDENS*

This is the sweetheart plant and has heart-shaped dark green leaves which grace its climbing or semi-trailing stems. It provides a useful background plant to set off the brighter plants in your display. It can grow up to about 2 metres (6 ft) high.

General Care: *Philodendron scandens* prefers a slightly shaded situation and can even grow quite happily under the staging in a pot, or in a hanging basket where, if allowed to do so, it will trail over the pot as well as climbing up any support that you can give it.

To avoid overwatering the plant, keep just moist in between waterings. In particular keep the plant on the dry side in winter to avoid any chance of root rot. The sweetheart plant can tolerate winter temperatures of 10°C (50°F). Plant it in soil-less compost in a 15 cm (6 inch) pot, potting on every other year until in a 25 cm (10 inch) pot.

Propagation: In time the plant may become rather leggy and replacement plants should be propagated from it in May or June. Trim back wayward growth and cut into pieces of stem with a leaf and about 2.5 cm (1 inch) of stem above and below the leaf. Dip the bottom piece of stem into hormone rooting powder and insert between three and five in a 9 cm (3 inch) pot of peat-based seed compost. Once rooted, the cuttings can be left in the pot to grow on, making a more compact, better-formed plant.

Pests and Diseases: Mealy bugs, root mealy bugs and, to a lesser extent, aphids and red spider mites, may sometimes infect the sweetheart plant, but it is not often attacked.

PILEA CADIEREI*

Pilea cadierei, perhaps better known as the aluminium plant, has crinkly grey and green, slightly pointed oval leaves. It grows up to about 30 cm (12 inches) and will complement the brighter plants of your collection.

General Care: Although the aluminium plant is easy to

keep, it does have a few likes and dislikes. It prefers light shade, so avoid direct sunlight as this could cause leaf-yellowing or scorching. Take care with watering, as the plant can be overwatered fairly easily even though during the summer months it prefers a reasonably moist situation. In winter the plant should be kept on the dry side and watered far less frequently.

A minimum winter temperature of about 10°C (50°F) is required, though the plant will be more tolerant of low temperatures provided that it is not wet at the roots. Grow it in 13 cm (5 inch) pots of John Innes No. 2 potting compost, or a soil-less compost. Feed every two weeks in summer with weak liquid fertilizer.

Propagation: The aluminium plant is very easy to propagate. Simply cut or pinch off shoots about 5-7.5 cm (2-3 inches) long, dip into hormone rooting powder and insert about five cuttings to a 9 cm (3½ inch) pot of potting compost. Rooting is fairly rapid and should take only about two to three weeks during the spring and summer. Pinching out the tips of the shoots also helps to encourage a compact and better-formed shape.

Pests and Diseases: Aphids, mealy bugs and root mealy bugs sometimes attack.

PITTOSPORUM*

The pittosporum is an attractive evergreen shrub with glossy leaves, sometimes grown outside in favourable areas. It is not very hardy and is normally killed by the frost, but it does, however, make a good greenhouse plant, provided you can afford the room. Its foliage is very popular with flower arrangers. There are plain green and variegated forms.

General Care: Pittosporum likes a very well-lit situation to bring out the best in the colour of its leaves. Keep the compost moderately moist but do not overwater. In the winter, keep the compost drier and the plant will then tolerate temperatures down to around 7°C (45°F). It can be grown in good garden soil or John Innes No. 2 potting compost. Trim the plant to maintain its shape and to keep it compact.

Propagation: Cuttings about 7.5-10 cm (3-4 inches) long may be taken in mid-summer. Use semi-mature side shoots that are neither woody nor tender and fleshy. Dip the cuttings into hormone rooting powder and then insert singly into 9 cm (3½ inch) pots of seed compost. Keep at around 20°C (68°F) until rooted and grow on until the root system is well formed. It is probably better to leave the plants in these pots until the following spring when they should be potted into 13 cm (5 inch) pots of potting compost.

Pests and Diseases: Pittosporum is not normally troubled by pests or diseases.

Pilea cadierei (aluminium plant)

PLATYCERIUM*

Perhaps better known as the stag's horn fern, *Platycerium bifurcatum* is an unusual fern with fronds that look just like the antlers of a stag. It is a tree-living fern, and ideal to grow in a hanging basket or wired to a piece of cork bark filled with compost. It can, however, be grown just as easily under the staging. It grows to a height of 45-75 cm (1½-2½ ft), with a similar spread.

General Care: Platyceriums are very adaptable and, unlike most other ferns, will tolerate a higher light intensity, although a slightly shaded situation is best.

Allow the compost to dry out a little in between waterings and certainly keep it drier during the winter than in the summer. In the winter, avoid temperatures lower than 10°C (50°F). It is best grown in a compost of 2 parts fibrous peat, 1 part spagnum moss and 1 part fibrous loam. Good drainage is essential.

Propagation: Platycerium can be propagated from the spores that are released from the brown patches on the underside of mature frond tips. When these tips are visible, and become darker and more pronounced, tap the frond over a sheet of paper. The spores, once collected, look like fine dust and can be sown on the surface of a half pot filled with a mixture of equal parts peat and loam-based seed compost, or in a peat-based seed compost. Place the pot in a polythene bag and keep at about 21°C (70°F) until the spores have germinated. Pot on singly when large enough to handle into 9 cm (3½ inch) pots in a similar compost.

Pests and Diseases: Scale insects are the most likely problem.

SANSEVIERIA*

The mother-in-law's tongue, or *Sansevieria trifasciata* 'Laurentii', is a very hardy succulent that takes up little room and yet provides a colourful addition to your collection. It grows about 50 cm (20 inches) tall and has bold, green and yellow striped leaves. During the summer, the plant may produce a spike of greenish-white fragrant flowers.

General Care: Mother-in-law's tongue loves sunlight and is happiest in a well-lit situation in the greenhouse. Although easy to keep, do take care with watering, for the plant is relatively easy to overwater. Allow the plant to dry out completely between waterings.

During the winter, the plant should be kept almost completely dry; water it only if you maintain a temperature around 13°C (55°F) or to avoid dehydration. Otherwise the sansevieria will tolerate temperatures down to 10°C (50°F). Grow it in 13 cm (5 inch) pots of soil-less compost or John Innes No. 2 potting compost. Feed monthly in summer with weak liquid fertilizer.

Propagation: Propagate the plant by using offsets when they are at least 10 cm (4 inches) tall. To do this, moisten the compost and tease apart the small plant, using a sharp knife to sever any stubborn connections. Pot up the pieces either singly or together to make a more compact-looking plant, using potting compost. Do take care, though, not to use too large a pot, and be extra careful with watering for the first few weeks after potting up the cuttings.

You can also root leaf cuttings. Cut a leaf into 5 cm (2 inch) sections and insert them – right way up – in moist potting compost. Pot up once they have rooted.

Pests and Diseases: Sansevieria usually remains free from pests, although the flowers can sometimes be attacked by aphids.

TRADESCANTIA*

The tradescantia is an attractive trailing plant that is available in several variegated forms with cream, green or purple leaves. Unfortunately, it does tend to become rather leggy with age and is better as a young plant.

General Care: Tradescantias can be grown in a number of ways, either as pot plants in their own right on the staging amongst the rest of your plants or as hanging basket subjects. Whatever you decide to do, be sure to give them as much light as possible, otherwise the colours will dull and the leaves will become very green.

Water freely in summer, but keep them just moist in winter, at a temperature of 10°C (50°F). Either grow in John Innes No. 2 potting compost, or a soil-less compost.

As a tradescantia gets older, it becomes leggy, with stems devoid of leaves. Any new lush growth is generally well away from the pot, which gives the plant an untidy appearance. Keep it pinched back to encourage bushiness, and remove shoots that lose their variegation.

Propagation: When the plant becomes leggy, trim it back, taking each shoot as a cutting. Each cutting should be trimmed to a length of about 5 cm (2 inches) before being inserted, three or five to a 9 cm (3½ inch) pot, in John Innes No. 1 potting compost. Rooting should take only about two or three weeks and the plants can be left to grow on in the same pot, where they will form compact, well-balanced plants.

Pests and Diseases: Tradescantia is rarely troubled by pests, which makes it one of the easiest plants to grow.

Sanseviera (mother-in-law's tongue)

FLOWERING PLANTS

There is nothing quite like a greenhouse full of flowering plants, providing a feast of colour and splendour throughout the year.

The greatest show occurs from spring to summer, though certain varieties, such as carnations and chrysanthemums, can be encouraged to flower throughout the year. These do, however, require special treatment, and the greenhouse needs to be heated at colder times of the year.

Even if you want to economise on heating, you can still grow astilbe, bulbs, hydrangea and polyanthus over winter for early spring flowers. Followed by fuchsia, geranium and impatiens for early summer. Begonia, cyclamen and solanum can be grown for late summer to early autumn flowering, but from October onwards they will require some warmth. If you don't want to heat the greenhouse, find a position for them in the home. Solanum produce attractive orange fruits which last over the festive Christmas season.

A greenhouse is particularly useful for promoting early flowers on plants, such as spring bulbs or polyanthus.

Flowering plants are ideal companions to fruit and vegetables, for most varieties share a liking for fairly high light intensities. To provide a decorative note throughout the year it is worth devoting some space to flowering plants even if your main priority in the greenhouse is vegetables or fruit.

AMARYLLIS*

The amaryllis, or hippeastrum, is a bold winter-flowering plant that produces up to four beautiful large flowers on a tall stem. These range in colour from white to pink and red, and each flower measures up to 10 cm (4 inches) long and across. The broad, flat leaves can grow rather long and strap-like, but the plant rarely grows more than 60 cm (2 ft) tall.

General Care: The hippeastrum should be grown in as much light as possible, otherwise it can become very leggy. To encourage it to start into growth, provide gentle heat and water sparingly until the plant is in active growth. As it starts to grow from the bulb, take care with watering, as it can be relatively easily overwatered in the first few weeks. Thereafter the plant will require increasing amounts of water, and a weekly liquid feed. After flowering the plant should be allowed to grow until the leaves begin to yellow. It should then be kept dry through the dormant period during the autumn and early winter before starting into growth again.

Pot the bulb in a 13-17 cm (5-7 inch) pot of John Innes No. 2 potting compost, leaving about one third of the bulb exposed. The bulbs need a minimum temperature of 13°C (55°F).

Propagation: Hippeastrums can be propagated from seeds or offsets. Offsets will flower sooner but are not quite so numerous. To grow them, simply separate the offsets from the plant and pot on singly.

Seedlings are more numerous, but usually take longer. Sow the seed when ripe in half pots of seed compost and germinate at about 21°C (70°F), potting up singly in potting compost in 9 cm (3½ inch) pots to begin with and finally into 13 cm (5 inch) pots. Plants raised from seed may take three years to flower.

Pests and Diseases: Mealy bugs sometimes affect the flowers of the plant.

ASTILBE*

Astilbes, sometimes called spireas, can be grown outside but, grown under glass, they will flower much earlier and provide a splash of colour in the late months of winter. The bright flower plumes vary in colour from white through pink and rose to red. They are borne on finely cut dark green foliage.

General Care: Astilbes love light and water. To get the best from the plants, grow them in the lightest situation possible in the greenhouse and water very frequently. Do not, on any account, allow the plants to dry out otherwise they will dehydrate and they may not recover. To prolong the flowering period, try to keep

Pink flowering amaryllis (Hippeastrum)

General Care: The Indian azalea should be kept in the lightest position possible in the greenhouse with a minimum winter temperature of about 10°C (50°F). Watering is most important and on no account should the plant be allowed to dry out. Keep it in 15-20 cm (6-8 inch) pots of lime-free compost. The conditions of high humidity and high light intensities that are usual under glass help to encourage the plant to produce flowers in profusion.

After the plant has flowered, it can be placed outside from May onwards when frosts have finished, until September when the plant should be brought back under glass again. To grow the azalea outside during the summer, plunge it into a peat bed, still in its pot and keep moist throughout the summer months. Syringeing the plants with water daily from December onwards will encourage profuse flowering.

Propagation: The Indian azalea is not very easy to propagate, although it can be raised from seed or cuttings with difficulty.

Pests and Diseases: Aphids can be a particular nuisance on the flowers.

BEGONIA*

There are many different varieties of begonia that can be grown in your greenhouse. However, the large-flowered and hanging varieties that are tuberous rooted will probably give you most pleasure. The flowers of each are large and

the plants at about 13-15°C (55-59°F).

When flowering is finished, if you wish, you can plant them out in the garden for the summer, bringing them back into the greenhouse about October. As astilbes are fully hardy, there is no need to worry about a minimum winter temperature. Keep them in 13 cm (5 inch) pots of John Innes potting compost No. 2.

Propagation: The best way to propagate astilbe is to divide the clumps in spring with a sharp knife, potting each piece up separately into a pot of potting compost. The crown of the plant should be left just

proud of the compost surface.

Pests and Diseases: Astilbes are particularly prone to attack by aphids, which seem to enjoy not only the leaves but the flowers as well.

AZALEA**

The Indian azalea or *Rhododendron indicum* is not frost hardy, but it grows well in the greenhouse, and makes a good display during the winter months. The plant flowers in spring and comes in a wide range of colours from white through pink to salmon and red. With care the plant may last in flower from six to eight weeks.

highly coloured and will give a magnificent display during the summer in colours that range from white to pink, salmon, yellow, orange and red.
General Care: Whichever variety of tuberous-rooted begonia you grow, take particular care when planting and growing them for the first few weeks. The large-flowered tuberous rooted begonia can be grown in 13 cm (5 inch) pots, whereas the trailing variety can be grown in similar pots or in hanging baskets.

In February or March, lightly fill the containers with peat-based potting compost and plant the tubers on the top, convex surface down, concave surface up. Leave the top of the tubers proud of the compost and moisten the compost. Keep the tubers at about 18°C (65°F) until the shoots start to appear. They can then be grown on at a more moderate temperature around 15°C (50°F) or lower, but do not allow the temperature to drop

Display of orange and red flowering begonias

below 10°C (50°F) otherwise the plant may rot.

Begonias like a light but slightly shaded situation, so avoid prolonged exposure to the sun. Take care to ensure that the plants do not dry out; they require a fair amount of water.

After flowering, from mid to late summer, allow the plants to die back to the tuber and then dry out the compost. Gently lift the tuber and store in dry peat over winter at a temperature of around 10°C (50°F).

Propagation: Begonias can be propagated from seed sown at around 20°C (68°F) in half pots filled with seed compost. Prick out and pot up the seedlings singly in a potting compost when large enough to handle.
Pests and Diseases: Begonias may occasionally be attacked by aphids, particularly on their flowers and buds.

BULBS*

During the winter months, it is an excellent idea to make use of your greenhouse to force spring bulbs into early growth to provide you with a feast of colour whilst the bulbs in your garden are often still buried under snow. Tulips, crocus, hyacinths, daffodils and narcissi can all be successfully grown with the minimum of care. What is more, you can use the previous year's growing bags or they can be grown in pots, troughs or any other suitable container.
General Care: Having chosen your container, fill it with a suitable compost such as John Innes No. 2 potting compost, bulb fibre or last year's growing bag compost. Plant the

bulbs in the container; hyacinths should have their top halves above the compost, whilst tulips, crocus, daffodils and narcissi are buried so that their tops are about 5 cm (2 inches) below the surface of the compost. Keep the compost moist and cover the container with a bucket or other material to keep out the light. Then simply leave until the shoots are about 5 cm (2 inches) tall. Remove the cover and expose the bulbs to full light, keeping them adequately watered. Within a matter of a few weeks, the bulbs will flower and will provide a real spectacle.

After flowering, you can either allow the plants to die back to their bulb until the following spring or you can plant them in the garden.

Propagation: The best way to propagate bulbs is from young offset bulbs produced by the parent. Pot them up into John Innes No. 1 potting compost, and they will flower a year or two later.

Pests and Diseases: Occasionally the first aphids of the year might attack your spring bulbs, or sometimes a passing slug or snail may make the most of an early spring feast!

CALCEOLARIA*

Calceolarias have curious 'inflated' balloon-like flowers that range from yellow to orange and red, and are often spotted. The plants are low growing and sport the flowers on relatively short stems.

General Care: Calceolarias love cool, light airy conditions and therefore prefer a well-ventilated greenhouse. They are not at all happy in hot, dry

conditions. To get the best from your plants, try to prevent them from drying out and, if anything, keep them moist most of the time. A temperature range of 10-15°C (50-60°F) is ideal.

Calceolarias are normally grown as annuals from seed, providing a fairly long season of colourful and unusual flowers before fading. If kept over winter, they need a minimum temperature of 7°C (45°F).

Propagation: Calceolarias are fairly easily raised from seed germinated in the early

Yellow-flowering calceolaria

spring. Sow in trays or half pots of seed compost and maintain at about 18°C (65°F). The seedlings should be pricked out when large enough to handle and potted up singly into potting compost using a minimum sized pot of 9 cm (3½ inches), a more suitable size being 13 cm (5 inches).

Pests and Diseases: Aphids are particularly fond of calceolarias and a close watch should always be kept for these pests. Whitefly can also be troublesome.

CAMPANULA*

The campanula most grown in the greenhouse is *Campanula isophylla*, commonly known as the 'bellflower'. It has green-grey heart-shaped leaves and is available with white or blue flowers. It makes a magnificent hanging basket plant.

General Care: *Campanula isophylla* is fairly adaptable and grows equally well in full light or slightly shaded situations. It does, however, prefer a relatively cool position and is not at all happy under hot, dry conditions. During the spring and summer, try to prevent the plant from drying out, but conversely take care not to overwater.

After flowering, trim the plant back at the end of the summer and keep it on the dry side in winter at a minimum temperature of 7°C (45°F). It

Carnations need a well-lit position

should be grown in 13 cm (5 inch) pots or hanging baskets of John Innes No. 3 potting compost. Campanula may also be grown outside during the warmer months of the year, although it is more likely to put on a good show of flowers under glass.

Propagation *Campanula isophylla* is relatively easily propagated from cuttings about 5-7.5 cm (2-3 inches) long, taken in April. Dip into hormone rooting powder and insert in a mixture of 2 parts of a loam-based seed compost to 1 part of fine sand. Insert three to five cuttings in a 9 cm (3½ inch) pot.

Pests and Diseases: Campanulas are sometimes troubled by aphids.

CARNATION*

Carnations and dianthus provide relatively easy-to-grow subjects for the greenhouse. The colour range varies from white to pink and red; and many newer varieties have striped or dark-edged petals. Some have a magnificent clove scent.

General Care: Dwarf varieties of dianthus can be grown in 13 cm (5 inch) pots of John Innes No. 2 potting compost. Carnations tend to grow taller and are happier grown in a growing bag. Depending on the size of the bag, plant them 10-15 cm (4-6 inches) apart, approximately 12 to a bag, and provide support with canes or mesh. Only the central bud of each shoot should be allowed to develop if large blooms are required.

Dianthus and carnations do

not like too much water, but they should not be allowed to dry out completely. Light is most important, for these plants like plenty of direct light and will grow leggy, producing less flowers, in the shade. Over winter keep them at about 4°C (40°F), trimming back as required to avoid unnecessary straggly growth at a time when space should not be wasted.

Propagation: Propagation can be achieved by cuttings taken during the spring and summer. Use side shoots, about 7.5-10 cm (3-4 inches) long. Dip into hormone rooting powder and root in seed compost and fine sand in a 2:1 ratio. Pot up the rooted cuttings in 7.5 cm (3 inch) pots.

Alternatively you can raise some varieties from seed by germinating seed in January at around 18°C (65°F) in a half pot of seed compost. Pot up when seedlings are large enough to handle.

Pests and Diseases: Red spider mites, aphids and thrips may sometimes attack.

CELOSIA*

Celosias, commonly called cockscomb, are annuals that flower through the summer, after which their life-cycle is completed and the plants die. The feathery flowers range in colour from yellow to red and are borne on plants about 20 cm (8 inches) tall. They provide a splash of colour in the greenhouse.

General Care: Celosias love lots of light and should be exposed to maximum sunlight, so do not hide them in any shady corners of your greenhouse. They also have a fair appetite for water and should not be allowed to dry out. The flowers last for quite a time before fading, after which the plants should be disposed of. Grow them in 9-13 cm (3½ -5 inch) pots of John Innes No. 1 potting compost.

Propagation: Celosias are easy to raise from seed in February. Sow seeds in a half pot filled with seed compost, lightly covering the seed, and keep at about 18°C (65°F). When germinated, the seedlings should be potted up singly in 9 cm (3½ inch) pots of potting compost and grown on.

Pests and Diseases: Celosia may be attacked by aphids.

Celosia (cockscomb)

Display of assorted chrysanthemums

ment gives the plants an artificially short day and long night and thus encourages them to flower out of their natural season.

Propagation: Chrysanthemums are easily propagated in spring by taking cuttings about 7.5-10 cm (3-4 inches) long. Root them in 9 cm (3½ inch) pots of seed compost and allow to root well and grow on a little before planting up in a growing bag.

Pests and Diseases: Chrysanthemums are occasionally subject to attack by aphids, red spider mites, leaf miners, whitefly and thrips.

CINERARIA*

Although the correct name for this plant is *Senecio cruentus*, it is almost always listed as cineraria. A well-grown plant when the leaves are almost submerged beneath a mound of vivid daisy-like flowers in late winter and early spring, it is one of the most splendid sights in the greenhouse.

General care: The plants are best treated as biennials – sow them one year to flower the next, then discard them.

Cinerarias do not need much heat – 10°C (50°F) is ample, and it will not matter if the temperature drops a little below this. They do require shade from direct sun; a bright but shaded position, and a humid atmosphere, will produce good plants.

Propagation: Sow the seed in half pots from April to June. Cover with glass or polythene and keep moist and shaded until they germinate. When

CHRYSANTHEMUM*

Chrysanthemums come in an enormous variety of colours and forms: orange, pink, purple or red, and in tight pompoms or loose sprays. The small chrysanthemums grown by specialists as houseplants have been sprayed with growth-retardant chemicals, but the amateur will find that chrysanthemums need a fair amount of space and are perhaps happiest when grown in a growing bag in a greenhouse. They normally reach a height of 1.2-1.5 metres (4-5 ft).

General Care: In spring plant in growing bags, allowing about 12 plants per bag. The chrysanthemums will need plenty of light and a moderate temperature, although when established they will tolerate temperatures around 7°C (45°F). Keep the compost in the bags moist and do not allow them to dry out. The plants will require support in the form of canes or a mesh frame. Normally, they will flower as the days shorten in October and November, although they can flower at other times of the year with the correct treatment.

To make chrysanthemums flower out of season, cover them up with black polythene overnight a few hours before it is dark, and remove the cover several hours after sunrise. The black polythene should be placed *over* the plants and not *on them*, so you will need to construct a light frame. The procedure should be repeated every evening until the flower buds have formed. This treat-

about three leaves have formed prick off into seed trays or small pots. Gradually move the plants on into 11 cm (4½ inch) and then into 15 cm (6 inch) pots. A peat-based or loam-based compost can be used. Feed the plants from autumn until they come into flower.

Pests and Diseases: If aphids do not try to make a meal of your cinerarias, you are lucky. Be vigilant, and spray with a suitable insecticide as soon as you notice them.

CYCLAMEN*

Cyclamen grow well in a greenhouse under the right conditions. Cyclamen, such as the silver-leaved strain with colourful foliage, and the diminutive mini-cyclamen are both available in a wide range of flower colours from white to pink, rose, salmon, red and lilac. They grow about 15-20 cm (6-8 inches) high.

General Care: Cyclamens like cool, light, airy conditions, so remember to ventilate the greenhouse well and do not allow the plants to become too hot. Keep them reasonably moist and avoid the compost in the pots drying out. They usually flower in the winter and continue to do so for several weeks.

After flowering, the leaves start to yellow. Stop watering and let the corms dry out. When the plants have rested for a few weeks, they may be started into growth again.

Do not allow the temperature to fall below 7°C (45°F), and aim to maintain a temper-

Red and white flowering cyclamens

ature of 13°C (55°F). When individual flowers or leaves die, remove them, otherwise they will rot and allow grey mould fungus (botrytis) to infect the plant.

Propagation: Cyclamen are propagated from seed. Sow the seeds in August or January at about 18°C (65°F) in a half pot of seed compost. When the seedlings are large enough to handle, pot up singly in 9 cm (3½ inch) pots of John Innes No. 1 potting compost. After a few months, they can be potted up into their final 13 cm (5 inches) pots, this time in John Innes No. 2 potting compost. When planting, take care to plant the corms proud

of the surface of the compost and do not bury them.

Pests and Diseases: Cyclamen are subject to attack by aphids, thrips and botrytis.

ECHINOPSIS*

The echinopsis is a popular cactus that grows to a height of 15 cm (6 inches). It is globe shaped and has prominent ribs. The flowers are truly magnificent and tend to dwarf the plant. Sometimes they are scented and the colour range varies from white to pink and yellow. Although the flowers last for only a few days, they are usually produced in sufficient numbers to give a good display.

General Care: Fortunately, echinopsis is very easy to keep and very tough. This makes it a superb cactus to grow in a cool greenhouse, provided it is frost-proof. During the winter, echinopsis should be kept cool and dry at a minimum temperature of about 7°C (45°F), although it may tolerate lower temperatures. During spring, as the light increases and it becomes warmer under glass, the cactus should be watered, allowing the compost to dry out in between waterings. Within a few weeks there will be a magnificent display of flowers.

Echinopsis should be grown in 10-15 cm (4-6 inch) pots of John Innes No. 2 potting compost, and given maximum light.

Propagation: Echinopsis are easily raised from seed, but you will have to be patient and wait a few years for them to become large enough to flower. Sow the seed in March in a half pot or seed tray in a mixture of seed compost and fine sand in a 4:1 ratio, sprinkling a little fine sand over the seed. Keep at about 20°C (68°F) until the seeds have germinated, then pot up singly when they are large enough to handle.

Pests and Diseases: Mealy bugs and root mealy bugs sometimes attack echinopsis.

EPIPHYLLUM**

The epiphyllum or orchid cactus is a magnificent cactus, producing some of the largest and most exotic flowers in the plant world. The flowers range in colour from white to yellow-orange, pink, lilac and red and are borne on green fleshy stems in spring. The blossoms measure from 5-15 cm (2-6 inches) across. The stems are flattened and have wavy edges, growing to a height of 90 cm (3 ft).

General Care: Epiphyllums are certainly worthy of a place in your greenhouse, especially as they need little care or attention. Through the spring and summer they should be grown in a slightly shaded situation, unlike other cacti which generally prefer full light. They should be allowed to dry out in between waterings, but generally prefer a little more water than many other cacti. In winter, keep the plants on the dry side at a temperature of about 10°C (50°F). A cool, dry winter followed by a warm and more moist spring and summer helps to initiate a good flush of flowers.

Propagation: Epiphyllums can be propagated from stem cuttings or from seed. The cuttings taken in early summer should be dipped into hormone rooting powder and then inserted into seed compost to root.

Seed can be germinated in April at about 20°C (68°F), sown in a mixture of seed compost and fine sand mixed at a ratio of 4:1. When large enough to handle, the seedlings should be pricked out and potted up in John Innes No. 2 potting compost. The plants should be potted on until they are in 15-20 cm (6-8 inch) pots.

Pests and Diseases: Mealy bugs, root mealy bugs, and sometimes aphids, may attack the plants.

Tall-growing fuchsia plants

FUCHSIA*

Fuchsias are extremly popular flowering plants that bloom for much of the summer both indoors and outside. The colours range from white, pink and red to a vivid magenta and deep violet. Plants can be tall-growing, bushy, or trailing. They vary in height from 15 cm (6 inches) to 60 cm (2 ft). Under glass, it is worth growing some of the less hardy and more choice varieties.

General Care: Fuchsias like a well-lit position in your greenhouse and should not be shaded at all. Try to ensure that they are kept relatively moist, and do not allow them to dry out. Pinching out the growing tips helps to maintain balanced, bushy growth.

Fuchsias will happily tolerate low temperatures over winter during their dormant period, although there are many varieties that prefer protection from frost. They must be kept dry until regrowth appears in spring. Pruning back in the autumn encourages better shaped plants for the following season.

Fuchsias should be grown in 15-20 cm (6-8 inch) pots of John Innes No. 3 potting compost.

Propagation: Fuchsias are extremely easy to propagate from cuttings of young shoots, about 7.5 cm (3 inches) long, taken in spring or summer. Dip them into hormone rooting powder before inserting into potting compost, preferably one cutting to a 9 cm (3½ inch) pot. Leave them to grow on, potting up as necessary.

Pests and Diseases: Fuchsias are prone to attack by aphids, whitefly and red spider mites.

Pink and salmon coloured geraniums (pelargoniums)

GERANIUMS*

The plants commonly known as 'geraniums' but more correctly 'pelargoniums' – are very easy to grow. Like fuchsias, they make excellent flowering pot plants. There are many varieties suitable for growing in the greenhouse, and they fall into three main groups.

Zonal pelargoniums grow fairly large – up to 1.5 metres (5 ft) if allowed to, and hold their flower stems well clear of the plant.

Regal pelargoniums are about 40-50 cm (16-20 inches) high and bushy in habit.

Ivy-leaved pelargoniums are trailing in habit and suitable for hanging baskets.

General Care: Geraniums prefer an airy, well-lit position in the greenhouse and should not be kept too warm. Watering should be carried out with care, as overwatering can cause rapid death. The plants should be grown in 10-15 cm (4-6 inch) pots of John Innes No. 2 potting compost. During the summer, the plants may be placed outside, although they must receive protection from frosts in the winter. They are relatively happy with a winter temperature of about 7°C (45°F) provided that they are kept on the dry side. Trimming back the plants in the autumn will help them last the winter satisfactorily.

Propagation: Propagation is easy. Take cuttings about 7.5 cm (3 inches) long in late summer, dipping into hormone rooting powder and then into a 9 cm (3½ inch) pot of seed compost.

Some varieties can be grown from seed germinated in February in seed compost at a temperature of about 18-20°C (65-68°F), potting up when large enough. Choose suitable F_1 hybrids of the Zonal type if you want them to flower well in the first year.

Pests and Diseases: Certain varieties may be troubled by whitefly, botrytis (grey mould) and a rust fungus.

HIBISCUS**

The Chinese rose, *Hibiscus rosa-sinensis*, is a truly exotic plant growing to a height of 1.8 metres (6 ft) with superb large flowers that measure about 10 cm (4 inches) across. The colours vary from pink to salmon and red. Although short-lived, usually only a day or two, these flowers are produced in profusion. The foliage is dark green with the exception of the variegated variety which has green and white foliage. The red flowers of this variety are far less numerous, but last longer.

General Care: Hibiscus like a lot of light and thrive in the warm, well-lit conditions of a greenhouse. They are, however, sensitive to temperature fluctuations which can cause rapid flower bud drop. Keep them relatively warm in summer at around 18°C (65°F), and moist. Occasional trimming of the plants will help to maintain well-shaped plants, followed by hard pruning in the

early part of winter when hibiscus should be kept on the dry side and at a temperature of about 10-13°C (50-55°F). They should be grown in 20-30 cm (8-12 inch) pots of John Innes No. 2 potting compost or a soil-less compost.

Propagation: Hibiscus can be propagated, but they require a lot of care. Take tip cuttings, 7.5-10 cm (3-4 inches) long, in summer. Dip into hormone rooting powder and then insert into 9 cm (3½ inch) pots of seed compost. To reduce water loss from the cuttings, either mist with tepid water or cover with polythene until rooted. When fully established and grown on reasonably well, pot up into 13 cm (5 inch) pots of potting compost.

Pests and Diseases: Aphids can be a nuisance; red spider mites may also be a problem.

HYDRANGEA*

Although hydrangeas are normally grown outside, they also make good pot plants if grown carefully. The wide range of colourful and showy flowers make hydrangeas one of the most attractive flowering plants from early spring to late summer.

Grow in a pot as a small specimen with one large bloom, or in a tub as a branching shrub up to 1.2 metres (4 ft) high.

General Care: Hydrangeas like lots of light and, as their name suggests, they also like lots of water. Dehydration of the compost in the tightly massed fibrous rootball can cause severe damage, and even kill the plants. They should be grown in 15-20 cm (6-8 inch) pots of John Innes

No. 2 or No. 3 potting compost. If possible, keep in a cool part of the greenhouse otherwise they may become too leggy and soft. Blue-flowering varieties should be grown in lime-free compost. Watering with aluminium sulphate or alum helps to keep the blooms blue, and prevents them from turning pink or purple, which they do if the soil is alkaline. (Do not try to 'blue' pink or white varieties.)

The occasional application of Sequestrene will also help to combat effects of iron deficiency, which shows as a yellowing of the leaves between the veins. After flowering and at the end of the summer, hydrangeas should be pruned back fairly hard to overwinter satisfactorily, and kept just moist in a cool but frost-free position until the leaves begin to show in January or February. They can then be brought into a warmer position and watered freely.

Propagation: Hydrangeas are easily propagated from non-flowering shoots in July. Dip the cuttings into hormone rooting powder and then into a mixture of equal parts seed and potting compost. Dehydration of the cuttings may be reduced by misting them with tepid water or by covering with polythene. Pot the rooted cuttings up one to a 9

Blue-flowering hydrangeas

cm (3½ inch) pot of John Innes No. 2 potting compost and overwinter in a cool place.

Pests and Diseases: Hydrangeas may be attacked by aphids, red spider mites, mildew and eelworm. The latter deforms the leaves and reduces vigour. Plants affected by this pest are best destroyed, for control is difficult.

IMPATIENS*

The impatiens grown as a pot plant is the popular 'busy Lizzie'. It is very easy to grow and provides a long-lasting display of flowers throughout spring and summer. The foliage varies in colour from clear green to variegated and even purple; the flowers range from white to pink and red. Some of the plants can grow to a height of almost 60 cm (2 ft), but most modern varieties are much more compact than this.

General Care: Impatiens will grow well in partial shade but appreciate good light provided that it is not too strong through unshaded glass. They also require copious amounts of water; if allowed to dry out they will dehydrate and die. During spring and summer occasional pinching or trimming will encourage the plants to maintain a better shape, otherwise they tend to become leggy.

In late autumn, trim the plants back by as much as half to two-thirds and keep them on the dry side, then they will tolerate temperatures down to 7°C (45°F). Water more freely again when the warmer temperature and increased light of spring is conducive to renewed growth.

Grow in 13 cm (5 inch) pots of soil-less compost or John Innes No. 1 potting compost.

Propagation: Impatiens are easy to propagate. You can either take 7.5-10 cm (3-4 inch) long shoots and root them in a tumbler of water, or to do it more correctly, dip the cutting into hormone rooting powder and insert into a pot of seed compost. Whichever procedure you adopt, pot up the rooted cuttings into 7.5 cm (3 inch) pots.

Pests and Diseases: Impatiens are prone to attack by aphids, whitefly, red spider mites and mildew.

MAMMILLARIA*

Of all the cacti grown, mammillaria must be the most popular. It is fairly typical of what most people imagine a cactus to be with tubercles and spines arranged in spirals around the plant. The plants grow from 5-20 cm (2-8 inches) high depending on species. It is fairly free-flowering in summer with the flowers ranging from white to pink, rose-pink, lilac-pink and yellow. The arrangement of the flowers is normally in a ring around the top of the plant.

General Care: Like most cacti, mammillaria likes lots of light all through the year, with a reasonable amount of water throughout the spring and summer. Allow the plant to dry out in between waterings. During the winter, it should be kept on the dry side and at a

Pink and red impatiens (busy Lizzies)

temperature of about 10°C (50°F). This treatment is important in encouraging the plant to flower the following year. Most mammillarias, with the right treatment, will flower every year.

Propagation: Mammillaria may either be propagated from offsets teased away from the mother plant in summer and potted up separately in a mixture of 4 parts seed compost to 1 part fine sand, or from seed sown in spring in the same mixture and lightly covered with fine sand. A temperature of around 20°C (68°F) is required until the seeds have germinated. The seedlings should be left in the container until large enough to handle, and then potted up singly in 7.5 cm (3 inch) pots of gritty compost such as 2 parts John Innes No. 2 potting compost to 1 part coarse sand or grit. Pot on to larger pots in spring.

Pests and Diseases: The mammillaria cactus is subject to attack from mealy bugs and root mealy bugs.

POLYANTHUS*

With so much happening in your greenhouse during the spring and summer it is useful to know that polyanthus can make a good bridge between the winter and early spring. The leaves are only slightly larger than those of a wild primrose, but the flowers are grown on strong stems held clear of the foliage and come in vivid colours of white, yellow, pink, red or blue. They flower from Christmas to Easter.

General Care: Polyanthus are easy to grow and also frost-hardy. Growing the plants

Blue polyanthus – in flower from Christmas to Easter

under glass helps them to flower earlier. Polyanthus should not be cossetted and they prefer cool, well-lit conditions. They should be kept moist at all times, but without waterlogging the compost. Grow in 10-13 cm (4-5 inch) pots of John Innes No. 2 potting compost. Once flower stems are seen, feed weekly with liquid fertilizer.

When flowering is over, and certainly by the time you need the space in the greenhouse, from March or April onwards, you can remove the plants and plant them in the garden if you wish, to flower there next spring.

Propagation: Polyanthus may be propagated by division after flowering, or from seed. Seed should be sown in spring in a half pot or tray filled with seed compost and lightly covered. Keep moist and at a temperature of about 18°C (65°F) until germinated. When large enough to handle, prick out the seedlings and pot up separately in 9 cm (3½ inch) pots of potting compost. Pot into their final size pots by autumn.

Pests and Diseases: Polyanthus may be attacked by aphids and botrytis (grey mould) which causes black or brown leaf spots.

REBUTIA*

Rebutia is quite an amazing cactus that produces a mass of flowers around the base of the plant, almost dwarfing it. Although this tiny globe-shaped cactus grows only about 5 cm (2 inches) in diameter, the mass of white, yellow, orange or red flowers that it produces virtually every year makes it a must for the greenhouse collection.

General Care: The rebutia is one of the easiest cacti to keep, and requires no special treatment. Like most cacti, it prefers a well-lit situation and to be allowed to dry out in between waterings during the spring and summer. In the winter, it should be kept almost completely dry and at a temperature around 10°C (50°F) as this will help to encourage it to flower the following year. It prefers a rich compost with added grit or sand, and it is usual to grow several plants in a 15 cm (6 inch) half pot or shallow pan. The flowers appear in early summer and are produced in profusion. In the evening the trumpet-like flowers close up, only to re-open the next morning for several days until they finally die.

Propagation: Rebutias freely set seed and this can be easily germinated when sown in a half pot or tray containing a mixture of 4 parts seed compost to 1 part fine sand. The seed should be lightly covered with fine sand and kept reasonably moist at a temperature of around 20°C (68°F) until it has germinated. Pot up the seedlings when large enough to handle.

Pests and Diseases: Mealy bugs, root mealy bugs and aphids may attack rebutias.

RHIPSALIDOPSIS*

Not all cacti are 'spiky barrels'; *Rhipsalidopsis gaertneri*, the Easter cactus, grows to 45 cm (18 inches), has flattish green pads and a few bristles at the end of the pads. It is naturally a tree-living cactus and requires slightly different treatment from its relations. The beauty of the Easter cactus lies not in its strange foliage and unusual appearance but in the magnificent display of flowers that the plant produces each year. The blossoms are superb, 5-6 cm (2-2½ inch) long red trumpets that literally cover the plant with a superb blaze of colour. It flowers, as you might expect, in March and April.

General Care: In order to encourage the plant to flower well, it should be kept on the dry side in winter, watering only to avoid dehydration. A temperature of around 10-13°C (50-55°F) is suitable. In spring, the warmer condition will mean that the plant requires more water, although it should not be kept constantly moist. Keeping the greenhouse damped down with water will provide the humid conditions it prefers. Feed weekly with dilute liquid fertilizer while flowering.

Unlike many other cacti, rhipsalidopsis does not like too much direct sunlight and should therefore be placed in a position where it has some light shade. As it lives perched on branches of trees in its natural habitat, it does not need an ordinary compost, but is best in a mixture of leafmould and sandy grit. Grow it in 13 cm (5 inch) pots.

After flowering, the plant will produce new growth in the form of little leaf pads that grow past the withering and rapidly dropping dead flowers. It can be stood outside in the summer in a shady place.

Propagation: The Easter cactus can be propagated from mature leaf pads, gently pulled from the plant. Dip these into hormone rooting powder and then insert two or three pads to a 9 cm (3½ inch) pot of seed compost. Once rooted, leave to grow on in the same pot.

Pests and Diseases: Easter cacti may be attacked by mealy bugs and root mealy bugs.

SAINTPAULIA**

Saintpaulias, the popular African violets, form a close rosette of fleshy, hairy leaves from which pretty flowers arise in a wide range of colours – usually purple/blue, but also white, pink, wine-red, light blue, and dark blue. There are even bi-coloured and frilled forms.

General Care: African violets prefer a temperature of about 20°C (68°F), shaded from direct sunlight. You can even place them beneath the staging. Humidity is important but avoid splashing water on the leaves, which are easily marked. Water the plants from below, placing the pot in a saucer and allow it to soak up what it requires within about 20 minutes before pouring away the surplus.

A stubborn African violet can be coaxed into flower by keeping the plant on the dry side for six to eight weeks, watering only if it looks like drying out and dying. Then gradually increase the water, and feed every two weeks with tomato fertilizer at about quarter strength.

Propagation: Take leaf cuttings. Select a mature leaf, and cut it off cleanly at the base of the leaf stalk close to the centre of the plant. Cut back the leaf stalk to about 3-4 cm (1½ inches) and lightly dip into hormone rooting powder. Gently insert the stalk into a 5 cm (2 inch) pot of seed compost, leaving a small space between the base of the leaf and the compost surface. Cover the leaf with polythene. The cuttings should root in about six to eight weeks, but it may be as long again before plantlets emerge. Pot on into 9 cm (3½ inch) pots.

Pests and Diseases: Aphids and mildew can be problems during spring and summer; botrytis (grey mould) is a risk at any time.

Pink saintpaulias (African violets)

287

Solanum capsicastrum (winter cherry)

SELENICEREUS*

The selenicereus is a magnificent cactus to grow in your greenhouse. The flowers are superb, varying in colour from white to yellow, scarlet or mauve and measure up to 20 cm (8 inches) across, often with a fantastic scent. *Selenicereus grandiflorus*, which grows about 1.8 metres (6 ft) tall, is called the 'queen of the night' as it flowers at night.

General Care: To grow this selenicereus successfully, provide the plant with support and a well-lit position. During the winter, keep it on the dry side and at a temperature of around 13°C (55°F), watering only to prevent dehydration. Water more frequently during the spring and summer, allowing the plant to get on the dry side before re-watering.

Provide support in the form of canes or a trellis, for the growth habit can be rather straggly. It can also be grown against the wall of the greenhouse. Finally, you will need a torch! The splendid flowers of the selenicereus open at night and you will only see them at their best if you go to look at them then. It is well worth the trouble!

Propagation: Selenicereus may be propagated from cuttings in a similar way to rhipsalidopsis, or from seed germinated at about 20°C (68°F) in a mixture of 4 parts seed compost to 1 part fine sand. Prick out and pot up singly when large enough to handle.

Pests and Diseases: Mealy bugs and root mealy bugs sometimes attack this plant.

SOLANUM*

Solanum capsicastrum or winter cherry is a fairly compact plant from the same family as the tomato. It bears small white flowers and has rich green leaves. Once pollinated the plant produces orange, cherry-like fruits that look attractive and decorative. The fruits are inedible and indeed poisonous. It grows to a height of up to 45 cm (18 inches).

General Care: The winter cherry is very easy to grow, provided it is given plenty of light and is not allowed to dry out, particularly during the critical time of flowering and the period of fruit setting. It is hardy enough to be grown outside for the summer but should be given protection under glass from September onwards. By early autumn the fruit will appear and will gradually colour to provide a magnificent display over the Christmas period. Spraying the plant with a mist of tepid water during the flowering period will help to 'set' the flowers and will encourage a better show of fruit. Feed every two weeks with dilute liquid fertilizer from June until the fruits ripen.

Over the winter period, this solanum is happy with a minimum temperature of around 10°C (50°F), which makes it an easy and colourful plant to grow in the greenhouse at a time when little else is happening. It is grown in 13 cm (5 inch) pots of John Innes No. 2 potting compost and is usually treated as an annual.

Propagation: The winter cherry is easily propagated from seed germinated in seed compost at about 18-20°C (65-68°F) in the spring. When large enough to handle, prick out and pot up the seedlings separately in potting compost. Pinch out the growing tips to produce bushy plants.

Pests and Diseases: Solanums are occasionally attacked by aphids and are particularly prone to white fly.

STREPTOCARPUS*

Streptocarpus or Cape primroses are rather unusual flowering plants of low habit, growing to 20-30 cm (8-12 inches) in height. They produce pink, red, purple or lilac primrose-like, but tubular, flowers. The longish leaves radiate in opposite directions generally in pairs.

General Care: Streptocarpus should be kept at about 10°C (50°F) over winter, and just moist. From March onwards they prefer a slightly higher temperature but should not be exposed to full light all the time because they appreciate a certain amount of light shade.

Water freely in summer. The plants will then flower from May right through until October. Grow in 13-20 cm (5-8 inch) pots of John Innes No. 2 potting compost or a soil-less compost.

Propagation: Streptocarpus can either be propagated from seed or from leaf cuttings. Seed should be sown at about 21°F (70°F) in seed compost in half pots or seed trays in spring, potting the seedlings up singly in 13 cm (5 inch) pots of potting compost.

Leaf cuttings are taken in a most unusual way. Cut off a semi-mature leaf (not one too old or too young). Cut the leaf in half down the central main vein and then cut each half into pieces about 2.5 cm (1 inch) wide. Dip the area of the main vein into hormone rooting powder and then lightly insert into seed compost in seed trays or half pots containing a mixture of peat and sand. Cover with polythene or apply a mist of tepid water to reduce water loss. When rooted, pot up singly in 9 cm (3½ inch) pots of potting compost.

Pests and Diseases: Aphids can be a problem.

Streptocarpus (Cape primroses) and Saintpaulia

FRUIT AND VEGETABLES

It is hardly surprising that the most popular things grown in a greenhouse are edible.

Sadly, many people tend to grow only tomatoes or – if they are a little more adventurous – cucumbers or peppers. However, with very little special care you can grow all sorts of exciting fruits and vegetables, such as apricots, courgettes, grapes, melons and even peaches.

To achieve good results it is not necessary to heat the greenhouse to an expensive extent. In fact, if grown in their natural season, the majority of fruit and vegetables manage without any artificial heat at all. Lettuce, rhubarb or strawberries can be grown with nothing more than sufficient heat to keep out the frost. For early or out of season crops, the greenhouse must be heated to the required temperature.

Effective use of space is essential when growing food crops under glass, to obtain a maximum yield. You may find that even with the best planning you wish that you had arranged things differently. Growing bags provide some flexibility because they can be moved relatively easily, unless of course the crops in them have become too tall.

Pots and troughs are also useful and, in the same way as growing bags, they isolate food crops from each other, reducing the likelihood of soil-borne diseases spreading. This can be a major problem with food crops grown under glass and planted in the border soil. Some plants will grow quite happily in border soil, but it is particularly important in the case of tomatoes to sterilize the soil in between crops, or avoid the problem altogether by using pots or growing bags.

APRICOTS*

Apricots are well worth growing in a greenhouse whether free standing or lean-to, provided you can give the plants enough room. Growing apricots under glass not only helps to ripen the fruit which would otherwise be more difficult and stubborn to ripen outside but also has another major benefit in avoiding frost damage to the flowers which bloom in February, earlier than most fruit trees.

General Care: Although apricots may be grown in pots for the first few years, they have such active root growth and so large an appetite, that they quickly out-grow their pots and are better in the border soil of the greenhouse. To save space, it is a good idea to buy fan-trained plants to grow against the lean-to wall or side of the greenhouse. Start the plants off in 25 cm (10 inch) pots of John Innes No. 2 potting compost and then move into larger tubs or into the border soil. Keep the plants well watered through the spring and summer and feed occasionally with tomato fertilizer.

It is not really necessary to prune in the first year but in the second year growth can be cut back by one third to a half to encourage compact growth and fruiting. Fruit set can be increased by hand pollinating the apricot flowers with a small artist's paint-brush, brushing the pollen of one flower onto the centre of another. Fortunately, it is quite sufficient to have only one plant as apricots are self-fertile. To produce better fruits, it is worthwhile thinning out the fruitlets to about 20 cm (8 inches) apart in June. The fruits can be harvested in

Ripe apricots – ready for harvesting

August when they are fully ripened and easy to remove.

Over winter, the plant should be kept cool, down to about 2°C (35°F), and a little on the dry side.

Propagation: Apricots can be propagated from apricot stones germinated at about 20°C (68°F) in 9 cm (3½ inch) pots of seed compost, buried about 5 cm (2 inches) deep. Leave the plants to grow on and pot up into larger pots when they are big enough to be transplanted.

Pests and Diseases: Apricots are subject to infection from peach leaf curl and leaf spot. You will need to spray with a copper compound to control peach leaf curl, following the manufacturer's instructions.

fruits should be harvested when large enough – about 10 cm (4 inches) in length and of a good colour. It is advisable to cut the fruit from the plant with a sharp knife rather than simply pulling it off.

Propagation: Germinate the seed in February at about 20-21°C (68-70°F) in either a seed tray or half pot of seed compost. Prick out and pot up the seedlings singly in 9 cm (3½ inch) pots of potting compost and grow on. Then, when about 15-20 cm (6-8 inches) tall, plant the aubergines in growing bags or pots of John Innes No. 2 or No. 3 potting compost.

Pests and Diseases: Aubergines are subject to attack from whitefly, red spider mites and occasionally botrytis (grey mould). The latter is a problem often caused by poor and damp growing conditions.

COURGETTES**

Courgettes grow particularly well in a greenhouse. Actually, courgettes are small marrows, or rather marrows that are picked earlier than they would be in the case of the more 'normal' sized vegetable. Varieties such as F_1 'Zucchini' and F_1 'Golden Zucchini' are good types to grow. They have a sprawling habit and they therefore take up quite a lot of room. However, if you like courgettes, then you probably will not mind the space they take up.

General Care: Plant them in growing bags, allowing about two plants to a bag. Take particular care not to allow the plants to dry out and to keep them well watered. Feeding should be started as soon as

AUBERGINES**

Aubergines are rather extraordinary plants, producing interesting fruits that are pear-shaped in appearance. The plants do not grow very tall but they do take up a fair amount of room. They can, however, be grown in pots or growing bags.

General Care: Grow the plants in either 20 cm (8 inch) pots, one to a pot, or growing bags, three to a growing bag. The plants like light and warmth. Although aubergines can be grown outside, they will grow far better under glass, produc-

ing more vigorous growth and more fruit of better quality.

The purple flowers should pollinate easily and fruit set should not be a problem. However, occasional misting with tepid water will help to increase the set if a problem is experienced. When the plant is large enough and the first fruit sets, start feeding once a week using a tomato fertilizer, applied at normal strength. As the plants grow, they will need support either in the form of canes if the plants are in pots, or a support frame if grown in growing bags. The

you have picked the first fruits, using a tomato fertilizer applied at the standard rate. The young marrows or courgettes are best harvested when they are up to 15 cm (6 inches) long. Harvesting the small fruits encourages the production of further fruits. If fruit set is found to be a problem, it may be encouraged with a small artist's paintbrush. Lightly tickle the flowers with the brush to transfer pollen from male to female flowers in order to pollinate them.

Propagation: Courgettes are best propagated by sowing seed in peat pots as this helps to avoid root disturbance when planting up later. In May sow one seed to each 9 cm (3½ inch) pot of seed compost, placing the seed on its edge in the moist compost without covering it. Keep the seed at about 21°C (70°F) to germinate and grow on in the individual pots until about 15 cm (6 inches) tall. Then transfer to the growing bags and grow on.

Pests and Diseases: Courgettes are subject to infestation of whitefly and red spider mites. They can also be infected with mildew.

CUCUMBERS**

Although cucumbers are a bit fiddly to grow, and can take up a fair amount of room in your greenhouse, they are worth experimenting with. Cucumbers grown under glass will produce fruits just like the ones that you can buy from the greengrocer rather than the ridge cucumbers with their characteristic rough skins that you would normally grow outside in the garden.

General Care: Cucumbers are rather susceptible to root rot problems which often occur when they are overwatered. To avoid this situation, it may help if you grow the plants in growing bags which have slits cut in the bottom edge of the sides to aid drainage. Plant two or three cucumber plants to a bag and provide support in the form of a growing bag support frame, canes, strings or wires. Strings or wires are probably the easiest method of providing support and work reasonably well. Anchor the string to the bag by tying it around the bag near each plant; then tie this to the greenhouse roof at a suitable anchorage point.

The plants should be planted during May to avoid frosts if your greenhouse is unheated, and when temperatures are about 15°C (60°F). Cucumbers prefer light shade and a humid environment. Keep the compost moist and start feeding with a tomato fertilizer as soon as the first fruits have been picked. Apart from training the plants around wires or whatever support you have used, you will need to work on the crops by removing any side shoots. Do not be too impatient for fruit; you will get better results by removing any flowers or fruit on the first 40-45 cm (16-18 inches) of stem and allowing ones above to grow normally.

All-female varieties are the best to grow as these will save you the trouble of pinching off the male flowers to prevent them from fertilizing the female flowers and spoiling the fruit. If fertilization takes place the fruit is bitter to taste.

Varieties such as 'Fertila', 'Monique' and 'Amstic' – all F_1 hybrids – are useful varieties that produce no male flowers. 'Amstic' is the most tolerant of lower temperatures.

Once the plants have grown to the greenhouse roof it is a good idea to let two to four side shoots trail down. This will help to increase the crop potential.

Propagation: Germinate the seed in February or March, one seed to a 9 cm (3½ inch) pot of seed compost. The use of a peat pot that can be planted directly avoids root disturbance. Keep the seed at about 21°C (70°F) to germinate, then grow on in the pot until the plants are about 15 cm (6 inches) high, when they can be transplanted.

Pests and Diseases: Cucumbers are prone to red spider mite, whitefly and mildew.

GRAPES*

If you can afford the time and space you might like to grow grapes in your greenhouse. Growing them under glass gives you the advantage of a more reliable crop than when grown outside, with larger berries and less susceptibility of frost damage to the flowers and young growth. It can be a delight to grow your own grapes, so they are probably worth the effort.

General Care: Grapes like a well-lit situation, and they should be planted in the greenhouse border soil and not in a tub or container. To save space, it may be worthwhile training them along the side of the greenhouse. Wires stretched along the length of the greenhouse and arched on sturdy posts placed at either end should provide a good support structure. In summer, when the plants bear fruit, maintain a temperature of 18°C (64°F). Keep the atmosphere humid at first, gradually increasing ventilation as the fruit nears maturity. Feeding with tomato fertilizer is useful but do not keep the grapes too well watered. During the winter it is advisable to let the vines be exposed to relatively low temperatures down to around 0°C (32°F) to provide the dormant season that they need.

Pruning grapes is an art in itself. In the autumn choose one main stem to grow on the framework and cut back all side shoots to about half their length. In subsequent years train side shoots and the main

Grapes are best supported by horizontal wires

shoot to the shape you want, but cut back all other shoots to two buds of new wood. These buds produce the flowers the following year. When the flowers appear in April and May, pollinate them with a small brush, brushing pollen from one blossom on to another. When the fruit has set, occasional thinning of the berries helps to increase the size of the remaining fruit, if you want larger grapes for dessert purposes.

Propagation: Although it is tempting to grow grapes from pips, you will achieve a better result from cuttings. When

Lettuce seedlings – ready for planting out

you prune back the grape vines in winter cut up the lengths into pieces about 25 cm (10 inches) long and insert them in the greenhouse border soil leaving the top of the shoot just above the surface of the soil. Use a cane or even a garden fork to make suitable sized holes for them. Then leave them to root and grow on, transplanting them when you wish, preferably about a year after insertion.

Pests and Diseases: Grapes are subject to attack from mildew.

LETTUCE*

Lettuce can be grown in a greenhouse at any time of the year and the quality is normally far better than when grown outside. Greenhouse lettuces are especially useful in winter, however, when shop prices are high and it is not possible to harvest an outdoor crop.

There are several types of lettuce: cabbage, crisphead, cos and 'cut-and-come-again'. Success or failure depends very much on the choice of variety if you are growing out of season. You must select a variety that is suitable for the temperature you can maintain (heat is not essential), and sow it at the recommended time. A good seed catalogue will suggest suitable varieties.

General Care: Lettuces can either be grown directly in the greenhouse border soil or in growing bags. Using the previous season's growing bags for growing lettuce after a tomato crop is a good idea and makes best use of your resources. Varieties such as 'Kloek' for spring cutting, 'Plus' for cropping from mid-October to mid-April and 'Fortune' for summer cutting are all good varieties, but follow the earlier advice on selecting a variety.

You can plant up to 12 lettuces, in two rows of six, in a full-sized growing bag, which is quite a crop from a bag that has already produced a crop of tomatoes. Grow them on, avoiding excessively wet, damp or cold conditions which could cause the lettuces to rot off. Lettuces like a well-lit situation in the greenhouse and should not be grown in shade. A temperature of 10°C (50°F) is needed for growing most winter-maturing varieties, but requirements vary.

Propagation: Lettuces should be germinated either in half pots or seed trays of seed compost. Sow the seed thinly and lightly cover with compost. Keep moist, and provide a temperature of about 13-15°C (55-60°F) until germinated. Avoid temperatures above this, otherwise germination may be inhibited. When the seedlings are large enough to handle, about 5-7.5 cm (2-3 inches) tall, prick them out and plant out.

Pests and Diseases: Lettuces are subject to attack from aphids, slugs, mildew and botrytis (grey mould).

MELONS**

Melons are interesting and slightly more unusual plants for the greenhouse. They can be grown either in pots or growing bags. However, the choice of variety is fairly crucial to success. Some of the varieties may be disappointing in this climate, but one that is certainly worth trying is the 'Ogen' melon, a Canteloupe type that is very suited to cool greenhouse culture.

General Care: Either plant the

Ogen melons are suited to cool greenhouse culture

melons in 25 cm (10 inch) pots of John Innes No. 3 potting compost or plant three to a growing bag. Keep relatively moist and start to feed with a tomato fertilizer when the plants are about 30 cm (1 ft) tall. Tie the plants to a support cane or framework. When the flowers open help the plants by tickling the flowers with a small artist's paint-brush, transferring pollen from male to female flowers. This will help pollinate them and encourage fruit set. As the fruits get larger tie them in nets to the framework to ripen, and ventilate well to prevent mildew. It is wise to settle for four melons to a plant, removing further fruits if they develop.

Propagation: Germinate the seeds individually in 9 cm (3½ inch) pots of seed compost, lightly inserting each seed on its edge into the surface but not covering it. To avoid root disturbance at transplanting, use peat pots, planting up when the plants have produced about four or five leaves.

Pests and Diseases: Melons may be attacked by whitefly or botrytis (grey mould).

MUSTARD AND CRESS*

Surely the easiest plants to grow must be mustard and cress. They provide a useful salad, garnish or sandwich filler at any time of the year.

General Care: The best way to grow mustard and cress is to sow the seed on to absorbent moist material such as blotting paper, paper tissue, cotton wool, or peat. Place any of these materials in a suitable container – a seed tray or plastic plant pot saucer are ideal. Sow the seed on to the surface of the material chosen and keep constantly moist. Be sure to check several times a day during warm, sunny conditions that the pots are not drying out, and within a few days the seeds will germinate.

White mustard will germinate quickly – within a few days – and can be eaten about a week after sowing, when it is about 2.5 cm (1 inch) high. Do not leave it any longer or it will become somewhat bitter. Cress takes a little longer. Although it germinates after about three to five days, it is usually not ready for harvest until two to three weeks after sowing. When mustard and cress are grown together harvest about 12 days after sowing.

Pests and Diseases: Fortunately, neither mustard nor cress should suffer from any pest or disease problem.

PEACHES*

Peaches should be grown in the same way as apricots. They need a fair amount of room, but growing them in a greenhouse is a good way to achieve a reasonable crop of fruits by ripening them more effectively.

General Care: Peaches may be grown in pots or tubs in the greenhouse, although they will grow better if planted directly in the border soil where the roots will not be so restricted and where the plants are not so likely to run short of nutrients. In the same way as for apricots, peaches can be trained in a fan shape against the greenhouse wall. To start the plants off, 25 cm (10 inch) pots of John Innes No. 2 potting compost can be used. The plants should be well watered throughout the spring and summer and fed with dilute tomato fertilizer.

After the first year, when pruning is not necessary, the second year's growth may be cut back to one third or half. In the same way as for apricots, fruit set may be increased by hand pollination of the flowers in March. This can be done easily by tickling the flowers with a small artist's paint-brush. Thin out the fruits in June if necessary and harvest the fruit in August or when it parts easily from the stalk. During winter allow the plants to be exposed to a temperature of about 2°C (35°F), and keep them on the dry side.

Peaches ripen more effectively in a greenhouse

Propagation In the same way as for apricots, peaches may be grown from stones planted about 5 cm (2 inches) deep in 9 cm (3½ inch) pots of seed compost, kept at about 20°C (68°F). Pot on when large enough to handle.

Pests and Diseases: Peaches may be attacked by peach leaf curl and leaf spot. Peach leaf curl is difficult to control once established, so it is worth spraying with a copper compound as a precaution (following manufacturer's advice).

PEPPERS*

Peppers are coming more into fashion as vegetables, although strictly they are fruits like tomatoes. These green or red fruits are produced freely throughout the summer and require little special care.

General Care: Peppers like warmth and light and do well in a greenhouse. Grow them either potted in John Innes No. 2 potting compost in 20-25 cm (8-10 inch) pots, or in growing bags, three to a bag. Peppers should be kept relatively moist and never allowed to dry out. It helps to spray the plants with tepid water during the flowering period. They should be fed with a tomato fertilizer when the plants have grown to about 15-20 cm (6-8 inches) tall, or as soon as the first fruits have set. When you have picked the first pepper, the plant will then 'break', producing side shoots from which future peppers will grow.

As far as the colour of peppers is concerned, the longer you leave them, the more time they are given to turn red.

Peppers are well worth space in the greenhouse

However, in order to get the maximum yield from your plants, it is better to pick them green and allow the plant to produce more rather than waiting and wasting crop potential. If necessary, provide support with a cane or framework.

Varieties worth growing are 'Canape' and 'Early Prolific' (both F_1 Hybrids), or for a yellow-coloured variety, 'Gold Star'. Peppers are not frost hardy and if your greenhouse is not heated, they should not be planted out until May.

Propagation: Sow in March in a seed tray or half pot of seed compost and lightly cover with compost. Keep at about 20°C (68°F) until germinated. When large enough to handle, prick out the seedlings singly into 9 cm (3½ inch) pots, using John Innes No. 1 potting compost. Grow on until about 15 cm (6 inches) tall before planting in growing bags or potting on.

Pests and Diseases: Aphids and whitefly can be problems.

PINEAPPLES*

Pineapples are only worth growing in a greenhouse if you are adventurous and curious to know how they grow. The chances of growing an edible pineapple are pretty remote, but the habit of growth is interesting with the small pineapple growing on a stalk from the centre of the rosette of spiky leaves.

General Care: Pineapples must have a well-lit position in the greenhouse. During the summer, they should be watered fairly regularly, being allowed to dry out a little between waterings. In winter they will tolerate temperatures down to 7°C (45°F) provided they are kept on the dry side. To encourage fruiting, cover the plants with polythene bags and place two or three ripe apples underneath each. After a week or so, remove the bags and the apples, and hope that the gas given off by the apples (ethylene) will have initiated the fruiting response. If they do not flower within a few months, repeat the treatment.

Propagation: The best way to propagate a pineapple is to cut the top off a fruit leaving 1 cm (½ inch) below the bottom rosette of leaves. Dust this with hormone rooting powder, then insert into a 13 cm (5 inch) pot containing a mixture of 3 parts seed compost to 1 part sand. Water infrequently until it starts to grow.

Pests and Diseases: Mealy bugs and root mealy bugs may attack pineapples.

RHUBARB*

Rhubarb is a useful plant, worth growing in the greenhouse in winter to provide a source of fresh material for culinary use. The effort necessary is minimal and you can grow, or rather force, it at a time when you probably have space free in the greenhouse.

General Care: During the winter, allow the rhubarb to be exposed to some fairly severe cold weather as this is important for successful forcing later on. If the winter is mild, dig up the rhubarb and expose to the frost for a few days. Then, during December, either place the crowns in a black polythene refuse sack and leave under the staging in the greenhouse, pulling the stalks once they have grown, or place in a box or other suitable container, planting in moist peat. Again, cover up the plant with black polythene until it has produced the sticks. A temperature of about 13-15°C (55-60°F) is suitable for forcing. After forcing, the clumps or roots of

Rhubarb can be grown or 'forced' under the staging

rhubarb will have been exhausted and should be disposed of.

Propagation: Rhubarb clumps are easily propagated. Simply use a spade and chop or lever the clump apart. Then plant or force as required. The best time to do this is during the winter.

Pests and Diseases: Luckily, rhubarb grown in the greenhouse is usually trouble-free.

STRAWBERRIES*

Both conventional strawberries such as 'Cambridge Favourite' and alpine varieties such as 'Alexandria' can be grown successfully in a greenhouse where they will produce an earlier crop than they would outdoors.

General Care: Strawberries do tend to take up a fair amount of space, especially if they are planted in the normal way flat on the ground. The best way to grow them, therefore, is either in a growing bag laid flat, planting two rows of five down the length, or alternatively with the bag on its end and slits, about 7.5-10 cm (3-4 inches) long, cut opposite

each other in pairs, to make a kind of strawberry 'barrel'.

Plant the strawberry plants in September and leave outside until January, when they can be brought under glass. Strawberries will flower in April. To encourage good fruiting, you can help pollinate the flowers by tickling with a small artist's paint-brush. With few insects around, this action in the early spring will help to ensure a better crop. Water as soon as the plants start to grow and keep moist while fruiting. Feed after fruiting with a tomato fertilizer. When the plants have fruited, the growing bag or pots, if you chose to use them, should then be placed outside.

Propagation: Strawberries can be propagated from the numerous runners produced in summer and potted up singly in 9 cm (3½ inch) pots of potting compost.

Alpine varieties can be raised from seed germinated at about 15-18°C (60-65°F). Prick out and pot up singly when seedlings are large enough to handle.

Pests and Diseases: Strawberries are subject to attack from aphids. These pests are a particular nuisance, because they also spread strawberry virus disease.

TOMATOES*

Of all the crops grown under glass, tomatoes are still by far the most popular. They are relatively easy to grow and, apart from the conventional types that take up quite a large amount of room, you can now grow smaller varieties that thrive well on the staging in pots.

General Care: Although tomatoes can be grown in border soil, they will grow far better with much less risk of any disease or infection by being planted three to a growing bag. Plant them up when frosts have finished if your greenhouse is unheated, when your plants are about 15 cm (6 inches) tall.

Keep the plants well watered in the bag and start feeding with a tomato fertilizer as soon as the first truss of tomatoes has set and the second truss is well on the way in terms of development. Pollination and fruit set might be a problem during the early spring and this can be helped either by spraying the flowers lightly with water or by gently shaking the plant to transfer pollen.

If you grow a normal variety, such as 'Moneymaker' or 'Eurocross A' which require support, you will need to pinch or rub out the side shoots, to encourage the plant to grow straight up. Support in the form of growing bag frames or strings tied around the bags and trained to the

Tomatoes – the most popular greenhouse crop

greenhouse roof will be important in taking the weight of the plants as they grow. Bush varieties such as 'Minibel' will only grow about 30 cm (12 inches) high and will not need to have their side shoots removed. They also grow well in 20-25 cm (8-10 inch) pots of John Innes No. 2 potting compost. The fruits are obviously smaller but taste very good.

Tomatoes need a temperature of about 15-18°C (60-65°F) when at the seedling stage but later they will tolerate a temperature down to about 10°F (50°F). Keep the plant well watered all the time they are fruiting as drying out can cause a disorder called 'blossom end rot', which causes the ends of the fruit to blacken and shrivel.

In the autumn, when the plants die, any green fruits can be encouraged to ripen by laying them in a warm place.

Propagation: Germinate the seed in the middle of March (or earlier if you heat your greenhouse) in seed trays or dwarf pots of seed compost covering the seed lightly. Keep at about 18-20°C (65-68°F) until germinated, then prick out and pot up singly when large enough to handle into 9 cm (3½ inch) pots of potting compost. Grow the plants on until 15 cm (6 inches) tall when they can be potted on or planted out.

Pests and Diseases: Tomatoes are subject to attack from whitefly, wilt diseases (particularly if planted direct into border soil) and botrytis (grey mould). Plants suffering from wilt are best destroyed and the soil or compost should not be used for tomatoes again.

CLIMBING PLANTS

Climbing plants are most useful in a greenhouse to provide natural, dappled shade and to fill the roof space.

It is, of course, essential to take into account the extent to which sunlight reaching the other plants is likely to be reduced by climbing plants. As a general rule foliage plants prefer heavier shade unlike flowering plants which require lighter shade. The passiflora or passion flower is most suiable if you want to create a dappled green, fairly heavy shade. At the other extreme, hoya and stephanotis – despite their fleshier leaves – are less densely foliaged and can be grown in parts of the greenhouse where more light is required.

Climbing plants are ideal for growing in association with a foliage plant collection. Both types will require some heat over the winter period if you are growing a more exotic collection, but with hardier species you can avoid expensive heating costs.

Keep the plants in containers so that they can easily be moved to other sites in the greenhouse. As far as support for the plants is concerned, you can use canes or thin wooden stakes in the early stages. Thin metal wires or horticultural twine are ideal for providing support from the bottom to the top of the greenhouse or along the roof to train the growth in a horizontal plane.

ABUTILON**
Strictly speaking, the abutilon or 'flowering maple' is not really a climber. However, its habit of growth is such that it makes an excellent background plant that grows up to 2 metres (6 ft) tall provided it is given some form of support. The hanging, bell-like flowers of the plant range from yellow to red in colour and are produced from May to October. Depending on the variety, abutilons have either green or variegated foliage.

General Care: Abutilons do not like hot dry conditions but otherwise they are reasonably easy to grow. Excessive amounts of sunlight may scorch the leaves, so some light shade should be given. The plants like to be kept reasonably moist during the growing season from April to late September. During the autumn and winter they require much less water, and should be kept on the dry side.

Abutilons will tolerate temperatures down to 10°C (50°F). Grow either in the greenhouse border or in 15-20 cm (6-8 inch) pots of John Innes No. 2 potting compost. Feed every two weeks from May to September with dilute tomato fertilizer.

Propagation: Abutilons can be germinated from seed. Sow in a half pot of seed compost in spring and maintain at a temperature of about 20°C (68°F) until germinated. Prick out and pot on singly into 9 cm (3½ inch) pots of John Innes No. 1 potting compost when large enough to handle.

Alternatively, propagate from cuttings, about 7.5 cm (3 inches) long, taken in summer and dipped into hormone rooting powder before inserting in 9 cm (3½ inch) pots of seed compost.

Pests and Diseases: Abutilon is subject to attack from aphids, red spider mites, root mealy bugs and scale insects.

BOUGAINVILLEA**
Bougainvilleas are quite extraordinary climbing plants that produce magnificent 'flowers'. The 'flowers' are in fact highly coloured bracts, ranging in colour from pink to orange red and even yellow. The small white true flowers are found in the centres of the bracts. The plants produce an abundance of bright bracts throughout the summer, for about three months. The plants grow to about 2.5 metres (10 ft) tall in pots or about 9 metres (30 ft) if grown in a greenhouse border, and provide a really superb addition to your collection, provided you have space.

General Care: Bougainvilleas are relatively easy to grow, enjoying a position in full light. During spring and summer, the plants must not be allowed to dry out or they may die. Occasional spraying with tepid water during warm dry conditions is beneficial.

During the winter, however, the plants should be kept on the dry side and watered much less frequently. They will then tolerate a temperature down to around 10°C (50°F). Following the winter, a light pruning back of shoots by about one quarter to one third will encourage compact, well-shaped growth from the spring onwards, but the plants will still require support either with a trellis, canes or strings. They should be grown in 15-20 cm (6-8 inch) pots of John Innes No. 3 potting compost.

Propagation: Bougainvilleas can be propagated by taking 7.5-10 cm (3-4 inches) long cuttings in summer, dipping into hormone rooting powder and then inserting into 5 cm

Flowering bougainvillea with its vivid pink bracts – these enclose the white 'true' flowers

(2 inch) pots of seed compost or a mixture of 4 parts seed compost to 1 part sand. Keep at about 24°C (70°F).

Pests and Diseases: Aphids, red spider mites and mealy bugs sometimes attack bougainvilleas.

HEDERA CANARIENSIS*

Hedera canariensis 'Variegata', the Canary Island ivy, is a highly variegated, large leaved ivy that is most hardy and grows very well in a cool greenhouse. The leaves are a beautiful blend of creamy-white and deep green, borne on red stems. The plant climbs well, requiring only a little support, for it tends to anchor itself on any suitable ledge or crevice that offers itself in the greenhouse. It can reach 6 metres (20 ft) in height in exceptional cases. Obviously you would cut it back before it came to this!

General Care: The Canary Island ivy should be grown in a well-lit position, although it will tolerate a little shade. As far as watering in summer is concerned, the plant may be allowed to dry out a little before being re-watered. During the winter the plant should, however, be kept on the dry side when it will tolerate temperatures down to 4°C (40°F). If the plant is kept too moist during the winter, it will become susceptible to root rot. Occasional trimming, even quite active pruning back, will encourage the plant to remain in a reasonably tidy shape. Grow it in 10-15 cm (4-6 inch) pots of John Innes No. 2 potting compost, or a soil-less compost. Feed monthly with a diluted liquid fertilizer in summer.

Propagation: Canary Island ivy can be propagated by stem cuttings in July. Take pieces of stem, each with about two or three leaves and about 3 cm (1¼ inches) of stem below the bottom leaf. Dip each piece

into hormone rooting powder and insert approximately five to a 9 cm (3½ inch) pot of potting compost. Cover with polythene or mist with water occasionally to reduce water loss. Grow on in the pot after rooting.

Pests and Diseases: The plant may suffer from red spider mites, aphids, mealy bugs, and root mealy bugs.

HOYA*

The hoya, sometimes called the porcelain plant, is a succulent that has fleshy leaves borne on woody stems. The plant's rather untidy growth habit is its only real failing; the

Flowering hoya (the porcelain plant)

beautiful white flowers of the hoya are often borne in clusters about 10 cm (4 inches) across, and look like a work of art created from porcelain – hence the plant's common name. It flowers from May to September.

General Care: Hoya needs substantial support, requiring a good trellis or wire and cane frame. It also dislikes too much direct light, preferring light shade. It is important to get the watering right, for this may be crucial to success. During the spring and summer, the plant should be kept relatively moist, although it must be allowed to dry out a little in between waterings. However, over winter the plant should be kept on the dry side when it will tolerate temperatures down to around 10°C (50°F).

Bud or flower drop may occur if there are severe temperature fluctuations or major changes in soil moisture content. Grow in 25-30 cm (10-12 inch) pots of John Innes No. 2 potting compost or a soil-less compost. Feed every three weeks with dilute liquid fertilizer in summer.

Propagation: Hoyas can be propagated by stem cuttings in June, each with one, two or three pairs of leaves. Dip the bottom of each stem cutting into hormone rooting powder and insert about three to a 9 cm (3½ inch) pot of seed compost. Grow on in the pot.

Pests and Diseases: Hoya is subject to attack by mealy bugs and root mealy bugs.

JASMINE*

Jasminum polyanthum, or indoor jasmine, makes a most attractive and easy to grow plant for the cool greenhouse. The dark green, finely cut foliage climbs well, provided the plant has reasonable support. In early spring the plant covers itself with the most attractive and exquisitely scented white flowers that last for a number of weeks. It grows to a height of 1.5-3 metres (5-10 ft).

General Care: Jasmine adapts well to either a well-lit, or slightly shaded, situation. It requires moderate support and can even be grown on a hoop if so desired. During spring and summer, take great care to ensure that the plant remains moist and is not allowed to dry out. Once it has finished flowering, the plant may be occasionally trimmed and trained. Surprisingly, it will grow at a tremendous rate once it has flowered and needs to be kept in check to prevent it taking over!

In winter the plant should be kept cool, at around 5-7°C (41-45°F) and a little drier than during the summer. It can be grown in the greenhouse border or in 25-30 cm (10-12 inch) pots of John Innes No. 2 potting compost.

Propagation: Jasmine can easily be propagated in March or September from top or stem cuttings dipped into hormone rooting powder and inserted three to a 9 cm (3½ inch) pot of seed compost. If small plants are preferred, cuttings taken in March can be potted up into 13 cm (5 inch) pots and discarded after flowering.

Pests and Diseases: Aphids tend to be the major pest of jasmine, particularly in the spring when the plant is flowering, or when it is generating new growth.

Jasmine (Jasminum polyanthum)

PASSIFLORA*

The passiflora, far better known as the passion flower, is a very bold plant with deep green leaves and curling tendrils that help it climb up to 9 metres (30 ft) in exceptional cases. The growth is vigorous and the abundance of greenery provides a mass of cover. The plant is at its best, however, when it produces its most unusual and beautifully spectacular flowers. Occasionally the plant will fruit under glass, particularly if it flowers freely.

General Care: Passion flowers grow in a well-lit situation, although they prefer a little light shade. Watering through the spring and summer is important and the plants must not be allowed to dry out, particularly when they are in flower, otherwise the buds and flowers are likely to drop prematurely.

During the winter, passion flowers should be kept on the dry side and will happily tolerate temperatures down to about 2°C (35°F). The plants will need to be kept in check and should be trimmed or pruned from time to time to stop them taking over the greenhouse!

Grow them in the greenhouse border or in 25-30 cm (10-12 inch) pots of John Innes No. 3 potting compost.

Propagation: Passion flowers are easily raised from seed germinated in spring at about 20°C (68°F). The seedlings should be pricked out and potted up singly in 9 cm (3½ inch) pots of potting compost when large enough to handle.

Alternatively they can be propagated from stem cuttings in July. Dip the stems into hormone rooting powder, then insert into pots of seed compost, three to a 9 cm (3½ inch) pot. Keep at about 20°C (68°F), and in a humid atmosphere until rooted.

Pests and Diseases: Passion flowers are sometimes attacked by aphids, mealy bugs and red spider mites.

STEPHANOTIS**

In many ways, stephanotis are similar to hoyas. Their leaves, flowers and even habit of growth are similar. The plants have deep green fleshy succulent leaves on woody stems, while the flowers are larger than those of the hoya but are fleshy and wax-like in appearance. The scent is absolutely amazing and makes these plants well worth growing in your greenhouse. They can reach 3 metres (10 ft) if trained up strings or canes.

General Care: Although stephanotis like a certain amount of sunlight, too much sun may scorch the leaves, so light shading may be necessary. Provide a minimum temperature of 18°C (64°F) in the summer. During spring and summer, keep the plants moist; do not let them dry out as this could cause the flowers and/or buds to drop.

Passiflora (passion flower)

In winter, the plants should be kept on the dry side, at a temperature not lower than 10°C (50°F). Apart from being trained up stakes or along wires, stephanotis can also be grown well on a hoop of wire. Grow them in 13 cm (5 inch) pots of John Innes No. 2 potting compost, or a soil-less compost. They can be grown in large tubs or in the greenhouse border if large plants are required. Feed every two weeks in summer with dilute liquid fertilizer.

Propagation: Stephanotis can be propagated from cuttings. Take these in May, dip into hormone rooting powder, then insert into seed compost and maintain at a temperature of about 18°C (65°F) until rooted. Pot up into 9 cm (3½ inch) pots of potting compost. Soft, young plant growth is not suitable for propagation purposes and it is therefore better to use the more mature stems as cuttings.

Pests and Diseases: Mealy bugs are probably the most common pest.

THUNBERGIA*

The thunbergia grown as a climbing or trailing greenhouse plant is also known as Black-eyed Susan. It produces a mass of colourful golden orange flowers with a brownish-black 'eye' at the centre of the flower. Unfortunately the foliage is rather bland and it is only the flowers that are appealing. Because the plant is an annual it dies after flowering. It will grow to 3 metres (10 ft) in exceptional cases.

General Care: Black-eyed Susan is easy to grow and can even be grown outside when all risk of frost has passed. The plant should be supplied with canes or wires to support its rather feeble, leggy growth and should be placed in a well-lit position. Water freely and do not allow the plant to dry out at any time. Grow it in 15-20 cm (6-8 inch) pots of John Innes No. 2 potting compost.

Propagation: Thunbergia is propagated from seed sown in March. To avoid root disturbance, it is better to sow directly

Thunbergia (Black-eyed Susan)

into a small pot of seed compost, sowing between three and five seeds in a 9 cm (3½ inch) pot. Thin to one per pot later. Germinate at about 20°C (68°F) and grow on in the pot. Pot up as necessary using potting compost.

Pests and Diseases: Thunbergia may be attacked by aphids and white fly.

INDEX

ACKNOWLEDGEMENTS

The following photographs were taken specially for Octopus Books Ltd:
Michael Boys 13, 30, 37, 43, 49, 59, 77, 117, 126, 127, 142-3, 147, 148, 152, 159, 175, 185, 186, 187, 193, 194-5, 197, 198, 199, 205, 207, 208, 218, 233, 237, 245, 294, 295;
Jerry Harpur 29, 33, 35, 50, 53, 54, 61, 63, 67, 68, 69, 78, 81, 83, 119, 139, 192, 220;
Neil Holmes 20-21, 55, 196, 200-1, 203, 206, 209, 211, 212, 213, 216, 217;
George Wright 27, 31, 39, 40, 41, 42, 45, 47, 51, 57, 58, 65, 71, 73, 76, 79, 80, 82, 115, 116, 125, 130, 145, 146, 167, 201, 251, 292;
Octopus Books Ltd 202, 279, 288.

The publishers would like to thank Bob Challinor for his permission to reproduce the following photograph: 14-5.

The publishers also wish to thank the following individuals for their kind permission to reproduce the photographs in this book:
Heather Angel 188;
Marie Louise Avery 221;
Brian Furner Photographic Collection 191, 214-5;
A-Z Botanical Collection 285, 286;
Jacqui Hurst 103;
Harry Smith Horticultural Photographic Collection 149, 273, 291.

Special photography by Neil Holmes 85, 118, 120-124, 128-9, 132-5, 137-8, 140-1, 153, 259, 271, 274, 278, 280, 284, 287, 289, 296-9, 301-5.

Illustrations by artists from The Garden Studio:
Josephine Martin 11, 12, 16-24, 25, 75, 232, 235, 236, 238-9;
Christine Davison 90-3, 244, 248, 250, 252-6;
Heather Dew 94-101, 104a, 240-1, 243, 246-7;
Felicity Kays 104b, 105-108;
Patti Pearce 86-9.

Illustrations by Lindsay Blow 158, 161, 163-6, 168, 174, 176-7, 179-180, 182-3.